A Man's Place

A Man's Place

Masculinity and the Middle-Class Home
in Victorian England

John Tosh

Yale University Press
New Haven and London

Set in Bembo by Fakenham Photosetting Ltd
Printed in Great Britain by the Bath Press, Bath

Library of Congress Cataloging-in-Publication Data
Tosh, John.
A man's place: masculinity and the middle-class home in Victorian
England/John Tosh.
Includes bibliographical references and index.
ISBN 0-300-07779-3 (alk. paper)
1. Men – England – History – 19th century.   2. Masculinity – England –
History – 19th century.   3. Sex role – England – History – 19th
century.   4. Middle class families – England – History – 19th century.
I. Title.
HQ1090.7.G7T67   1999   98–31422
305.31'0942'09034 – dc21   CIP

A catalogue record of this book is available from the British Library.

2 4 6 8 10 9 7 5 3 1

in memory of
Rosamond Estcourt Tosh (née Sillem)
1904–1995
historian

Contents

Illustrations

Acknowledgements

The origins of this book go back to an informal research group into the history of masculinity which met at my home in north London between 1988 and 1990, when the subject scarcely existed in Britain. The regular members of that group – Kelly Boyd, Norma Clarke, Graham Dawson, David Kuchta, Peter Lewis, Keith McClelland, Michael Roper, Jonathan Rutherford, Pamela Walker and Julian Wood – were an indispensable stimulus in the early stages; most of them contributed to *Manful Assertions* (1991), a volume of essays edited by Michael Roper and myself. As almost every chapter testifies, this book would also have been impossible without the previous work of Leonore Davidoff, Catherine Hall and James Hammerton, each of whom has provided warm encouragement and practical help. Philip Greven had faith in my research before I knew what it was about.

Conferences are now so much part of academic routine that their role in forwarding scholarship is taken for granted. As a relative newcomer to the field, I have good reason to acknowledge the supportive and open-minded community of gender historians. The 'Gender in Question' Conference at Essex University in 1993, the second Carleton Conference on the History of the Family in Ottawa in 1994, and the Royal Historical Society's conference on gender at York in 1996 have all left their mark on this book. I am particularly grateful to the Ecclesiastical History Society, whose kind invitation to address their 1996 conference prompted me to take a fresh look at the relationship between religion and domesticity.

I owe much to the individuals who allowed me to consult the private papers and photographs in their possession: Marguerite Meinertzhagen, Nicholas Meinertzhagen, Peter Newall, Teresa Lady Rothschild, David Stovin and Jean Stovin. Brian and Dorothy Payne were indefatigable and hospitable guides to the remarkable family papers of Dr John Heaton. I am also indebted to the Bodleian Library, Bradford Public Library, Bradford University Library, the British Library, the British Library of Political and Economic Science, the Cambridge Centre of South Asian Studies, Trinity College (Cambridge), Lambeth Palace Library, the Brotherton Library of the University of Leeds,

Liverpool Record Office, the University of London Library and Manchester Central Reference Library for access to manuscript collections in their charge. In identifying some of these sources I was greatly helped by the advice of Barbara Caine, Clive Dewey, Janet Douglas, Anthony Howe, Edward Royle, John Seed and Jenny Uglow. I am grateful to the library staff of the University of North London, and especially to Jo Tomlinson for her help with inter-library loans. Sabbatical leave awarded by the Research Committee of the Faculty of Humanities and Teacher Education enabled me to complete most of the writing. Alice and Frank Prochaska smoothed my path at a critical moment.

For advice on the text and the correction of errors I am most grateful to Lucy Bland, Michèle Cohen, Megan Doolittle, Simon Gunn, James Hammerton, Tim Hitchcock, Robert Shoemaker and Razia Yaqoob. I also received help and encouragement from Joanna Bourke, Treva Broughton, Bob Connell, Anna Davin, Anthony Fletcher, Deborah Gorham, Angela John, Ludmilla Jordanova, Denis Judd, David Newsome, Anthony Rotundo, Simon Szreter and Amanda Vickery. I owe a special debt to Michael Roper with whom I have discussed this project endlessly since the beginning, and without whose good-humoured and perceptive criticism the end product would have been very much the poorer. I am grateful to all involved in the production of this book at Yale University Press, especially my editor Robert Baldock. Lyn Greenwood compiled the index in the midst of many other commitments. It would be strange if my own family experience had not influenced my understanding of masculinity and domesticity. Nick Tosh and William Tosh helped in more ways than they are probably aware of, not least in keeping my feet on the ground. They will also understand why this book is dedicated to the memory of their grandmother.

John Tosh
London, March 1998

Introduction: Masculinity and Domesticity

Men make their living and their reputation in the world; women tend the hearth and raise the children. That division of labour has seldom been absolute, and today more than ever is regarded as a shackle from the past rather than a rational basis for society. But the underlying assumption about the proper – or 'natural' – roles of men and women has been profoundly influential in most cultures and in most periods of history. That being the case, what does masculinity have to do with domesticity?

The Victorians answered this question in a novel and affirmative way. Never before or since has domesticity been held to be so central to masculinity. For most of the nineteenth century home was widely held to be a man's place, not only in the sense of being his possession or fiefdom, but also as the place where his deepest needs were met. Questions to do with domestic affections and domestic authority permeated the advice books read by men, as they did the novels of Charles Dickens. In an age when, in the estimation of the Victorians, economic and social advance reached unprecedented levels, the men credited with these achievements were expected to be dutiful husbands and attentive fathers, devotees of hearth and family. The Victorians articulated an ideal of home against which men's conduct has been measured ever since. This book aims to show why this was so. Based on family records and didactic texts, it reconstructs how men of the Victorian middle class experienced the demands of an exacting domestic code, and how they negotiated its contradictions.

Because the home is small, confined and 'private', the domestic lives of men lend themselves to individualistic treatment, in the manner of biography. This has in fact been done for one of my case-studies, the family of Edward Benson.[1] In this book, however, episodes of home life are treated as a manifestation of gender. Of course gender is itself constructed through relationships, especially those of family. But how those relationships are formed, and what meaning they are invested with, are strongly conditioned by cultural expectations. Considered as a social phenomenon, male domesticity was more than the sum of individual experiences. Men's stance towards the home was influenced not only by the particular web of relationships they found themselves in, but by their sense of what was right and proper for themselves as men. The home was central to masculinity, as the place both where the boy was disciplined by dependence, and where the man attained full adult status as householder. The changes which occurred in men's relationship to the home during the nineteenth century marked a shift in gender identity as well as in family dynamics.[2]

This is less familiar ground to historians than it should be. One might suppose that, since most of the history which has ever been written is (as feminists express it) 'men's history', every dimension of that history would have been well aired by now. However, historical scholarship before the advent of second-wave feminism was characterized not merely by the exclusion of women, but by a strict gendering of the public/private divide. According to this perspective, the private sphere of family and household was women's – and thus outside history – just as the public sphere belonged to men – and should therefore be written about without reference to women. The women's history which emerged in the 1970s attacked both these conventions with great energy. It insisted that the private was part of history and set about re-creating the experience of women as wives and mothers; at the same time it demonstrated how women have been actors in the public sphere much more often than had been supposed. Not surprisingly, men's place in the private sphere did not initially form part of this feminist agenda. It began to do so when the scope of women's history was broadened to become the history of gender. Once the focus shifted to the structure of gender relations, rather than the experience of one sex, the family could be analysed comprehensively as a system, embracing all levels of power, dependence and intimacy. In that sense this book could not have been attempted without the achievements of women's history. Prior to the pioneering work of Leonore Davidoff and Catherine Hall in particular, very little research in British history had attempted to see the family as an historically formed, relational whole.[3] Only now can it be said that the 'private' is being reformulated to take account of men, in the same way that the scope of the 'public' has been progressively enlarged to take account of women.

But recent scholarship has done more than adjust the balance between public and private; it has called into question the validity of the distinction itself. The history of women is now well stocked with figures who routinely interpreted the distinction in surprising ways: the entrepreneurial widow, the rescue worker, the propagandist for moral causes.[4] Viewed in its full dimensions, the history of men sits even more uncomfortably with the private/public divide. Indeed much of men's power has resided in their privileged freedom to pass at will between the public and the private. As a social identity masculinity is constructed in three arenas – home, work and all-male association. Not only is the balance between them historically variable; analysing the connections between them soon reveals how each impinges on the other; what was lived does not necessarily bear much relation to our analytical distinctions.[5] Thus *establishing* a household creates the conditions for private life, but it has also long been a crucial stage in winning social recognition as an adult, fully masculine person; until women were admitted to the political process, to speak for one's family in the public arena conferred weight which was denied to the single man. Equally the man's duty to *protect* the home was more than an expression of power over his dependants; it implied collective measures alongside other householders, and thus underpinned the association of masculinity with physical self-reliance and personal bravery. *Providing* for the home is now viewed as a responsibility which takes a man out of the home – to the extent of paring down his other activities as a family member. But prior to the Industrial Revolution most paid productive work was carried on within the home, or in adjoining premises. The business of the household – be it farming, craft production or shopkeeping – often drew on the labour of wife, children, apprentices and servants; domestic relations were therefore also relations of production, and they were managed by the paterfamilias – at least in theory.

However, this is not the only reason why keeping order in the home was such a critical component of masculinity. From the Reformation until the eighteenth century there was a vigorous advice literature on the aims and methods of domestic patriarchy.[6] 'Patriarchy' has become an unfashionable term in recent years, as indicating a crudely reductionist view of sexual stratification. But, in its precise meaning of 'father-rule', patriarchy remains an indispensable concept, not only because men have usually wielded authority within the home, but also because it has been necessary to their masculine self-respect that they do so.[7] This was clearest with regard to the control of female sexuality. Men conducted extramarital relationships in the confidence that, morality aside, their family interests were not thereby placed at risk. But if a husband wished to be sure he was not providing for – or still worse passing on his property to – another man's child, then he must exercise surveillance over his wife's behaviour.[8] Early Modern society was merciless in pillorying men who appeared to have surrendered their mastery in this area, and an immense amount of litigation stemmed from the need to defend the sexual reputation of husbands (and wives also) from imputations of cuckoldry.[9] The man who was not master in his own house courted the scorn of his male associates, as well as economic ruin and uncertain paternity. It is not surprising that political thinkers held that the authority relations of the household were a microcosm of the state: disorder in one boded ill for the stability of the other.[10]

Less often mentioned in studies of domestic patriarchy is the stake men had in the masculine prospects of their sons. Recent cross-cultural studies have emphasized that full masculine status is the gift of one's peers; it builds on the foundation of boy-life outside the family, and is accomplished by economic or military achievements in the public sphere, often marked by a rite of collective, men-only initiation. A fine balance is struck between competition and comradeship as young men learn how to become part of the collective (male) voice of the community. But the success or failure of this progress to maturity reflects not only on the young man himself, but on his father. Fatherhood embodies hopes and fears about the future, in the sense that a man's place in posterity depends on leaving sons behind him who can carry forward his name and lineage. Whether that place in posterity is creditable or not depends on the son's masculine attributes – his manly character and his success in stamping himself upon the world. There is always a question mark over how well equipped sons are for later life. In Early Modern England, until such time as they were sent away to school or apprenticeship, boys lived under the parental roof. Parents in earlier centuries were clear that childhood could profoundly condition gender identity – even if they did not share the twentieth-century conviction that infants may be marked for life by their earliest interaction with adults. The position of girls was perceived to be relatively straightforward: provided they were raised in a domestic atmosphere and acquired the appropriate domestic accomplishments, there was no reason why they should not become good wives and mothers. But boys presented more of a problem. Like girls, they required maternal care in their early years – indeed the wearing of petticoats signalled a pattern of nurture common to both. But, unlike girls, they must be trained to stand on their own feet as a necessary foundation for manly 'independence'. Breeching marked the point at which the father was expected to take a more active hand in the raising of his son. How well he performed in that task affected not only his private satisfaction as a parent, but his social standing as a man.

The domestic sphere, then, is integral to masculinity. To establish a home, to protect it, to provide for it, to control it, and to train its young aspirants to manhood, have usually been essential to a man's good standing with his peers. *Domesticity* represents something else. It denotes not just a pattern of residence or a web of obligations, but a profound attachment: a state of mind as well as a physical orientation. Its defining attributes are privacy and comfort, separation from the workplace, and the merging of domestic space and family members into a single commanding concept (in English, 'home'). Domesticity in this sense was essentially a nineteenth-century invention. One can go further and say that it was an integral aspect of modernity: socially it was inconceivable without large-scale urbanization; culturally it was one of the most important expressions of that awareness of individual interiority which had developed since the Enlightenment.[11] Practised first and most intensively by the bourgeoisie, domesticity became the talisman of bourgeois culture, particularly in painting and novels. But it soon transcended this association, to become the goal of the conventional good life without distinction of class, subscribed to by all but the bohemian and the very poor. Domesticity not only defined people's material ambitions, but also filled their symbolic world in a new way. As John Gillis has put it, the family we live *by* became as important as the family we live *with*.[12] At a symbolic level the family became indistinguishable from the domestic space which it occupied. The home became the privileged site of subjectivity and fantasy: Gaston Bachelard, in his *Poetics of Space*, speaks of daydreams – the comforting illusions of continuity, protection and stability which bonded people so strongly to their homes.[13] There was special poignancy in images of returning home – particularly after exile or a lifetime's wandering. Home came to be identified with childhood, innocence and roots – indeed with authenticity itself.

Middle-class domesticity was in the ascendant throughout the Western world in the nineteenth century. In his classic account of the period, Eric Hobsbawm rightly treats the bourgeois family as one of the central institutions of the age.[14] Walter Benjamin succinctly summed up the phenomenon in France under Louis-Philippe:

> for the first time the living-space became distinguished from the place of work. . . . The private citizen who in the office took reality into account, required of the interior that it should support him in his illusions.[15]

Freud's work was essentially a commentary on the pathology of European urban domesticity, the only family system he knew well (which is one reason why his claims to universality must be handled with caution). But, as foreign observers were quick to concede, the domestic nation *par excellence* was England. The full apparatus of domesticity appeared there earlier than in any other country.[16] The English placed domestic values at the heart of their culture; they subscribed to them more earnestly, and they were probably more outraged when they were flouted. G.M. Young only slightly exaggerated when he remarked that, along with the representative principle in public life, the family was the only aspect of Victorian society which was not subject to serious critical assault.[17]

The nineteenth-century cult of the home is commonly associated with women and – often an afterthought – with children. The defining imagery is feminine. The best-known propagandists for domesticity were women, like Hannah More and Sarah Ellis. The intensification of the domestic ideal during this period is a major theme in women's history which has occasioned a vigorous scholarly debate. The range of activities open to women became narrower, and their access to the public sphere more restricted. On the other hand, since most middle-class women were wives and mothers before anything else, the greater prestige now attached to these roles tended to raise the status of women, and to endow them with greater moral authority.[18] Yet, important though these tendencies were, they represented essentially changes of degree since domestic life had always been women's concern. In the case of men, the tenets of domesticity if fully implemented meant a transformation. By elevating the claims of wife and mother far above other ties, domesticity undermined the tradition of a vigorous associational life with other men, and imposed a new constraint on men's participation in the public sphere. The domestic ideal was formulated and promoted by men, and it was frequently and sincerely endorsed in both their published writings and their letters and diaries. The full weight of Evangelical Christianity – essentially a *domestic* religion – was thrown behind it.

For two generations – from the 1830s to the 1870s – didactic writers in Victorian England were almost at one in declaring that bourgeois men not only had time for a domestic life, but a deep and compelling need of it.[19]

In one sense the cult of the home was strikingly at odds with the direction which industrial society was taking in the nineteenth century. Hobsbawm has called the middle-class family 'the most mysterious institution of the age'. Bourgeois society, he says, rested on freedom, opportunity, the cash nexus and the pursuit of individual profit; yet the family, as a collective unit based on reciprocity and strictly ascribed roles, denied all of these principles.[20] In the world at large the patriarchal model of authority had been largely superseded by the idea of contract – but it continued to flourish in the family. In fact these very contradictions hold the clue to the mystery. The nineteenth century was the first in which significant numbers of men of education and means experienced work as alienating: to be more precise, not so much their own work, as the polluted environment and the dehumanized personal relations which were associated with it. The marvels of technological and economic progress had been bought at an appalling social cost, as commentators never ceased to point out. The home owed its importance in men's lives to the refuge it offered them from these ills. It provided not only the rest and refreshment which any breadwinner needs, but the emotional and psychological supports which made working life tolerable. Much of this was – hopefully – provided by family ties, in a happy blend of love and order. Much also depended on what the home stood for in a less tangible way. Domesticity supposedly allowed workhorses and calculating machines to become men again, by exposing them to human rhythms and human affections. The very qualities which set the family apart from the prevailing social mores were what recommended it to middle-class men who were appalled by the disfigurement of industrialism, even as they struggled to profit from it.

However, this ascendancy was much less secure than it looked. The heavy moralizing of home ties conflicted with two longstanding aspects of masculinity. The first was homosociality – or regular association with other men. Moralists might dismiss this as indolent (and sometimes sinful) pleasure-seeking, but clubs and taverns were the forum in which masculine standing was appraised and recognized, and often a means of reinforcing gender privilege. The same purpose was served by the vast array of associations and committees by which the Victorians pursued more public goals, though these were easier to justify. But even they were vulnerable to the charge of diverting men from their domestic responsibilities. Men's associational life was open to moral reservations in a new and – for many – a troubling way. Secondly, domesticity was difficult to square with the traditional association of masculinity with heroism and adventure. In most settled societies there is a tension between the qualities men need to sustain the routines of production and reproduction, and the qualities they might need if their community is threatened from outside.[21] It is no coincidence that the heyday of masculine domesticity from the 1830s to the

1860s was for the most part a period of peace, when the country was untroubled by external threat. Middle-class men did not imagine that they were ever likely to be called to a life of adventure as soldier, sailor, emigrant or frontiersman. Their public ambitions were professional or entrepreneurial success – as 'captains of industry' but hardly captains of men. But there was a limit to how long this kind of denial could be practised; from the 1870s the view was increasingly heard that domesticity was unglamorous, unfulfilling and – ultimately – unmasculine.

Domesticity was also beset by serious inner contradictions. The expectation that men spend their non-working hours at home assumed a companionate marriage, based on love, common values and shared interests. Yet this was the period when belief in sexual difference was more absolute than at any time before or since. On a foundation of anatomical and physiological distinctions, intellect, emotions and character were all interpreted in a sexually polarized way, which was reinforced by the different patterns of education for boys and girls. Home was the place where, in theory, masculine and feminine were brought together in a proper relation of complementarity. This could mean many different things in practice. It might mean a rigid assertion of patriarchal control, or an acceptance by the husband of his wife's preeminence in the home. It often meant a lack of comprehension of each other's sexual needs. There was a tendency – though this must not be overstated – for fatherhood to be reduced to a providing role, since the relational nurturing aspects of parenting were deemed to be 'feminine'. Finally, considerable tensions surrounded the upbringing of boys, since their gender identity seemed threatened by the attentions of the mother; this was one reason why a rising proportion of middle-class youth was educated away from home.

The identification of masculinity with domesticity was never complete, and it was not likely to be enduring. Towards the end of the nineteenth century the strains became visible. Given the traditional religious support for household patriarchy, the rapid undermining of orthodox belief from the 1860s onwards was deeply unsettling of domestic order. Bourgeois men were increasingly disturbed by the identification of the home with the feminine, represented as the 'tyranny of five-o'clock tea'. They were also more sensitive to the traditional assumption that peer-group activity was the proper sphere of masculinity; club life and outdoor sports flourished as never before. There was a new wave of men's writing about domesticity, critical and even hostile. Perhaps most revealing, the old association of masculinity with adventure resurfaced in the era of high imperialism after 1880 – the period of Robert Louis Stevenson and Rider Haggard as well as Gordon and Kitchener. Domesticated masculinity came under mounting attack, as Englishmen were called upon to colonize the empire, and to defend it in difficult times.

In the end the nineteenth-century middle class established not so much a new masculine norm as a new dialectic between opposing tendencies. The Victorians articulated an ideal of home life against which men's conduct has been measured ever since, while at the same time clearly exposing the contradictions which have led to that ideal being widely questioned. Although many features of bourgeois domesticity in its heyday seem strange to us – its dependence on servants, its rigid regime for children, and its preoccupation with rituals – Victorian England is not called the first modern society for nothing. The middle-class family of those times was the first to grapple with what continues to be a central experience of daily life – the separation of home from work. The cult of home was the Victorians' response to this new experience.

PART ONE

Preconditions

CHAPTER ONE

The Middle-Class Household

On 31 March 1851 John Heaton proudly noted in his diary that the census enumerator had called that day and 'our baby's name was added to the list of the population'. Apart from two-month old Helen, the other occupants of 2 East Parade, Leeds, were John Heaton himself, his wife Fanny, two female servants and a stable-boy. For a man who had not married until he was 32, it was a moment to savour. This was the house to which he had brought home his new wife barely a year before, after a prolonged and stormy courtship. Now, with a child as well as a wife, his masculine standing was secure. By the time the next census was taken in 1861 there was further evidence of Heaton's rising status. The household now included four children and as many servants; there was also a resident governess. The family no longer lived in a terraced house close by the commercial centre of Leeds, but in a substantial Georgian villa called Claremont on the edge of the town. On most days John Heaton walked from the house to Leeds Infirmary where he was physician, or to the Medical School where he was a lecturer. Having been born 'over the shop' at the bookseller's business his father owned at 7 Briggate, he was keenly appreciative of the greater gentility he now enjoyed in an elegant merchant's house, standing in its own grounds, for which he had paid the considerable sum of £2,500.[1]

Dr Heaton's progression from crowded street to quiet and elegance was typical of the rising middle class of his day. The comfortable domestic circumstances he enjoyed by his late thirties were testimony to both parental support and his own professional abilities. Placed at 17 by his father as an apprentice with a Leeds surgeon, he had distinguished himself at Leeds Medical School, before completing his training at University College Hospital, London. Medicine enjoyed high prestige, along with the law and the Church. Membership of these 'old' professions was often taken to confer gentlemanly status, partly because of the requirement of formal education, and partly because giving advice or service for a fee carried little of the commercial taint attached to buying and selling in the market-place. In the course of the nineteenth century other professions secured recognition too, such as accountancy, engineering, surveying and architecture. All of them depended primarily on training and expertise rather than capital and entrepreneurial flair.

John Heaton could easily have found himself on the other side of the commercial/professional divide. If his father had not been so determined to advance his son, he would have groomed him to take over the bookselling business, or else apprenticed him to a manufacturer instead of a surgeon. The professions made up one great segment of the Victorian middle class, and to the extent that their number included men of letters and journalists, their cultural impact was assured. But strength of numbers lay with the men of trade and business. It was this entrepreneurial element which increased most rapidly during the first half of the nineteenth century and accounted for the largest number of fresh recruits to the middle class. The most successful enjoyed meteoric careers: Isaac Holden, one of the foremost woollen masters in the West Riding, had been born the son of a pit headsman and had gone to work in the mill as cotton piecer at the age of ten. By 1847, before he had turned 40, he had his own woollen worsted mill in Bradford, and within ten years he was known as 'the first comber in Europe'.[2] Such men were fabulously wealthy. They formed the provincial business elite of the country, often graced by an aristocratic-style mansion, a seat in the House of Commons, and even a knighthood (Isaac Holden secured all three). Below them were the owners of medium-size factories, the bankers, and the 'merchants', which usually denoted proprietors of wholesale and import-export concerns; these were the backbone of the commercial middle class. William Lucas took over the family brewing business in Hitchin in the 1830s; it made him a considerable figure in the town and enabled him, his wife and his nine children to live in some comfort.[3] Such men were squarely placed in the middle ranks of the emerging bourgeoisie, and they were sometimes known as the 'middling sort'.[4] Their counterparts in the countryside were the more substantial tenant farmers who leased extensive acreages and treated their operation as a business: they invested in agricultural improvements and looked to rising profits. In the Victorian period a middle-class dignity could hardly be sustained by men in these occupations on an income much lower than £300 per annum, and the same was true of members of the professions. Such an income could run to a commodious house and at least three indoor servants. The really successful professional or commercial man might earn anything up to £1,000 or more, in which case he was likely to maintain a horse and carriage with groom.

At the bottom came a broad base of less highly considered occupations, men usually on incomes between £100 and £300 and employing only one or two domestic servants. All of these occupations departed in some significant particular from the middle-class ideal: clerks because they were hired employees; shopkeepers because ready money passed directly between them and their customers; small workshop masters because they got their hands dirty. In the course of the nineteenth century this level of society became known as the lower middle class. It was, of course, very much bigger than the more comfortable stratum above: some 510,000 households, compared with 90,000, according to a careful computation made in 1867.[5] The distinctions of status and wealth to be found within the middle class were greater than in either the working class or the upper class. It is misleading to think of a unified bourgeoisie, and in some ways more realistic to accept the residual implications of the term 'middle' class. All the same, the middle classes were distinguished from the aristocracy and gentry because they worked regularly for a living, and from the working class because they did not stoop to manual labour. Within the moral economy of Victorian society these were significant distinctions. Moreover such a status was all the more valued because it could not be taken for granted. Despite the unmistakable air of prosperity which hangs over the middle class, especially during the mid-Victorian plateau of the 1850s and 1860s, contemporaries were keenly aware of how precarious all forms of business were. The risk of failure during a commercial downturn could never be entirely discounted. Isaac Holden's prospects as a newly independent master were almost blighted by the recession of 1847–48; he was seriously considering emigration when another manufacturer stepped in with the offer of a partnership.[6] The ranks of governesses in middle-class households were swelled by young ladies whose fathers had failed in business or had lacked the means to lay by a nest-egg for them.[7] Their presence was a pointed reminder to the family employing them of the risks to which they too were exposed.

★

Victorian domesticity carried such a heavy emotional load that its material prerequisites can easily be taken for granted. Yet the deeply felt appreciation of home as a place of peace, seclusion and refuge (to be explored in Chapter 2) would have meant little without certain standards of comfort, privacy and routine. Those cluttered domestic interiors for which the Victorians are so often mocked today reflect the range of activities which were now carried on in the home, each requiring its distinctive rituals and often its exclusive equipment: the daily act of worship, the instruction of young children, reading aloud at the fireside, music-making around the piano, the entertainment of friends and relatives to tea or dinner. But what these activities did not include was the production of the material surplus on which the household depended for its existence. Paid work was a prominent feature of the middle-class home: its smooth running depended on a great deal of back-breaking and monotonous labour performed by domestic servants. But the household was not, by and large, a productive unit. Its residents did not team up to provide goods or services in demand outside the home. The Victorian middle-class domestic unit represented the final and most decisive stage in the long process whereby the rationale of the Western family shifted from being primarily economic to become sentimental and emotional. More specifically, it reflected a steadily increasing separation of work from home. Today we can begin to see the reversal of this process as the electronic revolution makes it possible for more and more business to be conducted from home. But in cultural terms a physical gulf between home and work is still regarded as such a central feature of ordinary lives that we find it difficult to imagine a society where it scarcely existed.

Yet broadly speaking this was the situation until the end of the eighteenth century. One can detect indicators pointing towards the modern pattern a century or more before that. For example affluent merchants in London had long shown a taste for country residences, but these were second homes to which they only repaired at weekends and in slack seasons. London also boasted a rising number of men who worked in government departments or large capitalist enterprises and had no reason to mix home and work in their elegant West End residences. But London was exceptional in both its employment patterns and its wealth. Life was different in the provincial towns (and indeed in the less sought-after areas of London). Whether in trade or in one of the professions, middle-class men usually conducted their business and domestic life under the same roof, with no clear division between the two. In a town like Colchester, for example, traders, manufacturers and professionals lived in what one historian has called 'the business household', where the divide between working and domestic arrangements was minimal. Customers were seen, and deals struck, in the front parlour; apprentices slept in the upper storeys, sometimes alongside bedrooms converted into workshops; goods were stored in the basement and cellars. The pattern in the countryside was similar. The farm was managed from the farmhouse; the commercial side of the business was conducted in the parlour; a whole range of agricultural produce was finished or processed in the farmhouse; servants lived under the farmer's roof and ate at his table. The contrast between mid-eighteenth and mid-nineteenth century must not be exaggerated, and variations of region and occupation need to be borne in mind. Nevertheless the dominant tendency is unmistakable. From being a site of productive work, the household was increasingly becoming a refuge from it.[8]

The pattern of labour use is perhaps the most striking indication of the fusion of domestic and business worlds in pre-Victorian society. Masculine self-respect certainly demanded that a man provide for his family, and great shame was attached to one who 'failed'. But the requirement to provide did not carry the same exclusive connotations as the more modern notion of the breadwinner. In the eighteenth century men of the middle rank did not usually carry the burden of earning single-handed, nor did they think that they should. The typical bourgeois household comprised man and wife, children, and a range of subordinate non-kin, including apprentices, labourers and servants. The line between domestic work and business or professional work was blurred. Women were involved in production for the market, just as men took some interest in domestic matters. Women who contributed no labour to the household business, like wealthy leisured wives, attracted censure precisely because they were a deviation from the norm. The bourgeois wife often acted as her husband's junior partner in his business – working alongside him at the shop counter, for example, or during harvest time. The contemporary term which best summed up the wife's economic role was 'help-meet'. Often she had sole responsibility for some crucial aspect of the business, like the accounts book in a merchant concern, or the dairy and the poultry yard in a farm, or buying in raw materials for a manufacturing workshop. Widows sometimes took over their husbands' businesses, and it is clear that many were well qualified to do so through having shared so much of the work in a conjugal partnership. Children formed part of the family pool of labour too. They were at the beck and call of both father and mother to run errands and perform sometimes monotonous tasks. As for apprentices, they were attracted by the prospect of learning a trade, but there was usually nothing in their contracts to prevent them being set to housework, particularly when they were placed under the day-to-day care of the mistress.[9]

This type of working household had characterized the middling sort for some two or three hundred years. It was still widespread at the close of the eighteenth century, and it features very widely in the childhood memories of middle-class people who grew to maturity in the early years of Queen Victoria. John Heaton of Leeds recalled how he had been brought up in family accommodation adjacent to his father's bookshop, with a storage room for secondhand books and servants' quarters above. Edward Benson, the future Archbishop of Canterbury, had begun life in a house within the chemical works managed by his father.[10] Neither Heaton nor Benson idealized their childhood circumstances, but more sentimentalized memories appealed to a widespread sense of loss. In the 1880s Charlotte Sturge recalled how, early in the century, her father had bought a tannery on the edge of Coggeshall in Essex. It came with an adjoining 'good, old-fashioned, red-brick house' covered in climbing roses, and a kitchen garden which produced superb fruit. Father had time to teach his sons to swim and his daughters to ride, as well as pursue his business as a tanner.[11] That vision of the home as the site of work, nurture and leisure in a semi-rural setting recurs again and again in novels of the period, like George Eliot's *The Mill on the Floss* (1860) and Dinah Craik's *John Halifax, Gentleman* (1856). Victorian nostalgia was fed by many social and cultural changes, but none was more poignant for them than the transformation in the nature of home from a hub of integrated activities to a place of refuge. They expressed their ambivalence about up-to-date notions of family propriety and comfort by idealizing the domestic past.

Sentimentalized family histories and novels made the transformation seem more abrupt than it really was. The key change, on which so much else depended, was the shift in the focus of women's lives from the family economy to the private domestic sphere. Historians have come up with sharply varying accounts – mainly because of the wide variation between town and country, between regions, and between occupations.[12] During the eighteenth century there seems to have been a growing tendency for wives of the middling sort to withdraw from the business activities of the household when affluence allowed them to do so.[13] But the mid-Victorians were broadly correct in believing that their own lifetimes had witnessed a vital stage in the story. Taking the middle class as a whole, the pace of change was particularly pronounced during the first half of the nineteenth century – the period of most intensive industrialization in Britain.

However, this does not mean that the separation of work from home can be attributed directly to 'the factory'. Most middle-class men worked in occupations which had nothing to do with factories, and those who did were often in no hurry to move away from them. When Isaac Holden began looking for his own mill in 1845, he turned down a promising one at Shipley because his wife objected to the mill-house.[14] (In Elizabeth Gaskell's *North and South* Manchester cotton master John Thornton also lives with his mother in the mill-house.) In fact first-generation manufacturing entrepreneurs often lived on site because they valued on-the-spot supervision of their businesses before everything else; it was the second generation which shunned the mill-house and lived in style elsewhere. The trend in favour of a separation of home and work was driven less by the factory than by the pace of economic growth in the towns generally. As more and more businesses were concentrated in the urban centres, noise, smell and other forms of pollution increased. The heart of a manufacturing town became less attractive as a place to live. Commercial land values increased at the same time, thus encouraging the sale of the remaining residential properties. In Bradford, for example, only 7 per cent of bourgeois householders lived in the town centre by 1851; most of them were to be found in quasi-suburban residential districts.[15] On grounds of both amenity and economy, middle-class men preferred to maintain a residence away from their place of work.

Away from one's place of work might mean no more than leasing a terraced house in a square or crescent adjacent to the commercial district, as in London's ever-expanding West End. But during the decades immediately before and after Victoria's accession, it often meant a secluded semi-rural neighbourhood. In Manchester the out-of-town villa was already fashionable among the commercial classes by the 1830s. Edgbaston in Birmingham, laid out in the 1820s, was another early example. This was the suburb proper, but to begin with the pleasures of seclusion were limited mainly to people who were sufficiently affluent to keep a carriage. The real change came with the transport revolution of the early Victorian period. Railways out of the main cities were rapidly developed from the 1840s. By the 1850s the horse-drawn omnibus was responding flexibly to the commuter market, to be joined by the horse-drawn tram in the 1860s. It was these innovations which largely determined the pace and direction of suburban growth. The bus and the tram extended the social scope of the suburb to include not only the middle class but the upper reaches of the working class too. Speculative builders threw up properties within the range of every level of middle-class income: the villa for the successful businessman or lawyer, the semi-detached (an invention of the 1790s) for the large shopkeeper or accountant, the terraced house for the clerk or schoolteacher.[16]

Yet the separation of work from home was far from total. Its effects were most noticeable in the commercial classes, with manufacturing not far behind. But in some occupations the nature of the work allowed for much greater continuity. This was clearest in the case of the clergy who conducted church business from their homes, prepared their sermons and received their parishioners there. Doctors saw patients and made up prescriptions in their own homes. Lawyers continued for some time to combine home and office. Writers and 'men of letters' also worked at home, often heavily reliant on the unacknowledged secretarial assistance of a wife or a daughter. At the other end of the social scale were those on the margins of the middle class who might dearly wish to move away from their place of work but could not afford to do so. This was especially true of shopkeepers who depended heavily on unpaid family labour during working hours. It is worth bearing in mind that, as late as 1851, middle-class families who lived away from the workplace were still outnumbered by those who lived over the shop or immediately adjacent to their work premises.[17] But even here the domestic atmosphere was enhanced by a careful distinction between rooms identified by function. The office or surgery was likely to be set apart from the rest of the household; the ideal position for a clergyman's study was just inside the front door, so that visitors could be admitted without disturbing the rest of the household.[18] Thomas Carlyle reinforced his professional identity as 'man of letters' by having a soundproof study constructed at the top of the house. The same careful attention to the cordoning off of domestic space was to be seen in the countryside. There was a spate of farmhouse rebuilding, as farmers put pressure on their landlords to build better appointed residences with a dignified approach which did not pass through the farmyard. The separation of work from home may have been a more protracted and tortuous process than is often allowed, but the long-term trend is clear. Advice books may not be reliable as a mirror of behaviour, but it is nevertheless significant that during this period most of them took it as read that the men in the households they were addressing were out at work for most of the day.[19]

★

The most critical precondition of middle-class domesticity was the withdrawal of the wife from direct involvement in the productive work of the household. The idea of a marital working partnership was virtually at an end among the Victorian bourgeoisie. Once breadwinning had been removed from the home, it soon came to be accepted that wives should have nothing to do with it. For as long as work could be represented as something which all members of the household performed, the wife had been able to take her part without loss of status. Once work was located outside the home, the implications of intruding in the public sphere and perhaps forgoing her husband's protection were disturbing. His lonely status as breadwinner confined her to the role of home-maker rather than help-meet. The strength of this prejudice can be judged from the fact that it rubbed off on women for whom team-work alongside the husband was still a realistic option. Thus farmers' wives, if their husbands' means could stretch to it, withdrew from work directly connected with the farm, leaving the poultry yard and the still-room to lowlier persons. There were exceptions, such as shopkeepers, but the blurring of domestic and working roles was exactly what undermined the claim of these people to middle-class status. The influential advice-book writer Sarah Ellis asserted that no shame should attach to women who worked in their husbands' businesses; but in the same breath she acknowledged their 'moral courage', which gives some idea of the prejudice they were up against.[20] By the late 1830s when Ellis was writing, home and work were coming to be seen as independent spheres; if the husband's role was not entirely confined to work, the wife's role was certainly seen as falling within the home.

This polarization had important implications for the composition of the household. If its functions were domestic, then anyone employed in the business was out of place there. Of course this logic was not clear to everyone, and the decline of living-in among commercial employees was gradual and patchy. As late as 1833, when the young Daniel Macmillan took a three-year situation as a salaried shopman with a Cambridge bookseller, he lived in his house, ate all his meals with him, and went with the family to chapel on Sundays.[21] However, conventions were changing fast, especially for appren-tices. Despite a steady decline during the eighteenth century, the institution of apprenticeship remained an indispensable means of training and a source of cheap labour. But it was becoming detached from its traditional association with paternalism and dependence. Living under the roof of the master, subject to his authority, was the visible sign of a pre-industrial personal nexus, all the more appropriate when the apprentice and his master were of similar social background. But the business nature of the relationship was now seen to disqualify the apprentice from mixing on an equal footing with the family. When Sarah Ellis addressed the women of the commercial classes in 1843, one of her most impassioned passages was an appeal for motherly care to be shown to young apprentices; she knew that there were only a few 'noble and beautiful instances' of mistresses who behaved in this way.[22] By this time apprentices were more likely to be boarded out, or left to fend for themselves. The Young Men's Christian Association, founded in 1844, was intended explicitly to provide these young men with a substitute for the moralizing influence of their masters' homes from which they were now excluded.[23] In the countryside the removal of employees from the master's household was no less marked. During the late eighteenth and early nineteenth centuries the custom of hiring 'bed-and-board' farm servants for a year disappeared from the south and east of the country (though it survived for longer in the north), to be replaced by the day-labourer system, as farmers strove to minimize their labour costs. The shared meal in the farmhouse survived longer, but it conflicted with the aspiration of tenant farmers and their wives to live in bourgeois gentility like their urban counterparts. Economic calculation and status-seeking combined to overturn the traditional integration of domestic and agrarian life.[24]

New notions of domestic decorum also tended to exclude the lodger. The taking of lodgers had been commonplace in eighteenth-century middling households. Now it placed the mistress of the house in the invidious position of putting a place in her family up for sale, and it seemed a scarcely tolerable invasion of privacy. The important exception was the lodger who was also related to the master or mistress of the household: unmarried women and young men apprenticed away from home often lived with kin, paying their way but counting for much of the time as 'family'. It was the purely cash nexus between mistress and lodger which reflected badly on the household. Allowances could also be made for a respectable widow in straitened circumstances. But otherwise the taking of lodgers tended to suggest that domestic decorum had been sacrificed to financial necessity – a painful admission for any bourgeois family to make. Conversely, individuals who moved from house to house as lodgers were less than full members of middle-class society; in all save the financial sense they were dispensable to the families who offered them bed and board, and their membership of the household was highly qualified.[25]

The exclusion of apprentices, farm servants and lodgers left one remaining significant category of non-kin – living-in domestic staff. Servants had for a long time been regarded as a badge of middle-class status, since their presence implied that the wife was spared some of the drudgery of housework and thus had time for entertaining and display. In the Victorian period the association between servant-keeping and middle-class status intensified. The only major exception was in the northern industrial towns, where the numbers of servants were held down by a bourgeois ethic of self-denial, combined with alternative sources of employment for potential servants.[26] Cooking, which had once been within the compass of the lady of the house, was now thought to be beneath her. Second only to the kitchen as a focus of domestic labour was the hearth – appropriately enough in view of its symbolic importance to the home. Coal had to be fetched, the grate cleaned, the fire laid, and the fire-irons and fenders polished. More fastidious standards of personal hygiene and cleanliness took their toll in human labour expended on such tasks as carrying water, laundering clothes, dusting surfaces and polishing furniture. More demanding wardrobe requirements increased the amount of sewing to be done in the home. The single maid-of-all-work was often taken to be the dividing line between the most marginal middle-class household and the labouring classes below, yet such a person could carry out only a small proportion of all these tasks. The standard establishment for a securely based bourgeois family was three live-in servants: a cook, a housemaid and a nursemaid (or sometimes a parlour-maid). Wealthy households employed the full 'below stairs' complement of butler, footman,

housekeeper, several maids, coachman, groom and gardener. The employment
of male servants was a mark of superior status since they usually cost more than
female servants, and since the largest proportion did stable work, indicating that
the master owned a horse and carriage. Male servants were deemed more
difficult to manage, especially by the mistress, so the wife's undivided
responsibility for domestic matters tended to intensify the preference for an all-
female staff.[27]

The Victorian middle-class household represented a new departure not only
in the number of servants employed, but in their segregation from the rest of
the household. It was comparatively rare for the wife to work alongside her
servants. Her role was to issue instructions, and because she was often ignorant
of practical domestic skills (especially cooking), incompetent servants could
reduce a household to disorder. Servants were emphatically not 'one of the
family', except perhaps in the case of a long-serving superannuated nanny.
Recent intensive demographic work suggests that a higher proportion of
servants in such households were related to their employers than has been
realized, but this was certainly not the norm.[28] For the most part servants were
of a lower class; indeed most of them were young women of very humble
origins only recently arrived from rural areas, with whom their employers had
no desire to pass the time of day. They were accommodated in the attic or the
basement, often in shared rooms, designed to impinge as little as possible on the
rest of the household. In well-appointed houses kitchen, pantry and scullery
functioned as a segregated working zone reserved for the domestic staff. The
architect Robert Kerr clearly articulated the assumptions which informed this
arrangement in 1864: 'The family constitute one community; the servants
another. Whatever may be their mutual regard and confidence as dwellers
under the same roof, each class is entitled to shut its door upon the other, and
be alone'.[29] Up-to-date notions of decorum and privacy dictated that servants
be kept at arm's length. Yet at the same time their conditions of service were a
world away from the contractual and impersonal nexus which was held up as
the model in the world outside.[30]

There was, however, one employee in the household who could not so
easily be held at a distance. This was the governess. Her anomalous status
occasioned much heart-searching. Here was a young woman of respectable
family (though usually an impecunious one) performing paid service within the
home for people of her own class. Any family wealthy enough to afford three
servants, and with daughters to educate, was likely to regard the hire of a
governess as the only option. Immense thought was given by advice-book
writers as to how a family in this position should treat a person of such awkward
standing. The contradictions were never resolved, and the relationship continued to be found stressful by governesses themselves and also by their
employers until well beyond the Victorian era. The governess was the most
glaring exception to the convention which placed a clear divide between family
and domestics.[31]

The sense that notions of 'the family' were being narrowed down to correspond more closely with what we mean by the 'nuclear' family is confirmed by linguistic usage. In previous centuries 'family' had been most often used to mean either 'lineage' (in the sense important to a gentleman of title and land) or 'household' including all its inmates, whatever their rank or status. As recently as 1755 Samuel Johnson had given as one dictionary definition of 'family' 'those who live in the same house'. Early Modern England had no word meaning 'all the household except servants'. By the early nineteenth century, however, 'family' was filling precisely this gap. The new usage reflected both the rapid decline of live-in apprentices and farm labourers, and the growing tendency to segregate domestic servants from the family proper. The only remaining confusion concerned more remote blood-kin, typically adult siblings of the master or mistress, or grandparents. The chances of a middle-class household including such people were quite high. According to the 1851 census, the proportion of bourgeois households with co-resident kin was as high as 30 per cent in some towns. Grown-up children usually continued to live with their parents until they married – except in the case of sons seeking their fortune elsewhere or daughters put to governessing. The shorter life expectancy of this period meant that when those parents died, their younger children were quite likely to be unmarried. The logical course for these adult spinsters and bachelors was to move in with a sibling who *was* married. The presence of an uncle or aunt 'thickened' the kin structure of the household; a widowed parent 'lengthened' it. Extended kin (especially of the former kind) had an ambivalent status – usually dependent, but still part of the family and often called upon to deputize for an absent mother or father.[32]

The more rigidly domestic characterization of the home and its occupants was reflected in room use. Middle-class homes no longer had rooms devoted primarily to business, except in the case of some professional men. Cellars for commercial storage, workshops and offices were less and less common. Instead there was a proliferation of single-purpose rooms for domestic use, as notions of privacy and function became more exacting. Here the nineteenth-century middle class was building on the new standard of comfort which had been set by the wealthy since the Restoration period. In more affluent homes the complement of rooms might run to: dressing room(s), drawing room, morning room, dining room, breakfast room, and a library or study. Lower down the social scale the size of rooms was of course much reduced, but the instinct was always to replicate as far as possible the proliferation of rooms in wealthier homes: a reception room which could be divided in two, a scullery separated from a breakfast room, a room (however tiny) for the maid, and so on. The garden had a slightly ambiguous status. On the face of it a place reserved for relaxation and exercise, it could on occasion be colonized by the husband as an open-air study or as a place for conversing with business or professional colleagues.[33]

The move to the suburbs also brought about changes in household routine,

1. The garden as workplace: Edward Benson at the Master's Lodge, Wellington College,
1860s.

particularly in meal times. When men lived over the shop or across the yard, they came home to dinner at midday as a matter of course. Around 1840 the dinner hour for bourgeois families in Leeds was still 2 p.m. As late as the 1860s William Byles, proprietor of the *Bradford Observer*, used to return home on foot for dinner at 2 p.m., having ordered the joint on his way into work; he would then take a nap and go back to the office at 4 p.m.[34] But by this time Byles's daily routine had ceased to be typical of professional men. Dinner was now more usually served in the evening, at 7 p.m or 7.30. In polite circles the new fashion was attributed to the Duke of Wellington, who was said to have introduced into England his habit while on campaign of not sitting down to table until the day's fighting was done: the late dinner time was 'the social monument of the conqueror of Waterloo'.[35] But among the middle class the late dinner hour was an adaptation to the requirements of the commuting husband. As fewer men chose to live within walking distance of their work in the manner of William Byles, dinner around 7 p.m. tended to become standard practice. A man who worked in commerce was likely to be tired and very hungry by that time, having taken no more than a sandwich or a biscuit in the middle of the day. Dinner was also the focus of entertainment. Until the latter part of the century there were few restaurants in London and other big cities, while chop-houses and coaching inns were considered unsuitable for ladies. There was therefore heavy emphasis on the dinner party, adjusted according to taste and pocket, once a month being perhaps a reasonable average. Meals at home between breakfast and dinner, on the other hand, became more closely identified with the womenfolk: luncheon at around 1 p.m., and afternoon tea – though this might signal the arrival home of the breadwinner. With work away from home extending over six days, Sunday assumed even greater significance than before as the day of repose and retreat.[36]

Entertaining at home was conducted by middle-class Victorians with considerable formality. It was one of the many sins with which they were reproached by the rebellious post-Victorians. Etiquette manuals offered advice on how to behave when the domestic circle was suddenly enlarged by the addition of company from outside. Guests came usually by invitation only. The outside appearance of the house was unwelcoming, with the front door kept firmly shut and any caller required to state his or her business to a servant.[37] Advanced notions of domesticity had not always been associated with this stand-offish attitude. The eighteenth-century gentry and upper bourgeoisie had practised a more informal sociability, in keeping with the fluid boundary between living space and work space. Business associates might be entertained at breakfast, and visitors drop in unexpectedly. The bourgeois house often presented the appearance of a thoroughfare.[38] This tradition persisted for some time. At Clapham Common around the turn of the century the houses of the leading Evangelical families were open to each other, and the children treated them as common property.[39]

The reason why seclusion and privacy were carried to their High Victorian extreme had to do with status anxieties. As the middle class expanded, people became more and more preoccupied with their precise standing within it, and this sensitivity was often intensified by denominational distinctions. The institutional expression of these anxieties was the social call, when ladies exchanged visits and left cards, or not as the case might be, as a means of identifying which channels should be kept open and which ones must be blocked. The end result could be a pitifully confined pool of acquaintances. John Ruskin's parents were so sensitive on this score that there was scarcely a house in Herne Hill to which they could happily permit their son to go.[40] Formality towards visitors to the family home reflected the same uncertainty. As increasingly fine distinctions were introduced between suburbs of graded exclusiveness, and between housing of graded style and amenities, the home came to be treated not only as a refuge but a fortress – a development nicely caught by Dickens in his portrayal in *Great Expectations* (1861) of Mr Wemmick, whose suburban house was actually protected by a drawbridge. Ultimately the separation of home from work was matched by the separation of home from the neighbourhood community.

★

The changing character of the household conditioned middle-class family life during the Victorian period in ways which went far beyond matters of space and locality. In the first place, the home now received much more attention as a badge of social position. Already by the 1830s the kind of household described here had become not simply a by-product of middle-class status, but an essential qualification for that status. Occupation, or 'calling' in more elevated usage, was the nub of middle-class masculine identity, it is true. But domestic circumstances were the most visible and reliable guide to a man's level of income (and thus his success in work), as well as being a mirror of his moral character. These considerations were particularly important for those who had risen recently in the class hierarchy and lacked social confidence. Sarah Ellis's many advice books in the late 1830s and 1840s were addressed primarily to women in this situation. She did not mince words about the class significance of a properly appointed home: 'gentlemen may employ their hours of business in almost any degrading occupation and, if they have the means of supporting a respectable establishment at home, may be gentlemen still'.[41] In other words a non-working wife, a complement of servants and a tastefully furnished house reserved for domestic pursuits might be a more convincing demonstration of class status than a man's business or profession. There is a sense in which the bourgeois wife existed to show off her husband's capacity to keep her in leisure and luxury.[42]

The problem was that the social value of domestic amenities was subject to an inexorable process of inflation in a way that occupation was not. The situation was not unprecedented: it can be traced back to the new consumerism of the wealthier middling sort in the eighteenth century.[43] But the expanding size of the middle class in the nineteenth century intensified the gradations of status within it, and the importance of the visible evidence on which these distinctions were made. Furnishings became more sumptuous, the principal reception rooms more cluttered. By mid-century hardly a bourgeois drawing-room was without a piano. The horse and carriage – first one horse, then two – became an insistent marker of social rank. The library and the best bedroom, as well as the drawing room, were designed to impress the visitor. Young couples were set on beginning married life with a home which was at least as well appointed as their parents', and the time taken to accumulate the necessary resources tended to push the age of first marriage for both men and women of the middle class up and up.[44]

It would be hard to imagine this degree of sensitivity about the position, scale and contents of the home if work and living space had still been thrown together in the traditional manner. Living over the shop, or in an apartment behind commercial premises, was hardly conducive to an ethic of display. Nor did it allow for regular moving house, since most places of business did not lend themselves to being uprooted. In Victorian England, on the other hand, moving house was one of the surest signs of moving 'up' (or 'down'). Detached from the place of business, the home was free to become a finely tuned and flexible indicator of social status. A change of aspiration or income was quickly reflected in a better address; an over-ambitious move would be short-lived, resulting in a compensating move 'down'. Deciding to move house was comparatively easy, since nearly all middle-class families lived in rented accommodation. Many families experienced a move several times. John Heaton was unusual only in being able to make what counted as a substantial leap from a modest terraced house to a villa with a walled garden. This restless quest for status explains much of men's nostalgia for the home of their dreams, and their sentimental attraction to childhood, when home was imagined to have been as a 'real' home should be.

The new conditions of middle-class living had an even greater impact on the nature of marriage. Much of the rest of this book will be an elaboration of this theme. But two fundamental implications can be pointed out at this stage. The first concerns the changing character of family authority. In pre-industrial bourgeois society, family authority is correctly described as 'patriarchy'. The logic of a productive household dependent on the labour of family, servants and apprentices was a pyramidal structure with the father at the top. His job was to take decisions about production, to deal with the relevant outside parties (suppliers, customers, tax authorities, etc.) and to organize the labour resources of the household, administering discipline when needed. His authority depended on his control of production and his daily presence in the home. Economic practice assumed a patriarchal organization, while religious belief strongly reinforced it. Keeping order in the household was a key attribute of patriarchal power, and the man who failed to do so was the butt of merciless lampooning. Conversely the dignity of the wife was held to be subject to the constraints of patriarchy. The traditional notion of 'help-meet' correctly identified her as a support and partner, but not an equal to her husband. She was accountable to him for her management of the household, as she was for any part of the productive process which she carried out. The separation of home from work was clearly incompatible with patriarchy in this traditional sense; the key question was whether patriarchy would be redefined or diluted as a result. Renewed emphasis on the effort and sacrifices of the breadwinner bolstered masculine status in one respect, but what of authority in the household itself? Was this now wielded by the wife according to some conception of separate and equal spheres? Did the husband preserve the dignity of his position by retaining authority in specific areas like the housekeeping accounts and family discipline? Or were the implications of the separation of home from work so unsettling that household authority became a battleground?

But marriage is about companionship as well as authority. This was the second area in which the changing character of the household proved highly significant. Late eighteenth-century didactic writers had laid great stress on the need for affection in marriage. 'Keep it constantly in mind that the happiness of marriage depends upon a solid and permanent friendship', urged Hester Chapone, one of the most enduring of these authorities; she also advised the young wife to make her husband 'your first and dearest friend'.[45] Time spent in each other's company was a prerequisite. Something of Mrs Chapone's ideal might be attained by couples who were constantly in society together, as was not uncommon in elite circles. Among the middling sort, friendship between spouses was more likely to be the by-product of a working partnership in the home. This was one possible dimension of the system of family production. Under the same roof for much of the day and jointly engaged in the household enterprise, husband and wife at least shared a body of common concerns, whatever their differences of temperament and taste. But by the early nineteenth century this situation could no longer be taken for granted. The daily experiences of husband and wife were more likely to diverge sharply, as he laboured in an unfamiliar and unseen working environment for six days a week, while her life was given over to activities which often seemed to him to be either trivial or 'feminine' (or both). Eighteenth-century moralists had attacked affluent bourgeois wives for being idle drones. Their Victorian successors did not seriously question women's withdrawal from work; they tended instead to criticize the frivolous use which some non-working wives made of their leisure.[46] The very fact that the position of wife could be discussed in these terms underlines the gulf which now separated her life from her husband's. The polarization of breadwinner and home-maker, with divergent educational paths to match, loaded the odds against fulfilling marriages. In tandem with the undermining of patriarchal authority, this made for an unstable framework for married life.

CHAPTER TWO

The Ideal of Domesticity

When the Victorians sang 'Home Sweet Home', when they sagely repeated 'Home is where the heart is', and when they warmly commended the home life of their own dear Queen, it is clear that they were expressing more than their appreciation of food, shelter and rest; they were giving voice to their deep commitment to the *idea* of home. Comfort, privacy and time spent in the home, more sought after by the Victorians than by any previous generation, were regarded not as ends in themselves, but as means to realizing a domestic vision. To be without these benefits was to experience 'homesickness' – a word which only entered general currency at the beginning of the nineteenth century.[1] Domesticity in its fully developed form offers a moral view of the world. It places a high premium on the quality of relationship between family members – that is to say all family members related by blood or marriage. And, beyond the realm of everyday human contact, it points to the emotional power which the very idea of home exercises over its inmates, as memory, as fantasy, and through affecting images. In all these dimensions, prescription and practice were taken to unprecedented lengths by the Victorians. Not of course *all* Victorians: the pieties of domesticity were a sick joke to slum dwellers, and at the other end of the social spectrum they were scarcely relevant to the great aristocratic families for whom large-scale hospitality was an extension of political and dynastic activity by other means. It was middle-class people above all others who strove to live by an exacting standard of home life, and who accepted (mostly without question) the defining place of home in their culture. They found their everyday lives enriched and impoverished in new ways.

The time spent in the home and the significance attached to activities there were premised on a belief in the supreme importance of domestic affections, or, to be more precise, familial affections. Companionate marriage stood at the heart of the Victorian ideal of domesticity. Marriage was assumed to be voluntary, not arranged or imposed, and to be for love, whatever secondary motives might be involved. The prevailing trend in marriage choice is nicely exemplified in the case of the Heaton family. When John Heaton the bookseller was looking for a wife in 1814, he applied to the Congregationalist minister for a recommendation (which he accepted); thirty years later their son, John Heaton the doctor, fell in love with a merchant's daughter and had to run the gauntlet of her family's opposition for four years before they could marry.[2] Personal choice should rest on romance, as well as shared interests and calculations of material comfort. As for the relationship between husband and wife, traditional notions of patriarchy might suggest that marriage had more to do with authority than affection. But in Victorian discourse this was a false antithesis. The advice books which set the tone of early Victorian marriage recommended that spouses share each other's burdens and take – as well as receive – advice; but they left no doubt that the husband should be master.[3] In fact the romantic ideal of marriage was not based on equality. It assumed that sharply distinguished roles could be deeply satisfying to both parties: to the husband on account of the emotional support he received from his wife, and to the wife because of the window on the wider world which his education and experience made available to her. Romantic love, in short, was conceived as the attraction of opposites, bound to each other by ties of complementarity.

Children completed the circle of affection. Victorian homes were 'child centred' not because children called the tune (they very rarely did), but in the more literal sense that their needs, as perceived by adults, determined so much domestic activity. Whether they passed their time in the specialized zone of the nursery, or were more fully integrated with the rest of the household through pressure of space, children were the focus of family life. In more affluent families much may have been delegated to nursemaids and governesses, but young children were mostly confined within the home and seldom far from the parental eye. Mothers usually undertook the early instruction of infants, while fathers added homilies and discipline of their own. Both mothers and fathers behaved with much more playfulness than has generally been admitted. Their pleasure in play was part of a wider instinct that they themselves might learn something from the innocence and spontaneity of little children. Childhood was central to Victorian family culture both because children's needs were pitched so high, and because their company was held to confer a blessing on the adults around them (see Chapter 4).

If companionate marriage and the raising of children were to flourish, so went the common wisdom, they needed not only space but seclusion. The 'family circle' beloved of the didactic writers was intimate and inward-looking. Hippolyte Taine correctly summed up the view prevailing in the 1850s when he wrote:

> Every Englishman has, in the matter of marriage, a romantic spot in his heart. He imagines a 'home', with the woman of his choice, the pair of them *alone* with their children. That is his own little universe, *closed* to the world.[4] [emphases added]

The implication was that outside the conventional family unit of parents and children a fully human life could not be realized. As Henry Mayhew put it, the bachelor returned to his lair of an evening; only the married man dwelt in a home.[5] Ultimately the power of home rested on the twin authorities of nature and religion. The home was ordained by nature because its function and structure predated civil society and were the precondition for its reproduction. It carried the authority of religion because the family was the medium through which the divine purpose had worked in both the Old Testament and the New, and most of all in the life of Jesus Christ himself. 'The holy and blessed ties of home' was a phrase which fell quite unselfconsciously from the lips of the Victorians.[6] The holiness lay not only in the divine provenance of home ties, but in their moral wholesomeness – indeed their active power to inspire in both adults and children a moral life. At its most elevated, the idealizing of home extended to the belief that domestic virtues would triumph over a heartless world. It was because so much was credited to the saving power of domestic life that home lay firmly at the centre of the Victorians' moral world.

These were the characteristically Victorian attributes of domesticity. Indeed, to read the self-satisfied effusions which poured off the press of the day, one would suppose that they had been invented by the Victorians; as one historian has observed, it is as though 'the people of England before 1837 had lived in a sort of nomadic promiscuity'.[7] In fact there was much more continuity with the past than the conventional dichotomy between 'Victorian' and 'Georgian' would suggest. In royal portraiture the fusion of domestic and dynastic elements, which we regard as the very essence of Victorianism, began under George III.[8] An increasing interest in the home was evident among the middling sort of eighteenth-century London.[9] Companionate marriage was common in both aristocratic and upper bourgeois circles by the end of the century.[10] The Victorians inherited a liberal discourse from the Enlightenment which laid down that in marriage, as in the body politic, authority should rest on reasonableness and shared values, not on the exercise of force. Thus Hester Chapone, still widely read in the 1830s, did not question the husband's right to obedience, but she insisted that he 'have such an opinion of his wife's understanding, principles and integrity of heart as would induce him to exalt her to the rank of his *first and dearest friend*'.[11]

Children of the wealthier classes had experienced a lighter, more indulgent regime in the home since the mid-eighteenth century, based on a new respect for the state of childhood. More portraits were painted of them, and more toys and books produced for their edification and delight. The sanctification of home, to which the Victorians might be thought to hold a unique claim, is to be found in the domestic poetry of William Cowper as early as the 1780s; and Felicia Hemans, probably the most popular poet of Victorian domesticity, had been in full flow in the second decade of the century and was dead by the time the Queen ascended the throne.[12] Since the 1790s the funerary monuments of military and naval men had regularly paid tribute to their 'domestic virtues', sometimes ahead of their martial qualities.[13] The middle-class appeal of domesticity in the full sense just described varied according to region and occupation. It was still relatively new to the self-made entrepreneurs of the northern industrial towns in the 1850s, by which time professional and commercial families in the south had already brought up one and sometimes two generations of children in the new ways.[14] There was also a comparable time-lag among middle-class people in the countryside, especially tenant farmers.

Yet mid-century observers like the American R.W. Emerson and the Frenchman Hippolyte Taine who took domesticity to be a defining attribute of English culture were not mistaken.[15] The ideal of home life had by this time acquired immense cultural authority. While a consistent strand of domesticity is to be found in both aristocratic and bourgeois circles throughout the eighteenth century, it was only in the 1830s and 1840s that the ideal of home was raised to the level of a cultural norm. For the middle class above all it had become *de rigueur* to practise significant elements of that ideal, while those sections of the working class and the aristocracy which resisted it were often perceived to be at odds with the national character. The reaction against domesticity which would in due course set in among both sexes was still two decades away. What has to be explained is why the early part of Victoria's reign should have been the high point of idealized home life. For this purpose a deeper timescale is needed, stretching from the 1840s back to the turn of the century.

★

The separation of home and work described in the last chapter soon acquired psychological and emotional dimensions as well as a physical reality. Just because middle-class men were spared back-breaking manual labour did not mean that their work was congenial or undemanding. The hours were likely to be long; a position in commerce might mean being on one's feet or in the saddle for most of the day. More importantly, as work became detached from home, so its association with a heartless commercial ethic became closer. Early Victorian social comment is full of the chasm between the morality of the home and the morality of business. As Sarah Ellis sadly remarked, the men of her day had 'two sets of consciences . . . one conscience for the sanctuary, and another for the desk and counter'.[16] The world of business was seen as necessary, but morally contaminating. Whatever its rewards in profit, power or reputation, it exacted a heavy price in alienation. After depicting the 'destitution of comfort' endured by the lower middle-class man in warehouses and counting-houses, Ellis asked rhetorically, 'Are these the abodes of free-born and independent men?' Her solution was that men must be made whole again by the comfort and refinement of the properly ordered home.[17] Home provided the refuge from work in all its negativity. It offered bodily repose and human rhythms; it promised the comforts of love and nurture; and it was a reminder of a higher scale of moral values. So many of the treasured attributes of Victorian home life – its seclusion, its intimacy and its elevated morality – owed their appeal to the sense that none of these qualities was to be found in the utterly 'other' world of work. But the healing power did not come cheap: the virtues of home entailed a considerable outlay on the part of the hard-working breadwinner. As W.R. Greg sardonically put it, 'the merchant must be content to purchase the delights of domestic society and unanxious nights at the price of dying fifty thousand pounds poorer than he once expected'.[18] But, viewed as compensation for the emotional and moral costs of economic progress, the outlay was thought to be well worth the price. In reality Victorian bourgeois society included plenty of husbands who spared little time or thought for home life. But admiration for the public achievements of these men was tempered by disapproval of their negligence of the higher things of life.

However, the alienation experienced by Victorian men of the middle class was about more than work. It was not only the process and rhythm of work which exacted their toll. There was the ugliness and noise in which so much of it was located. Middle-class businessmen might live in quiet squares or leafy suburbs, but every day they must pass their waking hours amid the dirt and clatter and smells of an industrial environment. And there was a pervasive sense of social malaise. The changing quality of relations between mill-owner and man, or between master and apprentice, easily became intensified into a troubling sense that all the familiar social landmarks were being swept away in the rapid onset of an urban, individualistic society. Hierarchy and community, ultimately even faith itself, seemed at risk. In this alarming scenario the home, notwithstanding the significant shift in its own structure and function, was cast in the role of 'traditional' bulwark, the last remnant of a vanishing social order. Henry Mayhew remarked that the middle class regarded home as a place where 'all the cares and jealousies of life are excluded' and where reparation was made for 'the petty suspicions and heartlessness of strangers'.[19] Home stood for cooperation and for love, while modern society seemed dedicated to cruel and impersonal competition. In the most ambitious versions of this ideal the ennobling values of the home were destined to suffuse and transform the wider society.[20] Domesticity was a characteristically Victorian response to the damage which entrepreneurial capitalism had wrought on the fabric of human relations. And it was experienced just as keenly by men whose work was largely carried on in the home, as by those who laboured in the market-place.

Much of this sense of opposition between home and society was focused on the city. The early industrial city appeared as the summation of all the anti-social forces which threatened to engulf the Victorians. In the eighteenth century the principal associations of the city had been with economic opportunity and with the pleasure and instruction of society, or 'civility'. These associations persisted, but by the early Victorian period they were giving place to more frightening images. The speed and scale of urbanization had brought together myriads of people who were now apparently removed from the constraining structures of traditional society, and the all too visible extremes of urban destitution and demoralization graphically illustrated where this might lead. The city might be the place where money was made and the world went round, but for many its menacing social problems outweighed its cultural advantages.[21] The well-ordered home, with its welcoming hearth and its solid front door, furnished the most reassuring antidote to the alienation of city life. The Victorians loved to identify with the treasured place which these attributes of home had in the memory of the wanderer, the soldier or the sailor far from home. They continued avidly to read Felicia Hemans's immensely popular 'Domestic Affections' (1812):

> Bower of repose! when, torn from all we love,
> Through toil we struggle, or through distance rove;
> To *thee* we turn, still faithful, from afar –
> Thee, our bright vista! thee, our magnet-star!
> And from the martial field, the troubled sea,
> Unfetter'd thought still roves to bliss and thee!

That penchant for the exile's sensibility was reflected in the homecoming rituals of middle-class homes: the waiting wife and daughters on the threshold, the proffered slippers, the armchair ready at the fireside.[22]

But the most striking testimony to the middle class's ambivalence towards the city was its taste for country trappings. The idealization of the countryside as the realm of the natural and of organic communities originated in the eighteenth century; but the new urban culture of the nineteenth century heightened the appeal of this trope and enlarged its practical consequences. The constant vaunting of home tapped into a profoundly nostalgic longing for the simple, stress-free life of an imagined rural England. For the Victorian middle class the most desirable suburbs were not within walking distance of the centres of commerce, but far enough away to permit space, greenery and quiet. Roads should be leafy and hedge-bound, with open country or woodland within view. As one enthusiast for Edgbaston wrote in 1847:

> Glorious suburbs! long
> May you remain to bless the ancient town
> Whose crown ye are, rewarded of the cares
> Of those who toil amid the din and smoke
> Of iron-ribbed and hardy Birmingham,
> And may ye long *be* suburbs, keeping still
> Business at a distance from your green retreats
> And the tall chimneys of the Millocrat
> Outside your smiling border.[23]

Since family life was the rationale of the suburb, the ideal features of home and locality closely mirrored each other. Seclusion, refuge and repose in as rural an ambience as possible were the desired characteristics of the middle-class home.

Hence the passion for gardening among the English bourgeoisie of this period. The most sought-after property was the villa in its own grounds, set back from the road and approached by a winding drive, with gardens front and rear. Below that every gradation was to be found, down to the small garden at the back of a standard terraced house. Commercially produced garden accessories became widely available, notably the mechanical lawn-mower which was invented in the 1830s and intended for use by the master of the house. Moderately priced instruction manuals came in at the same period. *The Gardener's Magazine* was founded in 1826, followed by *The Horticultural Register* in 1831. The activity of gardening brought a man into closer touch with nature, while the results of his labours refreshed the soul and delighted the eye. That gardening should have been seen in this light is some measure of the emotional needs which the home was called upon to fill.[24]

The place of the home in bourgeois culture could be summed up by the proposition that only at home could a man be truly and authentically himself. While the workplace and the city crippled his moral sense and distorted his human relationships, home gave play to feelings of nurture, love and com-panionship, as well as 'natural' forms of authority and deference; it nourished the whole man. Every feature of home life was interpreted in these elevated terms. Samuel Smiles urged the merits of drawing-room music-making as involving all members of the family in an activity which was *harmonious* in both a moral and a literal sense.[25] Particular faith was placed in the healing power of Sunday as a sacred day dedicated to family life. Eliza Wilson employed a familiar trope when urging her fiancé Walter Bagehot to write to her on Sundays: 'Everyone, but especially men, are more themselves on that day; *you* have no Bank to jar you, and one can always go deeper into oneself when one has not been thinking of one's worldly affairs during the day'.[26] Countless writers expressed the belief in the restorative power of the family circle, but perhaps none with more heartfelt conviction than James Anthony Froude in his early novel, *The Nemesis of Faith* (1849):

> When we come home, we lay aside our mask and drop our tools, and are no longer lawyers, sailors, soldiers, statesmen, clergymen, but only men. We fall again into our most human relations . . . We cease the struggle in the race of the world, and give our hearts leave and leisure to love.[27]

Froude's paean to the home implicitly acknowledges the power of the other main constituent of middle-class manhood: occupation. Middle-class men certainly had a great deal invested in doing the kind of responsible and useful work which distinguished them from the supposed idleness of the aristocracy. Moreover they needed to rescue many of their characteristic occupations from the taint of money-grubbing and sharp practice. The work ethic and the emphasis on dignity of calling were an effective counterattack on deep-seated occupational snobbery. But Froude's impassioned comment – echoed by many others – is a reminder that not even prestigious professions like the law or politics offered a wholly secure identity. For the middle-class man work held deeply contradictory associations: on the one hand, pride in climbing the ladder of success, providing for his family, and acquiring the esteem of his peers; on the other, resentment of the time and toil required, fear of failure at the impersonal hands of the market, and revulsion from the morals of the business world. Home served to mitigate the harshness of these reactions. It could not soften the fear of failure. But it did explain and justify the labours of the breadwinner, and perhaps even the moral depths to which he must stoop, in order to sustain his dependants. And, it was claimed on all sides, home offered a morally wholesome environment to ease a man's conscience when ensnared by the corruption of the working world.[28]

★

> Pray for me that I may be enlightened and strengthened for the duties of this important and critical season. Hitherto God has wonderfully supported and blessed me; oh how much beyond my deserts! It will be a comfort to me to know that you all who are, as it were, on the top of the mountain, withdrawn from and above the storm, are thus interceding for me who am scuffling in the vale below.

The words are those of William Wilberforce, sometimes dubbed one of the 'fathers of the Victorians', writing to his family in August 1820 after political anxieties had caused him to cut short his holiday with them and return to London. Wilberforce's pious request is a reminder that the notion of home as a safe haven from worldly travail had a strong religious underlay, as indeed did the whole apparatus of nineteenth-century domesticity.[29] Memoirs of the period place so much emphasis on Sunday Bible-reading, daily family prayers, the keeping of spiritual diaries, and the uplifting death-bed scene, that it is tempting to reach for a reductionist explanation and to interpret the domestic side of Victorian religious observance as no more than a symptom of the social changes discussed in the previous chapter. But this is to underestimate the power of religious belief at a time when the inroads of modern Biblical criticism and evolutionary science still lay in the future. For their own reasons all denominations, with the exception of the High Church persuasion in the Church of England and the Roman Catholics, were placing fresh emphasis on the saving power of the godly household, and they had begun to do so before the separation of work from home had become widely prevalent. Much of the character of Victorian domesticity was defined by this religious input.

The spiritualization of the household had been one of the hallmarks of the Protestant Reformation. The shift away from the sacraments and from priestly authority highlighted the key role of the household in providing a framework of Christian discipline. And now that the clergy were married, their homes could (it was hoped) be held up as an example of sanctified family life. The routines of everyday became as important as, if not more important than, the rituals of public worship; family prayers might be as efficacious as prayers in church. The Reformers had been under no illusions that this new prescription was considerably more taxing for the laity than the old regime had been, and much sermonizing and didactic writing underpinned it in the late sixteenth and early seventeenth centuries.[30] For this very reason it proved impossible to sustain with its initial rigour. From the Restoration onwards, with important exceptions, there was a retreat to 'practical' religion, in which piety came to be equated with public worship and public actions. Family life was expected to reflect Christian belief – to be moral and decorous and enlightened. But the idea of the household as the powerhouse of faith was in abeyance. Few families practised family prayers.

This was the situation which the Protestant revival of the eighteenth century sought to address. Between the 1730s and the 1830s all denominations, including the Church of England and the Nonconformist sects, were galvanized by the Evangelical movement. This was a rekindling of the Puritan impulse, but with an individual and practical bent which marks it out as the product of a more entrepreneurial society. The newest and most energetic denomination was Methodism, founded in the course of John Wesley's peripatetic ministry to the poor. Posterity has strongly associated the Methodists with the labouring classes, but their social range extended to all but the upper ranks. In Lincolnshire and the Midlands they were strongly represented among the tenant farmers, and in the industrial north among the business class.[31] Methodism in its early days was considerably more unsettling of domestic and sexual conventions than it later became: Wesley himself had undermined marriage by commending celibacy, and he had given countenance to strong same-sex attachments.[32] But home was always central to the Methodist scheme of things. Wesley's original followers often assembled in houses because they had nowhere else to meet; the home of a preacher or a lay enthusiast had to do duty as a chapel. But the significance of the home went deeper. Methodism was a 'religion of the heart' which valued the spiritual feelings of the individual. In the relative intimacy of the small domestic gathering the soul could be bared, guidance sought and reproof administered. Intimate spiritual fellowship was vital in sustaining faith and commitment; in the homely metaphor of one of Wesley's preachers, 'when live coals are put together, the fire burns vehemently; but, when the coals are scattered, the fire dies away'.[33] In fact Methodism really originated not so much in the famous open-air preachings as in weekly cottage meetings. The association of the domestic and the sacred was intensified in the breakaway Methodist sects at the turn of the century which drew strong support from workers in domestic industry. But even when Methodism had become respectable, it retained its domestic bent. The Methodist community comprised a network of cells, or 'classes' of up to twenty members who met weekly in the home of the class-leader to share their spiritual experiences and seek comfort and strength from each other. Unlike the preacher, the class-leader could be – and sometimes was – a woman. The nucleus of a class was often the master or mistress of the house, with the rest of the family including servants furnishing the core of the membership.[34] In the early nineteenth century the class was more important than the chapel. Thereafter the chapel loomed larger, and classes often met there rather than in the leader's home.[35] But when, as in small rural congregations, a layman's parlour or kitchen had to serve as a chapel, Methodist writers recognized that improvisation of this kind captured something of the essence of their religion. Methodism continued to be, in part at least, a 'felt' religion, and the emphasis on domestic religious disciplines had a profound influence on the older Dissenting sects.[36]

The other main source of domestic religion was the Evangelical revival within the Established Church. This carried much greater social cachet, since its early nucleus was the group of wealthy mercantile families who settled at Clapham Common in the 1790s – the Thorntons, Wilberforces, Macaulays and Shores. William Wilberforce and Henry Thornton were MPs, and Wilberforce had the ear of the Prime Minister, William Pitt the Younger. The Evangelicals set out to reform society from the top. They certainly had considerable success in popularizing a more sober and spiritual pattern of family life than had been common among the elite of the previous generation. Evangelicalism, or 'serious Christianity' as its early adherents called it, was above all a religion of individual faith and practice. The believer must first of all achieve a state of mind in which he or she could experience the saving grace of God (though conversion was not necessarily sudden); thereafter the daily pattern of life had to be scrutinized for failures of love and duty, as well as for signs of God's unfolding Providence and continued blessing. The soul must be constantly examined and the marks of corruption rooted out. These spiritual goals were pursued through private prayer, meditation, diary-keeping and Bible study. A religion which stressed these practices was almost inevitably a religion of the home.[37]

But the mark of a fully Evangelical household – whether Anglican or Dissenting – was that the family bolstered the faith of its members by enforcing certain common disciplines. Early rising was practised in order to fend off the threat of idleness and to discourage too great a taste for bodily comfort. Sunday became a family day *par excellence*, but within the strict confines of sabbatarian observance; Wilberforce regarded Sundays at home as a means of identifying 'domestic tenderness' with religion, to the advantage of both.[38] Above all, family prayers expressed the idea that the godly household was a divinely appointed institution for promoting the spiritual life. Each day, usually in the early morning and sometimes in the evening too, the whole household including servants gathered for readings and prayers, chosen and recited by the paterfamilias. Handbooks directed him to pray that parents bring up their offspring in the knowledge of the Lord, that children obey their parents in all things, that husbands be loving and wives meek, that masters be just and servants obedient.[39] The clergy did not scruple to spell out the practical gains to be expected from order, deference and harmony, but there was more to family

2. Morning Prayers, *c.* 1840.

prayers than social control.[40] In Evangelical thinking the husband had a responsibility to sustain the faith of the converted and to show the way to those who were not – usually children and servants. In some families the sins of errant members were singled out for mention. In the theology of most Evangelicals the loving authority of the earthly father was seen as a microcosm of divine authority, sanctified by God himself. In a strange paradox even Nonconformists, who held to a rigorously non-sacerdotal interpretation of the ministry, referred to the household head as 'priest'.[41] One of the reasons why the revival of confession by the Tractarians (or Oxford Movement) aroused such hostility among Evangelicals is that it was seen to undermine the spiritual authority of the household head.[42] In practice the husband's sacred authority was balanced by his wife's high moral status which rested, as we shall see shortly, on the recently enhanced prestige of motherhood. Yet family prayers offered daily proof of the husband's divinely ordained authority, all the more necessary if his work took him away from the house for most of the week. That this convention, in almost complete disuse since the seventeenth century, should have become so widespread in bourgeois families by the mid-Victorian era is a striking demonstration of Evangelicalism's influence, and of the appeal of domesticated religion generally.

The climax of Evangelical domestic life was the death-bed. The 'good' death took place before an audience composed of close relatives and a servant or two. Inasmuch as they reproduced the domestic circle which had enveloped the dying person in happier times, they came to say farewell. But as those who were also closest to him or her in faith, their role was to provide spiritual support in a moment of extremity; in return they hoped to receive an uplifting last testimony (often committed to paper) from which they would derive spiritual nourishment. Death was domesticated in a further and – for the bystanders – quite crucial sense that Heaven was increasingly thought of as an extension of home, where family members would be greeted by those who had pre-deceased them, in eternal domestic bliss. By the middle of the nineteenth century the reunion of earthly families divided by death was the dominant popular image of Heaven. Family and faith were cast in an everlasting mutually supportive role.[43]

Pious Evangelicals tended to make light of the transition from this world to the next, since home in its spiritual sense encompassed both. Methodists, in viewing the godly household as a corner of Heaven upon earth, played down the terror of death. The real gulf was between home and world. For if home was the site of religious life, the world appeared in strongly drawn negative colours. It not only offered material temptation in plenty; it was also populated by people of no religion. The world was conceived as a 'mire' or a 'slough' where the faithless and the fickle provided fertile soil for the devil's evil designs. Even the most spiritually disciplined might be ensnared if exposed to the world for too long. The message was clearly proclaimed by the class meetings held by the Methodists in people's homes. They aimed at a complete separation from 'the world', which was why sympathizers who had not yet committed themselves to the faith were usually excluded.[44] Of course men had a calling to do good in the world, but the moral contamination which tainted most forms of work made it essential for them to exploit the spiritual resources of the home to the full. This was the point of Wilberforce's letter, quoted earlier, and it was also reflected in the physical layout of Evangelical homes. Quiet seclusion was highly valued. Clapham Common itself, which combined ease of access to London with a semi-rural atmosphere, has been called 'the first suburb'.[45] Edgbaston, the most sought-after suburb in Birmingham, had an Evangelical peer, Lord Calthorpe, as its ground landlord. There was, in short, strong religious validation for the middle-class conceit that the suburban home was really a rural retreat. As for the houses themselves, the Evangelical ideal was a bedroom for every member of the family, so that everyone, including children, could carry out their religious devotions in private.

Both Methodism and the Evangelicalism of the Established Church had their own theological rationale for locating so much of their religious observance in the home. The Methodists developed their approach over the second half of the eighteenth century; the Evangelical ministry to the Established Church took shape during the 1780s and 1790s – in each case before the separation of work from home or the sense of alienation from city life had fully taken hold. But the convergence thereafter is significant. Many who had lived in some bafflement through great changes in family and community life found understanding in the power and simplicity of the new religious language. That language was made widely available as Evangelicals seized every opportunity presented by the print culture of the day. Undoubtedly many families who followed some other strand of belief, or none at all, fell under its influence. Evangelicalism ennobled work as a struggle carried on in an ungodly world, while showing how domestic life could comfort and elevate the worker. The home might no longer be the site of production, but its deeper, more moral purpose now became clear. In drawing religion into the home at the same time as work was being taken out of it, the Evangelicals greatly intensified the hold of domesticity over the middle class and produced much of its characteristic tone and atmosphere.

★

Over the same period the shift in the perception of childhood had equally important implications for domesticity, but here was no return to an earlier pattern; the changes pushed adult–child relations in new directions which are with us still. The root of modern thinking on the subject is that each child is an individual whose distinctive character should be valued and nurtured; childhood itself is not only an inescapable preparation for adulthood, but a precious state which children are entitled to enjoy for itself and which adults cannot help envying. This way of thinking was entirely foreign to earlier periods. It gained currency in the late eighteenth and early nineteenth centuries, and it was central to Victorian domesticity. If childhood is precious, then it follows that the needs of children must to a considerable degree determine the regime of the household; and if the loss of childhood is a matter of regret to adults, then they are likely to spend more time with their children, in a spirit of enjoyment as much as duty. The most telling symbol of this outlook in Victorian England was the domestication of Christmas, which had previously had much more the character of a community festival. As John Gillis has pointed out, it was middle-class families, not the Church, which invented Christmas in the form we know it. The Christmas tree, newly imported from Germany, nicely illustrates both the shift to a more private, familial atmosphere and the blend of secular and spiritual. Christmas became a time for children, and also a time for adults – especially men – to become children again. Gift-giving, previously an act of charity for the benefit of the poor, was now directed at children within the home.[46]

Some of the groundwork for this child-centred outlook was laid by the parenting practices of the English elite as far back as the early eighteenth century. English parents of this class were famous – or notorious – for their pleasure in children and their petting and spoiling of them. Foreign visitors marvelled at how children were allowed to be the centre of attention, to their

3. The child-centred home: George Morland, *The Cottage Door*, early nineteenth century.

own detriment and the irritation of grown-ups. The commercial production of toys and children's books reflected an adult desire to play with children as well as instruct them. Changes in the structure of the bourgeois household are also relevant. If children no longer form part of a working team, then their distinctive needs are likely to attract greater attention. Moreover the gradual removal of all but domestic servants from the household sharpened the distinction between children and other dependants, and placed them in a more clearly defined position *vis-à-vis* the rest of the family.[47] But it was intellectual and artistic influences which placed the appreciation of childhood at the heart of middle-class culture and ensured its enduring appeal. First Rousseau, whose manifesto for the new childhood, *Emile*, was taken up in England almost as soon as it was published in 1762, and then the Romantic poets, especially Words-worth, set a new philosophical framework for understanding the child. By forging a link between childhood and nature, the Romantics conferred an integrity on what children do and what children feel, and they offered a compelling interpretation of that sense of lost innocence which draws so many adults to the company of children. The agnostic or pantheistic tendencies of Romantic thought were easily adapted to a more conventional system of belief by seeing the child as the newly minted creation of God. In the words of an anonymous contributor to *Blackwood's Magazine* in 1822:

> There is in childhood a holy ignorance – a beautiful credulity – a sort of sanctity that one cannot contemplate without something of the reverential feeling with which one should approach beings of celestial nature. The impress of the Divine nature is, as it were, fresh on the infant spirit – fresh and unsullied by contact with this withering world.[48]

It was in this sanctified form that the Romantic idea of the child secured the most widespread acceptance in Victorian England. Clearly, celestial natures ought not to be subjected to oppressive labour or other degrading treatment. The appropriate adult response was one of respect, even reverence, and during time spent in children's company something of their divinity might rub off on those around them. This outlook also intensified adult feelings of nostalgia for childhood, which became more strongly lodged in the home as its child-rearing functions became more visible and more highly valued.[49]

Within this context Evangelicalism is usually presented in stark antithesis to Romanticism, and with some reason. Evangelicals were above all concerned to bring up children so that they would lead disciplined lives and be receptive to God's grace. They attended to the adult in the making rather than the child in the present. According to this way of thinking children, far from having celestial natures, were born in original sin. The parent's task, as John Wesley and countless others asserted, was to break the child's will by enforcing absolute obedience and dependence. This goal was still being commended to parents by advice-book writers as late as the 1850s.[50] Confronted by what the Words-worthian might regard as innocent play, the Wesleyan saw only sinful self-will and frivolity.[51] Not all Evangelicals were so repressive. There was a moderate school which preferred the image of bending and shaping, rather than breaking the child's will, and they emphasized the careful nurture of children over time rather than the transforming experience of conversion. But each strategy exposed the child to intrusive control, made more relentless by the sobering fear that if death came before conversion damnation would follow.[52]

This spiritual alarmism was paralleled by an equally overdrawn sense of foreboding in the realm of psycho-sexual development. The late eighteenth and early nineteenth centuries saw the full flowering of the scare about masturba-tion, and childhood masturbation in particular. The panic was not Evangelical in origin, but it neatly dovetailed with Evangelical assumptions about the corruption of human nature. In England anti-masturbatory writing had enjoyed a high profile since the publication of *Onania* in 1708. The most influential Western text on the subject, Tissot's *L'Onanisme*, appeared in 1760. It was translated into English in 1766, and the very next year was pirated by none other than John Wesley in his pamphlet on the 'sin of Onan'. Tissot's book expressed greater conviction than ever before about the appalling physical, mental and moral consequences which it was thought would beset the later life of a child who indulged in the solitary vice. Apart from numerous remedies and precautions, the main lesson for parents was that children must be subject to constant surveillance. Tissot commended 'that vigilance, which an attentive and enlightened father exerts to know what is done in the darkest recesses of his house'. The same message was still being put out in the 1850s by William Acton in his influential *Functions and Disorders of the Reproductive Organs*. The medical discourse on masturbation assumed privacy within the home, as well as the parent's right to breach that privacy. The necessary watchfulness was premised on an intimacy between parent and child, or at the very least the careful vetting of a nurse for purity as well as attentiveness. The preoccupation with precocious sexuality placed the spotlight on the child in the home, just as surely as the Evangelicals' terror of early damnation did. Both fears were grounded in a pessimistic appraisal of children's natures.[53]

The contrast to the teaching of Rousseau or Wordsworth is obvious enough. But the Evangelical and Romantic approaches to childhood had something in common all the same. Protective seclusion was vital to both: to the Romantics because children needed a playground beyond the reach of the adult world; to the Evangelicals because children's delicate spiritual state was so vulnerable to corruption. The logic of Evangelical doctrines about man and salvation was to place children near the centre of domestic attention, just as the Romantic sensibilities did for quite different reasons. Salvation required a huge early investment by proxy. Infant wills could be neither broken nor shaped without a great deal of time and patience. The child in an Evangelical household faced a constant stream of prayers, readings, catechisms and homilies. Communication could also be two-way: many parents encouraged questions and doubts, dealing painstakingly with them. Nor was parent–child interaction confined to these serious matters. Evangelical family life has often been dismissed as joyless and repressive. But this reputation is partly due to the subsequent spread of the externals of Evangelical observance, like family prayers and 'the English Sunday', which could weigh very heavily on the young. Reminiscences of Evangelical childhood in the heyday of the movement strike a lighter note. There was no ban on pleasure for its own sake, only on morally dubious diversions. Parents balanced their inflexible religious routines with playfulness; parties were given and holiday trips undertaken. Evangelicalism was serious-minded but not inherently killjoy. In the most attractive households, like those of the Thorntons or the Wilberforces, one has the impression of Evangelical earnestness striking a balance with an underlying spontaneity and affection which drew on eighteenth-century elite practice.[54] Evangelical and Romantic attitudes were evidently more compatible in practice than in theory. The Congregationalist minister John Angell James was one of the most influential didactic writers of the early Victorian period; in numbering both 'the nursery of virtue' and 'the playground of childhood' among 'the blissful associations' of home, he neatly combined the principal ideological ingredients of the Victorian idea of childhood.[55]

The centrality of children in family life is borne out by the evidence of diary-keeping. The Manchester Unitarian and future novelist, Elizabeth Gaskell, kept a detailed record of her eldest daughter's first year in the 1830s. Her fellow Mancunian, the Methodist Joshua Pritchard, had done something very similar fifteen years earlier, documenting every sign of spiritual progress in his daughter from the age of eighteen months. Diaries like these may reflect a diversity of religious and philosophical perspectives, but they share a common preoccupation with childhood. This did not necessarily mean that parents were in the continuous company of their offspring. All except the humblest middle-class family would expect to delegate some childcare to servants – sparingly as in Mrs Gaskell's case or very liberally as with the wealthy bourgeois. What the child-centred culture of Victorian England required was that parents should give careful attention to the domestic arrangements for their children's upbringing, and should give them their undivided attention during their daily periods of contact, as the Gaskells and Pritchards patently did.[56]

★

Perhaps inevitably, the separation of home from work entailed a very clear-cut notion of sexual roles, especially for husbands and wives. Yet the separation of the sexes regarded by so many Victorians as normal or natural went much further than a practical distinction between breadwinner and home-maker, and for reasons which, once again, have their roots before the economic changes around the turn of the century. The dominant belief in Victorian England was that women were not only inferior to men, but fundamentally different from them. They were not just a few notches lower on the scale of rationality or resolution, but set apart from the superior sex by natural endowment for specific tasks requiring distinctive attributes. Traditionally in Western society men had regarded women not as essentially different, but as less perfect versions of themselves. In Early Modern England women had been conventionally represented as less rational, less constant and less restrained in controlling the passions than men were. These assumptions were consistent with the medical conventions of the day. According to the Galenic tradition of humoral biology, men were 'hot' and 'dry', while women were 'cold' and 'wet'; these were distinctions of degree rather than kind, with disturbing implications of uncertainty in the middle ground. Reproductive differences were seen in the same light. Women's organs were believed to be analogous to men's, except that they were located inside instead of outside the body; women, like men, produced semen and they needed to experience orgasm in order to conceive.

The Galenic tradition began to be dismantled by medical writers as early as the sixteenth century, but it was only very gradually that a new reproductive theory took shape, emphasizing menstruation and spontaneous ovulation. There are grounds for questioning how widely this new knowledge was established even in the mid-nineteenth century.[57] The shift in popular under-standing of sexual character, on the other hand, is better documented and more central to an understanding of Victorian domesticity. It had its origins in the eighteenth-century rise of 'sensibility'. This reflected a new fashion for analysing human behaviour in terms of the nervous system instead of the humours. In both philosophical treatises and novels, women were represented as possessing keener nervous sensibilities than men, and ultimately as having a distinct nervous system which made for a distinctive sexual character. By the end of the eighteenth century the mental differences between men and women were increasingly stressed. As Mary Wollstonecraft complained in 1792, the writers of her day asserted the superiority of men 'not in degree, but essence', arguing that 'the sexes ought not to be compared', since 'man was made to reason, women to feel'.[58] On one level 'feeling' and 'sensibility' meant refinement; expressed as taste, this encouraged the female consumerism which was a marked feature of bourgeois domestic life in the eighteenth century. But in the early nineteenth century it was the moral implications of fine sensibility which counted for most. Women's openness to the emotional life around them and their quickness in reading the feelings of others gave them special qualities in the moral sphere. Some commentators put this eminence down to women's innate superiority; others conceded that men started life with the same moral nature but lost out through prolonged exposure to greed, envy and hatred in the market-place. But whatever its explanation, the moral gap between husband and wife was widely acknowledged.

Not surprisingly, woman's sexual nature was adjusted to conform with this moralized femininity. Modesty, instead of being a discipline imposed by men on the lascivious sex, came to be seen as an inner quality which arose from a lack of sexual desire. The medical discovery in the 1840s that conception did not require female orgasm merely reflected assumptions about woman's sexuality which had been current for two generations. The medical authorities differed as to how much passion was natural to women. The most-quoted contemporary opinion on this subject is Dr William Acton's in 1857, that 'the majority of women (happily for them) are not very much troubled with sexual feeling of any kind'.[59] Acton has been variously described as the voice of conventional wisdom and a crank on the margins of medical respectability. No doubt a wider range of views was heard in the consulting-rooms of the day, and it is clear that Acton did not speak for all his colleagues. But he certainly struck a chord with the public: his books went though many editions and were frequently cited. One reason for this was that, however uncertain medical expertise might be, the passionless woman was by now firmly established in respectable middle-class culture – in art and poetry as well as the common wisdom expressed in advice books. One should stress the qualification 'respectable'. Conveniently for bourgeois men, passionlessness was not a quality of women of the street: their sexual appetite was rather read as evidence of their corruption. Nor was the new orthodoxy necessarily accepted by the lower middle class, or at least those who fell outside the ambit of church or chapel. In the music halls which clerks, tradesmen and workers frequented so much in the

Victorian period, narratives of courtship and sexual adventure were premised on an assumption of equal libido between the sexes, and they sometimes portrayed women as predatory and insatiable. But above this social level there was a wholesale retreat from the traditional view of women as the lascivious sex, and this shift was of course central to women's claim to a higher morality.[60]

Passionlessness and morality were brought together in the enhanced prestige of motherhood from the late eighteenth century. The higher medical profile given to the ovum made generation seem less subject to the man's determination, and more like a natural process unfolding inside the woman. But much more influential was the new discourse about breast-feeding. The arguments in favour were, to begin with, largely practical and child-oriented: that it was a less risky means of feeding than the alternatives, and that it was the best way of establishing an enduring bond between mother and child. It was largely for these reasons that the breast became the most visible and most emphasized marker of sexual difference. But by the early nineteenth century breast-feeding had acquired a weighty moral dimension as well: it symbolized the unstinted altruism which was unique to mothers. In his *Advice to Mothers* (1803) William Buchan made it plain that breast-feeding was a test of selfless dedication. As Sarah Lewis put it in 1839, maternal love was 'the only purely unselfish feeling that exists on this earth', in other words the nearest earthly approximation to the love of God. Moreover the mother, as example and instructress, had unique opportunities and unique aptitudes to mould the moral development of the young, which made maternity 'the most powerful of all moral influences'.[61] For this demanding role to be fully realized, character and training were needed, as well as instinct. But if girls were not born with all the required qualities, their predisposition to acquire them as they grew up was believed to distinguish them sharply from boys. In common discourse no clear line was drawn between the moral and natural functions of motherhood – they tended to be fused together in a cultural icon of formidable authority, the Angel Mother. By the 1830s this interpretation of female character was no longer confined to Evangelicals who had made the running at the turn of the century; it was almost a cultural commonplace. Nearly all the outpourings about motherhood which appeared at this time increased the sense of women's privileged otherness. Nothing did more to mystify and sentimentalize the appeal of home as a sanctum which conferred on men benefits they could not find elsewhere.[62]

If the passionless moral mother now represented the epitome of femininity, the implications for men's sexuality are much less clear, and for the significant reason that they were much less written about.[63] Women were still 'the sex' – the bearers of most discourse about sexual difference. Men, as controllers of that discourse, were the invisible subject directing attention at women as object, and also the unspoken standard by which women were judged.[64] Yet the effect on men of the shift in understanding women's nature was of great significance. Traditionally men's responsibility for their desires and their actions had been tempered by women's reputation as the lascivious sex. Now that womanhood was redefined as passive and inert, the burden of sexual responsibility was carried by men alone. They were credited with the prime role in both intercourse and conception. Within the culture of respectability at least, men became the sole bearers of sexuality. This was no small burden. In an age when the world of nature appeared to be yielding to human control on every front, sexual passion stood out as an untamed and potentially destructive natural impulse. Later in the century the characterization of sex as the beast within every man would be made more palatable as a key evolutionary mechanism in the Darwinian world-view. But the early Victorians could reconcile themselves less easily to the burden of sexuality. Both Christian precept and the discourse of reason inherited from the Enlightenment declared that sexual passion should be controlled and rationed. Several leading writers of the period, notably Carlyle, Tennyson and Browning, expressed deep fears of the sexual energy within man and the consequent fragility of manhood itself.[65]

This need for restraint was expressed as a fear of excess which permeated Victorian thinking about sex. Despite grave medical reservations, it was widely believed that the male body was endowed with a fixed quantity of sperm, and that too much indulgence would either cause impotence or drain energy from other functions of the mind or body. This view of the male sexual economy underlay the vigorous polemics against masturbation and nocturnal emissions, and was sometimes carried over into anxiety about over-frequency of inter-course, even in marriage. The good wife deployed her purity as a means of cooling her husband's ardour, and so protected him from the dangers of over-indulgence. Men who disregarded this call for moderation carried a heavy load of guilt and anxiety, usually without being able to share it. Men's sexual predicament in Victorian times was that their sexual energy was assumed to be very powerful, while the legitimate avenues for discharging it were very closely circumscribed.[66]

★

Victorian middle-class culture was constructed around a heavily polarized understanding of gender. Both character and sexuality were seen in more sharply gendered terms than ever before or since. And the place where these yawning differences were made functional and intelligible was the home. Other, more public venues for the encounter between the sexes aroused varying degrees of misgiving, but in the domestic setting, so the theory went, masculine and feminine found their proper relation of complementarity. As Ruskin was to put it in *Sesame and Lilies* (1864), that hugely influential set of reflections on the meaning of home:

> Each [sex] has what the other has not: each completes the other, and is completed by the other: they are in nothing alike, and the happiness and perfection of both depends on each asking and receiving from the other what the other only can give.[67]

Home was inseparable from the rhetoric of sexual complementarity. The elevation of the Angel Mother cut the moral pretensions of men in the home down to size, and their significance as parents was correspondingly diminished. At the same time the association of masculinity with reason, authority and resolve was consolidated, together with their dissociation from the feminine. Again and again the dichotomies of energy and repose, intellect and feeling, resolution and adaptability, were seen to divide humankind into two quite different elements. The feminine home was the place for nurture and love, the masculine world for restless energy and rationality. Sarah Lewis told her own sex:

> Let men enjoy in peace and triumph the intellectual kingdom which is theirs, and which, doubtless, was intended for them; let us participate in its privileges without desiring to share its domination. The moral world is ours, – ours by position; ours by qualification; ours by the very indication of God himself.[68]

Nor were men unwilling to agree, provided it was understood that the morality in which women shone was a private morality, confined to the home and its environs. The public sphere was left to them, while the services and support they looked for in the home were elevated by the most solemn validation known to man or woman. The outcome of all the heavy moralizing about woman's nature was a set of clear conventions about the division of labour in family life. The husband was to govern, the wife to manage; the husband to provide, the wife to distribute; the husband to inform, the wife to nurture.[69]

However, it was one thing to structure the representation of home in this dichotomized way, and quite another to make reality conform. As a code for living, Victorian domesticity was shot through with contradictions. Some of these can be attributed to the material conditions outlined in the previous chapter. The home was supposed to be inward-looking, focused on the most intimate and compelling of human needs. But for the bourgeoisie the home was also the prime means of affirming social status – a medium of display intended to impress visitors and neighbours. The home was meant to represent a complete antithesis to the values of the world of work, yet it was a point of pride to most wives to make the household routine conform to a punctuality hardly less strict than that of the shop floor. Class pride and discomfort with the cash nexus required that domestic servants should be segregated and invisible, yet their presence at every turn (for example at family prayers) affirmed a more organic relationship with the rest of the household. Middle-class culture was supposedly more child-centred in this period; yet the effect of employing specialist nursery staff was that more affluent parents, at least, saw less of their offspring than they had done in the days when no great to-do was made about the sacred state of childhood.

Above all, the common labelling of home as 'the woman's sphere' obscured the true relationship between home and gender. A superficial reading of the

4. Victoria and Albert as a model of domesticity: Edwin Landseer, *Windsor Castle in Modern Times*, 1841–5.

dichotomies of masculine and feminine character might suggest that home was entirely given over to female influence. The popular image of Victorian domesticity is almost entirely focused on women and children, suggesting that their needs were its governing rationale. Our retrospective picture is dominated by the hearth and its female votaries. The reason is that so much contemporary representation was tilted the same way. The new domestic advice literature on childcare, household management and the direction of servants was addressed exclusively to women. The presiding image of the Victorian Christmas was the Virgin and Child. 'Home Sweet Home', first performed in 1823 and later immortalized by Jenny Lind and Adelina Patti, was drawn from an opera about the abduction of a girl from her village home. Perhaps the most powerful symbol of all was the blameless and bourgeois home of the Queen herself, in stark contrast to the irregular lives of her immediate predecessors.

It is easy to lose sight of how much of this culture was determined by the needs of men. Often they appear as marginal figures only – as the absent breadwinner or the worshipper on the edge of the charmed circle. Yet even at the cultural level appearances are deceptive. The theme of 'Home Sweet

5. Mother and children as an icon for male contemplation: 'Home Comforts', the frontispiece of Sarah Ellis, *The Women of England* (1843).

Home' was *exile* from home; given the disciplines of work, this had much more resonance for men than for women (John Howard Payne, the American librettist who wrote the words of the song, had led a notably peripatetic existence). The theological basis of the Christmas story may have been the virgin birth, but by the 1860s Father Christmas was a popular counter-attraction. For all her association with domestic propriety, Queen Victoria disliked babies and was bored by the details of parenting. In the Prince Consort she could happily rely on the most domesticated and conscientious of husbands: 'Dear Papa always directed our nursery and I believe that none was ever better.'[70] Advice literature for men did not deal with the minutiae of domestic management, but it plainly indicated why home mattered so much. The married man's self-respect, wrote H.C. O'Donnoghue in 1828, is 'kept alive by finding that, though all around is darkness and humiliation, yet there is still a little world of *love* at home, of which he is the *monarch*' (emphases added).[71] Mastery and affection answered to deep-seated masculine needs.

None of this should be cause for surprise. If the role of the home in Victorian culture was to make complementary the polarities of sexual difference, it must surely have expressed men's aspirations, as well as women's. As the foregoing account has shown, the elaboration of the idea of home answered to profound changes in the experience of men. Alienation from work was essentially a man's predicament. Alienation from the city affected both sexes, but when a household moved to the suburbs it was the commuting husband who was most often reminded of the dehumanizing quality of urban life. Order and love – the two vaunted principles of Victorian domesticity – were exactly those qualities which men found lacking in the public sphere. The 'religion of the heart' has rightly been seen as opening a window of opportunity for women;[72] but initially it was experienced and led by men, and men continued to be drawn to the proposition that the home is the proper place to cultivate one's spiritual and emotional well-being. As for the revaluation of childhood, this may well have entailed a bigger mental adjustment for men than for women, since children had always been central to women's lives.

The Victorian ideal of domesticity was in all respects the creation of men as much as women. 'Woman's sphere' was a convenient shorthand, not a call to exclusivity. Given that cultural power was concentrated in the hands of men, the domestic ideal reflected masculine as well as feminine sensibilities. How far the reality of home life embodied these sensibilities is another question. It could only be a qualified correspondence because no reality could have matched the depth of emotional need invested in the idea of home. The Victorians were driven by their sense of social alienation to set up an exacting standard which hardly anyone could meet. Yet, as this book will show, that standard permeated men's practice and produced a distinctive domestic culture.

PART TWO

The Climax of Domesticity,
c. 1830–1880

CHAPTER THREE

Husband and Wife

In May 1867, in the course of the House of Commons debate on the Second Reform Bill, John Stuart Mill tabled the first ever parliamentary motion for a gender-blind franchise, proposing that the word 'person' should be substituted for 'man' throughout the bill. It was the climax of a lifetime's commitment to the cause of women's emancipation. In his speech Mill not only appealed to arguments of political justice; he also placed the issue in the context of the changing character of marriage:

> Women and men are, for the first time in history, really each other's companions. Our traditions respecting the proper relations between them have descended from a time when their lives were apart – when they were separate in their thoughts, because they were separate equally in their amusements and in their serious occupations. In former days a man passed his life among men; all his friendships, all his real intimacies, were with men; with men alone did he consult on any serious business; the wife was either a plaything or an upper servant. All this, among the educated classes, is now changed. The man no longer gives his spare hours to violent exercises and boisterous conviviality with male associates; the two sexes now pass their lives together; the women of a man's family are his habitual society; the wife is his chief associate, his most confidential friend, and often his most trusted adviser.[1]

Mill commended this growing intimacy and trust in marriage because he had immense faith in the value of women's companionship, such as he had happily experienced with his wife Harriet Taylor. But this beneficial effect depended on women being equipped with a breadth of outlook and knowledge of the world. As long as they were denied the vote, women would remain ignorant of public affairs and would undermine their husbands' sense of public duty. Mill asserted that warm companionate marriages were not just a private good – they necessitated a broader definition of the public sphere. In the debate which followed Mill's speech, none of his opponents dissented from his glowing picture of marriage, though they disputed the inference he drew from it. The prophet of high-minded radicalism on sexual questions was for once articulating the common wisdom. Domesticated husbands and supportive wives had by this time become central to the self-image of the Victorians. They defined what marriage was taken to be about; they were a central feature of the Victorians' supposed superiority over both their Georgian forbears and their contemporaries in other countries.[2]

It is not difficult to see where this flattering self-image came from: it was the practical, 'commonsense' expression of the ideology of domesticity. Mill's generation liked to believe that their domestic relations were about love, comfort and morality; Victorian men in particular tended to speak of marriage in terms which distanced it from the authority and formality associated with patriarchy in the past. Of course plenty of allowance must be made for window-dressing. On the lips of men of less integrity than John Stuart Mill, glowing testimonials to the pleasures of companionate marriage readily invite the charge of hypocrisy. But, as the previous chapter showed, there is no doubt that companionate marriage corresponded to deeply felt needs in men: they constantly signalled their allegiance to it in every representational and didactic form available. A more compelling question is how far these needs were met, and how far they conflicted with other expectations of marriage.

★

Husbands looked to a partner in life to whom they could pour out their anxieties, their doubts and their aspirations. Home was felt to be the only place where the vulnerability that lay behind the public mask of strength and imperturbability could be shared with someone else. The sympathetic ear and soothing tongue of the wife were regarded as much the most important dimension of the healing power of home. As long as these qualities were in evidence, failings in other areas might be overlooked. Contemplating her forthcoming marriage to the up-and-coming writer and banker Walter Bagehot in 1858, Eliza Wilson was nervous about her inferior intellectual attainments. 'But I will hope on, for a sympathising heart must be of more value in a wife than a powerful intellect.'[3] This was a role for which women received much coaching in the advice literature of the day. They were told emphatically not to expect full equality of emotional support. When the husband returned from work, the wife must be all attention to lighten his load and calm his spirit, and she must present a demeanour of 'cheerful complacency'; but this was not the cue for her to bring up her domestic worries, which could only disturb his hard-gained repose. The needs of the husband took priority. The wife's obligation to minister to them was the quid pro quo for the material sustenance and protection she received from him.[4]

Victorian culture gave a distinctive twist to the duty of the wife to provide her husband with loving support. What today we treat as an emotional need was seen then as a *moral* need. The emphasis laid by the Victorians on moral tone was, if not entirely new, unparalleled in its intensity. We have seen how this was the powerful legacy of the Evangelical movement, and how its appeal was greatly strengthened by a widely perceived crumbling of moral values in the market-place. Outside the ranks of the frivolous and hedonistic, middle-class Victorian men expected their homes to stand for a moral vision of life which would affect their own sensibilities for the better. In keeping with the current elevated notions of womanhood, the custodians of this moral flame were the women of the home – perhaps a mother or a sister, sometimes a favoured daughter, but most often the wife, who was seen as owing a sacred duty to her husband in this respect. That this was now regarded as the chief practical duty of a wife is suggested by the changed usage of the term 'help-meet': previously applied to the wife in her economic role of producer, it was now applied to her moral functions. In 1843 the Bradford Baptist minister Benjamin Goodwin reminded his twenty-eight-year-old son, still a bachelor:

> you have no 'help meet', no one when you retire from the warehouse to whisper in your ear thoughts of holier and better things, to encourage you in domestic devotions, but you are left a prey to all the unchecked solicitudes of business, from the morning light to far in the evening shades, if not also on your solitary pillow.[5]

The son married soon afterwards.

'Help-meet' was not the only term to shift its meaning in the light of the new conditions of bourgeois marriage. It was at this time that 'angel' acquired its feminine and largely domestic associations. Originally a divine messenger, the angel was now seen as a selfless minister, whose mere presence had an uplifting effect on the moral needs of others. The qualification added in the phrase 'the angel in the house', popularized by Coventry Patmore's sequence of poems (1854–63), was almost superfluous. Women who visited the poor or the sick were certainly 'angels', but the home was the first and most essential sphere for a woman's angelic mission, and philanthropy only the application to a wider field of those virtues whose prime rationale was the needs of husbands and children. Men could not be angels in this sense – nor could they be described by any other term which had the same morally elevating associations.

The redemptive power of the home was, of course, the subject of a vast quantity of prescription, whether given in private (as in Goodwin's case) or directed at the public through advice books. More significant is the evidence that it structured much of the interaction within marriage itself. Many husbands looked to their wives to provide an active moral intelligence to underpin their working lives in an uncertain or disturbing environment. On the eve of his marriage in 1843, Archibald Tait, beset by perplexing problems in the running of Rugby School, impressed upon Catherine Spooner his crying need for her help. 'Oh my dear girl, I do look to you to be my good Angel . . . you shall be my stay & hinder me, with God's help, from being worldly.' Catherine pledged her support, but she was much more tentative in putting forward any needs of her own. That was to be the pattern of their marriage. In his devotional journal Tait prayed that God would enable Catherine to help *him* but reflected little on what she might want in return.[6] Many a young man warned his fiancée, as the publisher Daniel Macmillan did in 1850, to be prepared for unspecified faults and weaknesses in her beloved, requiring future sympathy and support.[7] Both Macmillan and Tait were men of profound faith, but sentiments of this kind were not confined to the devout. The young doctor James Paget, exposed to the surgical wards of the early Victorian metropolis, told his future wife Lydia North in 1837 that he hoped to find in her his 'spiritual nurse'.[8] After two and a half years of marriage John Heaton of Leeds admitted to his wife Fanny that he often felt 'disturbed, or angry, or misanthropic'; 'I hope you will "preach" to me whenever you feel prompted to do so, that you may instil some of your goodness into me and make me somewhat more like yourself'.[9] That preaching should have been admissible within marriage is some measure of the moral expectation which was laid on their wives by bourgeois Victorians. Of course not all were as ready as Fanny Heaton to meet the need. Writing in 1880, Frances Power Cobbe asserted: 'the higher *moral* good of the husband occupies wives comparatively little'. By this she meant that wives were more likely in practice to urge their husbands to pursue their own interest with scant regard for the moral consequences. But the very way Cobbe framed her denial shows how strong the convention of the moral wife was. Husbands expected it, and many wives strove to understand it and live up to it.[10]

But home was also the place for comforts of a less elevated kind. Men expected from their wives a clean and well-ordered house, an inviting fireside, an appetizing table, and soothing attentions in the sick-room. All this was implied in John Heaton's appreciative description of Fanny as 'the presiding genius of cheerful regularity'.[11] Daniel Macmillan, enumerating his blessings in 1853, concluded: 'and then to have a quiet home, and quiet evenings with one's wife, all that one requires, and all without great toil and anxiety'.[12] Comfort without exertion was the key. As the bestselling Baptist writer William Landels put it, 'Man has no aptitude for domestic duties, and so long as they require to be done – that is, so long as the world lasts – woman will be required to do them'. That was a much more acceptable message than the minority view that domestic burdens should be shared.[13] Yet the services of wives could not be taken for granted. Ill health frequently removed them from the scene. Post-partum complications often made childbirth a major disruption of household routine; comparatively minor illnesses got out of hand much more easily than they do today; and the lifestyle of the bourgeois wife brought in its train chronic ailments like headaches and stomach disorders. For these the medical prescription was usually a change of air or a taking of the waters. John Heaton's appreciation of his wife's 'cheerful regularity' was all the keener because she spent so much time with her own family or in spa towns – often twelve or thirteen weeks in a single year. During these periods, until his eldest daughter was old enough to take over the running of the house, Heaton had to hire and fire servants, pay the bills and supervise the younger children – 'left to do the drudgery and keep the pot boiling while the rest get away for health or for pleasure', as he grumbled in 1871.[14] During the same period in the Lincolnshire Wolds Elizabeth Stovin believed that her poor health owed much to her husband's damp and dark farmhouse, and she frequently abandoned it for her parents' more comfortable residence twenty miles away. Husband Cornelius wrote to her during one November absence: 'It is cool work entering my empty bedroom at night. You may be sure I wrap round me the bedclothes pretty close ... It has been comfortless for me through the night by reason of the cold'.[15]

That is about as close as most Victorian husbands were likely to get to acknowledging the prime physical comfort offered by marriage. Even between loving intimates good taste dictated a reticence about sexual matters. This has allowed posterity to take a very negative view of the erotic side of Victorian marriage. Middle-class husbands, so the argument goes, found their main sexual outlet in the prostitutes who were so widely available, while their wives were confined within an ideology of 'purity' and good for little more than raising children. It is not difficult to find instances which bear out this depressing stereotype. In 1873 Georgina Potter married the wealthy banker Daniel Meinertzhagen. Daniel was a man of the world, and sexually complaisant women were not the best preparation for marrying a sheltered 23-year-old. The wedding night was a disaster; in their son's words, 'mother in her puritan chastity could not respond to father's exuberance'. Thereafter Daniel spent as little time as possible under the same roof as his wife, often staying at his bachelor apartment in the Albany, Piccadilly. He performed his 'duty', and ten children were born to the couple, but Georgina's sisters were probably correct in their suspicion that Daniel's sexual needs were met elsewhere; one of them, Beatrice Webb, damned him in retrospect as 'narrow-minded and narrow-hearted and a downright selfish impracticable husband'.[16] However, the notion that 'respectable' husbands routinely cheated on their wives is a figment of the post-Victorian imagination. Of course married men did use prostitutes. But, as we shall see in Chapter 6, the vast scale of prostitution in Victorian society primarily served the needs of *unmarried* men of all classes, whether these were confirmed bachelors, or (more typically) those postponing marriage until they enjoyed the required income. The needs of married men accounted for only a small proportion of the trade.

For the most part husbands looked primarily to their wives for sexual fulfilment. The conventions of courtship strongly encouraged them in this direction. The association of marriage with romantic love was well established by the Victorian period. It is true that bourgeois men tended to choose women who were of their own class, or slightly better, and they often married into families with whom they had a close business connection. But in most cases this was less a cynical bid for upward mobility than a reflection of the limited social contexts in which members of the opposite sex could be met. The Victorians expected to marry for love, and as Peter Gay has shown, erotically charged courtship letters are not hard to find.[17] This expectation was partly formed by an extensive popular advice literature which assumed that full conjugal relations should be a pleasure to both parties.[18] The early Victorian period admittedly saw some spirited advocacy of celibacy for men from the Tractarians, but this was balanced (and possibly outweighed) by a strong pro-sensual backlash: Charles Kingsley celebrated married love as the essence of divinely authorized masculinity, and some Evangelical writers were only a little less forthright.[19] It was common for men to approach the wedding day with the keenest anticipation of the sexual delight to come. Other men must surely have thought what Kingsley said: 'Do I expect to marry an *angel*, passionless, unsympathizing? No! My wife must be a woman – subject to like passions with myself!'[20] The relevant question to ask is what were the prospects of translating these erotic yearnings into reality.

Sometimes the wedding night rudely dashed these longings, and a long haul of sexual frustration was the outcome. Respectable girls were often brought up in complete ignorance of the facts of life, or they knew just enough to be terrified of pregnancy. For these wives the honeymoon could be so traumatic that sexual relations were ever thereafter blighted. That seems to have been true of Daniel and Georgina Meinertzhagen, with the consequences already noted. But virginity and feminine modesty were not necessarily a barrier to a sexually satisfying marriage. This was most famously true of the premier couple in the land, Queen Victoria and her serious-minded, equally inexperienced consort. Contemplating the empty bed after Albert's early death, the Queen reflected, 'What a contrast to that tender lover's love!'[21] No doubt the odds were stacked against newly-weds more heavily than they are today. But educated men were brought up to show chivalrous consideration towards women, and in sexual terms this translated into tenderness rather than 'exuberance'.

The clearest evidence we have of sexual fulfilment in marriage is the expression of acute physical longing in correspondence when couples were separated. Joshua Pritchard was a devout Methodist whose work as an excise officer took him away from his Manchester home for extended periods. After eighteen years of marriage he still found these separations extremely trying. As a saved believer he was confident that he would never really be parted from his wife, any more than he would be parted from Christ, but this made the physical separation no easier to bear. From London in 1836 Joshua vividly communicated his aching sense of deprivation: 'Bless you Mary, I love to be at home, I now wish you were with me, I am sitting by the fire alone. O bless you my Love, my Dove, my Dear one, my best, my sweetest . . .' He fondly recalled his 'bloom of youth' when Mary had first fallen in love with him, and concluded 'thank God our Love is not abated'. These are not the words of a man whose passionate ardour was rebuffed by passivity or forbearance on his wife's part. Indeed he feared rather that his 'passionate Spirit' might distract Mary from higher things.[22]

During the 1850s Isaac Holden kept his emotions under better control than Joshua Pritchard, but he was in some ways even more direct in his letters to his second wife, Sarah Sugden. Like Pritchard, both Isaac and Sarah were confirmed Methodists. Isaac's business ambitions kept them apart for several months each year. These regular absences took their toll on Isaac. To 'taste in imagination the sweet conjugal feeling' was not enough; the memory of her 'spirited and affectionate embrace' made him 'long to squeeze you well'; he found himself in bed at night thinking of her 'with heart warm and something else as warm'. On her side Sarah was not offended by this overtly sexual language. In the privacy of her bedroom, she imagined them 'entwined in each other's embrace' and she longed for the warmth of his flesh. The pair seem to have enjoyed a good sexual understanding, even though for Sarah physical intimacy only began when she married Isaac at the age of 45.[23]

Silence on such matters was much more typical – as for example in John Heaton's letters to his often-absent wife which are almost entirely without erotic charge. This may point to a physical void at the centre of their lives. More likely it reflects a reluctance to commit such matters to paper, and possibly speech too. The plain truth is that we are never likely to know much about the sexual lives of Victorian couples, because they alluded to it so little themselves. The evidence is so patchy and contradictory that a case can be made with equal confidence for fulfilment or frustration as the norm. Either of those positions is a distortion of reality.[24] A sounder course is to cite the contradictory conditions which pushed marital sexuality in different directions, and to settle for considerable variation in this most private of spheres. We know that for middle-class spouses sex was for the most part confined to the marriage bed. But we are in no position to hazard an estimate of how much sexual fulfilment was found there, or how one-sided it may have been.

★

The blessings of companionate marriage were about intimacy and leisure. The foundations were meant to be established during the wedding journey or honeymoon, which originated in the late eighteenth century and was an established convention by the beginning of Victoria's reign. Thereafter the most important prerequisite was that husband and wife would routinely be in each other's company a good deal. Extended meal times, music-making, reading aloud – and by mid-century the ritual of afternoon tea – were all intended to promote the companionate ideal. When it came under strain the blame was sometimes laid at the wife's door, on the grounds that her commitment to 'visiting' and other philanthropic work led her to neglect the family.[25] But the key issue was how much time the husband spent at home. There was no doubt about the high value which in theory was placed on men's leisure in the home. There is an unmistakable tone of complacency about the London clerk who told readers of the *Daily Telegraph* in 1868, 'When not employed with extra work from the office, I am cutting my grass, sticking my beans, doing carpenter's work, drilling my children in music, or mending their toys'.[26] His upper middle-class counterpart probably substituted music-making and reading aloud for carpentry and repairs, but the moral imperative was comparable. Men's commitment of time to the home was more than a matter of personal preference, however. The lower middle-class husband working for an exacting employer, or the factory-owner on the verge of ruin, could not linger at the fireside – though this did not save them from the reproach of neglecting the domestic sphere.[27] As we saw in Chapter 1, members of the professions were likely to spend much more time at home than businessmen or office workers because so much of their work was carried out there: the clergy tended to live in tied houses and work from home; doctors set up their practices at home, and so on. Independent professional men of this type nearly always used a room at home which served as office, library and interview room according to need. The 'study', as it was usually called, was not so much sited *within* the home, as carved out *from* the home. Reserved for the husband's exclusive use and often out of bounds to the rest of the family, it conformed to the principle of separate spheres by removing his work from the domestic atmosphere. The study allowed a man to become buried in his work at the expense of his family, just as much as the manufacturer who kept long hours at his factory. For William Gaskell, the Manchester Unitarian minister, the study served as a retreat for intellectual pursuits as well as the chapel office. Elizabeth complained that when William was at home she only saw him at meal times, since 'by his own free will he would never stir' from his study.[28]

Nor was the stay-at-home husband necessarily conducive to family harmony. In fact he could be positively destructive – as Samuel Butler brilliantly conveyed in the fictional portrayal of his father in *The Way of All Flesh* (written mainly in the 1870s, but based on recollections of the 1840s and 1850s). Theorists of the ideal marriage might commend the home-loving and home-living husband; practical advice-writers were not so sure. Dinah Craik knew what worked best: 'I beg to ask ... if it is not the greatest comfort possible when, the masculine half of the family being cleared out for the day, the house settles down into regular work and orderly quietness until evening?'[29] Behind that lightly turned put-down was a justifiable concern that the husband who spent too much time at home would assert his authority in ways which made unfair demands on other family members. As memoirs of the period show, the husband who used his study to work was frequently at large in the rest of the house, making irksome demands for quiet and punctuality.[30] A satisfying companionate marriage was best served by the husband who regarded the home as the first call on his leisure but who spent his working hours elsewhere.

Whether or not the material conditions for companionate marriage were translated into experience turned mainly on two issues: patriarchal authority and sexual difference. Household authority had been a benchmark of adult masculinity for hundreds of years. In pre-industrial society to be head of a household, and to be visibly head of it, was essential to masculine status, and the man who could not keep domestic order counted for little among his fellows.[31] This remained the case in the Victorian period. In 1841 responsibility for completing the census return was laid on the 'occupier'. A court ruling a few years later defined the occupier as one who could 'retain his quality of master, reserving to himself the general control and dominion over the whole house' – a turn of phrase which nicely implies that since mastery could not be taken for granted, it reflected credit on the occupier who exercised it.[32] Rank insubordination on the part of a wife was a gross slur on her husband's manliness, and the henpecked husband was still a figure of fun. In 1845 *Punch* ran a hugely popular series by Douglas Jerrold called 'Mrs Caudle's Curtain Lectures', a biting satire on the nagging wife and the belittled husband; the context was the early Victorian lower middle class, but the angle on sexual politics was hardly novel.[33] To these traditional notions was now added the more distinctively Victorian appreciation of domestic order as compensation for the apparent crumbling of order in society at large. Social alienation called for reassurance in the most intimate sphere of men's lives. As we saw in Chapter 2, the well-ordered home rose in men's valuation as traditional hierarchies elsewhere buckled under the strain of rapid economic and social change. In short, traditional and novel concerns combined to set a high premium on domestic patriarchy.

Acceptance of patriarchy was certainly not unqualified, however. It was rejected in radical and free-thinking circles, especially where the influence of Robert Owen was still felt. Even within respectable society there was room for dissent. The Unitarians in particular subscribed to a theory of dual headship of the family. Elizabeth Gaskell found herself wishing that William would *command* her: 'I am sometimes coward enough to wish that we were back in the darkness where obedience was the only seen duty of women'.[34] In middle-class society generally the reservations were less about the principle of patriarchal authority than where its boundaries should be set. The most contentious issue was the traditional association of patriarchy with correction. Between the 1820s and the 1870s there was a rising tide of revulsion against wife-beating and other forms of physical-force patriarchy. Middle-class Victorians were almost as shocked by lurid tales of physical assault in the home as they were by the violence of master against slave or of humans against animals. Much of this indignation was displaced on to the working class; exposés of 'wife-torture' were written, and reports of the magistrates' courts scoured for evidence of the scale of the problem in the poorer industrial districts. Far less was said about the extent of domestic violence in the middle class, which is why it is so difficult to speak confidently about it now. But bourgeois Victorians could not remain in ignorance of the problem, given the space accorded to marital breakdown in the press. Under the Matrimonial Causes Act of 1857 divorce was transferred from the jurisdiction of the Church to the civil courts, where it was handled more expeditiously and more cheaply. As a result a steadily increasing number of middle-class people sought divorce or separation, and their stories were reproduced at length in the daily newspapers, with no intimate detail spared.

For middle-class wives cruelty – both physical and mental – was the ground most commonly cited in making a petition to the court. There is nothing like repeated reminders of the shocking reality of matrimonial abuse to fuel intolerance of it. Opinion had moved on this issue well before changes in the law of patriarchy were made in the 1870s and 1880s.[35] But this did not mean that the patriarchal principle was being jettisoned. Quite the reverse. The excesses were not read as disturbing proof that patriarchy was rotten to the core; they were seen as an embarrassing aberration which brought marital authority into disrepute. On this reading, the patriarchy principle was compromised by the failure of some men to conduct themselves in the home with due chivalry and restraint. In fact the lurid courtroom tales of cruelty seem to have had little perceptible impact on the support for patriarchy among women. The principle that husbands held ultimate and overall domestic authority was accepted by almost all female advice-book writers of the period, including those who were intent on raising the status of wives. Indeed it remained unchallenged until the feminist onslaught at the end of the century. Women at marriage often spoke of passing from the authority of a father or brother to that of a husband; those who had gained greater autonomy *vis-à vis* their parents spoke of surrendering their independence.[36]

What justified this subordination was the protection and material support supplied by the husband. That too was in keeping with patriarchal tradition. Directing a domestic labour force for a common productive end had given men the strongest rationale for domestic authority, while providing structures and routines by which it could be enforced. Yet domestic production was becoming an anachronism among the early Victorian middle class. The labour that continued to be performed within the household not only went on behind the householder's back; it was hardly classified as 'work' at all. That dignified label belonged exclusively to the work which *he* carried out, usually away from home, for a salary, fee or wage. This was what justified the husband in demanding the deference and obedience of his wife and children. Failure to provide was unmanly and undermined the claim to authority. Hence for a wife to make this charge against her husband was to strike him at his most vulnerable point – sometimes at the cost of inciting him to violence. In other words, the prestige which had previously belonged to the head of the domestic team was now attached to the 'breadwinner', a new term which featured prominently in the public discourse of the early Victorian period.[37] It carried then – as it has continued to do since – the unmistakable inference of justifying men's privilege and power in the home.[38]

But it was one thing to be master in one's own house, and quite another to attend to every detail of its organization. In the last resort no one disputed the husband's responsibility, since it was his money and his authority which were at stake. The question was whether the wife acted as a trusted manager or as a closely supervised inferior. The message of the most widely read didactic writers was clear: while the husband provided for the family and exercised the governance of it, *management* of the family belonged to the wife.[39] Two clerical households illustrate divergent responses to an almost identical situation. When Archibald Tait was headmaster of Rugby in succession to Dr Arnold during the 1840s, his wife Catherine not only had total control of their family finances, but took over the accounts of the school as a whole. Twenty years later Edward Benson, as the first head of Wellington College, caused to be inscribed over the door of the Master's Lodge the Latin motto *Proesis ut Prosis*, meaning 'Take charge here that you may be of service'. He was as good as his word, scrutinizing his young wife's somewhat erratic accounts, castigating errors and extravagance, and pointing out trivial lapses in domestic order. Tait was nearer to the norm than Benson. To descend to the level of detail that Benson did was undignified (as it was in the slightly later instance of Leslie Stephen).[40] Life was made easy for Tait by his wife's financial flair, but it was generally felt that the wife should have effective control of the finances and, if need be, she must learn on the job by painstaking trial and error. This was a matter not only of domestic efficiency but of female dignity. In legal disputes between spouses the husband who removed his wife from the day-to-day management of the household badly prejudiced his case.[41] The American writer Richard G. White was close to the mark when, after visiting England in 1876, he observed that the reason why wives had household affairs more absolutely in their hands than in America was because the husband was so obviously master of his house; his delegation of accounting responsibility was a sign of strength rather than weakness.[42] The wife's effective management of the household under the overall control of her husband was a practical application of the principle of separate spheres.

However, when husbands spent more time at home, the separation of spheres tended to break down, and patriarchy was less acceptable to those at the receiving end. This was tellingly revealed by the proceedings of the new Divorce Court. A number of women petitioners were prompted to brave publicity by the belief that their domestic sphere had been brutally encroached on. Only husbands who spent a good deal of time at home were likely to attract an accusation of this kind. In the case of the engineer John Curtis and his wife Frances in 1858, John was a committed and opinionated father whose attentions to the children were construed as an intrusion on his wife's sphere. His most pointed response to her protests was to replace her as household manager with a young servant. This was the action not of a roving ne'er-do-well, but of a home-loving husband whose domestic interests drew him into an abuse of his power. Ten years later a similar assertion of patriarchal power was enforced by the Anglican vicar James Kelly. In a *cause célèbre* which occupied the Divorce Court for five months, it transpired that he had installed a housekeeper to perform all his wife's domestic duties.[43] This abuse of patriarchy, though not common, is nevertheless highly suggestive. Men were expected to spend more leisure time at home than ever before. Evenings and Sundays were billed as domestic time for the conscientious husband, but they also gave him much more scope to assert his mastery over the household. A meddlesome or combative man was likely to do much more damage at home than when hanging out with his cronies in the town. He might disrupt the family's financial arrangements, or come between the wife and her servants, or between her and the children. The theory of patriarchy, on which there was little dissent, then became an intolerable reality. Conventional wisdom held that home was the wife's domain, but that the wife must be subject to her husband. The contradiction was obscured when work or pleasure kept the husband away for most of the time. It became potentially explosive when he was constantly at home, even when he strove to be a 'good' husband and father.[44]

★

If the problem of patriarchy was as old as marriage itself, sexual character as understood by the Victorians was a comparatively recent concern. We saw in the last chapter how a 'two-sex' model had been gradually supplanting time-honoured notions of homology between the sexes. Both body and mind were now sexed. A formidably comprehensive range of antitheses was inscribed on the distinction between the two sexes, in ways which cast doubt on how much meeting of the minds there could ever be between a man and a woman. There has probably never been a time when the differences between male and female were so rigidly interpreted as the early and mid-Victorian period. To what extent the experts were believed is impossible to know, but considerable doubt must be thrown on their impact if only because experience so often contradicted them. Perhaps the early stages of love were confined to the wondering worship of difference, but marriage was likely to supply repeated evidence of sensibilities and aptitudes which crossed the gender divide. In 1874 Cornelius Stovin was reminded how little his wife conformed to conventional womanliness; after she had made a taxing journey through wind and snow, he told her

> We need not come to you in search of effeminacy of character. You are a true enterprising tourist. Storms cannot quench your ardour . . . Accomplishment and endurance are your two watchwords. You love action more than contemplation though you blend judgement with action. Your active preponderates over the reflective power. You believe in business tact and energy carried to the goal of success in life.[45]

The Stovins illustrate another consideration tending to undermine the perception of sexual difference – a shared involvement in the husband's work. It is of course true at a general level that the trend was towards the complete detachment of work from home, and some husbands made a fetish of this. Edward Barrett kept his wife and eight children (including the poet Elizabeth Barrett Browning) in rural seclusion and in total ignorance of his precarious Jamaican business interests. In the 1870s when Henry Ashbee ran a City export firm, there was a rigid family rule that his wife should never set foot in the premises, even though the business had been set up by her father.[46] These were

6. Cornelius and Elizabeth Stovin in later life.

men who occupied the higher reaches of finance. Hippolyte Taine had much the same category in mind when he remarked that, unlike in France, the English husband 'considers that he has the right to tell her nothing of his business'.[47] But lower down the social scale men were not always so secretive. The logic of occupational 'marrying-in' was that wives often knew a great deal about their husbands' work. This was most true of the clergy, since so much church work was transacted in the home, and much of it touched on philanthropy and moral welfare. Nevertheless the Revd Mandell Creighton anticipated some difficulty in this area. 'The nuisance of married life', he wrote to his fiancée in 1871, was that

> strive as I may or as you may, still the practical side of life must be much more prominent to me than to you. I shall have a number of things to do; whereas your sphere will be all within my reach and knowledge, mine on the other hand will not be in your reach entirely.[48]

Apart from Creighton's easy confidence that he would have a perfect grasp of his wife's concerns, the significant point here is that he took it for granted that she would be party to much of his work. And so in fact it proved: Louise Creighton laboured as a historian alongside her more famous husband, and when he died she demonstrated a fine command of his ecclesiastical and scholarly work in her two-volume biography.[49]

The line distinguishing the economic roles of husband and wife became blurred wherever occupational endogamy prevailed. Victorian wives were often the daughters of pre-Victorians whose work had been located in the home or close by. Such women picked up a practical grasp of the trade, sometimes intensified by a close relationship with the father, and they often married one of his business associates. In Lancashire, for example, the wives of cotton masters possessed a pool of largely unacknowledged expertise in the textile trade.[50] Much the same was true of farming. As explained in Chapter 1, farmers' wives at this time were withdrawing from practical farm work in order to clinch their claim to respectable bourgeois status. Yet because endogamy was pronounced within the farming community, wives generally knew a good deal about the ins and outs of agriculture, and they were a source of advice (or reproof) to their husbands. It was Elizabeth Stovin who spotted that her husband's foreman was not up to the job and needed closer supervision. 'I have according to your wish risen early and looked more sharply after my men', Cornelius reported in 1876.[51] With their quarrels over money and health, the Stovins were not a harmonious couple; but this only made their common interest in farming all the more important as the cement which bonded their marriage together.

Probably the most reliable basis of companionate marriage – and also the clearest rebuttal of the two-sex theory – was shared cultural interests. Often this was what had brought the couple together in the first place. Education was therefore vital. As John Stuart Mill recognized, domesticity was a doubtful blessing if the wife's education lagged badly behind the husband's. There was certainly little cause for complacency regarding middle-class boys' education, since there were still huge disparities among grammar schools, public schools, and most of all the private boarding establishments. But prior to the late nineteenth century the position was incomparably worse for girls. Formal schooling was comparatively rare, and the education which girls received at home from mother or governess was often weighted towards 'accomplishments' at the expense of intellectual development. In later life Mary Benson was still saddened by how little companionship she had been able to offer Edward Benson during the early years of their marriage in the 1860s: 'of large interests, of knowledge, of initiative there was scarcely any'.[52]

But in practice there was much more to women's education than the demeaning stereotype of the ignorant novel-reading wife allows. Professional men like doctors or the clergy tended to pay rather more attention to the mental progress of their daughters. In some denominations – notably Unitarianism – there was a strong tradition of female self-improvement which took the form of ambitious programmes of reading in history, philosophy and political economy. Many women attended courses of public lectures and kept up with the journals. They learned foreign languages, sometimes to a reasonable reading fluency in French or German. And there was a fine line between proficiency at the keyboard or the sketchbook and an informed critical interest in music and art. In these circles intellectual convergence between spouses was far from uncommon, and the strict demarcation of sexual character to be found in the didactic literature was considerably toned down.[53]

These were the circumstances which Mill had in mind when he judged that husbands and wives were no longer 'separate in their thoughts'. But there were two marital situations in which awareness of sexual difference was likely to be more pronounced. The first was when a serious–minded and perhaps hard–working man was married to a woman of little education and few interests. This was the context for a vigorous and enduring discourse directed against the 'frivolous' wife (though sometimes the husband was held to share the blame through treating her like a pampered pet instead of a rational friend). Sarah Ellis was the most widely read proponent of this perspective. Her string of advice books in the late 1830s and early 1840s was directed at women in the lower reaches of the middle class who in Ellis's view were most likely to be given to vanity, affectation and idleness. In their preoccupation with the superficial markers of social status, such women were blind to their higher duties. Improved education was essential so that they might become 'not only equal but interesting and instructive companions to men'.[54] By the 1860s concern had shifted to the leisured women of the upper middle class who regarded a profusion of servants as an excuse to pursue the full-time life of hostess. Significantly there was now much less concern about the damage this might be doing to marital relations; it was the claims of children (and to a lesser extent philanthropy) which counted.[55] The truth was that 'frivolity' was no respecter of sex. Daniel Meinertzhagen, who spent his ample leisure shooting and fishing in the day, and playing billiards and cards at night, was a great deal less 'serious' than his wife Georgina with her spiritualism and her interest in science. The higher reaches of business and the City were full of husbands like Daniel. There was little to choose between these men and the inveterate socialite and shopper in London's West End. The attempt to foist frivolity on women as a marker of sexual difference was never very convincing.[56]

Sexual difference was more heavily underscored by the second and opposed tendency of placing married women on a moral pedestal *vis-à-vis* their husbands. One could argue that the moral wife had as much, or as little, grounding in reality as the frivolous wife. But 'the moral wife' was not only an ideologically loaded label; she represented an applauded ideal with immense prescriptive power. Without question many husbands were very gratified to be the recipients of moral uplift, and many wives relished supplying it. The problem was that the moralizing tendencies of Victorian culture made this transaction carry a much greater burden of meaning than it need have done. Husbands bore the taint of moral contamination by the market-place. Wives, on the other hand, were graced if not with inherently superior moral natures, then certainly with conditions of relative seclusion which kept their moral insight unclouded. Here was the basis of a character gap which both husband and wife might interpret in terms of 'natural' sexual difference.

The demand for emotional and moral support which husbands made on their wives was potentially an overwhelming one, given the stresses of work and the troubling intimations of a moral vacuum outside the home. Many wives were crushed by it. But husbands were adversely affected too. Psychological reassurance and refuge from the hard world outside are what children turn for to their mothers. Given the immense prestige of motherhood at this time, it is not surprising that for men the wife became hopelessly confused with the mother. Both the imagery and the identification became blurred. The popular icon of the Angel Mother had as much – if not more – resonance for husbands as for children. As the scholar churchman Arthur Stanley told his fiancée in 1863, 'You must be my wings. I shall often flag and be dispirited; but you, now, as my dear mother formerly, must urge me, and bid me not despair when the world seems too heavy a burden to be struggled against'.[57] He was then in his mid-forties. Other husbands spoke of laying their head on the wife's breast for comfort.[58] Sarah Ellis advised wives never afterwards to allude to those moments when their husbands had come to them in a state of tearful collapse. But clearly many men derived gratification from playing out their maternal fantasies. It seems to have been during the 1850s that the practice of some middle-class husbands not merely referring to, but addressing their wives as 'Mother' first became a matter for comment.[59]

The sexual implications of this amplification of the mother-figure were not promising. Victorian notions of motherhood were so deeply identified with purity that any identification of wife with mother was likely to make her a highly equivocal object of desire. Indeed according to conventional notions of sexual difference this was no bad thing. Beatrice Webb recalled that her mother's role had been to keep her father Richard Potter 'from animal self-indulgence'; he would return to kneel penitent before 'the ascetic purity of his wife' whenever he strayed.[60] A thin line must have divided this policing, restraining role from a complete embargo on sexual relations with the forbidden 'mother'. On her side, a wife brought up with an unquestioning belief in the purity and innocence of womanhood was likely to have to shed a great many inhibitions before she could fully enjoy sexual relations with her husband. In these instances the perception of sexual difference distorted the emotional relationship between spouses and loaded the odds heavily against sexual fulfilment.

★

The Benson marriage illustrates some of these themes well. Edward was 30 when he married in 1859, soon after taking up his appointment as headmaster of the newly founded Wellington College. Mary was 18. Edward had had plenty of time to reflect on what he owed to Mary. He had known her since she was seven, and had come to an 'understanding' about their future together when

7. Edward Benson, 1867.

she was only 12. As a man troubled by a strong libido, he saw her innocence as his best means of resisting temptation of thought or deed. He told her on the eve of their marriage, 'you know me, and your sweetness and simple purity have been God's angels to me, and I know they always will be'. In later life Mary realized that part of Edward's motive in choosing her had been 'to preserve himself from errant feelings in love'.[61]

The wedding night was a disaster. His sexual need was pressing, but his inexperience matched hers, and his desire was complicated by a complex web of identification. Not only did he already see her as his Angel Mother; Mary was also his second cousin, whom he had long ago cast in the role of surrogate sister after his own favourite sister had died of typhus. The honeymoon was deeply traumatic for Mary: 'how I cried at Paris! ... The nights! I can't think how I lived', she recalled years later. All her life she bitterly reproached herself with never having learned to love with 'that strong human passion' which Edward had. Only after more than ten years of marriage did Mary begin to discover her sensual side, but in a manner which excluded Edward entirely; it was women friends who mattered now, leading eventually to a full lesbian

8. Mary Benson, 1860.

relationship. Meanwhile Edward's passionate nature was thwarted, while his strict moral principles ruled out any substitute (including masturbation). Almost certainly this contributed to his neuralgia and his black depressions, which periodically cast a pall over the household.[62]

Mary's appointed role was of course to care for Edward through these vicissitudes. At first she felt desperately inadequate to the task. 'I have not yet deserved the privilege of being his comforter: I never feel my own want of womanliness so much as when he is in trouble or ill', she wrote in her diary. Edward reproached her for her lack of tenderness. In fact he reproached her with a good deal, including (as we have seen) alleged incompetence as domestic manager. Scenes of this kind, when Edward expressed his patriarchal displeasure, usually took place in the same study where correction was meted out to schoolboys. Mastery and dependence alternated in an uneasy switchback. After sixteen years of marriage the dynamics began to change. Mary experienced an acute spiritual crisis and rebirth, quite independently of Edward's pastoral guidance. In 1878 when their eldest son died suddenly, she proved the more resilient of the two, and Edward leaned gratefully on her fortitude and her spiritual understanding. From then on, the younger sons recalled, Mary became more skilful in soothing her husband's irritability and moderating the effects of his depression. He also began to consult her and rely on her judgement in public as well as family matters. Edward remained very much in charge at home, a husband and father who was easily offended. But Mary was now indispensable in maintaining Edward's formidable public energies at full tilt. His legendary capacity for work (he rose to become Archbishop of Canterbury) was probably also in part a displacement of his frustrated libido. Domesticity exacted its toll, but it also directed Edward's energies into channels which he found richly rewarding.[63]

Edward's need for comfort and reassurance was intense. Like many others he came to terms with his dependence by constructing his wife as mother. 'Would you were here', he wrote to her on the eve of their marriage, 'and that I could lay my head on your breast & be comforted, as you have comforted me, for I am filled with shame'. Mary would gather him to her breast, intuit his unarticulated needs and regulate the emotional equilibrium of the household. Given the power of the maternal ideal and the ambivalence about acknowledging carnal desire, Victorian men were more drawn than most to the appeal of the wife-mother. But at the same time Mary never lost her character of child-wife. The earliest years of their friendship had placed an indelible mark here. Rather than minimize the age gap between a girl not yet in her teens and a man in his mid-twenties, Edward had drawn attention to it. He corrected her faults of character, and he took in hand her education in subjects like architecture and geography. Not surprisingly the young Mary viewed him as a father-figure rather than a lover, her own father having died in the year she was born. She never entirely lost her awe of him.[64]

In Edward's case, therefore, relating to the wife as an Angel Mother was only part of the truth. Paradoxically she remained also a child whose subordination should be beyond question. In fact the two positions were intimately connected in ways which had a much wider resonance. The greater a man's dependence on his wife for counsel and comfort, the greater the strain on his sense of masculine self-sufficiency, and the greater the temptation to compensate for this by the arbitrary exercise of domestic authority. Husbands negotiated this contradiction between dependence and dominance by relating to their wives in quite distinct modes. When asserting his authority the husband acted as a patriarch; in turning to his wife for support his conduct was more like that of a child towards his mother. Dependence was only acceptable to the man's sensitivities if the woman was constructed as mother instead of wife. In Edward Benson's case these tendencies were intensified by the unusually tender age at which Mary had become bound to him and by his very pronounced preoccupation with 'purity'. But they reflected significant structural tensions in bourgeois marriage. In the American context this syndrome has been dubbed the 'patriarchal child'. It is a highly appropriate term to describe men like Benson.[65]

★

The Benson marriage is a commentary by implication on one other dimension of marriage, and that is religion. Edward's ambition to distinguish himself in the service of the Church was the driving force of his life; his passionate belief in the importance of dogma and discipline had obvious parallels in his family life. Mary's faith was deeply personal and mystical, and doctrine counted for little with her. In their different ways each was abreast of the religious tendencies of the day. Mid-Victorian England certainly allowed for a considerable diversity of religious sensibilities. The influence of the churches was still pervasive. Up until the 1860s at least, formal religious observance was the norm among the middle class, and couples usually worshipped at the same church. For some a common religious affiliation touched only the surface of their lives: it indicated no more than a lack of opportunity for meeting members of the opposite sex in any other context, and a judgement of where their social advantage lay. But even when allowance has been made for calculations of respectability, there was a formidable degree of sincere Christian adherence in middle-class society. It made a difference to the tone of marriage when both parties shared the same view of life in Heaven and on earth, particularly if they thought more of these matters than anything else. The tensions of the Benson marriage were certainly increased by the growing gulf between their personal stances on religion.[66] In contrast Joshua Pritchard's loving intimacy with his wife Mary in the 1830s was founded on a common Methodist devotion, most evident in their commitment to a spiritually intrusive regime for their children.[67] Archibald Tait and Catherine Spooner provide a striking instance of religious harmony. He was a convert from the Church of Scotland to an intensely devotional and practical Anglicanism; she was the daughter of an Evangelical archdeacon (who had also been William Wilberforce's brother-in-law). From their marriage in 1843 until her death in 1878, much of the Taits' spiritual life was conducted together, and their private journals demonstrate how close the convergence was.[68]

Yet religion was no guarantee of marital harmony. This was because it gave out such contradictory messages about the ordering of family life. Like the institution of marriage itself, almost all forms of Christian belief were shot through with assumptions of sexual inequality. St Paul's injunction, 'Wives, submit yourselves unto your own husbands, as unto the Lord' underpinned unequal marriage in countless devout households. William Austin, a salaried employee and Baptist lay preacher, recorded one episode of this kind during his life as a newly married man in the early 1850s:

> My beloved wife is all to me that I could require in most respects – in other respects she is improving. Bless the Lord. This evening I returned home, found my wife under the influence of a little temptation – rather dissatisfied and unhappy through having been alone all day. But I talked, we read and bowed at the Family Altar, the Lord broke her heart and humbled her before him so that we were greatly blessed.[69]

The Methodists brought a breath of fresh air into Christian practice, but they had no quarrel with this patriarchal conception of the Christian family. They looked back to the unyielding prescription of their founder: 'Whoever, therefore, would be a good wife, let this sink into her inmost soul, "My husband is my superior, my better: he has the right to rule over me. God has given it him, and I will not strive against God".'[70] But against this old-style patriarchy must be set the commitment of all the Evangelical churches to the power of the moral mother as the foundation of a godly family life. Once home was recognized as the prime site of 'the religion of the heart', the spiritual standing of the wife was bound to rise. If the husband reflected the authority of the Father in Heaven (often unseen but ever-present), the wife stood for Christian love and spiritual intuition. It was an open question whether the bedtime prayer of mother and child was not more important than the family prayers led by the father. The fact that the rituals of the death-bed were almost entirely in the hands of women reflected not only their dominant place in domestic management, but also their superior endowment as spiritual comforters.[71]

Religion might therefore inform and justify sharply differing interpretations of the marital relationship, even within the same denomination. There were husbands who, as the proceedings of the Divorce Court showed, invoked their divinely ordained power to justify extreme measures against their wives. And there were wives whose moral and spiritual prestige in the home displaced the husband's authority entirely. Between these two extremes could be found any amount of disagreement over the application of religious principles to the running of a household.[72]

★

Something of the way in which both marital conflict and its resolution were conditioned by religious considerations may be seen in the case of Isaac Holden and Sarah Sugden. Their encounter reflects the impact of the Industrial Revolution on the West Riding. Isaac got to know Sarah during his years as manager of a woollen worsted mill at Cullingworth, before setting up on his own in 1846. Sarah at this time was keeping house in nearby Oakworth for her brothers who also ran a mill, and she was well versed in the ways of the industry. The only social distinction between them was that Isaac had begun life in more humble circumstances, as a child piecer at a cotton factory in Paisley, but he had more than made up for that since, and as an entrepreneur abreast of the latest innovations in wool-combing he was destined to go far. The similarity of religion was closer still. Both Sarah and Isaac were formed within the tightly knit Methodist community – his upward path had been smoothed by his co-religionists at every turn, and her life beyond her brothers' house was entirely conducted within the world of class, chapel and circuit. Both had won recognition for their leadership qualities, she as a class-leader, and he as a possible candidate for the ministry. These elements of common background

9. Isaac Holden, about the time of his second marriage in 1850. Unfortunately no photograph of Sarah Sugden survives from the same period.

bore closely on their decision to marry. Isaac took for granted that his second wife, like his first, would be a Methodist, and a 'serious' one who would provide some moral ballast at home while he got his hands dirty in the business. Isaac also proposed to Sarah at a crisis point in his affairs. His first independent business venture was falling victim to the recession of 1847–48 and he was in desperate need of capital. After tortuous negotiations Sarah's eldest brother Jonas Sugden agreed to supply an infusion of funds as part of the marriage agreement.[73]

By the time they actually married in April 1850 Isaac had set up a new combing mill. It was daringly located not in Keighley or Bradford, but in France, where the manufacture of worsteds lagged behind the most advanced West Riding practice. Sarah was slow to realize the full implications of the move. Isaac intended to live at St-Denis and he looked to his new wife to run the household there and care for his four children. The marriage almost came unstuck over this misunderstanding. Isaac believed his business would never prosper if he wasn't personally in charge, and he would only contemplate visits to Yorkshire of a few days at a time. Sarah, on the other hand, believed that France was 'an unChristian country' and that both Isaac and she needed the spiritual support of the Methodist community. Her solution was that he should sell up, return to Yorkshire and enter the ministry. Until the quarrel was resolved, she spent most of her time at her brothers' house in Oakworth, repeatedly urging Isaac to 'soon come and settle among us'.[74] Early in 1851, after many painful exchanges, a compromise was agreed: Sarah would live at St-Denis on condition that she spent lengthy vacations with her own family at Christmas and in the summer. Until Isaac brought his business back to Bradford in 1860, the two were separated for at least three months of every year. Their letters to each other – once a week and sometimes more frequently – reflect the continuing resentments which this arrangement caused, as well as the growing affection and sexual longing already described.

Sarah took her stand on two principles, both embedded in her religious understanding. Firstly, she was alarmed at Isaac's devotion to material concerns. One of the issues which Methodist class-leaders were expected to address with 'godly jealousy' was the conflict between business and spirit. With that experience behind her, Sarah did not hesitate to remind Isaac of 'the awful danger there is of being too much entangled with the world'. Any man who was prepared to immerse himself in work in a Catholic country was, in her view, far gone in this direction. In the second place, the countervailing influence of home depended not merely on the immediate family but on the community of which it formed a part. Sarah herself could not contemplate living without daily access to her brothers and sisters and chapel associates, from whom she derived her 'spiritual enjoyment'. Sarah Holden comes over in this correspondence as self-willed and outspoken, but it would be wrong to interpret her firmness as a bid for independence. Her view of marriage was entirely conventional. When engaged to Isaac, she had looked forward to 'a proper yoke to bear' and disclaimed any wish to be 'a lawless subject'. Her aim in this dispute was not independence for herself, but the restoration of the sacred proprieties of life from which they would both benefit. Her sense that his salvation and her own were at stake gave her the power to speak out.[75]

Isaac, on the other hand, was a workaholic in love with his factory: he had only to 'come within the sound of the dear old combing machines' and 'the old passion comes over me' and all other concerns (including his wife at home) were forgotten in a moment. How he ran his business, and where he located it, were matters between him and Divine Providence (in later life he claimed to have been guided to the site of his first French factory by a dream). Sarah's views were therefore beside the point. But on the question of where she should live, Isaac was more conciliatory. He certainly did not discount the importance of home; his invocation of 'its sweet social intercourse and its reciprocal duties of affection and fidelity' was an impeccably Evangelical sentiment.[76] He saw no reason why a good English home could not be created in France. But he refrained from ordering Sarah back, as was certainly his right. He knew that if she returned to St-Denis they would probably both be made miserable, whereas if she remained in Yorkshire one at least of them would be content.

> I feel willing to allow *you* to decide when you can *willingly* and cheerfully come to me ... Therefore my dear Sarah enjoy yourself so long as you can be happier without me, and do not decide on coming till you can be happy with me.[77]

It was a generous gesture and it worked. Within two weeks Sarah was on her way to France, with the bones of a working compromise agreed. Isaac believed instinctively that his wife's autonomy should be respected, and he quickly learned that this was also the path to securing her compliance.

In the Holdens' case closeness in religion permitted wide differences of interpretation along gendered lines. Isaac and Sarah breathed the same atmosphere of prayer, homily and hymn-singing, and the Methodist community was almost the only social world they knew. Yet each was able to strengthen their position by appealing to sincerely held religious notions – he to the guidance of Divine Providence over his work, and she to the sacred power of home and neighbourhood. In the end it was that same shared sense of religious identity which enabled Isaac (and to a lesser extent Sarah) to respect the other's perspective. It may be that their solidly grounded affection and the erotic appeal which each held for the other would have been enough to pull them through a rough passage: there is no way of knowing. But what they set down on paper certainly suggests that the intensely felt aspirations of Methodism were what ultimately kept them together as a genuine partnership.[78]

★

The Holdens' final return to England in 1860 was a fitting symbol of the triumph of middle-class domesticity. What had kept them divided were the rival claims of work and home. Sarah lived by the sanctity of domestic and family ties; Isaac located his gender and class identity in his occupation, and whatever avowals he might make to the contrary, he gave short shrift to any other call on his time. But by 1860 Isaac was already grooming his eldest son to take over the day-to-day running of the business, and he would soon be casting around for positions in public life which did not require the same slavish devotion to routine. Isaac and Sarah settled in Oakworth, close to the Sugden family. They were able at last to lead the life of a God-fearing couple in the midst of the active Methodist community in which Sarah felt so much at home. By the 1860s Isaac's uncompromising, almost obsessional devotion to business was less acceptable as a badge of bourgeois virtue than it had been in his youth. The punishing work ethic of the first generation of self-made entrepreneurs was giving way to more relaxed attitudes among their sons who enjoyed inherited wealth. When Bradford had adopted as its town motto *Labor vincit omnia* (work overcomes everything) in the 1840s, it had fairly reflected the personal code of its leading citizens, but the succeeding generation applied it less literally. There was more to life than ledgers and bills of lading.[79] This was in some ways the central feature of middle-class masculinity at this time. Men refused the logic of separate spheres, that they be full-time breadwinners and accumulators who appeared at home only for the minimum hours of physical restoration. Indeed the doctrine of separate spheres, which has been more dogmatically asserted by modern scholars than it ever was by the Victorians themselves,[80] is particularly misleading here because it loses sight of the distinctively masculine privilege of enjoying access to both the public *and* the private sphere. Middle-class men proclaimed their need to spend a significant proportion of their adult lives at home, and to a remarkable extent they did so.

In this sense John Stuart Mill's talk of a companionate consensus reflected a key shift in masculine mores. But how the husband defined his expectations and his duties during the hours when he was at home was much less clear and much more contentious. Patriarchy was alive and well. Men did not stop wishing to exert domestic authority just because the material conditions of traditional patriarchy had largely disappeared. It remained close to their conception of masculine self-respect and continued to find considerable support in the prescripts of religion. While women did not usually question their husbands' entitlement to household authority, their desire for trust and intimacy made them less ready to tolerate husbands who treated them as underlings. Conjugal domesticity gave ample opportunity for disagreement as to how patriarchy might be applied in practice. The household finances, the hiring and firing of domestic staff, the management of the children, could all become areas of dispute, with the wife interpreting her husband's interventions as an unwarranted intrusion on her sphere. Most disruptive of all was the husband who felt that his self-respect required a constant demonstration of authority, almost regardless of the occasion for it. The bland injunction of the advice books that patriarchal authority should be tempered by domestic affection was not a very helpful guide.

Jeanne Peterson, reacting against the bogeyman of the Victorian paterfamilias, has described marriage in the professional classes as a partnership of shared culture and shared involvement in work. She has produced some striking instances of harmonious cooperation (including references to 'our work' and 'our career'). But this attractive picture needs to be kept in proportion. It was only possible when the wife could identify closely with her husband's occupation and actively assist him in it. Even in the Church this was by no means the general rule, as the case of the Bensons shows. Elsewhere it was much less probable, as most wives knew little of their husbands' working lives and were inhibited by social conventions of female propriety from exploring them.[81] For most Victorian couples, the husband's career was more likely to emphasize the gulf between them than to unite them in a shared endeavour. Above all, the conventions of domesticity saddled husbands with unreasonable expectations which burdened their wives and distorted the relationship. Men's desire for psychological support and moral uplift tended to make wives feel inadequate, and it sat uncomfortably with the patriarchal principle. It was also liable to set up a destructive tension in husbands who could not reconcile their emotional dependence with the requirements of manly self-sufficiency. That Edward and Mary Benson should have been in thrall to this contradiction while both being so convinced of the merits of domesticity is especially poignant.

Yet the most significant point about early and mid-Victorian marriage is that these tensions were contained within an ideal of domesticity whose hold over the middle class remained undiminished. This after all was what struck foreign observers so forcibly. They noted both the dominant place of domesticity in public discourse and its realization in everyday life.[82] The ideal was inseparable from adherence to any and every Christian denomination. It also ranked high in the hierarchy of moral virtues proclaimed by the most admired agnostics of the day, like George Eliot and John Ruskin – which in some ways is a more telling indicator of the undisputed hegemony of domesticity. The incessant repetition of didactic propaganda on this subject through the period does not mean that the message was falling on deaf ears. Most of it was addressed to young men, in the entirely realistic conviction that the rising generation stands in recurrent need of being informed of its proper duties. Of course there was plenty of fraying at the edges. The middle class, like the aristocracy, always included a sizeable minority who were unreconciled to the comforts of home and preferred to lead an intensely homosocial life instead (see Chapter 6). But prior to the 1880s public discourse gave little quarter to this kind of rebellion. The self-image of the middle class was consistently domestic. Men manoeuvred within that image, but there is little evidence that they were yet inclined to call it into question.

CHAPTER FOUR

Father and Child

Of all the qualifications for full masculine status, fatherhood was the least talked about by the Victorians. The question of whether to marry – and even more *when* to marry – regularly featured in public discourse. The importance of dignified, independent work was endlessly proclaimed. The moral qualities attributable to manliness were the stuff of sermons and homilies. By comparison, little attention was given to the duties and delights of fatherhood. Only in the late Victorian period did this reticence begin to be undermined, as fathers experienced overt challenges to their domestic preeminence (see Chapter 7). One reason why fatherhood received so little emphasis before that time is that, according to the fairly rigid categories then current, parenting took place in the private sphere, largely secluded from observation and intervention. It might also be argued that fatherhood was seen as an intrinsic or 'natural' constituent of masculinity, and hence beyond the scope of analysis or critique. But this was true only up to a point. Beneath the surface fatherhood held a decidedly ambiguous position in the culture and practice of Victorian family life. In fact its location in the private sphere was the nub of the problem. For if public and private were really separate spheres defined by gender, then parenting must fall exclusively to the woman's lot. If, on the other hand, the virtues of domesticity laid a claim on both sexes, fatherhood became a telling touchstone of men's commitment to the home. Since both these views coexisted in the Victorian middle class, there was a great deal of uncertainty about what was expected of fathers. Were they a remote back-up for the mother's efforts? Did they offer their children something distinctive and essential? Or was their role to duplicate as closely as their natures permitted the services performed by the mother? Men weighed these questions within a culture which placed a very high value on motherhood; but they were also deeply conditioned by the belief that begetting children is integral to a fully formed masculinity. It is thus hardly surprising that the experience of fatherhood was highly varied – and certainly not to be contained within any stereotypic image of 'the Victorian father'.

★

According to Catharine Beecher, the great American champion of domesticity, man's labours in the public world of work were motivated by 'the desire for a home of his own, and the hopes of paternity'.[1] Outside the courts of law paternity was a concept little discussed by the Victorians, but Catharine Beecher was surely right. Among men's impulses, desire for the ultimate demonstration of virility, and ambition to endow the future with one's own offspring, are comparatively impervious to cultural variation, and they do not appear to depend for their power on cultural reinforcement. These feelings existed alongside the more often expressed anxieties of prospective fathers about their wives' health or the imminent increase in the charge on the family budget. Charles Kingsley was ecstatic about his first child – 'My little baby, the next link in the golden chain of generations, begotten of our bliss'.[2] This was a private joy, to be shared (as in this instance) with the wife alone and certainly not trumpeted abroad. But the public impact mattered too. Husbands without children suffered a loss of masculine status, and this taint is perceptible in the public reaction to prominent men in this condition, like John Ruskin and John Stuart Mill.[3] Childless businessmen were known to falter in their ambitions later in life, from a growing sense that their present power and reputation meant little without someone to hand them down to. The successful quarry owner Samuel Holland made a late marriage which proved childless. His relative passivity in politics and public life seems to have been conditioned by his sense of reproductive failure, and when he died in 1892 he left his estate to a favourite nephew, mortified that his considerable wealth could not be enjoyed by a direct heir.[4] Equally traditional was the prejudice in favour of sons. Men looked for an offspring who would continue the family name and transmit the attributes of masculinity to posterity. Whatever comfort and support a daughter might be expected to provide in later life, few men shared Kingsley's happiness at the arrival of a daughter as firstborn. A more typical response was that of John Heaton in 1851. Presented with a daughter, Helen, he noted in his diary, 'I was considerably disappointed that the baby was not a boy' and promptly took himself off to the Leeds Conversation Club for the evening. Five years later the tone was very different: 'Fanny gave birth to a *Son & Heir* – John Arthur Dakeyne Heaton. This event was the occasion of great rejoicing'.[5] It is significant that this first son was given his father's Christian name (though to avoid confusion he was never actually called John).[6] The naming of children, especially sons, was a matter for the father, reflecting his concerns about lineage, descent and heredity. Both the prejudice in favour of sons and the preference for well-tried names were established patriarchal features of the propertied classes.

What did change in the early part of the nineteenth century was men's relation to childbirth itself. Medical lore dating back to Aristotle attributed the key role in reproduction to the potency and agency of the male: he was the progenitor of life, while the female was the passive carrier. The Christian notion of God the Father greatly reinforced this way of thinking. Social practice in Early Modern society reflected the same message. Before and after the birth

10. John Heaton more reconciled to his baby daughter: an ink sketch of Helen, aged seven weeks, 1851.

the mother was rigidly secluded; the father was the central figure in the social drama of childbirth, celebrating with family and friends, arranging the baptism and hiring a wet-nurse. He was confirming his manhood as well as performing his patriarchal duties. From the late eighteenth century, however, scientific enquiry began to place more emphasis on conception as a natural process which unfolded within the woman's body, with the ovum rather than the seminal fluid holding the key to the mystery of generation. Childbirth came to be seen as the fulfilment of a woman's femininity rather than a disruption to her performance of the duties of wife. This was one reason why the prestige of motherhood was on the increase, and it meant that the mother as the bearer of the child became the central figure, rather than the father as bearer of the family name. Instead of being the master of ceremonies and focus of public attention, the father was on the way to becoming the nervous bystander of recent times.[7]

Paradoxically, however, he was now more often found in the delivery room. Traditionally the seclusion of the mother-to-be had extended to her husband, who was not present during the birth – though he was likely to be the first person to enter the room after the happy event. By the 1840s it had become commonplace for husbands to be in attendance during the birth itself. Prince Albert's presence at the Queen's first confinement in 1841 was much commended at the time, and judging by comment in the medical press it appears to have followed rather than led practice in respectable society. This pattern, which remained prevalent during the rest of the century, has usually been interpreted as evidence of companionate marriage: husbands stayed with their wives out of anxiety for their perilous ordeal, and in order to offer comfort and assistance. These considerations were particularly strong in the case of young husbands in the first flush of romantic devotion. But it is likely that men's presence at the birth was also a statement about paternity, a means of staking a claim to be at the centre of family life at a time when motherhood was being placed on a pedestal.[8]

Often what was uppermost in the mind of the expectant father was the added burden of material provision. Middle-class fathers were seldom on the breadline, but they certainly faced job insecurity, and failure in business was all the more traumatic if there were the needs of children to be taken into account. Errors in the course of business might cost a man's dependants dear. Even without the threat of penury, the need to provide children with a richly endowed start in life might well be experienced as a heavy burden (as it frequently is today). Childbirth was therefore a moment when awareness of a father's material responsibility was particularly intense. But that sense was integral to the whole experience of fatherhood. Full acceptance as a man in society depended on manifestly possessing the independence and the resources to be a household head. What had always been a key qualification for adult masculinity became if anything more absolute during the nineteenth century, as the scope of patriarchy in the home was whittled away. Didactic writers lost no opportunity of impressing on children the sacrifices that father had made for them. 'How often,' wrote John Angell James in 1851 in *The Young Man's Friend*, 'when bearing the heat and burden of the day has he wiped away the sweat of his brow, and exclaimed, with the smile of hope, "Well, my boy will one day reward me for all this".'[9] A generation later the same message was being addressed to boys. The novelist Marianne Farningham reminded them of the obedience and honour due to fathers who 'have toiled and deprived themselves of many comforts for your sake'; home life depended on 'that active brain and those busy hands. If he stops, then the whole must stop.'[10]

In the minds of Victorian children, though, the father's role as provider was symbolized less by his unseen labours than by his newly enhanced role as giver of gifts. Family birthdays were celebrated as never before, and presents between family members quickly became an essential part of the Victorian Christmas. Among the aristocracy and gentry, fatherhood was traditionally associated with largesse; expensive treats, foreign excursions and the settling of sons' debts all bore witness to the sovereignty and benevolence of the paterfamilias.[11] In the middle class there was a more specific association between gift-giving and work. The father's outlay on some expensive or unusual item expressed the structure of the family economy perfectly: as the biggest and the most eagerly awaited gift, it reflected the value of his labours and his privileged access to the market-place. Writing to his wife Mary from a posting in Nottingham in 1835, the Manchester exciseman Joshua Pritchard looked forward to a suitably expansive home-coming. He sent 'lots of kisses' to the children and 'scores for you'; 'I have a pin-cushion for Emma, a watch for Thomas, & lots of Baa Lambs for John' (Thomas was of course the oldest).[12] Mary Pritchard was in no position to match this kind of outlay. Conversely, the forgetting of a child's birthday was a sobering reminder of the stresses which work and public responsibilities might impose on a dutiful father.[13] Presents from father were the prime symbolic evidence of his exclusive duty as provider for his children. In the late Victorian period the traditional figure of Father Christmas would be transformed under American influence into the most compelling symbol of paternal largesse (see Chapter 7).

Father Christmas mirrored earthly realities in more ways than one. 'Absent' for 363–4 days in the year, he was a poignant, if distorting reminder of the contradictions of everyday fatherhood. Certainly by the 1870s, when Father Christmas was beginning to assume his modern shape, the father who worked away from home was decidedly the middle-class norm. For the Victorians this was the central shift which distinguished father–child relations in their own day from the time of their grandparents. Father was no longer a habitual presence in a working home, but someone who appeared only at certain times and on certain days. And because these appearances were both predictable and well spaced, they were marked by ritual. The most elaborate and solemn was the daily reading of family prayers. As we saw in Chapter 2, this practice dated back to the Puritan heyday of the seventeenth century, but its characteristically Victorian forms and its wide popularity were the achievement of the Evangelicals. Regardless of whether the meaning of the words registered, family prayers served to sustain a hierarchical ethos in the household. As an adult on a visit to his family home in 1864, the barrister Arthur Munby mused on the impact of this familiar ritual:

> This evening at nine we had prayers in the library as usual: my father sitting at the centre table & reading for the twentieth time one of those good sincere old sermons, full of the simple Calvinistic Protestantism of thirty years ago. . . .
> The master of the house, every year more reverend & more worthy, sitting in the same room amidst his family and servants, reading thus gravely and with undoubting faith: such a scene so long repeated gains from habit and affection a sacredness and sublimity which has little to do with the merit of the things read, though it reflects a certain beauty upon them also.[14]

That scene continued to be typical of middle-class family life until the 1880s. Sometimes it was the key spiritual experience of the day; sometimes it was an empty shell. But it was hard to escape the message that the father was both set apart from – and set in authority over – the household.

But the rituals which most accurately reflected the real standing of Victorian fatherhood were those of return, recognizing the respect and welcome due to the breadwinner on his release from work. In *Over the Bridge* (1955) Richard Church recounted the family tradition surrounding his grandfather, Benjamin Orton, who had been goods manager at St Pancras Station in the 1870s:

> The ritual was always the same. There would be a loud, single blow on the front-door knocker. Either Grandmother or my uncle, as the heir, would then open the door and wait at the threshold. Grandfather would enter, thrust his umbrella into the stand, and pass his hat to the attendant member of his family. It was a tall black hat, of dull felt. Then he was helped off with his overcoat. Having inspected his daughters, to ensure that they were still safe and virginal in his bosom, he was ready for supper, which everyone secretly prayed would be to his liking.[15]

In this recurring scene lasting a few minutes, Orton received the attentions due to a working father. He was ritually unburdened of the insignia of his occupation which sustained the life of the household. He was formally presented with all his dependants for inspection. Everyone else's routine was interrupted in order to mark his arrival, and they were forcibly reminded that the principal goal of their domestic labours was to secure his comfort. In other homes the younger children were primed and presented to their father with toys or picture books – a brief evening spectacle to round off his re-entry into the home.

The regular times spent by the father in the home were taking on a ritualized quality. As John Gillis has pointed out, it was in the nineteenth century that the concept – if not the term – of 'family time' originated. Family time denoted those periods in the day when the whole family was together, which in practice meant when the father was able to join everyone else. In affluent households this could mean no more than the single hour before dinner each evening when the children passed out of the nanny's keeping for a brief (and sometimes rather stilted) encounter with their parents. In the middle class as a whole there was less formality and more interaction, but from the father's point of view there was still something special about family time. It was neither work nor leisure, but a moment of being 'with the family', when propinquity was as important as activity (whether that was reading, music or conversation). The inexorable demands of the father's working day gave a new lustre to the time he spent in the company of his children – Sundays, Christmas and (with increasing regularity) family holidays. This accounts for the static, almost sacralized quality of so many visual representations of the Victorian family.[16]

The significance of both 'family time' and the rituals of return depended on a recognition of what occupied the father the rest of the time. Work was culturally upheld as the essence of fatherhood, the prerequisite of all other domestic functions. Many commentators took it as read that performing this central function effectively disbarred fathers from other aspects of parenting. Sarah Ellis believed that, because middle-class fathers were seldom present at home, an 'almost double responsibility' was placed on mothers. The picture of fatherhood conveyed in the contemporaneous *British Mothers' Magazine* was of a little fireside sociability at the end of the day, and otherwise an almost complete delegation of parenting to the mother.[17] Others noted this trend with indignation. The historian J.R. Seeley, in roundly criticizing the father who 'elects to perform his parental duties entirely in the counting-house', echoed a score of didactic writers.[18] But whether commentators acquiesced or objected, the convergence of fatherhood and breadwinning was widely recognized as a fact of modern life.

Yet the representation – much less the reality – of fatherhood was never reduced to breadwinning alone. Fatherhood was always more broadly conceived than that, partly on account of the weight of tradition, and partly because the new value placed on childhood by both Romantics and Evangelicals implied a more complex relation between father and child. One traditional responsibility was the protection of domestic dependants, particularly children. Sarah Ellis was moved by the thought of seeing the father's 'stronger powers of protection brought into action to defend the little helpless one from heedlessly inflicted pain!' (though she was reticent about the source of this pain).[19] As the one who owned the house or (more likely) the lease, it was the father who secured the roof over his children's heads and was the first line of defence against intrusion or danger. But the father was often protector of his family in the figurative sense of shielding them from knowledge of what was disturbing or threatening. The real world might include the shadow of business failure, leading perhaps to foreclosure on the family home, or the onset of a wasting and ultimately fatal disease in the father himself. According to this construction, it was for the father to bear unpalatable truths unaided, maintaining his wife and children in carefree happiness – as Edward Barrett did when contemplating the collapse of his West Indian business interests.[20] Given the lurid polarization in Victorian culture between home and street, the role of protector also meant preserving the family from 'impurity' – that is, from any taint of sexual impropriety or sexual knowledge. Comparatively few fathers were called upon to put this aspiration into practice, but they bore the ultimate responsibility for maintaining the conditions in which their wives could perform their moral mission within the home. Partly because of the purity dimension, the role of protector was strongly gendered. It was premised on the vulnerability of home-dwelling wife and daughter, and it was sentimentalized accordingly. In Sarah Ellis's reflections on daughters, the father 'folds her tenderly in his arms, toils for her subsistence and comfort, and watches over her expanding beauty that he may shield it from all blight'.[21] Cradling an infant girl and defending her virginity when grown were the images of the protecting father which appealed most deeply to middle-class Victorians.

★

Like provision, protection suggested primarily a duty performed in relation to the outside world: it was the business of those who knew the public sphere and the consequences (good or bad) which it might have for the home. Family memoirs sometimes portray the Victorian father as essentially a public being, enjoying immense prestige at home, but out of place and ill at ease in all but the most formal domestic settings; the head of the household's life centred on his actions in the world, leaving only a small place for the home, and the smallest of all for its youngest occupants.[22] That very interaction with the world might indeed disqualify the father from a fully interactive role at home. In her bestselling novel *John Halifax, Gentleman* (1856) Dinah Craik gave an idealized and tear-jerking portrayal of a public-spirited entrepreneur who melted at the sight of his newborn daughter and watched over her when she was ill. But her comments about real family life were much more hard-nosed. Of the father she wrote: 'His very selfishness, or call it selfism, his hardness and masterfulness, are, in one sense a necessity, else he would never be able to fight his way and protect those whom he is bound to protect.'[23] According to this view, the very distortions which the father's personality endured in the public sphere disqualified him from full human relations with his children.

Yet Craik was unduly pessimistic. There is abundant evidence of fatherly concern and involvement with the day-to-day raising of children. The middle-class man who resolved the conflict between home and business by retiring early in order to attend to the needs of his children was a familiar aspect of Evangelical domesticity.[24] The records abound in nurturing and playful fathers, men who both delighted in their children and put their love to many practical tests. Inconsistent as these patterns may be with stereotypic notions of the Victorian paterfamilias, they were closely in tune with the new attitudes towards children described in Chapter 2. The Romantic view of human nature, broadly associated with Rousseau and the Lake Poets, held that grown men (like grown women) retained the child within, and that this inner child should be nurtured through enjoying the company of actual children, rather than denied through repression. For the sake of both adults and children, parents and their offspring needed to spend more time in each other's company, not for instruction only, but for the realization of their full humanity. As alienating conditions of bourgeois work became more prevalent, the redemptive power of the child was more widely recognized. Men felt morally reinvigorated by contact with the purity and innocence of children. For some the moral inspiration of children was central. The Glasgow shipbuilder William Denny believed that the care and love which his four children under ten needed from him 'guards me from evil and makes me wish to rise step by step in duty and love'.[25] Others were deeply influenced by the full Romantic cult of the child. The publisher Alexander Macmillan recalled how in the 1860s he found daily refreshment in the sight of his two-year-old son Willie, surrounded with his sisters, and the household servants kneeling round him, and listening to grave wise speech – prattle we call it – or to merry laughter mixed with the ineffable sweet serenity or the playful sparkle of the intense blue eyes.[26]

The spontaneity of the child and the worship which this elicits from adults perfectly convey the idea of the child-centred home in its Victorian form.

How far did this desire for the company of young children lead middle-class fathers to trespass in the nursery? Is 'trespass' the right word? There was certainly a tradition of avoidance. In 1772 William Buchan had observed that most men were much better informed about what went on in their kennels and stables than what went on in the nursery.[27] Any practical responsibility for infants involves some readiness to surrender to another's will – a prospect which, it has been suggested, was distasteful to gentlemanly notions of masculinity in the eighteenth century.[28] Lower down the social scale, among men of the middling sort, the prejudice was less marked. The father who fed his babies by hand and tended them through illness – the 'nursing father' – was by no means uncommon. The Essex silk manufacturer George Courtauld reminded his grown children, 'I have been a nursing father to you all'.[29] The words recall a famous passage in William Cobbett's *Advice to Young Men*:

> How many days, how many months, all put together, have I spent with babies in my arms! My time, when at home, and when babies were going on, was chiefly divided between the pen and the baby. I have fed and put them to sleep hundreds of times, though there were servants to whom the task might have been transferred.[30]

Cobbett's memories, like Courtauld's, referred to the opening years of the nineteenth century. But *Advice to Young Men* was published in the 1830s out of a keen sense that the nursing father, like other traditional manifestations of English manhood, counted for less and less. One reason was hinted at by Cobbett himself; after fondly recalling the hours he had spent with his children he added quickly, 'yet I have not been effeminate'. It was a hard line to hold. As the gendered character of man and woman, of father and mother, became more polarized, there was less tolerance for paternal behaviour which appeared to encroach on the maternal role. When William Wilberforce was raising his family around the turn of the century, his relations of easy affection with his children were not a matter for comment. But by the time James Stephen wrote his biography in 1849 he felt obliged to stress that Wilberforce's tenderness had never 'degenerated into fondness' or been expressed 'by caresses or by a blind and partial admiration'.[31] By this time too a father's vigil over his child's sick-bed invited the epithet 'womanly', even from writers who approved of such devotion.[32] The nursing father was hardly likely to escape disparagement in this climate. Thomas Carlyle was an early proponent of the coming view. In 1824 he was appalled to find how fatherhood had changed his friend Edward Irving: 'Visit him at any time, you find him dry-nursing his offspring; speak to him, he directs your attention to the form of its nose, the manner of its waking and sleeping, and feeding and digesting'. Such things were properly 'the wife's concern alone' and hence 'piteous to behold' in a grown man.[33]

The other reason why fathers now had less practical experience with the very young has to do with the domestic management of children. One of the most tangible consequences of the growth of child-centredness in bourgeois culture at this time was that the rearing of infants now tended to be secluded from the rest of the household in a nursery, preferably staffed by specialist servants. The nursery was not a place where men felt at their ease. Among the aristocracy it had long been regarded as 'the kingdom of the dependent ruled by the dependent . . . the rule of the irrational by the irrational'.[34] The spread of the specialized nursery to the middle class seems to have had the effect of instilling similar attitudes there. While 'men of sense' in the eighteenth century had confidently laid down the bases of infant care, few now followed the Prince Consort's example in drawing up a nursery regime for his children. Fewer still lowered their dignity by spending much time with infants who tended therefore to see comparatively little of their fathers. In the more affluent households where nursery staff acted as barrier between father and children (sometimes between mother and children too) familiarity and trust could be in short supply. Looking back to his early childhood in the 1870s, Austin Harrison remembered his father as an intruder for whom the servants stood up when his big, bristly face appeared at the nursery door.[35]

Yet if Victorian fathers had little to do with the care of babies, it would be a great mistake to assume that this presaged a settled habit of detachment throughout a child's upbringing. As children grew older, they were less confined to the nursery, and as they gained in rationality and self-control a father's comradeship was much less open to the charge of effeminacy. Above all, fathers were licensed to play. The Victorian family Christmas has been described as a world turned upside down, when fathers could abandon the normal restraints and become like children for a day.[36] In many instances, however, Christmas was merely an intensification of familiar patterns of play. Even among Evangelicals patriarchal authority was not necessarily incompatible with playfulness. The memorial volumes to worthies like William Wilberforce and Adam Clarke emphasized their easy informality. As Doreen Rosman has put it, they acted as 'both paterfamilias and playmate', confident that their spiritual and moral authority did not demand an unrelieved solemnity.[37] When Joshua Pritchard was away from home, the sight that made him most homesick was other fathers 'tossing their children about'.[38] For a man like William Gaskell who was too reserved to express much verbal affection or sympathy, flying kites and playing pranks with his daughters offered an essential release.[39] Austin Harrison recalled those moments of delight when his somewhat austere father's repressed high spirits were suddenly released in a rampage, a bellow or a piece of play-acting: 'I liked him best when he roared'.[40] John Heaton of Leeds made comparatively little time for his older children, but he was completely won over by his youngest, Bob, born in 1868. From dressing in the morning until prayers in the evening, they were inseparable companions. Bob was to be seen in the carriage when his father went on medical rounds; he sang nursery rhymes in his father's study and played tunes on his stethoscope; the house resounded with shrieks as father and son chased each other from room to room.[41] Fathers who could not unbend in this way were sometimes keenly aware of their inadequacy. The Hertfordshire brewer William Lucas had seven sons and two daughters. He was proud of their attainments and took them on educational visits to London, but he knew he lacked the spark of companionship. He wrote in 1847, 'I feel at times much depressed from not being able to make myself so companionable as I ought to be with my children or getting free with them and I do not now expect to do it.'[42] His comment is revealing of the standard of easy paternal approachability which had penetrated Quaker circles by this time. Unrestrained spontaneity with children provided entertainment and distraction to men who, like Gaskell and Heaton, often felt burdened by their public duties. At a deeper level it was an affirmation of the childlike part of man which could only be experienced through the role of father in a domestic setting.[43]

★

Yet playfulness was never more than one facet of fatherhood. Authority, guidance and discipline continued to be viewed as central to the father's role. Masculinity, after all, was essentially about being master of one's own house, about exercising authority over children as well as wife and servants. Indeed rule as 'father' embodied the primary meaning of the term 'patriarchy'. Traditionally children were subject to their father because he provided for them, and because they had not yet attained the age of reason. The fact that children were now more sharply distinguished from servants, and were also less likely to work under the father's direction, certainly modified the character of their subordination, but daughters were still expected to serve their father and sons to obey him. 'I merely require to act' was how the didactic writer Christopher Anderson summed up his paternal right to unquestioning obedience.[44] Not without reason did Victorian boys customarily refer to their fathers as 'the Guv'ner'. The belief in untrammelled paternal authority ran deep. John Stuart Mill deplored the uncompromising way in which it was too often applied, as if, he complained, a man's children were 'literally, and not metaphorically, a part of himself'.[45] But few were prepared to join him in attacking a time-honoured entitlement which most people took for granted.

There was a much keener interest in the principles which should guide the exercise of a father's power. Middle-class fathers were constantly reminded of the onerous duties of parenthood. As James Anthony Froude sadly observed in 1847, 'You will find many fathers – substantially kind and good fathers – whose single guide in all they do for their children is the highest, most imperious sense of duty.'[46] The more worldly writers reiterated the obvious point that the foundations of success in adult life were laid in the self-discipline and morality acquired in childhood. Religious authors emphasized the need for spiritual discipline as well; if they were of an Evangelical persuasion they dwelt on the need to prepare the young for conversion and to avert the danger of damnation should an early death supervene.[47] Since the Reformation all strands of Protestantism were agreed in allocating ultimate responsibility for the spiritual and moral welfare of household members to the father. In some ways the Victorian era was one of strengthened paternal moral authority. The late eighteenth and early nineteenth centuries had seen a revival of the Puritan idea that the father was not only accountable for the religious welfare of the family but stood in place of God to his children.[48] If the analogy was pressed home, the implications were grim. In 1838, when Caroline Norton's campaign to reform the law on infant custody was reaching its climax, the journalist J.M. Kemble wrote: 'Remember that God himself has placed his greatest glory in being GOD *THE FATHER*; that the very existence of this world and this human nature of ours subserve the sole purpose of *his* paternity!'[49]

The comparison between earthly and heavenly fathers imposed duties as well as powers. Evangelicals in particular spent much time in prayer on their children's behalf. 'Tell the children that their Father had them all up before the throne of Grace', Joshua Pritchard told his wife in 1835. He urged them to pray themselves, holding up the example of his eldest daughter who had been taught to pray by the time she was two and had, he believed, died in the bosom of Jesus.[50] Many a father keenly awaited news that each child had in turn given his or her heart to God, thus signalling that his main spiritual duty had been accomplished.[51] In the most idealized versions, the earthly father was supposed to be for his children a prefigurement of the justice and wisdom of their heavenly Father.[52] At first this was a distinctively Methodist and Evangelical position, but it had far wider currency by mid-century. The most tangible evidence of it was the revival of the practice of family prayers.

But, despite the support of biblical authority, it was in precisely this area of spiritual and moral training that the tradition of paternal control proved most vulnerable. Since the mid-eighteenth century parental virtue had been displaced from the wise father on to the loving mother (see Chapter 2). From being little more than an intermediary between her husband and his children, the mother was recognized by the 1830s to be the moral force of family life, with her own spirituality and her own genius for the management of children.[53] Her distinctive role had first been defined in terms of breast-feeding, then in relation to the child's impressionable early years, until it was widely regarded as applicable to the whole span of childhood. There was no secret about what all this meant for fathers. Child-rearing advice literature in the eighteenth century had commonly been addressed to the father, on the assumption that he exercised the chief responsibility for his children's upbringing once the nursing stage was over; now it tended to be written for mothers alone, or for parents in such a way as to exclude fathers.[54] The founding text for the new perspective was *Emile* where Rousseau roundly declared: 'Ambition, avarice, tyranny, the mistaken foresight of fathers, their neglect, their harshness, are a hundredfold more harmful to the child than the blind affection of the mother'.[55] Milder versions of this sentiment were commonplace by the 1830s. Elizabeth Sandford said of the mother: 'None can supply her place, none can feel her interest; and as in infancy a mother is the best nurse, so in childhood she is the best guardian and instructress'.[56] Sarah Ellis was blunter: as wife, woman must accept second place to her husband, but as mother she could not 'be too dignified, or be treated with too much respect'. Indeed in Ellis's view there was a compelling symmetry about the allocation of parental roles: while mothers had the right instincts to build on, fathers lacked 'the nicety and tact to manage the minute affairs of domestic life, and especially those of individual feeling'; they were out of their depth because they lacked the moral resources for the job. Ellis's own discourse on motherhood accordingly included few references to fathers – in fact she made considerably more mention of the Heavenly Father than of his earthly counterpart.[57]

This transition in parental roles was reflected in a revealing change in vocabulary. There was less talk of 'authority' and much greater emphasis on 'influence'. Because the child's individuality was now more readily recognized, its upbringing had to be carefully adapted to its particular temperament, requiring observation and flexibility from day to day. 'None but a mother can effectually understand these particularities', pronounced Sarah Sewell.[58] The implications of character training pointed in the same direction. The watchword here was 'self-government': in the business and professional world of the nineteenth century, success and respect came to those who were guided less by external authority than by their own inner drive and their own moral sensibility. Self-government in the child was developed by the application of 'influence', not by the inflexible enforcement of boundaries. Once parenting was seen in these processual, developmental terms, fathers were inevitably sidelined, since they were less and less available for the extended periods of contact with children which the new wisdom required.[59]

Important practical consequences flowed from this change in the philosophy of child-raising. Family prayers continued to be an impressive expression of spiritual patriarchy, but there was growing competition from the more intimate and personal bedside prayers conducted by the mother, and by the 1880s the traditional family gathering would be in decline.[60] The father's educational role was at risk too. Any instruction about issues of morality and conduct was likely to be carried out by the mother. In a book dedicated to Hannah More, William Roberts declared in 1829 that the father's role was 'to guide domestic conversation, and to give to it its proper tone; to make it ... a mutual provocation to virtuous resolves and manly pursuits', yet this was the very area which mothers were now making their own.[61] The only aspect of the father's educational role which remained unimpaired was 'rational', as distinct from 'moral' instruction. Many middle-class women had cause to be grateful to their fathers for their literary and scientific education. Many more children received their first impressions of the world of politics from their fathers speaking over the newspaper and in some cases encouraging lively debate.[62] Few went as far as J.R. Seeley in recommending that fathers should educate their children at home, rather than consign them to the risky milieu of a school, but men's self-respect as fathers continued to be invested in a practical educational function.[63]

    The disciplining of children was subject to most change. Traditionally the head of the household had the right to beat his children, as he did all other dependants under his roof. Inflicting punishment was an unequivocal demon-stration that ultimate power resided with the father.[64] The early nineteenth century was a critical period in shifting attitudes towards the use of physical force in all relationships of power. The discourse of anti-slavery profoundly influenced popular attitudes to the treatment of children. The practical implications of Romantic notions of childhood tended in the same direction. To chastise the innocent 'child of nature' – or in the Christian adaptation the being who was 'next to God' – was deeply disturbing, most of all if it was done in the bosom of the family where love and empathy should prevail. James Payn maintained that if the necessity for punishment arose, the fault lay in earlier parental error. 'It is ourselves, not they, who do in reality deserve to be smitten.'[65] Legislation against parental cruelty towards children was not passed until 1889, but one of the reasons why the law could be changed was that by then the common wisdom had moved so far away from condoning corporal punishment in the home (though not yet in the school).[66] Breaking the will by the rod was distinctly out of fashion. Stern Evangelical moralists like Hannah More were to be found advocating mildness and quiet insistence, rather than the heavy hand of patriarchal authority.[67] The widely read American minister Horace Bushnell tried to hold the line by distinguishing between the mother's 'soft imperative' towards infants and 'the stiffer tension of the masculine word', directed at older children and 'connected with the wider, rougher providence of a father's masculine force'.[68] But by the time Bushnell's *Christian Nurture* was published in England in 1861, even this compromise looked out of date. As Linda Pollock has shown, there was a gradual but marked shift through the nineteenth century away from beating as a routine punishment.[69] The majority of texts assumed that the purpose of parental discipline was to bend and mould, not to crush. As the playwright Andrew Halliday put it in 1865, previously 'almost every father in Great Britain kept a strap, or a cane, for the special purpose of correcting his children'; but now 'he has relaxed his old severity of aspect, and become more human'.[70] The desired outcome was not a broken spirit, but a capacity for self-government, and this called for different methods. Once again, it was the mother who was thought best able to administer the appropriate, finely calculated punishments. Paternal discipline began to look like little more than a court of last resort, if that.[71]

★

Fatherhood was as profoundly changed as any other facet of middle-class manhood during the Victorian era. The law relating to fathers and its administration by the courts might be relatively unyielding,[72] but new social and cultural conditions were forcing an adjustment in old expectations and introducing new ones. Bourgeois notions of work and calling threw the role of father as provider into higher relief, and at the same time made it more difficult for men to do justice to the interactive dimensions of fatherhood. As fathers spent more time away from the home, they came to depend on their wives to devise and implement a suitable childcare regime. If they bucked this trend and attempted to retain something of their traditional domestic authority, they encountered the growing belief that the mother was the right person to bring up children, not only because she was usually present in the home for much more of the time, but because she possessed moral qualities which were exclusive to her sex. Both symbolically and practically the father's headship of the household was under threat. In other cultures men in this predicament have sought psychological substitutes for real fatherhood in social activities which exclude women: in nineteenth-century America, for example, the men-only clubs and fraternities were rich in paternal and generational symbolism.[73] Nothing on that scale developed in England, and the reason may be that, at the same time as fathers were being pushed from the centre of family life, many of the most powerful images in Victorian art and literature concurred in affirming the centrality of children and childhood to a fully realized humanity. Culture gave men a language in which to articulate the emotional satisfactions of fatherhood at the very time when conditions of employment and the new maternalism were making those satisfactions more elusive.

In face-to-face relations which are too private to be policed, much obviously depends on the particularity of the individuals concerned. But amid all the variety four patterns of fatherhood recur in the documentary record, suggesting that certain adaptations were widely followed. The first is absent fatherhood. This was by no means an entirely new phenomenon, given the exigencies of life at sea and in the armed services. But in the form we know today, of the father whose work and leisure interests remove him routinely from the emotional cross-currents of family life, it was essentially a Victorian develop-ment. The claims of domesticity might still be observed as regards the marriage itself, but everything to do with childcare was left to wife and servants. Authority and nurture went by default, as fathers took the line of least resistance, exploiting the mother's sense of responsibility while preserving their freedom from domestic constraints.

This was the outlook of Daniel Meinertzhagen, a comfortably placed London merchant banker who married Georgina Potter in 1873. Their first child was born in 1875, to be followed by nine more. Daniel was more often apart from his family than with them. When they were in the country, he had

11. The abstracted father: Daniel Meinertzhagen and his family, *c.* 1896.

business in town; when they were living in the London house, he vanished for extended shooting and fishing holidays with male cronies. In his letters home he would enquire dutifully after 'the chicks', but he was not to be diverted from his bachelor life by children's birthdays or by the need for regular contact between father and infant. 'I shall be quite anxious to see baby again now that he is well again', Daniel wrote home from Scotland in 1876. 'I hope he hasn't forgotten me, though well he might, the little wretch, as I have seen so little of him lately.' The sentiment of regret was little more than a sop to Georgina, as Daniel made a habit of taking sporting holidays whenever his light duties at the bank permitted.[74] When he was at home, Daniel appeared in the guise of benevolent uncle rather than responsible father. He handed out treats and enjoyed his children's affection, but he took no interest in their daily routines, and exerted little influence over their education. All this was left to Georgina, including the role of disciplinarian. Their son Richard recalled that there was 'never once even so much as an admonishment' from his father; neither was there a kiss (or not until he was an old man).[75] Daniel Meinertzhagen looked for an easy life, and the prevailing cult of motherhood provided him with a fairly convincing excuse.

From the point of view of women advice-writers, there was something to be said for a father who did not blunder in and upset his wife's delicate childcare regime. Fathers in turn derived some advantage from abdicating their parental responsibilities, in that they freed themselves from the prospect of failure in an activity which seemed a good deal less predictable than their professional or business life. But on any scale of masculinity, opting out was scarcely a solution. It made the husband something less than master of his own home. He became entirely dependent on his wife for the upbringing of his children, and was placed in an unacceptably passive position. It is a measure of Daniel Meinertzhagen's indolence that he appears to have been untroubled by this consideration – as he was also by the moralists' claim that absent fatherhood would reap a bitter harvest of failed sons and wayward daughters.

Absent fatherhood tends to be emphasized by historians because it prefigures a practice which has been so widespread during the twentieth century,[76] but it needs to be considered alongside the other three patterns to be found in the nineteenth-century middle class. At the opposite end of the spectrum from the absent father stood the tyrannical father, so dear to the hearts of the debunking post-Victorians. His stance towards the family might be a matter of personality – a compulsion to masterful and repressive behaviour in any social arena which endowed him with some authority. In that sense tyrannical fatherhood is a recurrent type, still to be found today. But the structure of middle-class Victorian family life supplied further reasons for this pattern. Repression was one response to the shift in the balance of familial authority which had been going on since the beginning of the century. Faced by the formidable moral prestige of motherhood, some men sought to shore up their own self-esteem by making an issue out of those areas which they could still control. To insist that the routine of the household should be subordinate to every aspect of his own convenience, to enforce tight controls on family expenditure, to treat family prayers as a means of keeping his dependants in subservience, and to mete out regular and painful punishments to his children, were all means of bolstering a man's domestic authority in his own eyes and the eyes of others. Some fathers appeared almost pathologically unable to see familial relations in anything but terms of authority. Harshness and inflexibility were the result.

Mention of the 'Victorian paterfamilias' is still likely to bring to mind oppressive behaviour of this sort. It is, however, not easy to substantiate. The best-known examples, like the fathers of James Anthony Froude and Samuel Butler, depend on autobiographical material composed many years later, without much contemporary corroboration.[77] The most promising source is the records of courts of law: the Divorce Court, where unreasonable conduct towards children was often at issue; and Chancery, which handled cases of custody and guardianship.[78] The case of John and Frances Curtis was heard before both courts in 1858–59. In the course of testing the grounds for a judicial separation and for removal of the children from their father's custody, the courts heard a great deal of evidence about John Curtis's tyrannical behaviour. This has recently been uncovered by James Hammerton and Megan Doolittle.[79]

The marriage dated back to 1846. John Curtis was a civil engineer. His wife Frances Flood was the daughter of a barrister and JP. This was a significant distinction in terms of middle-class status. John belonged to a new profession, his father-in-law to one of the oldest in the land. Frances's family were never reconciled to the match, and they regularly cast aspersions on John's ability to maintain their daughter in appropriate style. In the course of the next six years five children were born to the Curtises, three of whom survived. The growing family put pressure on the household resources. In 1851 John Curtis moved his family to New York, partly to better his prospects, and almost certainly to distance himself from his meddlesome father-in-law. He underestimated his antagonist. On receipt of his daughter's litany of complaints about John's cruel and unreasonable behaviour, Frederick Flood travelled to New York and had John committed to a lunatic asylum. Frances then abandoned John and took the children to her family home in Ireland. The couple never lived together again. John's attempt to remove the children from Frances's care by force resulted in the separation suit of 1858.

John Curtis's alleged cruelty towards the children featured prominently in the grounds which Frances advanced to support her petition for separation, as well as in the separate suit for custody. Both cases included much uncorro-borated evidence on the part of Frances Curtis. But not all of it was denied by John. Amid a string of stories, three things were beyond reasonable doubt. John was physically violent, being given to striking children aged two and three on scant provocation; he steadfastly refused to allow them to be baptized; and he sought to dislodge Frances from her maternal dignity by installing a servant in her place.

At the root of this behaviour was John's faltering and beleaguered self-esteem as household head. His capacity as breadwinner was doubted; indeed he appears to have doubted it himself, else why resort to the drastic step of emigration? Frances's continued reliance on her father for advice, and latterly for material support, exacerbated John's insecurity. So far as the children were concerned, it was never denied in court that John was preoccupied with them; Frances described him in 1852 as 'wrapped up in the children'.[80] He appears to have vested so much of his own identity in them that he could not allow Frances to prevail in anything which related to their upbringing. His obsession with his domestic authority seems to have disturbed the balance of his mind, though the 'brain fever' which caused him to be confined in asylums on two occasions is open to alternative interpretations. John insisted on determining the children's discipline, their medical treatment, and their religious upbring-ing. His eccentric religious position – he was a church-going Anglican who rejected infant baptism – is important here because it led him to challenge his wife in the spiritual and moral sphere which was by now seen as a female preserve. Forbidding Frances access to the children while they were placed with

12. W.P. Frith, *Many Happy Returns of the Day*, 1854.

a young servant was completely consistent with the usurping fatherhood which now characterized John's behaviour. It did more than anything else to destroy his prospects of saving the marriage in court, though it did not prevent him from retaining custody of the children after he was separated from Frances.

Between these extremes of absent and tyrannical fatherhood lay two intermediate positions which probably had far greater currency in the Victorian middle class. The first of these was the father who was 'absent' not because he was physically removed from the home, but because he withheld intimacy from his children. The distant father is much more frequently encountered in family memoirs of the period than the oppressive father. He appears in paintings of the period too. In W.P. Frith's *Many Happy Returns of the Day* (1854) the father is the only one at table not engrossed in the family celebration, suggesting a semi-detached presence. The distant father exemplifies the ambivalence with which so many men viewed their paternal role. In the more polarized view of sexual difference which was current by the 1830s, the emotional warmth and physical tenderness which young children so easily elicited from adults were confused with feminine softness and sensitivity. Fathers feared for their own manhood. They were often even more concerned about the manhood of their sons. As will be explored more fully in the next chapter, the transition from boy to man was fraught with tension. Somehow boys had to be prepared for the insecurities of adult life within the security of the family, and equipped with a confident manliness after passing many years in the feminine ambience of home. This requirement was widely interpreted along lines which confirmed the gender gap between mother and father, as fathers strove to convey through their own conduct something of the harder world which their children would encounter later. They held back from an easy confidence or a rough-and-tumble familiarity, believing that their role was to prepare their children for more formal relationships and more rigid expectations. 'Forming character' is a recurrent theme of paternal reflection.[81] It was an anxiety which weighed with any father who recognized his responsibility not only to protect and provide for his children, but also to oversee their preparation for adult life.

Edward Benson is a poignant example. He was a man of strong passions and strong attachments, to his six children no less than his young wife. After his death, when his sons perused the many bundles of letters and diaries, they found abundant evidence of their father's love 'streaming out towards us'. But their own recollections were very different. While growing up in the 1860s and 1870s they had been starved of intimacy with him. Benson was an imposing and inhibiting presence in the home. His work as headmaster and later bishop was manifestly important, and eminent public figures were frequently invited to the house. He spent long hours in his study. Although they only went to the study when summoned for reproof, the children were always aware of his presence there because he was so intolerant of noise. As both father and priest, Benson took a serious view of his children's moral training. He frequently corrected their faults and took every opportunity to give them a moral lesson. Benson tended to sabotage his own well-meant efforts to be playful with them. Innocent pleasures were killed by a word of disapproval; flippant remarks encountered stony silence. As Fred (E.F. Benson) recalled, 'we sat on the edge of our chairs and were glad to be gone'. His brother Arthur agreed: 'In those days he seemed to me more censorious than affectionate. How *can* children understand that they are loved, unless it is shown them plainly?'[82]

Benson withheld practical expression of his love for what, to him, were compelling reasons. Fatherhood was an onerous responsibility. Children – especially boys – had to be prepared to hold their own in a competitive and impersonal society which would place a high premium on self-government. As someone who had begun life as the impecunious son of a bankrupt, Benson was certainly alert to these worldly considerations. But it was the moral training of children which weighed upon him most. As a thoughtful and ambitious churchman, Benson was keenly aware of the growth of secularization and the decline of social morality. If the traditional supports for individual morality were withering away, it followed that the responsibility of the family to instil strong principles was even more compelling than before. Benson was in no doubt what that demanded of a dutiful father: watchfulness and hard-heartedness, rather than fondness and indulgence. That he did violence to his own emotionally demonstrative nature seemed to him a price worth paying. He was less aware of the damage which this style of parenting did to its intended beneficiaries.[83]

These priorities were reversed in the case of the fourth pattern of nineteenth-century fatherhood. The intimate father set more store by the transparency of spontaneous relations than by the disciplines of restraint. Through anxieties about the future and tensions between the parental roles, the intimate father held to the value of tenderness and familiarity, both to himself and his children. He wandered into the nursery at will, instead of requiring formal presentations. He observed the antics of his offspring for pleasure as well as reassurance. In 1872 J.R. Seeley watched appreciatively as his little daughter Fanny pulled herself upright by the back of the sofa and formed her first words; nine years later she was still 'wonderfully interesting'.[84] The intimate father praised, he laughed, he romped; by the 1860s he might even answer to the name of 'Daddy'.[85] He might be a pushover, as Seeley was. More often, easy familiarity was balanced by a respect for discipline and routine, as in the case of the entrepreneur Richard Potter who lavished affection on his nine daughters (including Beatrice Webb) but required his comfort and convenience to determine the household regime.[86]

Cornelius Stovin also struck a fine balance. He was a conscientious Methodist, much preoccupied with the workings of Divine Providence when he was not worried about the prospects for his farm and his wife's poor health. He often thought about his four children's future, and he attended to their early lessons in 'self-government'. Yet his attitude towards them, as recorded in his diary during the 1870s, was anything but joyless and denying. He did not confine them with fixed expectations. 'If I can give them full scope for the activity of their entire nature that there may be no faculty run to waste or remain dormant, their life will most probably be more enjoyable and happy.' Stovin's outlook on childhood was unequivocally Romantic. Of his third child Frank, aged two, he wrote: 'He is a splendid divinely constituted ray of sunshine to brighten my lonely hours. He laughs and sings and chatters and enjoys life as if he were on the borders of Paradise.' Stovin was unperturbed by the demands that babies placed on everyone around them. When Frank was a few weeks old his father remarked in appreciative wonderment, 'He seems to have revolutionised the whole household. Every other interest has more or less to bend to his. At present his sway is almost royal.' Stovin bottle-fed babies without demur and nursed them through illness. He believed in self-expression. 'Every kind of innocent playfulness is encouraged.' And not merely encouraged, but shared, as father and two-year-old son ran leaping around the kitchen. Stovin took seriously his children's spiritual and moral development, but 'childlike joyousness' remained at the centre of his vision of childhood.[87]

Stovin's active involvement in practical parenting was to a considerable extent explained by his family circumstances. His wife Elizabeth was frequently ill, especially after childbirth, and she periodically went back to her own family for rest or convalescence. As Stovin complained, good domestic servants were hard to come by in this remote part of Lincolnshire, so there was limited scope for delegating childcare. As a result the little ones were not 'imprisoned in the nursery' and they received much more attention from their parents. But there was nothing forced or reluctant about Stovin's performance as an engaged father. There is no evidence in the diaries that his loving tenderness towards the children placed his sense of manliness under strain. The redeeming power of children was an article of faith which he found fully borne out by experience. It provided the sparks of joy and vitality in what was all too often a life of toil and anxiety.[88]

★

Amid these contrasting vignettes it is easy to forget that fathers then, as now, were bound to their children by powerful and primitive emotions which took their toll, regardless of attitudes to the practical job of parenting. Men who had for years been used to the sight and sound of children in the home faced the 'empty nest' with great sadness. Edward Benson remarked to his wife in 1881, 'What the blessings to us of those children were! And now I do not know how to look on to the years without little children.'[89] Children had been a regular backdrop to his domesticated working life. But the sudden silence in the home was felt no less keenly by Henry Ashworth whose working hours were spent at his cotton mill near Burnley. In 1861 his last remaining daughter was married on her parents' thirty-ninth wedding anniversary. Writing to his friend Richard Cobden, Ashworth sadly commented how it was now necessary for him and his wife 'to consider our lonely condition bereft of all young people and left alone in that big house'; married children, he reluctantly conceded, had 'duties of higher import than that of being companions to two old people'.[90]

The centrality of fatherhood in men's lives was never more tellingly laid bare than in bereavement. It has been somewhat naively assumed by some historians that in the days of large families and heavy child mortality parents were comparatively detached from their offspring and philosophical when they died prematurely.[91] No one who has read the agonized outpourings of distraught fathers in this period could make that mistake. 'I see her in every corner of the room – in every part of the house – her dolly – her couch. Oh the agony of pain which these remembrances excite', wrote the Bradford minister Benjamin Goodwin after the death of his young daughter in 1849.[92] Grief was no respecter of different approaches to fatherhood. When Cornelius Stovin's son Denison caught scarlet fever at boarding school in 1874, he feared the worst (as well he might). 'To see him thrown so far out of my own and his dear mother's reach and to have become so complete a burden to his friends shook my manhood. Tears would rush up from the fountain of grief within me.'[93] Edward Benson's anxious detachment from his children made no difference when the eldest, Martin, died of meningitis at the age of 17 in 1878; for a while his self-discipline and his faith in God's purposes lay in the balance, as he tried to come to terms with the shattering of all his hopes.[94] John Heaton was no less devastated when his second daughter May died suddenly in 1878. 'My heart ached with actual physical, as well as mental pain, and I felt too truly that happiness would no more be mine, but that I shd go sorrowing all my days'; it was a loss which continued to appear 'in fresh lights' before time began its healing work.[95]

For most Victorian fathers, children were an insistent, if not always a demanding, part of their emotional lives. Aspirations of personal immortality were vested in the young. Fathers recognized in their own offspring reflections of the children they had been, and sometimes still were. Many of them wholeheartedly welcomed the opportunity which children offered to be 'off duty', to lay aside the dignity of the responsible public man in an interlude of spontaneity and play. Besides these emotional benefits, fathers secured the satisfaction of fulfilling a crucial criterion of adult masculinity – the ability to feed, clothe and shelter children. The child who was successfully raised to the point of a good marriage or a respectable occupation brought social reputation to the father. Some of these aspects, like providing for and protecting children, were uniquely the father's; others, like the emotional investment in children and the responsibility for their moral training, were shared with the mother, and sometimes contested with her. The role of father was not a late and superficial addition to the middle–class man's identity. It touched his manhood at many different points. It brought pain and pleasure, sacrifice and empowerment, shared endeavour as well as competition. Small wonder that the practical and emotional problems posed by bringing up children were so keenly felt.

CHAPTER FIVE

Boys into Men

I recommence my diary under rather different cares than those on which I last wrote. I have at length obtained the grand object of my wishes, the anticipated deliverance from & compensation for all the passing annoyances to which I was subject at Manchester. I am in London.

Edward Herford was 19 years of age and beginning the final stages of his training as an attorney when he wrote this entry in his diary in February 1835. The pent-up frustration of submitting to the indignities of parental discipline, and the excitement of living away from home for the first time, mark this out as the reflection of a youngster on the threshold of manhood. Edward's father, John Herford, was a prosperous Unitarian liquor merchant, with firm views about how his sons should conduct themselves under his roof. They were expected to make do with a meagre allowance, to be in bed by 10.30 p.m., and to defer to their father's conventional liberal opinions. Edward bridled at all these restrictions. He fumed at his father's parsimony; he sealed the door to his bedroom in order to stay up late undetected; and he reacted indignantly to his father's complacent claim to be the friend and companion of his children. Most significant of all, he challenged his father's declared principles, first by announcing that he would be a *radical* lawyer, and later by abandoning Unitarianism in order to become a High Church Anglican.[1]

There is something almost timeless about this story of filial rebellion, as though the compulsion of sons to level with their fathers bridges the gulf between our own day and the 1830s. Edward's awareness that he entered into quarrels with his father as much 'for the sake of contradiction' as from principle strikes a particularly modern note. But there are three less familiar aspects which should give us pause. First, Edward's radicalism may have caused offence, but his choice of the law as a profession was what his father had insisted on. Edward had been compelled to abandon his original ambition to be a surgeon – an assertion of patriarchal authority for which in the longer term he was profoundly grateful. Secondly, Edward's arrival in London in 1835 did not signal the end of his confinement under the parental roof. Four years later, when his training was over and he returned to Manchester to take up a legal appointment, he was back in his father's house, still chafing at 'the most unaccountable ill feeling & intolerably arbitrary conduct of my father', and he appears to have remained there until his marriage. Lastly, one figure was conspicuously absent from the story – Edward's mother. She had died when he was 16. A mother's mediating influence was conventionally looked to for a softening of the tension between a father and a son entering manhood – a piece of common wisdom which is certainly borne out in this instance.[2] Then as now, the passage of boys to manhood was deeply marked by their parents, but parental roles were different. Fathers exercised much more authority over their sons' choice of profession or business than they do today, while mothers – often justifiably – were credited with immense moral and emotional influence. And the power of each parent was immeasurably increased by the convention that – unless study or employment took them far afield – sons lived at home for as long as they remained unmarried.

★

The progress of the middle-class boy from infancy to manhood was marked by a sequence of well-defined stages. First came the acknowledgement, at the age of six or so, that he was not only a child but a *male* child and therefore entitled to wear breeches or trousers. The modern reader is still pulled up short by photographs of the infant Robert Baden-Powell or Robert Louis Stevenson in what to us is girls' dress. Every middle-class boy wore petticoats during his earliest years, just like his sisters. There is in fact good reason for our surprise. In many ways petticoats for boys were a conservative residue of the past, rather than an accurate indicator of Victorian attitudes to gender. Prevailing conceptions of a deep divide between the sexes were founded on a theory of *natural* or biological difference. Logically this extended to children and should have encouraged markers of sexual difference from birth. This may be the reason why relatively little was made of breeching – the moment when a boy put away his petticoats, usually at about the age of six. There are comparatively few references to breeching in the family documents of the time. The emphasis is less on the ritual than on its consequences. Phil Holt, aged six, was described by his father as 'looking very sturdy & well – he strutts about in his knickerbockers and speaks in a deep important voice and gives himself such airs that he constantly makes us laugh'.[3] In the Early Modern period, on the other hand, breeching had been a great event, marked by ceremonial dressing and often the donning of a sword.[4] It corresponded with a view of gender as an identity acquired over time. The Victorians also thought of masculinity – and to a lesser extent femininity – as something which developed over an extended period, but they had a surer sense of innate sexual difference. Breeching meant less to them than to their forebears. And it mattered not so much for its symbolic importance as its practical consequences.

Once out of petticoats boys' horizons expanded. Greater freedom of

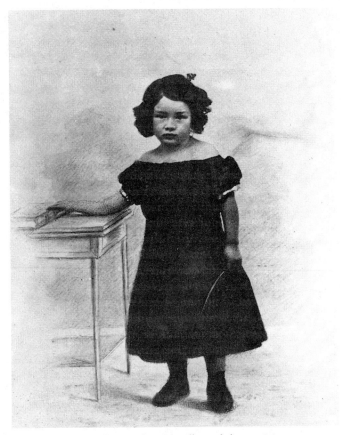

13. Robert Baden-Powell, aged three, 1860.

movement allowed them to spend more time out of doors, to engage in rough-and-tumble, and to team up with other boys. Above all, breeching heralded the start of school. Nursery lessons alongside their sisters came to an end. Few boys were educated at home after the age of six or seven. Earlier in the century the more fastidious parents, like those of Tom Macaulay or John Ruskin, sometimes kept their sons out of school on the grounds of religious scruples or class sensitivity. William Cobbett had asked how boys were ever to 'learn to talk and act like men' if they were confined to the society of boys during their school hours. But home education became increasingly rare during Victoria's reign. By 1872 J.R. Seeley's belief that educating boys alongside their peers retarded rather than advanced them was distinctly eccentric.[5] The complaints of Evangelical writers that school taught boys to despise the weak and to scoff at their sisters went largely unheeded.[6]

The majority view was that school prepared boys for the wide world in a way which home tuition could not match. At a practical level the foundations for an occupation were laid there. These included not only the relevant academic subjects, but a training in mental discipline. The engineer Joshua Murgatroyd told his 13-year-old son that boys were better equipped to succeed at business if they had learned 'to fix their thoughts on what their mind ought to be engaged with' – something which school was best fitted to teach.[7] There was also the long-held belief that school was an indispensable introduction to the company of males. It taught a boy to rub shoulders with his peers, to experience competition, and to bend to public authority. In smaller schools, like the private boarding establishments run by the clergy, a boy whose father was distant or dead could sometimes find in his teacher a surrogate parent. That consolation was much less likely in a public school, where the emphasis was on learning to 'shift for oneself' in conditions which sometimes approached brute anarchy. In the 1830s public school was far from being the typical education of middle-class boys, apart from the sons of the clergy. But as the number and standing of the public schools rose, the very distinctive masculine socialization which they offered became the defining experience of the upper middle class.[8]

Except for the tiny minority destined for university, most middle-class boys ended their formal education in their mid-teens. Training for a business or profession now began. At an age when many of them had scarcely entered puberty, boys began to keep long hours at work, surrounded by people much older than themselves. There was little concept of adolescence in the modern sense of an extended transition between childhood and adulthood. Parents, employers and teachers were often intent on forcing their charges through the remaining stages to manhood as quickly as possible – a distinctive feature of English upbringing much noted by foreign observers.[9] In the past the transition had not been so abrupt. When work was located in the home, children could be acculturated to it gradually from an early age. But as work became separated from home, a more formal induction was indicated, sometimes coinciding with full membership of a Dissenting congregation or first communion in the Church of England.[10] The young man would be ceremonially introduced to the workplace and his first position, say as a clerk or a junior buyer. But most fathers were denied the satisfaction of bringing their sons into their own line of business. The majority of young men had to be placed elsewhere. Sometimes this was by means of a formal apprenticeship, as in medicine or engineering. In business and commerce the aspirant was just as likely to find himself taken on in a menial capacity without the security of apprenticeship, in the hope of working up to a more lucrative and responsible position.

How big a step boys felt the entry into the world of work to be depended largely on whether or not they continued to live at home. This was taken for granted in the case of boys placed under their fathers. William Byles was proprietor and editor of the *Bradford Observer*. When his eldest son William left school in the mid-1850s, he was taken on at the newspaper and worked there until after his father died forty years later; he lived at home up to his marriage at

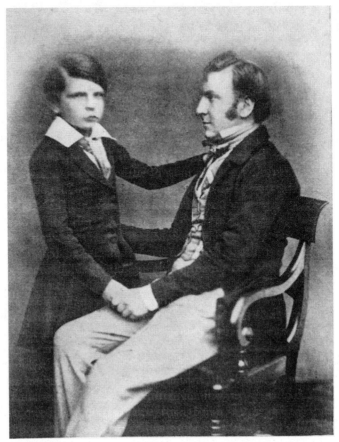

14. William Byles and his son William P. Byles, late 1840s.

the age of 25. William Byles's youngest son Frederick recalled that in the 1870s
when he and Arthur were following in their eldest brother's footsteps, 'we still
had our pegs on the hat-stand at home'. The same was true of George and John
Ashworth who started work as youngsters in Henry Ashworth's cotton-
spinning business in the 1840s, and did not leave home until they married at 41
and 35 respectively.[11] Living at home was also the obvious option for youths
who were working elsewhere in the same town. But even young men who
succeeded in setting up their own businesses often continued to live with their
fathers. During the 1840s John Young ran his own chemist's shop in
Sunderland and was a Methodist preacher, but despite these markers of adult
status he continued to live under his father's roof.[12]

The greatest challenge was reserved for those boys who moved to a strange
town and had to fend for themselves. The preferred solution was to have the
boy live either with his employer or with a kinsman. William Maynard was

apprenticed to a Bradford stuff merchant in the 1850s; he lived as a lodger in the house of his cousin William Byles and eventually married his daughter.[13] But for many this kind of extension of family living was not available. James Watts – a future mayor of Manchester – came to London in the 1820s and shared accommodation with another Manchester lad. He found that London was creating 'a desire in me that I never felt before for business', but neither the place nor the people were congenial to his pious outlook on life. 'The young men here are no company to me – they go of a Sunday to Places of all kinds of amusement. . . . Let me flee from them.' He survived homesickness and moral scruples to return home and enter business in Manchester.[14] The apprentices whose company James Watts shunned were certainly testing the boundaries of respectable conduct, yet they enacted only a pale reflection of the tearaway, rumbustious behaviour for which apprentices had been notorious in previous centuries. In fact the more decorous behaviour of apprentices by this time is a striking indication of the popular reformation of manners which Francis Place traced over the first decades of the nineteenth century. Social concern about apprentices was now focused not so much on the threat they posed to order as on their welfare. The temperance societies directed much of their activity at young men. The Young Men's Christian Association, founded by Non-conformists in 1844, was intended to provide social and reading facilities in the towns for apprentices and shop assistants who lacked the amenities of a regular home.[15]

Traditionally sexual misdemeanours had featured prominently in the bad reputation of apprentices. This was still reflected in the concern of the YMCA and other Evangelical bodies with the 'moral dangers' to young men. In theory the threat was dealt with by a strong commitment to purity, instilled since childhood, and able to withstand temptation until the wedding night. But what was the reality? Medical writers took the view that early sexual activity was physically undermining, and the churches were no less insistent as to its moral dangers. Once a boy had reached his teens, much depended on the father's attitude, since the sex education of boys was generally considered to be his responsibility. Many fathers did nothing; some endorsed the full repressive rigour of the purity ethic; and some communicated a man of the world's view of the pleasures and dangers of sex in the market-place.[16] The varied pattern of advice given reflected the diametrically opposed attitudes to sex of the pious and the worldly-wise. The latter almost certainly provide the more accurate guide to practice, despite the most strenuous counter-discourse of the moralists. The interval between puberty and marriage averaged ten to fifteen years for middle-class youth. During that time middle-class girls were off limits. The cult of female purity, not to mention the physical restrictions placed on respectable women, allowed little opportunity for any degree of physical intimacy with a girl of comparable background.

Sexual experience meant crossing class lines – beginning possibly in the home itself. Domestic servants were sexually vulnerable, and their illegitimate offspring attracted a good deal of charitable attention. There were undoubtedly instances of the 'young master' taking sexual advantage of his position. But it is now clear that the great majority of female servants who became pregnant were involved with men of their own class. The single mother from this background was more likely to be serving in a lodging-house with a steady turnover of transient males than to be employed in a conventional bourgeois household.[17] For most young men of the middle class sexual experience was to be found not in the home, but on the streets. In all the major towns of England prostitutes were readily available, graded to suit every pocket. Young men were the prime market for commercial sex, especially those removed from home constraints; the decline of 'living in' appears to have been linked with an increase in illicit sex on the part of apprentices.[18] Anthony Trollope, recalling his experience as a penniless clerk without family or respectable female friends, was able to admit that he had become a prey to the temptations of 'loose life' because it was known that young men in this predicament commonly did so. Trollope was not the only commentator to represent the sexual behaviour of young bachelors as a surrender to low instincts in the absence of appropriate social diversion.[19] What he omitted to mention was the power of peer pressure. Sexual intercourse amounted to a *rite de passage* to manhood, and repeated intercourse was a form of display intended to impress other males. Those who resisted this convention were either men of low libido, or paragons of self-control, usually sustained by their membership of churches and improvement associations like the YMCA. They were a significant minority, but a minority nonetheless.[20]

Sexual activity enhanced masculine status, but the complete transition to manhood depended on marriage. A fondness for female society could be indulged as a bachelor among the *demi-monde*; only marriage could yield the full privileges of masculinity. To form a household, to exercise authority over dependants, and to shoulder the responsibility of maintaining and protecting them — these things set the seal on a man's gender identity. For Edward Herford, as an aspiring Manchester lawyer, they had the merit of completing his independence from his father, and he was only held back by his clumsiness as a lover (including an impractical preference for girls very much younger than himself).[21] The bachelor was sometimes envied for his freedom from responsibility, but he occupied a marginal status, always in danger of being regarded as less than a man because he had renounced the office of patriarch. One strand of early Victorian literature, exemplified by Carlyle, glamorized a monastic ideal of celibacy, but this had more resonance with creative men fascinated by the idea of sublimation than with those in more mundane occupations. The celibacy embraced by the High Church party in the Church of England at this time seems to have done little to commend their cause among the generality of men.[22]

For most middle-class men the question was not whether to marry, but when. The answer usually erred on the side of caution. Material calculations were of the utmost importance. Young men could not expect to be earning much more than their keep until they were 22 or 23 at the earliest. It was several years more before they could accumulate enough to afford the outlay on a household, as a result of professional success, entering into a partnership or setting up an independent business. Middle-class couples did not begin married life in the equivalent of today's bed-sitter. They expected to enjoy amenities which were comparable to those of their parents – a point on which the bride and her parents were often adamant. For men this delayed marriage to the late twenties and beyond.[23] Angus Holden, eldest son of the mill-owner Isaac Holden, began eyeing the field in 1853 when he was 20. He complained that girls were put off by the family home being in France, and he blamed his stepmother's parsimonious housekeeping. But what really held him back was his lack of independent income. Not until he and his younger brother became partners in their own mill in 1860 did Angus marry Margaret Illingworth, the daughter of another mill-owning family; he was then 27.[24]

But the attitude of a young man to marriage was a very emotional matter as well. On the one hand, love or loneliness might press him forward into matrimony. On the other hand, there was much to make him hold back. The attractions of middle-class girls, so peerless in theory, often dissolved in a practical sense of sexual difference and incompatible interests. Men were unprepared for the power which courtship suddenly placed in the woman's hands, and resented the sense of losing control. They feared being drawn back into the feminine routines of domesticity which they associated with child-hood.[25] For some men marriage threatened the end of other kinds of emotional intimacy. One that tends to be discounted today is the bond between brother and sister. The social contacts of children and adolescents with the opposite sex were often so restricted that kin offered the only emotionally sustaining relationships. Significantly, where the law did not forbid marriage between relatives, as in the case of cousins, it was quite common: witness Edward Benson and Mary Sidgwick, and Henry and Sara Coleridge.[26] Relations between brother and sister, being based on daily contact, were potentially even more intense, as in the well-known case of Thomas Babington Macaulay and his two sisters. Macaulay's reference to his 'blameless and amiable' affection has not deterred historians from speculating about the incestuous element in these relationships. In most cases it is impossible to come to a conclusion on this point. What cannot be denied is that intimacy between siblings was quite common, and that it could delay or – in Macaulay's case – eliminate the prospect of marriage.[27]

Even more common were intimate friendships between young men. These were a further consequence of carefully policed contacts between males and females, and the attraction of young men to each other was enhanced by the generally superior quality of their education compared with that of girls. In any society where women are regarded as markedly inferior or different, close friendship between males is likely to flourish. Christian tradition extolled the virtues of spiritual love between men, and familiarity with the Greek classics reinforced the message that what men could give each other was better than anything a woman could offer. The young Mandell Creighton shared with an undergraduate friend his reflections on this topic:

> Of course at a certain age, when you have a house and so on, you get a wife as part of its furniture, and find her a very comfortable institution; but I doubt greatly whether there were ever many men who had thoughts worth recounting, who told those thoughts to their wives at first, or who expected them to appreciate them. I should like to hear from Tennyson a comparison of his feelings towards Arthur Hallam and towards his wife.[28]

In Creighton's view there was clearly no contest. It took five years, and the intellectual challenge of a girl he met at a lecture by Ruskin, to change his mind.

Creighton took it for granted that Tennyson and Hallam were the epitome of a fulfilling spiritual friendship. Posterity has not been so sure. *In Memoriam*, the poem which Tennyson wrote in heartfelt tribute to his friend, certainly lends itself to a multi-layered interpretation in which there is ample room for the erotic as well as the spiritual.[29] And what applies to this most celebrated couple extends by implication to the entire genre of male friendship. The extravagant language employed between friends may have been born of literary convention, or it may have been the closest that men of conventional moral conscience could get to expressing carnal affection. Although the phenomenon of male friendship surely subsumed a fair amount of overt homosexual feeling, it is seldom possible to know whether this was so in particular instances. Yet however important the place of male friendship in the lives of young men, it was not a secure basis for a fully achieved masculine status. Only marriage could be that. Those who were more attracted to unfettered friendships than to the power and privileges of the domestic patriarch might avoid marrying at the earliest opportunity. But indefinite delay was not a comfortable option for anyone who respected convention. Without marriage, neither formal majority at 21 nor material self-sufficiency was enough to confer a fully fledged masculine status.[30]

★

Endlessly played out in thousands of cases, there is an easy predictability about this process of ascent to manhood. How boys become men takes on the appearance of the natural, or at the very least becomes the social norm. Yet the reality for individuals was anything but routine. Becoming a man involved detaching oneself from the home and its feminine comforts. It required a level of material success in the wider world which was so often represented in threatening and alienating terms. And it depended on the recognition of manhood by one's peers in an atmosphere which had as much to do with competition as camaraderie. Attaining manhood could not therefore be blandly described as a natural process, or a matter of filling one's allotted niche. It made more sense to represent it as a period of conflict, challenge and exertion. The Victorians were little disposed to underestimate the difficulties. The pronounced individualism which marked their thinking about morality and society led them rather to play up the challenges posed by the attainment of manhood. In a pamphlet entitled *How Men Are Made* (1859), the popular Baptist writer William Landels declared that men 'do not simply grow'; they are made 'not by passively yielding to an internal pressure, but by the putting forth of an internal force which resists and masters, if it cannot change, the outward'. In a later reworking of the theme he added, 'that man was never worth anything who simply *grew* into a man by passive growth, as the acorn grows into the oak'.[31] As a Nonconformist minister Landels naturally emphasized a *moral* activism which was not to everyone's taste; but the embattled individualism reflected a very widespread experience.

So too did the stress on personal qualities. Boys became men not only by jumping through a succession of hoops, but by cultivating the essential manly attributes – in a word *manliness*. Energy, will, straightforwardness and courage were the key requirements. Sometimes there was an implied claim to natural endowment; more often a manly bearing was taken to be the outcome of self-improvement and self-discipline. This aspect was explicit in what was for the Victorians the key attribute of manliness – independence. The term meant more than freedom from patronage (its principal association in the eighteenth century); it suggested autonomy of action and opinion. Edward Herford reflected on the meaning of the word in his diary. For him it meant 'not vulgar low-born independence, but [a] tolerable opinion of yourself hidden under a very modest demeanour, and not the least sense of shame or fear of doing that which is not morally wrong'.[32] Independence could only be acquired at the cost of competitive relations with one's peers. This was a recurrent theme of paternal homilies. The Liverpool cotton broker and politician Robert Holt habitually wrote in these terms to his eldest son, Richard: 'You must fight for your places [in class] as we have to do in the Town Council'.[33]

Independence and the moral qualities on which it depended were uncontentious. But manliness had bodily associations which were less universally acclaimed. Self-defence, whether individually or as part of a collective assertion, placed a premium on physical prowess and readiness for combat. At the beginning of the nineteenth century duelling was still regarded as a test of manhood among propertied people, with fist-fighting fulfilling a comparable role at the other end of the social spectrum; there was credit to be gained from being quick to defend one's honour, and still more from quickly disposing of the challenger. Popular forms of sport, or 'manly exercises', kept men in a state of alertness and physical fitness, ranging from fox-hunting and cricket to archery and rowing. First impressions of an individual were strongly conditioned by physical indicators – countenance, voice and hand-clasp could (and should) all be 'manly'. But a manly appearance suggested more than physical health and strength; it indicated virility. In common usage manliness always presumed a liberal endowment of sexual energy, and this feature was commended quite independently of the moral issue of male sexual conduct. There was in fact a strong tradition at all levels of society that, in young men especially, the libido *should* be released in full relations with the other sex. 'Conquests' were part of the accepted currency of manhood – a perception which was particularly clear when fathers expressed pride in their sons' escapades. Body and sex accounted for the oldest and in many ways the most prestigious aspects of manliness. They were reflected in the field sports and high-class prostitutes of the aristocracy, as well as the fist-fighting and the assertive courting practices of the labouring poor. These were the qualifications for manhood invoked in wartime, and they retained considerable allure in peacetime as well.[34]

Not surprisingly, the Evangelicals set out to clean up physical manliness, like other expressions of popular mores. Their reformed version, vigorously promoted by virtually all the churches during the Victorian period, set a new moral standard. The fatal flaw in the traditional notion of manliness from the Evangelical standpoint was that it was built on *reputation* and therefore involved playing to the worldly standards of one's peers. Instead of this dangerous chimera the Evangelicals substituted *character* – the inner moral resources of a man which should determine his dealings with the world. 'Manliness is superiority and power certainly,' Isaac Taylor conceded in his *Advice to the Teens* (1820); 'but it is power and superiority of character, not of vociferation'.[35] The traditional vocabulary of manliness – words like 'sturdy', 'vigorous' and 'robust' – was redefined to include a moral as well as a physical dimension; this was particularly true of 'courage', now interpreted to mean standing up for what is true and right, rather than showing physical guts. Character was formed by two areas of experience, moralized work and moralized home. Work acquired almost hallowed authority. Manly energy was to be focused not on anti-social self-assertion, but on occupation or 'calling'. The material reward for living by the work ethic was not only personal wealth, but true freedom from dependence or patronage. At the same time the Evangelicals aimed to destroy the sexual licence of the old physical manliness by anchoring masculine energies in the home. Under the new dispensation, to be manly meant not only maintaining and protecting a household; it demanded an attention to domestic relationships as well. Wife, children and servants all required a man's care and time, summed up in the picture of the paterfamilias conducting family prayers or sharing blameless amusements with his family at the fireside.[36]

The Evangelical intervention throws into high relief one of the central dilemmas of manhood in the nineteenth century – its relation to domesticity. In essentials the dilemma is a perennial one. Becoming a man means leaving women behind – or at least the women who have provided nurture in childhood. It entails renouncing the comforts of the hearth in favour of the rigours of an all-male public atmosphere. And, once a new household has been established, sustaining one's manhood depends on a pattern of life which is proof against any suspicion of petticoat government or unduly softened manners. These tensions had surfaced in the eighteenth century. Moralists like James Fordyce were very conscious of the difficulty of striking the right balance between the enervating allure of women's company and the boorishness of men's. The pamphleteer who spoke in 1779 of 'that dangerous parent' was referring not to the arbitrary or violent father, but the emasculating mother. Men were given to doubting their own or each other's manliness because of too great a fondness for home. Among the wealthy one of the recommendations of the Grand Tour was that it served to break the hold of domesticated femininity and instil masculine self-reliance in the young traveller.[37]

So there was nothing new about the tension between manliness and domesticity. But for those young men who were touched by Evangelical influence, the contradiction was intensified by the novel idea that domesticity was a *defining* attribute of manliness – and this at a time when home was associated ever more closely with women, and femininity was counterposed ever more sharply to masculinity. The Evangelical programme not only accepted a prominent role for women in the upbringing of boys, but commended it. As Mary Sewell remarked, boys needed 'the affections trained and developed to make good domestic men', and this required 'good, intelligent women'.[38] A subordinate but significant contribution was also expected from a sister in keeping their brother in the paths of virtue and exercising his protective instincts. 'To my two younger sisters', wrote Macaulay, 'I owe it that neither voluptuousness nor ambiton have, as I think, impaired the stamina of my character'; but for them, he maintained, he would have become a libertine.[39] For a boy brought up in an Evangelical family, home was also likely to be the scene of his conversion, and the feminine associations of this experience were hard to ignore; the abject acknowledgement of powerlessness and dependence which the convert must make was no doubt temporary, but it was alarmingly close to common stereotypes of womanly behaviour. However cautious we have learned to be about applying a simple model of separate spheres to real life, home was the women's sphere in a more emphatic sense in the nineteenth century than ever before, and boys grew up in a correspondingly more feminine atmosphere.

In Evangelical discourse the pivotal figure in a boy's upbringing was of course his mother. Some doubts were voiced. The Congregationalist minister John Angell James conceded that boys who became too dependent on the comforts of home might become 'pitiable spectacles of querulous effeminacy and helpless imbecility'. But the general drift of Evangelical teaching was to turn the received wisdom about the dangers of a mother's influence on its head. By the 1830s she was widely credited with the dominant moral influence over her son. She was considered better qualified to impart spiritual truths to him, notwithstanding her husband's formal role in family prayers. And her influence was supposed to hold him to a virtuous path even from beyond the grave.[40] When the attorney John Taylor's mother died in 1845, he prayed before her corpse that 'I might be enabled to resist and overcome the habits of drinking and smoking, and the company of gay and foolish companions with whom I much associated'.[41] Evangelicals were clear that a mother's responsibility extended to the manliness of her son. Thomas Binney went so far as to call her 'the father of the child'. 'Women are not to be men in character, ambition, pursuit or achievement: but they are to be *more*; they are to be the *makers* of men.'[42]

This exalted estimate of the mother's role accorded with certain practical realities. As bourgeois wives withdrew from the more irksome aspects of running the household, they had more time to attend to the needs of their children. They were less likely to experience competition in parenting as their husbands' work increasingly removed them from the house during the day. And if the sharpening of character differences between the sexes was reflected in a lack of companionship between wife and husband, she was all the more drawn to seek intimacy with her sons. But mother's exalted role should certainly not be taken for granted in practice. The moral zeal assumed in Evangelical portrayals of the mother was hardly a universal trait of middle-class women, and it was unlikely to be found among those who lacked a 'serious' upbringing themselves. Sons with any sense of their prospects in the wider world could scarcely surrender the definition of manliness to their mothers. Young men living away from home did not on the whole live by the morality they had learned at their mother's knee. As the facts regarding prostitution show, they were in reality strongly drawn to the older tradition of manly prowess. This point was implicitly conceded by the many Christian writers on manliness who felt obliged to distance themselves from the coarser associations of the word which were still current.

★

The vaunting of moral motherhood also begged the important question of how much influence was exercised by the father over his sons. Evangelicals like Sarah Ellis might write him out of the script, but the father was a crucial presiding figure, not only because he set boundaries and tried to enforce them, but because at a deeper level he had a personal stake in his son's attainment of masculinity. The previous chapter showed how fatherhood bore on a man's standing as breadwinner, protector and authority-figure in the present. But the inter-generational aspect was also vital. Posterity is often thought of as a consideration which weighs most heavily on men of position and power. It was the head of a large business or the owner of an estate who was likely to be most preoccupied by questions of inheritance. In that sense posterity mattered little to the majority of men in the middle class. But the transmission of masculine attributes and masculine status to the next generation was a matter of keen concern to every man who had male offspring, and it mattered all the more if he had little else to leave behind him. Sons have traditionally been seen as threatening the father with displacement and oblivion: that fantasy underlies the classic nineteenth-century accounts by sons of their upbringing, as well as

Freud's theory of Oedipal conflict. But sons also hold out the prospect of symbolic immortality, reproducing the name, the attributes and sometimes the occupation of the father. That prospect was all the more alluring at a time when the facts of demography made it unlikely that a father would live to see all his offspring in full possession of their adult status. In preparing sons for their place in a man's world the father's own manhood was at stake, mortgaged to the future.[43]

Much of this generational concern was focused on the ambition to establish a son in an honourable and rewarding occupation. This was the vital prerequisite of his future masculine standing. Boys were trained up to the business under the father's eye, or apprenticed to his choice of master, or 'placed' through kinship or patronage. Entrepreneurs like Henry Ashworth and Isaac Holden took it for granted that their sons' future lay in the family business. Isaac Holden's plan was to assist his two sons, Angus and Edward, to acquire a mill in Bradford, which he could well afford to do after ten years of profitable enterprise in France. He made two stipulations. First, he would not present it to them on a plate. *They* must decide on the kind of business, which allowed Angus to rile his father with the opinion that it should not be in some 'bubble' like wool-combing (the basis of Isaac's wealth). Secondly, he required that they show some aptitude in his employment first. 'I fear much', he wrote to Angus in 1859, 'whether ever you acquire those minutious and *careful, painstaking* habits which are necessary in a *manufacturing* business.' By the following year, however, Isaac had overcome his misgivings and was ready to dig into his pocket.[44]

It was this preoccupation with career and public standing which accounted for so much of the difference in the demeanour of fathers to their sons and daughters. Daughters were intended almost exclusively for marriage. The domestic charms with which they were expected to delight their husbands could be enjoyed by fathers now. The father could appreciate his daughter's dependence without qualification, bask in her admiration, and accept her personal services. Affectionate expression could therefore be encouraged in girls, while it must be restrained in boys, and this had implications for the conduct of father as well as children.[45] Isaac Holden's letters to his daughter Margaret were completely different in tone from his letters to Angus. They were very affectionate, full of tender solicitude for her spiritual welfare and appreciation of her warmth. Like many other daughters, Margaret relished her dependence; she gladly promised that she would always be with her father to care for him, though in the event she married long before his death. It seems clear that fathers found deep satisfaction in showing a tender, indulgent side to their daughters, which they felt unable to show to their sons without undermining their manhood. Looking back to her childhood in the 1870s Beatrice Webb recalled her father's 'extraordinary tenderness and charm'; no boy would have used that language, and few would have remembered anything which corresponded to it.[46]

As the previous chapter showed, fatherhood was no more an unchanging construct than motherhood was. The nature of men's stake in the masculinity of the next generation shifted in the course of the Victorian era. One of the most significant changes was the steady decline of occupational endowment. The father no longer had the same power to set up his son for life. From the 1850s onwards places in the public service were increasingly filled by competitive examination, and entry into the professions was coming to depend on regulated training instead of apprenticeship or patronage. The days when a trusted official like James Mill could ease his son John Stuart Mill into a junior appointment (and a lifetime's career) at India House were over. Middle-class fathers were obliged to think less about trade or family contacts and more about education. The passport to a good career was now a carefully laid academic knowledge which would carry a boy over a succession of hurdles leading to a professional qualification. Middle-class employment diversified and became more bureaucratized, reflecting the impersonal quality of urban industrial society which weighed on so many Victorians.

The power of fathers to endow their sons with an occupation may have been in decline, but their masculine standing was no less bound up with the prospects of the next generation. The less control a father had over those prospects, the keener his sense of insecurity. During the Victorian period the anxious father becomes a recognizable type. The anxiety did not just focus on the health and survival of the children, for which indeed there continued to be good cause. It concerned above all the prospects of sons in adult life. The novelist Thomas Hughes, looking back on a lifetime of family preoccupations, treated the contrast between a mother's love and a father's 'anxious affection' as a truism hardly worth discussing.[47] Expressions of anxiety were in nearly every case focused on sons, not daughters, and were usually to do with the anticipated vicissitudes of their future lives. 'Anxious affection' exactly characterizes the Baptist minister Benjamin Goodwin's attitude to his son John. The letters between father and son, reproduced in Goodwin's *Reminiscences*, record his intense concern at each stage of John's progress in life – his spiritual growth, his choice of university, his entry into business, his marriage and his performance as breadwinner. 'Whenever any good is to be enjoyed we long for your participation in it', wrote Benjamin in 1840. 'You are all that we have of earthly friends – the nearest and dearest of all.' William Lucas was a prosperous Quaker brewer in the Hertfordshire town of Hitchin. By 1847 he and his wife Eliza had completed their family of nine. The eldest son was destined for the family business, but the future of the rest was uncertain. William wrote that he had no desire to see his seven sons rise above 'the middle rank of life', but he still felt 'an inexpressible anxiety' that they turn out well; of his two daughters he made no mention.[48]

Uncertainty about the prospects of achieving masculine independence placed an even greater emphasis on personal qualities. Fathers might regret the decline in their power of endowment, but this only intensified their concern about the other aspect of a father's traditional duty to his son – to train him in manliness.

To the Victorians this seemed a more difficult task than ever before. They believed that the economic discipline of the market-place was placing entirely new stresses on the individual, at a time when the traditional props of social hierarchy and revealed religion were also beginning to crumble. For a young man embarking on adult life in these challenging circumstances self-government was the key. A resilient, self-reliant character, able to rub shoulders with all sorts and to handle any situation, was an absolute prerequisite – and one not easily ensured by even the most responsible parent. The precise emphasis varied according to the balance of moral and material considerations. The Anglican vicar John Breay reflected in 1838:

> I can truly say that the older my children grow, the more difficulty do I find in the discharge of parental duties. The best mode of attempting the formation of character occupies much of my thoughts. With respect to the girls, the path appears to me comparatively clear; but the boys, who must eventually mix with a variety of characters, occasion me much anxiety.[49]

Breay was most exercised by the sexual dangers his sons faced. Other fathers pitched their anxieties at a more worldly level and worried about how resilient their sons would be when exposed to the full blast of competitive individualism.

This is the context in which to interpret one of the most significant shifts in the culture of manliness in the nineteenth century – the rise of the public school.[50] Until the early years of Victoria's reign, the public schools had been few in number and had ministered primarily to the landed elite and the Anglican clergy. They were a byword for harshness and immorality and about as far removed from a domestic atmosphere as could be imagined. Yet by the 1860s attendance at public school was almost *de rigueur* for the respectable professions, and it was no longer unusual in the business classes. Over thirty new or reformed schools had been added to the original seven, to cater for this increased demand. Given that the moral value of home was pitched so high, why was it deemed a mark of privilege for boys to be banished from its improving influence for three-quarters of every year for up to ten years of their lives? The explanation of this startling contradiction is that the public schools were changing for the better, while much of their traditional ethos now found favour with the middle class. Thomas Arnold's development of a reformed model at Rugby during the 1830s received widespread publicity. Abuses were checked, standards raised, and a moral tone was assiduously preached, if not always practised. The new schools were more academic and more orderly than their predecessors. Middle-class educational concerns were directly addressed. For some parents this was a matter of social status, the public school being seen as an opportunity for middle-class boys to acquire the accomplishments of a gentleman. Other parents took seriously – more seriously than it warranted – the claim that schools in the Arnoldian mould were Christian communities which instilled godliness and morality. For the majority, however, the appeal of the public schools was founded on two enduring preoccupations: in place of patronage and personal contacts they offered an academic preparation for university and for entry into the professions; and in complete contrast to the atmosphere of home and family they offered a crash course in manliness.[51]

Home and boarding school are always experienced in polarized terms, but how the difference between them was understood by bourgeois Victorians tells us a lot about their transition from boyhood to manhood. The most telling characteristic of the public school is that it was effectively a men–only sphere. Not only were women excluded from the school body or the teaching staff; they were effectively banned as points of emotional reference. Family photographs were frowned upon, as were fabrics and china which smacked of the feminine. No boy who valued his reputation would speak of mother or sisters. In *Tom Brown's Schooldays* (1857) Tom takes a robust attitude towards his delicate protégé Arthur: 'his blundering schoolboy reasoning made him think that Arthur would be softened and less manly for thinking of home'. Blundering Tom may have been, but his reasoning was the common wisdom of public schoolboys. As Leslie Stephen put it, 'the domestic affections' were 'mere nuisances which ought to be studiously suppressed ... to allow their existence to be manifest to others is a distinct act of indecency, if not of immorality'. The effects of this conditioning were not confined to school. It was observed that back at home boys became more formal with their mothers, more distant from their fathers, and more callous towards their sisters – tendencies which prepared boys better for the all-male society of the public sphere than for their future roles as husbands and fathers.[52]

Freed of female distraction, the schools could get on with their real job of instilling manliness. Much was made in the propaganda for the schools of *moral* manliness, the implication being that the development of the boys was along Christian lines. This was pious aspiration rather than reality. What was said in chapel was no guide to what went on in the dormitories. It is doubtful whether any school succeeded in enforcing a regime of moral manliness, or certainly not for long. Arnold fought an uphill battle against lying; the next generation of headmasters focused their anxieties on 'impurity', by which they meant not only the sexual corruption of younger boys but over-familiarity between age-peers.[53] But provided these matters did not reach the proportions of a scandal, the majority of fathers who sent their sons to public school were unperturbed. For them, moral manliness was a secondary consideration. What counted were the time-honoured attributes of sturdy manliness which long predated the Evangelical offensive. The key was independence. Learning to 'shift for yourself', to be resilient, to rub shoulders with your peers, to stand out from the crowd if need be – these qualities were an essential preparation for life, including public life. The training process could begin very young. Christopher Oxley Parker was just nine when he was sent to preparatory school in 1863. 'I was very much pleased with you today,' his father wrote. 'Considering that it was your first separation from home you behaved manfully. I could plainly see that your heart was full but you bore yourself bravely through, and a little overflow at the last was only to be expected.'[54] The touch was sensitive, but the message clear – and other fathers were less understanding. The promotion of 'independence and manliness of character' was singled out as a prime virtue of public school life by the Clarendon Commissioners in 1864.[55] It was closely associated in the minds of Victorian fathers with physical toughness, especially endurance. The schools were known to be lacking in the barest comforts and sometimes dangerous to health; they also lived by the rule of the jungle, and acts of gross cruelty were periodically reported. But within limits this was the kind of regime which middle-class fathers wanted for their sons. What had been good enough for the landed class for generations was good enough for them. They looked to the confident, resilient and self-contained products of the school and worried little about how this was achieved. Like Edward Thring of Uppingham School, they believed that 'the learning to be responsible, and independent, to bear pain, to play games, to drop rank, and wealth, and home luxury, is a priceless boon'.[56]

As a statement about gender the Victorian public school phenomenon is clear enough. It was an admission on the part of middle-class fathers that they could not prepare their sons for the adult world as they had done in the past. They could not deal from their own resources with the new, more impersonal conditions of professional and business life, and they recognized that in a society which valued maternal influence so highly the odds were heavily stacked against an effective manly training at home. Manliness was best instilled by proxy, under the care of a surrogate father who could set to work without the distractions of home comfort and feminine charm.

★

How well did middle-class boys adjust to the differing, but supposedly complementary influences of home and school? For some the transition to the threshold of manhood seems to have been seamless, though hardly effortless. Edward Benson's eldest son Martin is a poignant example. Born in 1860, Martin was programmed by his parents from the start for a life of absolute purity and dedication to intellectual rigour. Nothing was left to chance and little to his own devising. He was closely supervised. Edward and Mary Benson believed that young children needed to be carefully watched in the nursery for signs of impurity; an early copybook of Martin's features the injunction 'Abandon immoral customs'.[57] At the age of ten he was sent away to an academic preparatory school. Edward's regular letters to the boy placed him under relentless pressure. His performance in class was carefully scrutinized and backsliding subject to severe reproof. On receipt of his very first school report, Edward wrote, 'this is a report I hope never to receive again'. In his next letter he broadened the moral: 'I could tell you of many and many a boy who might have attained great powers of mind and a full store of knowledge who has been obliged to leave school and go into some poor occupation, because he was inattentive to his lessons.' Martin was also expected to inform his father if there were any signs of gross immorality in the school: 'Be *sure* you let me know if there is the *least* budding out again of the Abominable'.[58] The pressure did not let up when Martin was back at home. The conversation between father and son was on religious and classical themes, with Edward making scant allowance for his son's need for fun and adventure. Four years later Martin won the top scholarship to Winchester. The pattern of admonition continued, but with mounting confidence on Edward's part that his son would realize all the hopes placed in him. Martin became a precocious and brilliant textual scholar, as well as an intensely spiritual believer. A close intellectual companionship grew up between father and son, indulged on long walks and rides in the holidays. Martin was destined for Cambridge and doubtless the career of scholar-churchman, like Edward.

But it was not to be. In February 1878, while at school, Martin Benson died suddenly of meningitis. Edward was completely devastated. His faith was placed under an even greater strain than his wife's, and the wound never healed. Meningitis was then known as 'brain fever' and often attributed to mental strain. Edward took this diagnosis bitterly to heart, reproaching himself too late for the burdens he had pressed on Martin, and thereafter his handling of the younger boys was more relaxed. It is tempting to speculate what would have happened to Martin had he not been struck down at 17. The strain might have told in other ways, as it did in the case of his brother Arthur and sister Margaret both of whom suffered mental breakdowns later in life. Filial rebellion seems unlikely. Martin had completely internalized the standards of his parents – both the purity which his mother had instilled since the nursery, and the spiritual and intellectual aspirations of his father. His story is a reminder that, in a culture which was not structured around generational conflict or the glamorization of youth, parents stood a much better chance of moulding their children's adult lives than they do today. Martin Benson's case was no doubt extreme, but many middle-class fathers forced the pace of development in the hope of a brilliant future, and many sons allowed the emerging shape of their lives to be determined in this way.[59]

Many sons, but by no means all. Arthur Heaton was also burdened by overreaching paternal expectation, but his reaction was rather less accommodating. His father, John Heaton, had an acute sense of 'line' and posterity which caused him both to research his own ancestry and to plan his children's future with care. His eldest son, born in 1855, was named John like his father and grandfather, though he was always known by his second name, Arthur. John Heaton led a very active public life which took him out a great deal in the evening. His wife Fanny was a conscientious mother, but due to ill health she was absent much of the time. Arthur was therefore much thrown on the company of his two elder sisters. John Heaton was dismayed by the contagion of femininity. He found Arthur to be 'petulant' at home and concluded that 'he required to be amongst other boys, to give him a more manly bearing & spirit'. So, at the age of nine, Arthur was sent away to school in Northallerton. Five years later, in 1869, he moved on to Rugby. As John explained to his daughter Helen, 'It is a large school, where there are nearly 500 boys, so he will have to stand up for himself there'.[60] But the outcome was not as John would have wished. Arthur applied himself neither to his work nor the kind of reading that was appropriate for a gentleman. Both his behaviour and his demeanour appeared to lack manliness, and to show him at a disadvantage compared with his friends. There was no improvement when Arthur went up to Cambridge in 1874, and John felt 'personally humiliated' by his son's uninspired performance in the Maths Tripos. When John died in 1881, Arthur was reading for the Bar without much energy, and with no clear path ahead of him.[61]

John Heaton was careful with money and resented having spent so much on Arthur's education to so little effect. But his concern went deeper. He had looked for an eldest son who would have the position and character to be an effective head of the family – 'to prove the comfort and support of my declining years, & then take my place and carry on my work with better effect & more worthily than I have done'. He cared deeply about Arthur's place in a family line which stretched back to the first recorded John Heaton in the early eighteenth century, and which, in John's vision, was destined for great things in the future. In a bitter recognition that this was not to be, he rewrote his will in 1879, dividing the estate equally between all three sons. But this was an exercise in damage limitation, not a solution. John Heaton went to the grave with the painful sense that his masculine standing was impugned by his eldest son's disappointing performance as a man and as a member of the family. On his side, Arthur rejected the standards of self-denying manliness to which his father subscribed; nor was he attracted to the dignity of head of the family. But given his financial dependence, passive resistance was the only stance open to him. He could be highly provocative, as when he spoke of emigrating to Australia and suggested that John would have done better putting him into trade than sending him to Cambridge. His final resting place as a lawyer in colonial Rangoon suggests a raffish taste for the exotic or a last-ditch attempt to earn a living; either case would have greatly depressed his father. A more radical rebellion was never really on the cards.[62]

★

Despite the *causes célèbres* of literary autobiography, filial rebellion was comparatively rare in Victorian England. The power of the father may have diminished, but it still counted for much. Fathers controlled the purse strings, and hence were able to determine their sons' disposable income, their access to education and training, and their place of residence. In an economically unstable world, middle-class youths did not lightly cast aside their financial cushion and peer into the abyss. Even Edward Herford, with whom this chapter began, confined much of his rebelliousness to the pages of his diary, and he baited his father rather than challenged him directly. Most young men did not push their luck even this far. In their own estimation Victorian fathers had good reason to watch their sons' growth to manhood with anxiety as well as anticipation. For sons in turn, that sense of the father's intrusive concern and his power to define – if not always exemplify – the meanings of masculinity conditioned their progress to manhood, no less than the moral influence of the mother.

The passage to manhood in middle-class England was marked by no common *rite de passage*. For young men of no fixed religious principles, there was sexual initiation with a prostitute, but this was completely rejected by those who came from godly homes. Entry into apprenticeship or employment was a major step for boys from the business classes, but increasingly irrelevant to those from professional backgrounds who stayed on at public school until they were 19 or 20 (and then often went on to university). Similarly, leaving home could happen as young as 15, and as old as the late twenties. Only the final stage of marriage was a relatively fixed point in the transition to adult masculine status, with economic pressures tending to push it into the late twenties. The journey to manhood began in domestic dependence and ended in domestic authority. In between these two versions of domesticity a young man needed to demonstrate to himself, his father and his peers that he could live without the comforts of home and the ministrations of its female inmates, so that when he came to form a household of his own he would do so on the right terms. He must set about securing the material means without which a socially reputable marriage was impossible. And he needed to acquire – and demonstrate – the essential manly qualities of energy, resolution and independence, which would secure his masculine reputation. All the while the claims of home, the values of school, loyalty to one's peer group and the charms of female company jostled for ascendancy in his life. The Victorians were not always realistic in their choice of means to smooth the path to manhood, but they were surely right in supposing that it was an inherently testing experience.

CHAPTER SIX

Convivial Pleasures and Public Duties

The Frenchman Hippolyte Taine remarked of England in the 1860s, 'Here, there is nothing beyond work conscientiously done, useful production, and a secure and convenient comfort in one's own home'. No doubt some allowance must be made for the fact that Paris under the Second Empire was a byword for publicly consumed masculine pleasures. But Taine was in fact accurately reflecting the self-image of middle-class England.[1] Domesticity for men implied a life spent, as far as working routines permitted, within the home or in the company of family. Once the requirements of material provision had been met and responsibilities towards employer or partner discharged, moral discourse allowed for no higher claim on a man's time than his home, with the exception of divine service. Both pleasure and duty took on a strongly domestic tone in the works of didactic writers. The claims of the wife were pitched high. More confined to household duties than had been the case in the past, deprived of her husband's company during his working hours, and often a prey to boredom, she was entitled to every attention from him as soon as his time was his own. She was encouraged to expect this attention not only because it was her due, but because it was the channel through which her husband would find the intimacy and comfort so painfully lacking in the outside world. Middle-class men were expected to be uplifted by the moral wholesomeness of home and refreshed by its innocent amusements.

A prescribed set of domestic activities for men corresponded with this principle. Moral responsibilities in the home were fulfilled by making family prayers the daily focus of domestic discipline and spiritual renewal, by giving instruction (both 'rational' and moral) to the children, and by holding up an example of self-restraint and quiet authority. Time must also be allowed for leisure pursuits, as a relaxation for the whole family, but most of all for the depleted breadwinner himself: reading aloud and music-making indoors; gardening and family walks outside. There was some scope for public entertainment *en famille*. Exhibitions and concerts attracted a mixed-sex clientele, as did the choral societies which rapidly expanded from their original base in chapel and church at this time. But the assembly rooms which had been such a marked feature of the late eighteenth century were in decline, and middle-class audiences at provincial theatres were also falling off, deterred by the traditional association of the stage with low life (the return of the theatre to middle-class favour began in the 1850s and 1860s). There was in short a definite reduction in the venues where middle-class couples could socialize freely.[2] The result was more entertaining at home. Within carefully circumscribed social boundaries, middle-class households received visitors, often assiduously. A couple on a middle-band income and with moderate social pretensions might give a dinner once a month, with visitors invited for tea on other days.[3] The routine of giving and receiving 'calls' was not confined to the ladies; when the husband was at home he might well take part, following the dress code for gentlemen and conducting conversation by the rules of etiquette.[4]

It was not a very exciting regime. The Victorians are noted for their belief that entertainment should be improving as well as diverting. Home carried such a heavy freight of moral purpose that domestic amusements were often taken too seriously. Of course not everyone internalized these values. Provided visitors were excluded and the servants' discretion could be relied upon, the seclusion of the middle-class home permitted more informal and spontaneous activity, like the romps involving parents and children which were noted in Chapter 4. But the constraints of social propriety were never far away. Moreover the rituals of home life had an unmistakably feminine quality. Women featured much more prominently in domestic entertainment than men. Music-making should have been, as Samuel Smiles urged, an occasion for shared performance, but in practice gentlemen were not expected to play the piano in company, and most drawing-room songs were written for female voice.[5] The social side of domestic life was also regarded as falling within the wife's sphere. She was likely to be the one who planned the dinner parties and drew up the guest lists. She certainly controlled the calling ritual, whether or not her husband participated. The flow of visitors into the home was a matter for her social instinct and management skills. Within the domestic social space the husband was an actor, but he was not prime mover.

Once some allowance has been made for the formality of this pattern, it does not seem that unfamiliar today. Shorn of its moralizing edge, the ideal of domesticated manhood has never lacked devotees. Gardening and DIY are simply the most widely accepted forms of male domesticity in the recent past. It requires an effort therefore to comprehend the revolution in masculine mores which was required to bring this about. Pre-industrial society had provided many venues for male conviviality – the street, the racecourse, the theatre, the coffee-house, and above all the alehouse or tavern. Men who both worked and slept at home had every reason to go elsewhere for their leisure. In the late eighteenth century, to frequent the tavern indicated not so much a taste for dissipation as a sociable nature, and one which did not dwell unduly on class distinctions. All ranks of society frequented the tavern; the well-to-do and the professionally respectable (like the clergy) rubbed shoulders with their social inferiors; merchants still did business deals there.[6] Moralists were already urging married men to be more attentive to their domestic ties, yet only a minority of the middling sort heeded this advice. Masculine mores were comparatively broad-minded. The Birmingham businessman James Bisset wryly recalled how, as a young married man in the 1790s, he regularly played the fiddle at parties and 'was roaring myself almost hoarse at the tavern' while his wife pined at home.[7]

James Bisset's embarrassment at his youthful sociability is a measure of how different masculine mores had become among the entrepreneurial middle class of the 1820s. By that time men's place at the fireside was touted on every side. In 1828 John Angell James wrote, 'it is a sad reflection upon a man when he is fond of spending his evenings abroad. It implies something bad, and it predicts something worse'.[8] Such sentiments were echoed many times over by other Christian writers of the day. That they were also fully endorsed by radicals is striking testimony to the non-partisan appeal of the new social morality. Thus William Cobbett deplored the 'profligate abandonment of their homes' by men who frequented the ale- or coffee-house after the day's business instead of returning to the fireside.[9] The socialist William Thompson, a much more daring social critic, wrote in almost identical terms against 'the manly pleasures of conviviality' being enjoyed at the expense of the sorrowing wife 'imprisoned at home'.[10] That such urgings were periodically repeated throughout the Victorian period is a sure sign that old habits persisted,[11] but by the 1830s the ground of convention had nevertheless shifted. These were critical years in the public re-moralization of men's leisure. Even before the rise of the temperance movement, London taverns had become off limits for respectable bourgeois men, due to a greater sensitivity about class distinctions as well as the growing appeal of domesticity. In middle-class eyes taverns or pubs became associated with rough manners and drunkenness. This explains why in the early Victorian period there were hardly any pubs in the more desirable residential areas of the capital like Bloomsbury or Belgravia. A comparable withdrawal from taverns was taking place in the large manufacturing towns of the Midlands and the north, though the process was more gradual, with businessmen continuing to frequent taverns for lunches until the 1870s.[12] One reason why the early music halls which sprang up from the 1850s onwards were largely shunned by the middle class was that they were located almost entirely in pubs or adjacent premises. The picture only began to change with the appearance of better-appointed purpose-built halls towards the end of the century. The more glamorous music halls of late Victorian fame developed at about the same time as a new breed of saloon pubs which were also able to attract substantial middle-class custom. Until that time the middle class either restricted their drinking to home, or else renounced alcohol entirely – a widespread aspect of Nonconformity.[13]

The most visible forms of homosocial leisure certainly fell prey to more rigorous standards of respectability in the early Victorian period, but it would be a great mistake to assume that middle-class husbands were living out the code of domesticity to the letter. Taine's picture of men dividing their time only between home and work was greatly over-simplified. The lengthy years of bachelorhood established a taste for masculine companionship which marriage was unlikely to replace completely. As one prospective husband wrote to the *Daily Telegraph* in 1868, it was unreasonable 'for a man suddenly to change his whole manner of living, relinquish his position, give up the society of his friends, and settle down quietly with his wife, uncared for by the world'.[14] The writer – probably a clerk – was oppressed as much by limited means as by social convention, a reminder that those middle-class men who insisted on marrying before they were 'comfortable' faced harsh choices in their social life. For those who had the means, the joys of homosocial society were not to be lightly given up. In 'Mr Brown's Letters to His Nephew' (1849) Thackeray has old Mr Brown tell young Bob that a man cannot spend all his time with his wife, and no sensible woman would expect it. 'You can't be talking to Mrs Brown for ever and ever: you will be a couple of old geese if you do.' The proper husband is 'respected on the 'Change, liked by his friends, and famous for his port wine'.[15]

Most married men probably continued to relish this kind of gregarious sociability, but for all too many it was the sum total of male friendship. This was an important consequence of the rise of companionate marriage. John Stuart Mill doubtless overstated the case when he described the wife as her husband's 'chief associate, his most confidential friend, and often his most trusted adviser',[16] but time spent at home, and the expectation that there should be trust and openness between spouses, undermined the quality of other friendships. An early casualty of this trend was the close friendship between Thomas Carlyle and Edward Irving which had flourished in Scotland but did not survive Irving's move to London in the 1820s. No one valued the 'communion of man and man' more highly than Carlyle, and he keenly felt Irving's absorption in his young wife and baby as an exclusion, which left no room for the free-wheeling discussions on religion and literature they had always shared together; Carlyle reacted with sullen rage.[17] The sense that marriage and friendship were mutually exclusive became more pervasive in the course of the Victorian period. In 1871 Samuel Smiles approvingly quoted the sad conclusion of Nathaniel Hawthorne on this subject:

> In matters of affection there is always an impassable gulf between man and man. They can never quite grasp each other's hands, and therefore man never derives any intimate help, any heart-sustenance, from his brother man, but from woman – his mother, his sister, or his wife.[18]

This description corresponds closely with the predicament of the lawyer and writer Thomas Hughes a few years later. Hughes did not lack male friends, but confronted by the disastrous failure of his pet project of a public school settlement in Tennessee, he could divulge nothing to any of them. He managed to pen a letter to his lifelong friend Lord Ripon who was 3,000 miles away in India, but otherwise the whole burden of loss and humiliation descended on his wife.[19] The episode is a revealing measure of the power of domesticity against the culture of male friendship, since Hughes's whole life – from public school and university to Lincoln's Inn and the House of Commons – had been spent in an intensely homosocial atmosphere. Lower down the social scale the institutional supports for male friendship were much weaker.

★

One way in which married men tried to make a space for their male friends was by going on holiday with them. Later in the century – certainly by the 1880s – family holidays would become the middle-class norm, made possible by the rapid extension of the railway network and the development of a string of respectable seaside resorts from Brighton to Blackpool – though even then it was not uncommon for husbands to continue working in town and to travel down by train to join their families at the weekend.[20] But in the early Victorian period holidays were used as much to break the family mould as to reinforce it. Many middle-class men of impeccably domestic credentials were glad of a chance to get away from the family. In the mid-1830s the newly wed James Watts thought nothing of leaving his wife and baby daughter in Manchester while he went on a hunting holiday in Leicestershire.[21] William Gaskell, minister at the town's principal Unitarian chapel, was the fond father of three daughters and a son. He could not often be torn away from his parishioners and his study, but when he was, he insisted on a complete change and freedom from responsibility, which usually meant a walking tour with a male friend or relative. Elizabeth would have liked to accompany him more, but she recognized how much he benefited from these opportunities to 'bachelorize off comfortably guided by the wind of his own daily will'.[22]

For the wealthy husband who still valued his old friends, another option was to keep up a bachelor apartment in addition to the marital home. This was not necessarily concealed from the rest of the family, but the wife was emphatically excluded, though sons were sometimes allowed to visit. In the 1860s and 1870s the City merchant and bibliophile Henry Ashbee kept his formidable collection of erotica at his chambers in Gray's Inn Square, less than a mile from his main residence in Bloomsbury.[23] But that kind of outlay was rare. A much more typical bourgeois setting for male society was the gentlemen's club. Its origins lay in the Restoration period and it became an established feature of urban life during the eighteenth century. By the early years of Victoria's reign that long history was reflected in a variety of institutions which went considerably beyond the stereotype of the stately Pall Mall pile. The earliest clubs had been small dining and drinking fraternities which met in taverns, usually in a private room. When the writer Edward Kimber noted in 1750 that 20,000 Londoners forgathered every night in clubs, it was this kind of setting that he had in mind, and he was referring not only to men of the middling sort, but to the aristocracy and artisans as well. Although good company was of the essence, clubs were often invaluable in extending financial aid to a member in distress and in validating his credit worthiness.[24] Tavern clubs survived well into the Victorian period. In 1860 the Thatched House Tavern in St James's Street, London, hosted no fewer than twenty-six clubs. Select company in a private room offset much of the disrepute attached to taverns and pubs. But for the middle class the trend was emphatically away from the tavern club towards the subscription club in permanent (and secluded) premises. One or two aristocratic clubs of this type, like White's and Brook's, dated back to the eighteenth century. The foundation of the Travellers' Club in 1814 heralded a proliferation of such institutions for the more affluent middle class in London, and the major provincial cities were quick to follow. In the larger subscription clubs greater exclusivity was imposed by the cost of membership as well as by the need to be put up for election, and more amenities were provided: not just bars and dining rooms, but common rooms, reading rooms, billiard rooms, and so on.[25]

The middle class became club members *par excellence*. Clubs were finely graded according to status and income. The Sheffield Club was set up in 1843 by manufacturers and members of the professions; the petty bourgeoisie frequented the Sheffield Athenaeum, founded three years later.[26] Clubs of this kind were a world away from the libertine gatherings which had given clubs their racy reputation in the eighteenth century. They prided themselves on their respectability and their elevated tone. In 1849 the *Leeds Mercury* commended clubs like the Union in Leeds for providing 'a mutual surveillance and a favourable influence' on men who found it inconvenient to dine at home, thus protecting them from the dangerous anonymity of places of ill repute.[27] Although available membership statistics do not allow precise statements to be made, there is little doubt that the bachelor element of these clubs was dominant. In the course of the nineteenth century, as more and more urban middle-class families moved out to the suburbs, their bachelor sons tended to rebel against the lack of social amenities by moving into lodgings in town. A young man in this position could scarcely afford to set up a household commensurate with his class dignity. Membership of a subscription club was the ideal solution: it gave him an 'address' (including headed notepaper) and a dignified place in which to entertain, while allowing him to continue economizing in humble lodgings. It also served as a social springboard, promising not only congenial company but useful contacts with a direct bearing on a man's business or professional prospects.[28]

The tone set by bachelors was exactly what made clubs so appealing to the married man. Club premises were often described in quasi-domestic terms. The *Leeds Mercury* emphasized that the Union Club had 'an air of domestic comfort', with its 'handsome coffee-rooms and dining-rooms ... excellent kitchen, lavatory, bedrooms, bathrooms, etc.'[29] The seclusion, the service, the cuisine and the fireside society offered by a good club might be seen as a tribute to domesticity. But the analogy was misleading in a crucial sense. It was the very absence of constraining femininity which made the club so attractive to the married man. The kind of conviviality it offered was a release from the burden of keeping up domestic appearances. Why not enjoy good company and varied fare instead of being condemned to 'solitude and mutton cutlets' at home?[30] All-male drinking and dining, cards, billiards and 'man-talk' could be pursued in the club without distraction or interruption. Victorian clubs valued privacy and seclusion above ease of access and open sociability. In this respect the club bore some resemblance to the home: both can be seen as private spaces offering men a refuge from the market-place.[31] But fundamentally the club's rationale was as an *alternative* to home life, where an ethos of fraternalism replaced the ties of family. This polarity was a characteristic theme in 'Mrs Caudle's Curtain Lectures', Douglas Jerrold's satirical series which ran in *Punch* in 1845: Job Caudle is regularly taken to task by his wife for staying out late and frequenting the 'Skylark Club'.[32] An Essex doctor who, after a dinner at Fishmonger's Hall in 1842, complained that 'Clubs and Companies estrange men from domestic and social life and thus leave mother and child too much unprotected' was putting his finger on the key role of the club as the antithesis of home.[33]

There is no doubt too that attendance at the club could serve as a cover for less reputable forms of pleasure. Posterity, unconvinced by the Victorians' public appearance of self-righteous rectitude, has tended to assume that for men with money at large in the city, 'pleasure' meant consorting with women of easy virtue. Nineteenth-century prostitution has been the subject of a flood of scholarly works since the 1960s.[34] No aspect of Victorian topography is more familiar to the modern reader than the urban 'dens of vice', ranging from the squalor of Jack the Ripper's Whitechapel to the glitter and wealth of the Haymarket. Yet this literature has very little to say about the social identity of the clients. The reason is that the same reticence is to be found in the contemporary sources. It is not that a veil was cast over prostitution; but the medical, journalistic and anecdotal accounts focused almost entirely on the prostitute herself. The punter had the advantage of anonymity. He was not counted in the streets, or confined in a lock hospital or quizzed by rescue workers. Doubtless too the investigators and their readers found it less threatening to think of an undifferentiated mass of male clients than to visualize particular categories defined by age, occupation and marital status.[35]

The paucity of hard data has allowed an easy ride for that most enduring stereotype of the prostitute's client – the rich bourgeois husband cheating on his angel wife. Combining sexual hypocrisy with class oppression, this image was savoured as a telling blow against the moral pretensions of the Victorians.[36] Yet as a reflection of the typical punter it is very misleading. The most determined Victorian effort to regulate prostitution – the Contagious Diseases Acts of 1864–69 – was intended to protect the health of soldiers and sailors, most of whom were single and working-class.[37] Recent scholars are agreed that those who consorted with prostitutes were a representative cross-section of society as a whole: middle-class men were proportionately no more forward than lower- or upper-class men. In fact the majority of prostitutes serviced working-class men in conditions which would have repelled the better off. Middle-class men were as culpable as anyone else, but their needs cannot be held to account for the vast scale of Victorian prostitution. The idea that seduction by middle- and upper-class men forced most prostitutes on to the streets is also a myth. The overwhelming majority of prostitutes entered the trade for economic reasons, believing it to be preferable to other lower-paid work, or no work at all.[38]

The marital status of the average punter is more difficult to establish. Yet here too the Contagious Diseases Acts point in the right direction. Soldiers and sailors tended to be single as much because of their conditions of service as their lack of means, but delayed marriage for men was an extremely widespread phenomenon. It was certainly not confined to working-class men compelled to scrimp and save for years in order to amass the means to marry. In the middle class the critical factor was not the bare necessities of life but the insistence on comfort; postponing marriage was socially preferable to marrying on too low an income to live in the appropriate style. Young middle-class men therefore faced many years of sexual maturity before marriage, but nevertheless possessed the means to purchase their pleasures. It is hardly surprising that they were the prime market for commercial sex. Some youths took their pleasure when they could afford it, often with different girls and in different venues which preserved their anonymity. Others consorted with a 'regular'. At the top of the range (though much rarer than in France for example) was the kept mistress, sometimes maintained for years at a time by a confirmed bachelor and integrated into the rest of his social life. At Oxford in the 1840s the proctors' records suggest a figure of between 300 and 500 prostitutes in a city of 25,000 people; by far the most important clientele was the 1,500 students most of whom had good incomes and lived in all-male colleges where sexual exploits were constantly spoken of.[39] In essentials the picture was little different in other large towns, especially London which was large enough to sustain a real *demi-monde*. Public acknowledgement of these facts remained muted until the full implications of prostitution were uncovered during the campaign against the Contagious Diseases Acts in the 1870s and 1880s. But the truth was freely admitted in private. In 1848 Dickens and Carlyle told R.W. Emerson that 'chastity in the male sex was as good as gone', and Dickens added that if his own son were chaste he would think he could not be in good health.[40] In this respect, at least, there is good reason for thinking that traditional patterns of sexual behaviour were comparatively impervious to the moralizing imperative of the new middle-class culture. Unmarried men accounted for by far the largest share of the demand for the services of prostitutes.

Where does this leave the cheating husband of common repute? Of course married men did use prostitutes. Sexual incompatibility in marriage must have been common enough, whether on account of the wife's revulsion from sex or the husband's association of respectable womanhood with 'purity'. Husbands might enjoy an occasional 'night in Bohemia' when up in town late; they might frequent places of entertainment which traded on their sexual ambience; a small minority of bourgeois men, like the novelist Wilkie Collins, maintained an illicit second household.[41] Participation in the 'gay life' nearly always remained secret and was hardly ever recorded in diaries or letters between friends. Men covered their tracks well and doubtless colluded in keeping each others' peccadilloes secret. The principal forum in which some of the true facts came to light was the Divorce Court, where it was not uncommon for wives of many years' standing to cite venereal infection by their husbands. But even allowing for the 'tip of the iceberg' argument in relation to the tiny number of divorce cases, errant husbands were not the middle-class norm. It is highly significant that adultery with prostitutes – indeed adultery of any kind – was seldom mentioned in contemporary critiques of marriage. The feminists of the 1890s, who spared no sacred cow, did not level this charge; they reserved their anger for the bridegroom with a promiscuous past who brought venereal disease to the marriage bed on his wedding night. It is in fact unlikely that the needs of married men accounted for more than a small proportion of the trade in commercial sex.[42]

Daniel Meinertzhagen exemplifies the place which a bachelor style could hold in the life of a none-too-dutiful husband. Public school, university, the exclusive coterie of merchant banking, and extensive foreign travel on business had fixed his social tastes well before he married Georgina Potter in 1873 at the age of 31. Daniel's world continued to revolve round the West End clubs where he hung out with his City associates, and a range of choice fishing and shooting locations, to which he repaired with a group of old Oxford friends whenever possible. Daniel spent numerous weekends in this way, and usually a whole month in the summer, regardless of his wife's pregnancies or any other family consideration. Georgina adopted a light ironic tone in response to these desertions, but they hurt her deeply. 'I am neither surprised nor indignant that you are taking your departure from Rutland Gate on my arrival,' she wrote in October 1878. 'Quite accustomed to it, dear, and don't mind at all! In fact I am very glad you are going to have two days' shooting, and I hope they will be nice ones.' More poignantly, she wrote from a family seaside holiday:

> I shall be glad to get settled at home again with the children: and to see you again, dear. I hope you won't mind having us. I never feel quite sure that you are not better pleased to be free to go your own way, without me.

The hesitation was mere tact. Georgina knew very well what Daniel's preferences were.[43]

Daniel was an indulgent and popular father, but a somewhat abstracted one. He was happier with a gun or a rod than with his family. And when in London, rather than dine at home, he spent his evenings in a number of clubs which ranged from the stuffy to the risqué. For much of the time he did not even sleep at Rutland Gate, preferring his bachelor flat in the Albany, Piccadilly. 'What a nice idea!' Georgina remarked of one club engagement. 'I must be a member, and then on Derby night and sundry other nights I need not cry my eyes out at home.' A year later Daniel himself recounted wandering from one club to another on a summer's evening without finding anyone he knew, until he was obliged to settle for a game of billiards with the marker. Even this apology for a social life was preferable to being with his family down in the country.[44] In fact it was not only club life which drew Daniel to the West End of an evening, but the company of 'gay' women. Almost certainly he had notched up considerable sexual experience on his travels as a young man. His sisters-in-law observed his roving eye, and they were probably correct in believing that he found his sexual pleasures away from home. On one occasion Daniel's customarily vague allusions to his evening pleasures sailed quite close to the wind. In a letter to Georgina in April 1881 he described his excitement at being introduced to the Lotus Club, full of rich and rowdy friends and graced with the company of actresses – 'quite a new and different sort of life'.[45] 'My father loved to live light-heartedly', recalled Daniel's daughter Beatrice, in an engagingly indulgent phrase.[46] The children certainly enjoyed the sense of anticipation about their father's appearances, but Daniel's semi-detached family life placed an almost intolerable strain on his wife. It was a not uncommon story among the families of the wealthy.

★

Both club life and low life were features of urban middle-class society which long predated the nineteenth century. The most distinctive contribution of the Victorian middle class was its development of formal associations for *public* life. A fine line divided the club which aimed at no more than oiling the wheels of men's society from the association committed to the 'improvement' of its members or the reform of society. But the distinction was vital to the public standing of the bourgeoisie. It was the dedication with which like-minded men of the middle class forgathered to pursue intellectual, political and philanthropic goals which underpinned their claim to be public men and members of the body politic. In Bradford, for example, the years from 1821 to 1838 saw the foundation of a plethora of associations, including the Philharmonic Society, the Bradford Club, the Bradford Exchange, the Literary and Philosophical Society, the Caledonian Society, the Bradford Choral Society and the Bradford Cricket Club.[47] As the *Bradford Observer* put it,

> Nothing more vividly marks our civilization than the multiplication of separate societies and agencies religious, charitable, political, economical, educational, professional, friendly, recreative, and what not.[48]

Indeed the claim has been plausibly made that middle-class identity was essentially the creation of these voluntary associations.[49]

In some ways the church or chapel congregation might be regarded as the model. There were many men of the middle class for whom, like Cornelius Stovin, religion was the heart of associational life. Stovin was not only a chapel official at Binbrook Free Methodist chapel, but a qualified preacher much in demand with other congregations who seemed to appreciate what he called his 'torrent of rude, sometimes incoherent, eloquence'. Most of his spare time from the farm was spent on horseback, in chapel or at circuit meetings. The only other formal claim on his time was his voluntary work as a Poor Law guardian.[50] Membership of a congregation was certainly voluntary, in that the post-Reformation system of compulsory attendance at divine worship had long since disappeared, and in general the Victorian churches were characterized by a higher commitment to moral and social concerns than their eighteenth-century predecessors. But the analogy with the voluntary associations of bourgeois urban society must not be pushed too far. Church congregations were neither class-specific nor gender-specific. When all allowances have been made for the class topography of Victorian towns, a much wider cross-section of society was represented in most churches or chapels than members of the congregation would encounter in their social life. The lawyer or doctor might not pray next to the clerk and the shopman, but they prayed as members of a single congregation. Nowhere else were all sections of the middle class to be found regularly in one place. Segregation between middle- and working-class congregations was more common, but it was far from absolute. The principle of inclusiveness was still more emphatic as regards gender. Women were not only present, they were frequently in a majority of the congregation; and although formal positions of lay leadership belonged to the men, women led an active associational life within the church, with organized philanthropy as their special concern.[51]

The new voluntary associations, on the other hand, were socially exclusive, confined to men, and in many cases committed to transcending denominational divisions among the local middle class. In many ways the Masonic lodge was a more convincing prototype than the church, since it too was secular (or at least non-sectarian), restricted to men only, and closely associated with status and respectability in the community. In England the Freemasons were a development of the eighteenth century, when they were comparatively open to scrutiny. They continued to flourish in the Victorian period, though as their activities were more discreet we know much less about them.[52] By this time, however, they were heavily outnumbered by all-male associations which functioned openly. A rule-of-thumb distinction must be drawn between those associations which aimed to facilitate discussion and the self-improvement of their members, and those which existed to promote some public goal. Typical of the first category were the literary and philosophical societies which began in the late eighteenth century and rapidly proliferated in the major towns from the 1820s. In Manchester – the leader in this field – the 'Lit and Phil' had been founded as early as 1781 and had a strongly scientific orientation. In Leeds the cream of the professional elite belonged to the Philosophical and Literary Society, with premises at the Philosophical Hall in Park Row. A well-stocked reading room and an active, well-supported programme of lectures were characteristic of these societies. Subscription libraries and musical societies also belong in this broadly cultural category, though they were more likely to permit female participation, and partly for this reason carried less cachet.[53]

The second group of voluntary associations was much more varied – as varied as the public objectives of the middle class. These included political reform, moral reform, missionary work, welfare provision (notably hospitals) and civic amenities. Active membership of these bodies meant a great deal of unpaid work, but hopefully the grateful recognition of one's peers and the satisfaction of having contributed to the goal in question. In the 1840s and 1850s Edward Herford's career as city coroner of Manchester and municipal councillor marked him out as a public man, expected to take up other causes on a voluntary basis. With other middle-class reformers he was active in setting up Lyceums for working-class men, and later devoted himself to the National Association for Providing Freedom of Public Worship. In middle-class representation, the cumulative effect of this associational activity was of much greater public significance than anything which the municipal authorities might achieve.

There was never a more assiduous supporter of societies than John Heaton of Leeds. As a first-generation professional man with a private medical practice to build up, he might have been expected to have had scant time for cultural and philanthropic activities. But Heaton was no struggling outsider. His father had been the premier bookseller in the town, able to set his son up in his own house and to leave him a considerable capital sum.[54] John Heaton could therefore afford to confine his work as a medical practitioner and lecturer to the mornings, leaving the rest of the day to dignified non-paying pursuits. In later life he sometimes reproached himself for not having a large paying practice, but the truth was that he did not need it, and he got greater gratification from playing the part of a man of wide culture and public service.[55] The culture was certainly very inclusive. Heaton was a member of the Yorkshire Archaeological Society, the Royal Archaeological Institute and the British Association for the Advancement of Science. All his adult life he was an active member of the Leeds 'Phil and Lit', serving as president from 1868 to 1872 when the society reached the peak of its membership. On a less formal level, in 1849 he was a founder member of the Leeds Conversation Club, an elite debating society which met for discussion in members' houses by rotation. Heaton himself enjoyed entertaining leading citizens and visiting worthies, which was one of the reasons why he moved in 1856 from his terraced house in the centre of town to the greater dignity of Claremont. Holding dinners brought his wife and daughters into fuller contact with the Leeds elite, but their associational life functioned quite separately from his. Fanny Heaton was active in philanthropic causes, and she and her two daughters were elected members of the Leeds

15. The public man: John Heaton, painted by John Pettie in 1884 for the Council of the Yorkshire College.

Musical Soirées. The social circles of husband and wife might mingle at Claremont, but otherwise they occupied separate planes.

John Heaton's public causes were just as diverse, and probably more time-consuming. His position as founder member of the Leeds Improvement Society gave him a base from which to intervene in the controversy about the style of the new Town Hall in 1854 (he was one of the leading advocates of the inclusion of an imposing tower in the design).[56] But his speciality was educational causes. He devoted an immense amount of time to Leeds Grammar School (where he had been a pupil), the Yorkshire College (precursor of Leeds University), and the Leeds School Board. The only striking omission is the Church: Heaton had moved from the Independents to the Church of England while still a boy. He carried out the prescribed observances, but no more.[57]

Heaton's life was presented to the public in 1883 by the journalist Thomas Wemyss Reid as a commentary on the transformation which had overtaken Leeds since the 1830s. At some cost to his medical practice, so Reid claimed,

Heaton's selfless labours had both contributed to and exemplified the growth of Leeds as a city, a society and a public sphere.[58] What Reid's account obscured was the toll which this public activity took on Heaton's domestic life. We are given a reticent and glowing glimpse of a happy marriage and a playful father, but no inkling of what Heaton chose to sacrifice. On the day of his daughter Helen's birth in 1851, his diary entry reads:

> I was considerably disappointed that the baby was not a boy. The same Evening I was at a meeting of the Conversation Club at which a new Society 'The Leeds Improvement Society' was constituted; and I was made Honorary Secretary.[59]

Heaton liked to think that his daily routine brought him back home around six o'clock for tea and an evening spent with his family (dinner having been taken at 2 p.m.). Yet fireside moments of this kind happened so infrequently that they were a matter for comment in his diary. Heaton did not reproach himself with neglect of family duties, but he keenly felt the loss of leisure – the 'desultory idleness' which came his way all too rarely.[60] He wrote to his daughter Helen, now 22, in 1873:

> I pursue my usual hackneyed routine; seeing patients; attending meetings; looking after the affairs of all the family including your aunt Ellen, and providing for their wants and keeping things going as well as I can, and generally doing a great deal for other people and for uncommonly little pay.[61]

This was an oft-repeated complaint. Work, family cares and public duties conspired to rob him of leisure. In writing to Helen, he emphasized the domestic burden in order to play on his daughter's guilt, but it was 'attending meetings' which so often broke the camel's back. As he told his wife Fanny, evening engagements were so 'very destructive of time'.[62] The idea put forward by his biographer that Heaton's life was characterized by a fine balance between public activities and domestic pursuits does not bear inspection. John Heaton relished sociability and the satisfactions of a reputation as a public man, but he was well aware of the toll which they took on both his family life and his health.

★

Bourgeois Victorian culture found the conflict between fireside and homosocial pleasures comparatively one-sided, because virtue seemed so obviously on the side of home. But when homosocial ties were graced with the dignity of public duty, two undisputed goods were pitched against each other, and the conflict became more evenly matched. Neither sphere could be cultivated to the exclusion of the other without reproach. When Queen Victoria married Prince Albert in 1840, it was widely feared that the marriage would bring royalty into contempt – ironically in view of the Prince Consort's subsequent reputation as the embodiment of selfless devotion to the common good. John Ruskin's father, as shocked as anyone, told his wife, 'We must look to our domestic Circles & our own neighbourhood & let politics alone'.[63] Here the claims of home were held to justify a fastidious recoil from public affairs. This was a stance which did not go down well with the apostles of domesticity. As John Angell James put it, while married men should not need public amusements, they certainly owed public duties, and some sacrifice of domestic comfort might be called for.[64] But if the totally domesticated man fell well short of the mark, the workaholic was hardly less reprehensible. The man for whom work was everything, and who returned to his home only for food and rest, was pursuing a path of self-destruction and social irresponsibility. This was the charge which Sarah Holden had levelled at her husband during their prolonged quarrels about how much time they should spend together, and where. Isaac's resolve to 'stay close to the Business', at the cost of neglecting his wife, took him close to the limit of what was acceptable in a dutiful husband.[65]

Quite ingenious attempts were made to square the circle by showing how private virtue and public duty were mutually supportive. In the first place, patriarchal authority in the household was buttressed by eminence in the public sphere. It was a commonplace of Victorian obituaries that the public man was supported by a self-denying wife and admiring children. It would have been nearer the mark to say that the public reputation of the household head imposed on other family members. Many Victorian households bore witness to the belief that the 'great' man was entitled to special deference in his domestic circle. Of course much the same was conceded to the role of breadwinner, but attention to the *public* good placed the authority of the paterfamilias on a more exalted, even godlike plane. Children especially were likely to be overly impressed by their father's importance in the wider world. Writing of the Positivist leader Frederic Harrison, his son Austin recalled, 'Very early in life I grasped that my father was not only head of the family, but "head" of something outside as well'.[66] During the 1860s the sons of Edward Benson knew that their father's word as headmaster of Wellington College was law. They were awed by the string of eminent school governors who dined at the family table, and they were even more impressed when their father became a bishop in 1877. Small wonder that a dressing-down in Benson's study was so dreaded.[67] From this perspective the privileges of private patriarchy were no more than the public man's due. Younger men who achieved early public prominence were indignant if they were denied these privileges. John Heaton was outraged when his father-in-law-to-be rebuffed his suit in 1849 on the grounds that he was 'not a *public character*'. Heaton was already a keen society man and was at that very time canvassing for money to remove the debt on the Leeds Philharmonic Hall. As he told his fiancée Fanny, 'I don't think I know another person of my age [31] in the town who does so much public work of a gratuitous kind'.[68] The same argument might be deployed against an over-bearing father, though with less hope of success. In 1839 the young Edward

Herford was already a member of Manchester Municipal Council and heavily involved in the campaign for working-class Lyceums: 'my plans for the public good are all in good train'. Yet living under his father's roof he still found himself in a 'state of infantine subjection' which ill accorded with his public prominence.[69]

If high standing in professional or associational life enhanced one's domestic position, the converse was also true. The reputation of public figures was reinforced by evidence of a heartfelt commitment to domestic values. The man whose family life was in disorder or disrepute was thought unlikely to be an honourable or devoted public servant. One of the things which made the Victorians uncomfortable about the heroes of the previous generation was their disregard for the proprieties of domestic life. The adultery of Nelson and the philandering of Byron were a distinct embarrassment. The bourgeois public figure was expected to be not only blameless, but devoted. Politicians were commended for seizing every opportunity to hurry back to their domestic havens. Gladstone's much publicized tree-felling at Hawarden could be interpreted in many ways, but it clearly suggested the simple diversions of a home-loving patriarch. John Bright was another Liberal statesman who reaped credit from his reputation as a 'plain man' with strong family emotions.[70]

The remarkable case of General Henry Havelock, the hero of the Indian Mutiny, shows how avid the Victorians were for reassurance that a public man whose life could not be other than dangerous and peripatetic was at heart a domesticated husband. Havelock died in 1857, towards the end of a string of victories over the rebels in India, during which he had been saluted by the English newspapers as 'a second Clive'. He contradicted the military stereotype in several ways. He had risen from relatively obscure middle-class origins, and he was a pious Baptist. Above all, as Graham Dawson has shown, he was seen as a family man – the head of a Christian household whose first duty was to wife and children. Havelock had returned to an Indian posting six years before the rebellion, at the comparatively advanced age of 56. Already in 1848 he had contemplated retirement to a peaceful country cottage where he could enjoy family life without interruption. But in the end his domestic responsibilities demanded a different course of action. His early biographers emphasized that his motive in embarking on his final and glorious tour of duty was to secure the financial future of his wife and family when he died. There was a touching irony that this decision brought forward the day of his death, and a further irony that it also yielded a substantial widow's pension from a grateful nation which went far beyond Havelock's modest hopes of financial security. Public life in bourgeois societies is commonly supposed to be understood on its own terms, according to a public standard of rationality. The popular adulation of Havelock is striking evidence of how far the Victorian public was prepared to recognize the private springs of public conduct.[71]

Behind this foregrounding of private virtues lay the belief – or rather the pious hope – that they were fundamentally no different from the qualities required of men in public life, and that public service depended on a prior adaptation to the moral disciplines of domesticity. According to this view, training in 'character' at home was training for the public sphere too. This was the sense in which Thomas Hughes affirmed that domestic relations were the shrewdest test of manhood.[72] The young Walter Bagehot defended the institution of marriage to his friend Richard Hutton, arguing that, since the affections were an indispensable guide to human action, the 'strong habitual feeling of disinterested affection' between husband and wife was a vital aid to the performance of public duty.[73] Those men who had least regard for home, or no domestic circle at all, made the worst citizens, because they lacked those daily reminders of the necessity for responsible authority, mutual rights and mutual service, on which the well-being of the body politic depended. In that sense, 'family government underlies all forms of government', as the Revd S.S. Pugh put it.[74] If the household really was a microcosm of the body politic, it followed that those who governed their households well possessed political virtue and should be recognized accordingly. This argument was not immediately advanced by the new, virtuous middle class. It was given little stress during the prolonged political crisis which led up to the Reform Act of 1832. But after 1832 domesticity quickly became a talisman of civic virtue and a means of demonstrating middle-class superiority over the morally lax aristocracy. Indeed so prevalent was the idea that working-class leaders took it up as well, arguing that male artisans had cast aside the rough ways of the tavern and the street, and now exhibited the same home-loving qualities as their bourgeois counterparts. On these grounds all workers who were heads of household should exercise political rights too. This became one of the strongest arguments in favour of extending the franchise during the period between the First and Second Reform Acts (1832–67). 'What danger is there in giving the franchise to householders?' asked Richard Cobden in the House of Commons in 1848. 'They are the fathers of families; they constitute the laborious and industrious population.'[75]

Opponents of franchise extension could easily cite evidence to suggest that working-class household heads were not the responsible hard-working paragons whom Cobden praised. But by 1848 the reputation of middle-class manhood for domestic virtue was almost unassailable. The ideal of domesticity and the self-image of the Victorian bourgeoisie had converged to a remarkable extent. The paterfamilias was viewed as someone who ruled his household, and who spoke for his dependants when he made his contribution to ruling the country by casting his vote or by raising his voice in public. The implications for equality and openness within the household were not promising. Men's arguments for an extension of the franchise could easily be read as a further buttressing of patriarchal authority. It has been fairly said of John Bright's vision of household suffrage that it amounted to 'a confederacy of absolute despots', each supposedly exercising the same unquestioned patriarchal authority as Bright himself did.[76] But only a small minority of feminist campaigners made this case at the time. The link between responsible (male) headship of the household and responsible (male) citizenship was deeply rooted in mid-Victorian political culture, whatever the contradictions in the real world.

★

On a simple reading of 'separate spheres' the sharpest conflict in men's lives should have been between work and home. The more alienating the employment, the greater the tendency to conduct life in separate compartments. The classic literary expression of this split comes in William Hale White's autobiographical novel, *Mark Rutherford's Deliverance*, which draws on his own experience as a junior employee at Somerset House in the 1850s.

> I cut off my office life ... from my life at home so completely that I was two selves, and my true self was not stained by contact with my other self. It was a comfort to me to think the moment the clock struck seven that my second self died, and that my first self suffered nothing by having anything to do with it ... I was a citizen, walking London streets; I had my opinions upon human beings and books; I was on equal terms with my friends; I was Ellen's husband; I was, in short, a man.[77]

The poignancy of Hale White's divided identity turned on the need for both remunerative work and domestic life. Both were plainly essential to a fully realized masculinity, and the important thing was to maintain a balance between them.

When the demands of male sociability and public duty were added to those of work, the scope for conflict was intensified. Sarah Ellis, in speaking regretfully of the 'two sets of consciences' in many men – 'one conscience for the sanctuary, and another for the desk and counter' – underestimated the complexities.[78] As the historian H.L. Malchow has put it, many middle-class men had 'layered identities' corresponding to home, club, office, chapel and so on.[79] Each placed a premium on different qualities, and each was potentially in conflict with some or all the others. Men conformed to the standards set by their wives when at home, while honouring a very different code when in the company of other men. The smiling father might also be a harsh and inflexible employer. Often these tensions were spirited away in some bland formula. For example, Edward Baines of Leeds was a printer and stationer, a philanthropist, and an MP. After his death in 1848 it was said that 'the pure joys of domestic life, the pleasures of industry and the satisfactions of doing good, combined to make him as happy as he was useful'.[80] Some such trinity of virtues appears in countless memorials of the day. Other writers were more alert to the possibilities of hypocrisy in the life of a busy public figure. The biographer of the hosiery merchant and MP, Samuel Morley, stressed that 'Mr Morley was not one man in business and another at home'. Whether with his family at Stamford Hill or in the office in Wood Street, every task was to be done well, and not a moment of time must be wasted. Samuel Morley declined openings in public life beyond his seat in the Commons. 'He never allowed any public duties to come between himself and his family. For him, indeed, there was a time for everything, but that time was regulated by the claims of home.'[81]

The Bradford newspaper proprietor William Byles presents a particularly attractive instance of private and public demands being reconciled. In a family memoir of unusual vitality, his routines in middle age were recalled by one of his younger sons. In his fifties, with a large family, William Byles used to wake up his children and dispense bacon and coffee to the whole family. On his way to work at the offices of the *Bradford Observer* he did much of the shopping, personally selecting the joints of meat. He was back at home for dinner and a post-prandial nap, before returning to the office for the early evening. On Saturday afternoons he repaired (along with the Independent minister) to a friend's house for billiards, tea and a pipe. Sundays were given over to chapel, where he served as deacon and trustee. He attended meetings of the Bradford Philosophical Society and supported the subscription concerts. He made a point of accompanying his children to the dentist. He took part in family holidays, even if these were often no further afield than Ilkley. Domesticity, conviviality, cultural activity and a paid position of great local importance were brought together with little apparent strain. Only elected local office, an obvious ambition for a man of his influence, was kept at bay.[82]

Frederick Byles's account of his father commands considerable credibility because the detail is so fresh and specific. But without private manuscript records it is hard to know what allowance should be made for family piety. One cannot help asking, for instance, why Frederick has so little to say about his mother, who was long dead by the time he published the memoir of his father. The fact is that where we have letters and diaries, the fit between public and private is never as seamless as the published account suggests. William Gaskell was doubtless thought of in Manchester as a fortunate man able to carry out his work as minister from home and enjoy the attentions of his lively family. But evenings were filled with lectures, committee work and dinners with fellow ministers. He spent most of his daytime hours in his beloved study, 'out of which room by his own free will he would never stir', wrote Elizabeth. 'When he *is* at home, we only see him at meal times.'[83] From the opposite end of the religious spectrum, Edward Benson's mode of didactic moralizing, formed in the public sphere of church and school, was visited on his own children with little dilution; and consequently they grew up starved of the signs of affection. The stresses in John Heaton's life of public service have already been described.

Middle-class Victorian men were expected to be both paragons of domestic virtue and devotees of the common good. This tension between public and private exposed perhaps the most testing contradiction in the ideal of domesticity. For middle-class women the issue caused much less heart-searching. While never very far from the mind of the woman who aspired to cut a figure in the local community, the tension betwen private and public scarcely troubled her more retiring sister devoted to domestic duties, and commended for it in the advice literature of the day. Men, on the other hand, were in the privileged position of passing freely between home, work and the public sphere. Yet that very freedom set up the strain of competing demands. Most bourgeois men would have agreed that there was more to life than the conventional antithesis between home and work. Public duty on the one hand, and the pleasures of association on the other, demanded a space in men's lives, in ways which often transgressed the conventions of domesticity. In the last two decades of Victoria's reign the strains would become increasingly visible.

PART THREE

Domesticity under Strain, c. 1870–1900

CHAPTER SEVEN

The Decline of Deference

Middle-class domesticity in Victorian England could hardly be described as an unqualified endorsement of patriarchal privilege. For a majority of families, domesticity was premised on the practical foundation of the absentee breadwinner, while its ideological foundation was widely taken to be women's moral superiority. Both these elements – the material and the moral – served to enhance the status of wives. The prestige of motherhood was greatly increased; housewifery was redefined as the art (or even science) of household management; and the local standing of the family became more than ever dependent on the social skills of the wife. But, in principle at least, the prestige of patriarchy was undiminished. However much the running of the household might have fallen into women's hands, there was little disposition to challenge the master overtly in his private domain. The point is nicely made by the rituals of welcome which marked the husband's return each evening: they reaffirmed his domestic authority, while passing lightly over the female effort and initiative which had gone on in his absence. That the appearance of patriarchal prestige was upheld in this way explains in no small measure the success of the early Victorians in reconciling masculinity with domesticity.

In the late Victorian period this easy assumption of domestic patriarchy came under open strain. For the first time the legal *carte blanche* of the paterfamilias was subjected to significant inroads, by parliamentary legislation as well as judicial pronouncement. Male sexuality was the subject of unprecedented critique. The writers of advice books demanded higher standards of behaviour from husbands and tended to blame them when marriages came unstuck. The role and capacities of fathers were widely disparaged, and children of both sexes were less inclined to accept paternal authority. All of this was intensely scrutinized by the press, as every symptom of gender conflict or generational tension attracted analysis and polemic.[1] The relation of this vigorous public discourse to actual family experience was contradictory. On one reading, the reduction of patriarchal powers corresponded with a more relaxed domestic style, in which men were more accessible to their wives and children, and little disposed to use any of the powers which the law in theory conferred on them.

But that gentler pattern of family relations was far from universal in the late Victorian middle class. Many men who had themselves been brought up in an atmosphere of authority and distance could not imagine family life being conducted in any other spirit; others who doubted their own capacity to make workable relationships with women found reassurance in the legal powers of husband and father. From this perspective the public undermining of private patriarchy during the 1880s and 1890s was highly unwelcome. The merits of living in domesticity were no longer so clear to this generation of middle-class men, and (as the final chapter will show) increasing numbers either postponed marriage or else carved out a larger sphere for all-male society within marriage. At that point the characteristically Victorian culture of domesticity can be said to have entered a new phase.

*

So decisive a shift did not of course occur in isolation, but was intimately bound up with parallel changes in Victorian culture and society. The most obvious of these was the change in the position of women. Less often linked with the standing of men, but in some ways more fundamental, was the sea-change in the religious climate of Victorian England.

By the 1880s the Christian religion was subject to pressures which would have been inconceivable fifty years earlier. The early Victorians had been confronted by a sometimes baffling degree of denominational choice, and in many areas of life they had doubtless worn their religious profession lightly, but the authority of the Christian faith had not been in question, except among a tiny minority of free thinkers. The middle decades of the century proved to be a turning point. The new 'higher criticism' of the Bible from Germany compromised the credibility of holy writ as a historical record, including the life of Jesus himself. Advances in geology earlier in the century had already cast doubt on the presumed date of the Creation. The evolutionary biology of Charles Darwin, if accepted as the authoritative findings of science, exposed the story of the Creation in Genesis as no more than a cultural myth. One immediate consequence of these revolutionary developments in literary and scientific study was that a growing number of people were emboldened to question openly the morality of Christian doctrine. Darwin himself referred to God as 'a revengeful tyrant'. Only a small rump of Nonconformists now believed in the full rigour of predestination. Fewer and fewer intelligent Christians were prepared to accept eternal damnation. These Evangelical nostrums were now regularly condemned in print as morally offensive.[2]

This onslaught resulted in a relative decline in middle-class membership of the churches. Agnosticism surfaced in the 1860s and had become fairly acceptable in polite society by the 1880s. But for every intellectual like Frederic Harrison or Leslie Stephen who formally renounced Christianity, there were by the 1880s countless others who felt sufficient doubt or distaste to stay away from church and to abandon any regular spiritual discipline. Family life was probably even more influenced by the liberalization of belief on the part of the churches themselves. The response of the clergy to the various assaults on religion was complex. For some, the rising tide of doubt was a cue for the vigorous restatement of fundamentalist Evangelicalism – as in the recurrent 'revivals' and in the Salvation Army, founded in the 1860s. But a much more widespread response was to make official theology less vulnerable to moral attack by emphasizing its humanity. In both the established and Nonconformist churches there was less stress on the atonement, and more interest in Jesus as an exemplar. God was increasingly presented as an indulgent father instead of a stern judge. Social Christianity interpreted the religious life as a call to benevolence in the community rather than a daily discipline of introspection conducted in private.[3]

During the early Victorian period the dominant Evangelical strand of Christianity had strongly endorsed patriarchal authority. It had played up the all-seeing, all-judging power of God, and then cast the household head in the role of his earthly representative. Of course Evangelicalism also placed a heavy burden of expectation on the moral mother, with on the whole positive implications for women's domestic influence, and in practice the husband's working routine away from home projected his wife into a more prominent role. But her prominence was seen as complementing rather than supplanting the man's authority. In Evangelical thinking it was for the man to take the spiritual lead when he was at home, conducting family prayers and shepherding his household to church or chapel on Sunday. He remained the family's representative before the throne of grace, supported by an image of God the Father as puissant, distant and just. His word should therefore be final, however much he might consult his wife or be subject to her influence.

In the late Victorian period the Evangelical model began to seem like an embarrassing residue from the past. For many Christians it was at odds with the more accessible and indulgent pattern of heavenly fatherhood now stressed by theologians. The parable of the Prodigal Son provided a convenient reminder that God was a tender parent, as well as a king in majesty.[4] The moral for earthly fathers was clear. The judging, watchful father of Evangelical tradition seemed absurd and oppressive. As early as 1876 family prayers and grace before meals were said to be in decline, and this trend became very marked over the next generation. Domestic devotions survived longest in the form of bedtime prayers by mother and child: the Mothers' Union, which strongly advocated this practice, was founded in the 1870s and boasted a membership of 200,000 by the end of the century.[5]

It is no coincidence that the modern materialist figure of Santa Claus became established in England just as the spiritual underpinnings of paternal authority were shifting. As a personification of the festive season, Father Christmas had been known since the Middle Ages. In so far as he had any special significance for children, it was to commend the good and – just as important – chastise the naughty. In that respect he mirrored the familial authority of the paterfamilias.

"HERE WE ARE AGAIN!!"

16. Santa Claus as returning father: 'Here We Are Again!', *Punch*, 25 December 1880.

The association of Father Christmas with chimneys and stockings did not develop until the 1870s. Both the name 'Santa Claus' and the new emphasis on gifts were a largely unacknowledged import from the United States. The new form of Father Christmas was as strongly identified as the old one with the father in the family. In one of the first descriptions, dating from 1879, Edwin Lees reported on current practice in the West Country:

> On Christmas Eve, when the inmates of a house in the country retire to bed, all those desirous of a present place a stocking outside the door of their bedroom, with the expectation that some mythical being called *Santiclaus* will fill the stocking or place something within it by the morning. This is of course well known, and the master of the house does in reality place a Christmas gift secretly in each stocking . . .[6]

The presents miraculously conveyed by sleigh to every home in the land were free of any association with workaday toil. (The notion that Santa Claus had actually *made* the toys he distributed seems not to have caught on, unlike in America where this conceit appealed as a fitting symbol of enlightened entrepreneurship.) But the new version of Father Christmas certainly served to reinforce the status of the father as the source of material largesse. And like other forms of paternal gift-giving, it suggested that the mundane business of earning the family crust might in a moment be transformed into plenty, surprise and delight. The traditional association with discipline was weakened. Recalling his childhood in the early 1880s, John Lionel Tayler noted how much his Unitarian parents liked the idea of Father Christmas, because it expressed 'the spirit of unselfish hospitality, goodwill and fatherhood'; the harsher associations of the paternal role had no place. Father Christmas was now the apotheosis of the generous, indulgent father.[7]

For those in touch with the most advanced secular thinking, Darwinian biology was even more destructive of the traditional paternal role. The new evolutionary thinking swept away the awesome image of the Father as Creator. It also greatly increased the prestige of biological ways of thinking about social issues, including family life, and fatherhood did not emerge well from this. Analogies with the natural world confirmed the centrality of the maternal instinct and maternal nurture, while conceding little more than a procreative function to the father.[8]

There was a sense in which domesticity stepped into the place of religion. John Ruskin's 'Of Queens' Gardens', with its reverent invocation of the sacred power of home, is the representative text. First published in 1864, it was frequently reprinted and cast a long shadow over the late Victorians.[9] It was characteristic of most free-thinkers that they retained a fierce moral sense even as they jettisoned its traditional doctrinal underpinning. For them the home symbolized the moral verities of life no less – and sometimes more – than in the case of conventional believers. The atheist Leslie Stephen projected strong feelings of this kind on to his second wife, Julia Duckworth. 'You see, I have not got any Saints and you must not be angry if I put you in the place where my Saints ought to be,' he told her in one of his letters proposing marriage.[10] Ernest Newton reflected a widespread view when he told his colleagues in the Architectural Association in 1891:

> Nowadays, when all religions are assailed, and we believe in nothing very strongly, it is almost impossible to make our churches express anything more than a sort of galvanised enthusiasm ... Belief in the sacredness of home-life, however, is still left to us, and is *itself a religion*, pure and easy to believe. It requires no elaborate creeds, its worship is the simplest, its discipline the gentlest and its rewards are peace and contentment.[11] [emphasis added]

But the domesticity invoked by free-thinkers and rationalists was subtly altered from what their parents had known. Rationalists were not necessarily quick to

abdicate traditional paternal rights, as the story of Leslie Stephen's relationship
with his daughters demonstrates only too well. But the air of absurdity which
attached to Stephen's paterfamilial *gravitas* even then, one suspects, is an
accurate reflection of how conventions had changed. One of the main
psychological props of paternal authority had gone.

★

For largely independent reasons, the standing of children and childhood was
rising, as that of fathers and fatherhood was falling. The late nineteenth century
saw the working through of some of the major themes which had been
announced earlier in the century. This was in many ways the climax of the
Romantic view of the child as precious innocent, with Evangelical notions of
original sin retreating to the margins.[12] The late Victorians were even less
prepared than their grandparents to recognize childhood sexuality, and they
were all the more shocked when confronted with evidence of it. Sentimental
images of children, and especially little girls, proliferated. In Carolyn Steedman's notion of childhood as the authentic site of adult interiority, it is clear
that the late nineteenth century was a pivotal stage of consolidation in a process
of cultural adjustment stretching from the Romantic period proper to the inter-
war years.[13] The late Victorians went to considerable lengths to make reality
conform with their vision of childhood. The practical consequences were most
dramatic in working-class life, with the steady eroding of child labour, the
intervention of the state in cases of domestic cruelty from 1889, and the
enforcement of universal elementary education in the 1870s.[14]

But respect for the experience of childhood and the aspiration to enhance the
child's life chances transcended elite discourse about the poor. Childhood at all
levels of society was affected. In the case of the middle class, the most tangible
evidence of this was the prolonging of material dependence on adults. For boys
in comfortably off homes especially, the length of childhood was tending to
increase, as professional prospects dictated a continuation of schooling to 18 or
19, with often further study beyond that. There were far more respectable
young men in receipt of a parental allowance and subject to adult instruction in
the 1880s and 1890s than ever before. Less easily demonstrated, but nonetheless
profound, was the impact of imaginative literature for children. The best
writing for younger children (in a golden age for children's literature) strongly
sympathized with the imaginative lives of its readers. For older children, the
new mass-circulation magazines, notably the *Boy's Own Paper* with a circulation
of half a million in the 1880s, were eagerly read by middle-class as well as
working-class boys. Some of them may still have been cast in a somewhat
didactic form, but they certainly reinforced the awareness of childhood as a
separate stage of life.[15]

As these literary instances imply, much of Romantic thinking about
childhood was fantasy. But, as Hugh Cunningham points out, it was fantasy
with a strong appeal for men, and in those areas where paternal responsibility

for children was acknowledged their behaviour was affected.[16] Punishment is the clearest instance of this. No doubt the greater privacy of middle-class homes allowed abuse to go undetected, but the physical chastisement of boys by their parents offended against up-to-date notions of the care and empathy due to children; and in fact the evidence of diaries and autobiographies points to a steady decline of corporal punishment in the home.[17] There were certainly limits to the application of a Romantic view of the child. Upper middle-class fathers were not noted for their reluctance to consign their tender offspring to the rigours of public schooling. But all the signs are that higher levels of respect and consideration towards children prevailed in bourgeois families at the end of the century than at the beginning. This could hardly be achieved without some questioning of the powers conventionally vested in fatherhood.

*

If the enhanced standing of children unsettled the role of paterfamilias, the new confidence of women presented an overt challenge. It is well known that the late nineteenth century was a turning point in feminist consciousness; indeed in recent years the *fin de siècle* has become a byword for gender turmoil.[18] That sense of disturbance was keenly experienced at the time. It arose from men's sense that women were staking out claims and taking initiatives in more areas and with greater energy than ever before. As early as 1882 the trend towards sexual equality was sufficiently alarming for one male novelist to write a satire set in a twentieth-century Britain which has fallen under complete female sway and needs liberation by male leadership.[19] By the 1890s alarm at the new pretensions of women was common in conservative circles. The early and mid-Victorian period had certainly featured campaigns on specific women's issues, like the laws relating to married women's property or the guardianship of minors, and these had brought to prominence individuals like Caroline Norton and Barbara Bodichon. But in the late Victorian period the gains made by women in education, employment and personal freedom, not to mention the unfulfilled but vociferous demand for an equal political voice, suggested something much more formidable: a movement, even a revolt, sharing a common aspiration and graced by a galaxy of talent. From the mid-1880s until the end of Victoria's reign the 'sex question' was hardly ever out of the newspapers and journals.

The social context of this ferment lay in a problem which had caused great concern to the mid-Victorians – 'surplus women'. Common wisdom declared that the proper destiny of women was marriage, but the excess of females over males and the socially sanctioned practice of late marriage by men decreed that this destiny would elude an increasing proportion of middle-class women. The prospects for lifelong spinsters were not promising. As daughters they were expected to be a help to mother and a comfort to father. But in affluent households the proliferation of servants meant that there was little domestic work to be done, and helping mother might mean no more than accompanying her on calls and following her lead in voluntary charitable work. In the less well-off home it was highly unlikely that family resources would stretch to a lifelong income for an unmarried daughter. She faced the prospect of destitution or low-status (and low-paid) work such as governessing. The answer lay in education – as a means of dignifying the leisure of the rich spinster, and as a route to employment for those in more difficult circumstances. The number of girls' secondary schools founded in the second half of the century is a testimony to the work of pioneer women educationalists. But it also reflected the readiness of fathers to spend money on their daughters' education in order to protect them from the indignity of unendowed spinsterhood.

The new schools tended to be socially conservative. Education at Cheltenham Ladies' College or the new urban high schools may not have taught girls to question the gender regime of the day, but it certainly enhanced their job prospects. The small but growing number of women who proceeded to higher education were more likely to encounter radical thinking, but their main significance too lay in their impact on employment – in this case professional positions with a higher profile. At the same time changes in the economy increased the demand for female employees in schools, hospitals and offices. As a result the numbers of women teachers, nurses, secretaries and clerks grew substantially, while women made smaller but highly visible inroads into professions like journalism and the factory inspectorate. By 1891 some 240,000 women were reckoned to be in 'professional occupations', which covered all jobs considered suitable for ladies.[20] The working girl had become a familiar feature of offices and shops in all the big cities. Not all fathers were persuaded of the logic of this process. Sometimes daughters were compelled to contribute to the household income because their father had abdicated from the role of breadwinner, and feminist polemic made much of these cases.[21] More typical was the father who had good reason to doubt his ability to endow his daughter for life, and who encouraged or permitted her to follow a profession in order to ensure her material prospects.

This was the context for the emergence of the New Woman. The term was not invented until 1894, but it reflected trends which had been discernible since the 1880s.[22] Certainly smoking and cycling, the two most visible badges of emancipated womanhood, had been around for some years. The label was most convincingly applied to the young middle-class woman who not only had a job but maintained herself and lived on her own, or with another young woman, in an apartment or 'chambers'. This entailed a complete departure from the domestic obligations traditionally fulfilled by this age group, and was correctly summed up as 'the revolt of the daughters' – another coinage by the press of the day. The revolt reserved much of its animus for mothers, who represented exactly the model of womanhood which their daughters were renouncing, and who were the first line in the enforcement of domestic discipline. Indeed in some cases it was the father who encouraged his daughter to test the limits of convention: the social reformer and politician Eleanor Rathbone who began work in the 1890s in Liverpool under William Rathbone's wing is a striking example.[23] But the New Woman unequivocally represented a challenge to patriarchy. She sought to lead an independent life not so much from necessity as from choice. In office work, in journalism and to some extent in teaching, the New Woman's professional ambitions trespassed on male preserves of employment. Her insistence on appearing in public and private without a chaperon was a rejection of men's protection. Her claim to intellectual equality conflicted with deeply held assumptions about women's inferiority – the more so when it took an advanced feminist form. Most important of all, the New Woman's determination to live away from the parental home challenged traditional notions of domestic order, while her readiness to postpone or renounce marriage brought to the surface deep misgivings about the prospects for social reproduction. In short, the New Woman provoked because she refused to lead her life by the patriarchal rules.[24]

An independent life was echoed in independent thought. The last two decades of the nineteenth century were one of those periods when the gap between feminist writing and mainstream discourse was at its widest. In pamphlets and respectable journals, the position of the married woman was compared with that of the slave or the prostitute. A system which aimed to ensnare the woman like prey or to confine her to a gilded cage was 'disguised barbarism', in the words of Mona Caird.[25] The solution was variously presented as a drastic overhaul of domestic life, a new system of education, and – most threatening of all – the withdrawal of the state from the marriage contract. New Woman novelists like George Egerton and Sarah Grand embroidered these themes with a directness which sometimes smacked of overt sexual antagonism. Compared with the tenor of women's writing in the previous generation, this was heady stuff – intoxicating or terrifying or ridiculous, but never a matter of indifference.[26] Domestic patriarchy could hardly remain untouched. When every allowance is made for media distortion and rhetorical overkill, the New Woman was a tangible reality, daily encountered in the drawing room, as well as the office, the class room and the street. The advanced views on social and sexual questions with which she became associated were deeply disturbing to polite society. Cultural reaction verged on the hysterical. In particular, the work of male artists of the period, with its recurrent images of predatory seduction, suggests an almost morbid fear of women's sexuality. The mockery directed at the New Woman by the press in the 1890s reflected an acute anxiety that the new freedoms claimed by women in public would disrupt traditional notions of gender inequality in the private sphere.[27]

★

During the late Victorian period some very deep inroads were made into patriarchal power. The most clear-cut was the discrediting – and partial fencing in – of male sexuality. The Contagious Diseases Acts of the 1860s had stretched the double standard of sexual conduct to breaking point. The arbitrary treatment meted out to prostitutes (as well as innocent suspects) under the Acts only served to highlight the blind eye which society turned on their customers. Why, Josephine Butler asked, should women forced into vice by poverty bear the brunt of the criminal law, when the real cause of prostitution was the lax morals of young men? Her indignation was directed not only at the common soldiers and sailors whose health was the ostensible reason for the legislation, but also at the moneyed youth of the middle and upper classes who thought nothing of preying on those with nothing to sell but their bodies.[28] The campaign against the Contagious Diseases Acts tapped a strong current of Evangelical morality as well as avowedly feminist sentiments. Its success in getting the Acts partially suspended in 1883, and repealed three years later, encouraged a more ambitious programme. The state was now expected not only to negate the acceptance of prostitution which had been implied by the Contagious Diseases Acts, but to go on the offensive against it. Under the Criminal Law Amendment Act of 1885 there was a severe clamp-down on brothel-keeping, and the age of consent was abruptly raised from 12 to 16 as a means of restricting child prostitution. Most ambitious of all, the reformers aimed to carry the war into the enemy camp by transforming the sexual culture of men in the name of 'social purity'. This was taken to exclude a range of practices, including masturbation and homosexuality. But the central concern of social purity was the double standard. Its champions strenuously rejected the common wisdom that prostitution provided a necessary outlet for men's sexual drive, and asserted that the same standards of chastity were applicable to both sexes. The Social Purity Alliance had been founded as early as 1873, to be followed by the Young Men's Friendly Society in 1879. The movement assumed a much higher profile with the setting up in 1883 of the Church of England Purity Society and the White Cross Army under the energetic leadership of Jane Ellice Hopkins. These organizations urged men to take a purity pledge modelled on the temperance pledge. The numbers who did so, though recorded in their thousands, were modest compared with the huge impact of the temperance societies, but the propaganda was considerable. Ellice Hopkins wrote a set of pamphlets called 'The White Cross Series: For Men Only': *True Manliness* (1883) sold 300,000 copies in one year alone.[29] Social purity may have been a minority cause, but it undoubtedly brought a harsher spotlight to bear on male sexuality; where once there had been an accommodating silence, there was now exposure and condemnation.

In some ways this relentless critique was supportive of masculine domesticity. Josephine Butler was clear that the common factor which linked the unacceptable conduct of the sailor, the soldier and the university student was the lack of improving (and feminine) domestic influence. As one article attacking the Contagious Diseases Acts put it, the common soldier enjoyed 'in his barrack-room ... none of the comforts of domesticity – he is there compelled to herd indiscriminately with men whose bad example may exercise a pestilent influence on his own character'.[30] But although male domesticity was stressed as the solution to the vices of youth, it is hard to avoid the conclusion that the constant harping on sexual delinquency damaged masculine prestige in general. Men were toppled from their pedestal, leaving women's claim to moral primacy more convincing than ever.

In the opinion of Social Purity campaigners this adjustment in the moral economy of marriage had important implications for parental roles. The traditional expectation had been that boys be instructed in the facts of life and the rules of sexual behaviour by their fathers, since these matters were integral to manliness. (Austin Harrison recalled of his childhood in the 1870s that punishment and sex belonged to his father's sphere, while his mother had charge of clothes and sickness.)[31] Too often, according to the protagonists of Social Purity, that instruction had either not been carried out at all, or had been perverted by the complaisant morality of the 'man of the world'. The lax morals of young men bore witness to the negligence of generations of fathers. It was time for mothers to take the lead, by associating sexuality in their sons' minds with altruism, sacredness and motherhood itself. Boys must be *trained* in purity, declared Ellice Hopkins, and the mother was uniquely qualified for the role because her own person symbolized purity and altruism; if she had the courage to tackle these issues head-on, she would forge a link between sex and motherhood in her son's mind and so protect other women from the consequences of impurity.[32] A more secular version of the same demand was to be found among sexual radicals. Reacting to the child prostitution revelations of W.T. Stead in 1885, Olive Schreiner remarked, 'When we have pure strong mothers able to see the beauty and importance of the sexual side of life, we will have pure strong men able to guide themselves nobly'.[33]

Social Purity concentrated its fire on the immorality of bachelors and did not, on the whole, question conventional views of marriage. But the more radical feminists did not shrink from spelling out the consequences of vice for family life. The embarrassing issue of marital infidelity was largely sidestepped, but sex before marriage cast a dark shadow. Men with a 'past' risked blighting the domestic circle, since their venereal disease could later infect both wives and children. This point was passionately argued by several New Woman novelists of the period, notably Sarah Grand in *The Heavenly Twins* (1893).[34] Even without this poisoned residue of youthful immorality, men's sexual conduct in marriage was found wanting. Feminists complained, not that men sought satisfaction elsewhere, but rather that they burdened their wives with excessive sexual demands at great cost to their health and their personal autonomy. Public fears about the spread of syphilis lent credence to such views. From 1880 onwards Elizabeth Wolstenholme Elmy campaigned for the recognition of the wife's rights over her own person and for the legal acceptance of the offence of marital rape. These demands never received attention in Parliament. But if Dr William Acton is to be believed, middle-class wives were already asserting the right to withhold sexual access by the mid-1870s (he blamed it on the insidious influence of John Stuart Mill). The publicity given to views like Wolstenholme Elmy's can only have fuelled a wider discontent on the part of wives. Sexual emancipation in the modern sense was far from the agenda of late Victorian feminism. Since the double standard was so blatant, and the danger to life from childbirth and venereal infection so pressing, it is not surprising that feminists demanded that men conform to women's standards of purity, rather than that women should enjoy the same sexual privileges as men. Many came close to valuing continence for its own sake, and to seeing sex as no more than a distasteful prerequisite of maternity.[35]

That male marital sexuality was coming under mounting pressure at this time is also strongly suggested by the decline in fertility from the 1860s onwards. One of the most striking intimations of the modern world in the late Victorian period was the dramatic reduction in completed family size among the middle class. Couples who married during the 1880s were having 3.5 children on average, compared with 6.4 for those married in the 1850s.[36] Some wives were able to insist that their health required a reduction of child-bearing. Others valued the closer maternal relationship which would be possible with fewer children to care for. Family strategies were also influenced by the falling rate of mortality among children between the ages of one and five (though not yet among babies). But the explanation with the broadest application is that middle-class status was exacting a mounting toll on the costs attached to child-rearing, ranging from specialist nursery servants to boarding education, and that this pointed to concentrating the economic resources of the family on a smaller number of offspring. Although family size was a subject hardly ever broached in family correspondence, the argument about social status was almost certainly one which registered strongly with both parents: the wife, because she was more sensitive to the social standing of her family in the locality; the husband, because he held the pursestrings.[37] Predictably enough, there is even greater obscurity surrounding the means used to achieve family reduction. We know that practical handbooks circulated and that condoms and diaphragms were sold in considerable quantities. This last piece of evidence is probably misleading. The most recent (and most thorough) research concludes that the reduction in family size between the 1860s and the 1920s was essentially achieved by abstinence – sometimes coitus interruptus, but often abstinence in its full sense.[38] As we saw in Chapter 2, Victorian thinking about sex was permeated by fear of excess and the need for self-control, in marriage as in the single state. This resulted, in Simon Szreter's phrase, in a 'culture of abstinence'.[39] What happened in the late nineteenth century was that this regime of marital denial was reinforced by practical considerations of a material kind, as middle-class couples fell back on the most reliable means they knew of limiting their families to socially advisable levels. Ironically the sexual practice of the middle class was tending to converge with the demands of feminist purity campaigners. Uninhibited sexual expression by husbands in marriage was under pressure for material as well as ideological reasons.

★

Sexual conduct was not the only sphere in which significant legislative changes were made at this time. Even older than the campaign to restrict prostitution was the demand for a change in the law relating to married women's property. Under the law of *couveture* everything a wife owned or earned was the property of her husband, to dispose of as he pleased. First articulated as a national issue in the 1850s, this grievance was alleviated by two successive Married Women's Property Acts. The first, of 1870, conceded to wives control of any income earned after marriage – a measure primarily intended to benefit working-class wives. The second, more sweeping Act of 1882 allowed wives full control over property which they had possessed at the time of marriage; this included all forms of capital, and it greatly increased the financial autonomy of wives who came from affluent families. These were reforms on which virtually all strands of feminism were pulling in the same direction. Their demands happily coincided with other, quite different priorities of Gladstone's first two administrations which were not particularly sympathetic to women's issues: the 1870 Act was promoted as a means of checking the cost of poor relief, while the 1882 Act was intended to remove an anomaly in the relationship between equity and common law.[40] Yet the misgivings expressed by the opponents of the Acts showed how they touched a raw nerve. The 1870 measure, it was thought by some, would 'put a married woman on the same footing as a man' and would mean 'an entire subversion of domestic rule which had prevailed in this country for more than 1000 years'.[41] One parliamentary opponent of the 1882 Act warned of impending 'social revolution'; another believed that the provisions of the bill were so drastic that its implementation should be postponed for two years so that men who were contemplating matrimony might have 'time to change their minds when they found the law altered'.[42] This rhetoric was fully matched on the other side. The committee which had backed the 1882 measure hailed it as 'this first great victory of the principle of human equality over the unjust privilege of Sex'; they knew that the governing ethos was more significant than any compromises which had been made in the drafting of the bill.[43]

This sense that something fundamental had been achieved stood the test of time. In 1901, in a review of legal changes during the Queen's reign, Montague Lush remarked that none had been so great or so violent as those relating to married women. 'It is not that there has been an alteration, but a revolution in the law.'[44] Nor was this perception confined to the legal profession. Looking back to the 1880s, E.E. Kellett recalled, 'the Married Women's Property Act did much more than give women the right to own property: it gave them dignity in their own eyes'.[45] It was in psychological dimensions of this kind that marriage changed the most, enhancing the dignity of wives while bringing time-honoured patriarchal assumptions into question.

The Divorce Court worked to the same effect, as James Hammerton has demonstrated. Under the Matrimonial Causes Act of 1857 it was easier and cheaper for wives to seek redress against their husbands. But immense courage and self-possession were needed to do so. The stories of these wives were among the most harrowing that divorce judges had to hear, and they were widely reported in the press. Gradually the new offence of mental cruelty took shape in judicial pronouncements. The turning point was the 1869 case of the Revd James Kelly. His wife Frances's petition for a separation was granted not on account of any violent assault, but because his psychological tormenting was found to have gravely endangered her health. He had repeatedly made unfounded accusations against her; he had opened her letters; he had humiliated her in front of non-family members; he had deposed her from managing the household, and had set a servant to watch her. The effect of cases like this was to enhance public awareness of the dangers of untrammelled patriarchal power, and to raise the standards applied to the conduct of husbands.[46] The trend was exemplified in the advice books for husbands and wives. In many respects these were unchanged from their predecessors a generation previously. There was the same emphasis on the wife's duty to provide a morally wholesome home, and on the advantage to the husband of forsaking club life in order to breathe deeply of the improving home atmosphere. 'The door-sill of the home is the wharf where heavy life is unladen', as one writer put it in 1890.[47] But whereas the earlier texts had regarded wifely self-assertion as the most serious threat to marital harmony, the finger was now increasingly pointed at unmanly harshness. Higher expectations were also laid on husbands by the new stress on *mutual* conjugal passion as essential to a happy marriage. Geoffrey Mortimer asked in 1898, 'where is the intellectual and moral man who really believes in his conscience and reason that the Pauline teaching concerning woman is worthy of acceptance?' The answer was that he had been seen off by 'women of culture' who had 'ceased to regard themselves as mere ministers of men's sensual pleasure, the spoilt darlings of the home, in part slaves, in part playthings'.[48] Patriarchy as such was not being questioned, except by a tiny minority of feminists, but its legitimate scope was the subject of much critical debate.[49]

★

In more subdued fashion the same combination of legislative curtailment and changing prescription was affecting fatherhood. A man's freedom to do what he willed with his own was a principle traditionally applied to his offspring as well as his wife. He decided where they lived, in whose care, and under what religion; he had sole rights over the appointment of a guardian in the event of his early death; he determined their education (if any) and he could take possession of their earnings. All these were expressions of his 'natural' authority over his children. Given the reluctance of Victorian legislators to encroach on the sanctity of the home, the constraints imposed on paternal authority from the 1870s onwards represented something of a landmark. Much of the new legislation was framed with primarily working-class concerns in mind. Thus the introduction of compulsory elementary education in 1876 formally ended absolute paternal control over schooling, while the Prevention of Cruelty Act of 1889 set limits to how a father (or a mother) could neglect or abuse his children. But at a symbolic level these measures affected the status of fatherhood throughout society. The discharge of paternal duties was brought firmly within the reach of the law.

So far as middle-class families were concerned, the main legislative issue was the custody of children in the event of marital breakdown or the death of a parent. Husbands predeceased wives often enough for this to be a practical question of some importance, but it also raised a thorny issue which went to the heart of patriarchal convention. Under existing law fathers retained full rights over their offspring after a marital separation, and they had the power beyond the grave to choose their children's guardians. This principle was only very gradually and grudgingly encroached upon, in three Acts of 1839, 1873 and 1886. Under the last measure the deciding consideration became the child's welfare rather than the rights of the parents, though in practice the law was not always interpreted by the judges in this spirit. The slow pace of reform would seem to have conflicted with the Victorian reverence for motherhood. It was indeed a scandal to many – and not only feminists – that mothers, whose sacred responsibility was an article of faith, should have no say in a matter so central to their children's welfare as the choice of guardians: men, it seemed, had all the rights of parenthood, while women had only the duties. But any recognition of the mother's rights must necessarily encroach on the father's sole headship of the household, and this was the central principle of domestic patriarchy. The Infant Custody Act of 1886 was a watered-down version of a bill put forward two years earlier, under which parents would have been joint guardians of their children *during marriage*. One of the more moderate opponents complained that this bill 'started with the idea that the husband and wife were equal, a theory which was against scripture and reason'.[50] There was in fact no question of MPs accepting the feminist demand for equal custodial rights between parents – any more than they could stomach full economic equality between spouses. The father's rights while he continued to live with his wife were undiminished. But even a sequence of piecemeal changes, intended to do no more than minimize the worst anomalies in custody cases, called into question the traditional conception of domestic patriarchy. Rights over children, like rights over wives, had become conditional.[51]

This outcome can be seen as part of the onward march of liberal values into the more resistant recesses of social life. But it was also facilitated by an uncertainty about the proper functions of fathers. By the late Victorian period the attenuation of the traditional functions of the middle-class father was far advanced. He was more likely than not to be absent from the home for the working week; his moral leadership was widely perceived to have been eroded by the mother; mounting unease about corporal punishment discredited the traditional pattern of paternal discipline; and the father was less and less likely to be in a position directly to endow his son with an occupation or profession. Procreating and providing were practically the only paternal functions left unscathed. As the child-narrator of Helen Mathers's novel, *Comin' Thro' the Rye* (1875) exclaims, 'I can't think what fathers were invented for'; for good measure she also inveighs against family prayers.[52] Much of the social comment of the period echoed this remark. Claudia Nelson has shown how low an estimate of paternal feeling and competence prevailed among the contributors to periodicals. 'Fancy a man managing the nursery!' wrote the Revd Charles Dunbar in 1872. 'As Nature has not provided him with the power ... "of nourishing and bringing up children" he is evidently there as much out of place as a stork would be on the rugged tops of the steep "high hills"!'[53] The feminist Mona Caird was concerned by the vacuum created 'when men grow absorbed in the business of money-making, and have no time or ability to assist in the development of a higher type of manhood'.[54] If fathers were seen as bumbling amateurs or distant absentees, it is hardly surprising that the legitimacy of their authority over children was called into question.[55]

★

To say that domestic patriarchy in the late Victorian middle class was in crisis would be a wild exaggeration. It takes more than a few legal changes and an egalitarian tendency in the prescriptive texts to disturb longstanding assumptions about family order. The commanding heights of the traditional structure remained intact. The principle of joint headship of the household, so fervently desired by feminists, was a long way from being inscribed as a general principle of law. The double standard of sexual conduct still applied to the terms under which husband and wife could seek a divorce. The encroachment on a father's rights of guardianship only applied after he had died or separated from his wife; in a regular marriage his control over the children was virtually untouched. The agenda for legal equality within marriage remained a formidable one well into the twentieth century. Yet there is a perceptible change of atmosphere in family memoirs of the period, confirmed in many instances by the evidence of letters and diaries. Publicly aired issues to do with property, sexuality, cruelty and custody were often couched in almost pathological terms. But once allowance had been made for the tendency of the courts and the press to deal in extremes, these issues patently touched on everyday life, and they spoke to people whose dissatisfactions might otherwise have found no echo in public discourse.

The marriage of Henry and Elisabeth Ashbee, recently unravelled by James Hammerton, illustrates one way in which these connections were drawn. Henry was an affluent businessman with a conventional notion of separate spheres. There was no social contact between his household and his place of work, a City export firm. His wife never set foot there, even though he owed his partnership to the patronage of her family. Nor was there much contact between his family and his friends, who were more likely to see him at his chambers in Gray's Inn, where he also kept his vast collection of pornography. But Henry valued domestic life and he seems to have been a fond and dutiful father. He noted in his diary in 1875, 'My wedding day, thirteen years married, do not think it possible for any man to have a better wife, or nicer children, am perfectly happy'.[56] Yet within little more than ten years his marriage was in severe difficulties and his son Charles had broken with him completely. Despite his affectionate disposition, Henry was rigid and intolerant of dissent within the family. While these characteristics remained unmellowed by advancing age, the rest of the family were sensitive to the new thinking on social and aesthetic issues. As a Cambridge undergraduate Charles mixed with men of advanced views like Edward Carpenter and Roger Fry. He clashed openly with his father over his choice of career, and became estranged from him in 1886. Elisabeth, meanwhile, found her husband's control irksome as she developed her interests in avant-garde painting and poetry, and in women's education. She left her husband in 1893 after years of bitterness, and a formal separation was drawn up. But for the new legal climate she might have continued to submit to the marriage indefinitely. Charles's account sets his mother's courageous action in the context of the Married Women's Property Act of 1882, not so much because it enhanced her financial independence, but because it had contributed to a more egalitarian climate in which so drastic a step could be contemplated.[57]

Nor was the impetus for change merely negative. Many couples were inspired by a new vision of spousal equality along the lines advocated by feminists. This point was happily conceded by no less a scourge of patriarchal marriage than Elizabeth Wolstenholme. With her seven years of marriage to the manufacturer Ben Elmy no doubt in mind, she wrote in 1881:

> In every happy home the change is complete. There no husband claims supremacy, and no wife surrenders her conscience and her will. There the true unity, that of deep and lasting affection ... reigns alone.[58]

This was the model long professed by the Unitarians. William and Elizabeth Gaskell had managed a fairly convincing approximation of it. Elizabeth had signed the first petition for a Married Women's Property Act in 1856, and during her last years she exercised sufficient control over her earnings to secretly buy a retirement house for herself and William, which she sadly never lived to enjoy.[59] John Lionel Tayler, a medical doctor, recalled that women's oppression was an unquestioned assumption on the part of his kindly Unitarian parents when he was being brought up in the 1880s, though he and his wife would later renounce it in the cause of an individualist philosophy of human nature.[60] Others encountered egalitarian ideas only after they had grown up. Thomas Sanderson, a lawyer with leanings towards the abstract and the spiritual, was deeply influenced by John Stuart Mill's *The Subjection of Women* during his courtship of Annie Cobden in 1881–82; she may well have introduced him to

17. Thomas Sanderson in Siena, 1881, with Jane Cobden, Jane Morris and Annie Cobden.

the book, as she was reading Mill's *Autobiography* at the same time and was already involved in the women's suffrage movement. When they married, Thomas adopted her surname as well as his own, out of respect for her late father, the free trade campaigner Richard Cobden who had never had a son. On her urging, Cobden-Sanderson then abandoned the Bar and trained as a bookbinder, a craft which for many years he practised from home, with periodic assistance from his wife. During the time it took him to become established in his new profession, Thomas was dependent on Anne's income from her share of Richard Cobden's estate, which as a result of the recent law was under her undivided control. They remained intellectual equals, sharing books, reading to each other aloud, and discussing politics and philosophy. Their partnership extended to parenting, with Thomas attending to the detailed management of his eighteen-month-old son Richard.[61]

The change of atmosphere was most pronounced with regard to relations between fathers and children. This subject has suffered acutely from the attempt by the first generation of post-Victorians to distance themselves from their immediate forebears. The modernist script required not only rebellion, but an oppressor who justified that rebellion; Leslie Stephen, with his tyranny over the

18. The Playful Father, *c.* 1880.

household accounts and his insistence on selfless service from his children, casts a long shadow over the image of the Victorian father.[62] One still finds references to the 'blustering certainty of the late Victorian paterfamilias'.[63] This stereotype is not borne out by the didactic texts of the time, which signal a shift towards more interactive and less authoritarian patterns of fatherhood. There was growing endorsement of the Romantic idea of the child and of the dethronement of the surrogate Father in Heaven. In her advice manual, *Courtship and Marriage and the Gentle Art of Home-Making* (1893), Annie Swan commended those men

> who never grow old, who, while doing a man's part better than most in the world, keep the child-heart pure within them . . . The ideal father will be a boy in the midst of his boys all his days.

The father is urged to be 'a chum' to his son, and to impart moral lessons without preaching.[64] Although this was the period when 'Dad' entered common usage, Swan's cheerful counsel (possibly influenced by fashions in America) pushed the idea of companionate fatherhood to the limits of what was commonly understood in England. All the same, the general tendency of the family memoirs of the period inclines towards this end of the spectrum, rather than the grim patriarch of popular repute.

In some cases the liberalizing effect which the crisis of religious faith had on patriarchal attitudes is clearly visible. Daniel Meinertzhagen was indulgent to a fault towards his many children. He offered them little by way of guidance or advice. He made no attempt to regulate tensions within the family, such as the antagonism between his wife and his eldest surviving son. According to his sister-in-law, Beatrice Webb, Daniel treated his unmarried daughters as 'agreeable talented younger sisters'; he took no responsibility for them, and when they visited him in London they enjoyed 'a happy-go-lucky concert-going latchkey restaurant existence'. This was all of a piece with Daniel's religious observance. He never went to church when in town, and in the country he made no attempt to listen to the service, becoming absorbed in business calculations. His wife Georgina was drawn to mysticism and spiritualism and remained at home.[65] Edward Hopkinson also took his religious duties lightly. He had been brought up in Manchester as a Congregationalist, but by the turn of the century, when he had become managing director of a large engineering firm, he was a none-too-demanding Anglican. His daughter Katharine recalled that 'the males were never expected to perform religious duties unless they wanted to', and even in her own case this laxity was associated with some of her most vivid memories of companionship with her father: in winter, if the ice was thick enough on a Sunday morning, 'I was always allowed off [church] to go to skate with father, and the sense of truancy added a spice of pleasure to those expeditions across the frozen fields to Alderley mere'.[66]

Thomas Cobden-Sanderson, as well as attending to the care of his two children, also heartily appreciated their spontaneity, in a way which seems entirely in keeping with his rather vague optimistic pantheism. Of seven-month-old Richard he wrote:

> Dickie is developing rapidly. He is becoming conscious of himself. He now shrieks with the utmost vigour and the utmost delight, conscious of his shrieks and observant of our laughter and enjoyment. Shriek follows shriek, each prolonged till he is almost blue in the face and quite out of breath, and each is energetically worked out to the last and deepest note. He is very merry, very good-natured, with occasional bursts of temper and rage and insatiable of amusement. A most delightful boy.[67]

This was no mere sentimentality on the part of an absent father. Thomas worked at home, and Richard was a highly audible distraction who was also allowed to crawl about the workshop. Thomas was no less entranced by his daughter, born two years later. Of them both he wrote, 'I do not often mention them in my journal, but our life is full of them, and we ache with admiration

19. Thomas Cobden-Sanderson in his workshop with his two children, Hendon, *c.* 1890.

and delight'. When the children were in their teens, Thomas had the idea of setting up a family council, which would 'discuss our several naughtinesses and grievances, and propose plans for our common and several good'; like most of Thomas's brain-waves it got no further than the pages of his journal, but it expresses well the respect which he thought was due from parents to their children.[68]

The influence of Romantic thinking was not confined to those with easygoing or doubt-ridden belief. Comparable attitudes were to be found among the clergy. When the Revd Stopford Brooke became a father in the 1870s, he was resolved to let his children grow by 'their own divine vitality'. He proved as good as his word. Left a widower with seven children, he refused to pursue a method, preferring a *laissez-faire* approach. He respected his children's individuality, to the point of permitting his daughters to make their own marriages.[69] Thomas Darling, the High Church incumbent of a City of London church, made a particularly pointed rejection of traditional parenting. His own father, George Darling, was a Scots Presbyterian doctor settled in London, who had been determined to pass on his faith and his moral code to his children. His letters had been sharp and admonitory. Thomas married late in life, and he was in his sixties when his two sons, Kenneth and Malcolm, were born in 1879 and 1880. He seems to have been determined to rise above the negative associations of an elderly clerical father. He wrote regularly to the boys when they were sent to boarding school (at the age of nine). His letters are chatty, affectionate and full of incident, especially relating to dogs. Family celebrations were keenly anticipated. Thomas did once dispatch a lecture on the meaning of Whitsun, and he was inclined to harp on dietary matters, but there is very little of the preacher in these letters. He was also sensitive to the emotions surrounding family separation. In January 1890 he told the boys, 'Your vacant places remind us all of your absence, and none of us like to look at them, especially Mother, who particularly dislikes passing your empty bedroom'. Two years later, when Kenneth left prep school for Eton, Thomas sent a letter of heartfelt condolence to the lonely younger brother, Malcolm, to arrive on his first morning back at school.[70] The tone is a world away from the letters written by Edward Benson to his son Martin fifteen years earlier (see Chapter 4).

Thomas Darling died in 1893 when his sons were still schoolboys. It is interesting to speculate whether he would have performed the traditional paternal duty of preparing his sons for the temptations of the flesh. His widow did not flinch from the task. Writing to Malcolm shortly after his Confirmation, she prayed that he and Kenneth might

> both receive strength to keep your vows & also keep your bodies pure & holy as the Temple of the Holy Ghost. Is it not wonderful to think how you were both made *whiter* than snow that happy day.[71]

Mary Darling might have written in the same vein even if her husband had still been alive, for by this time Christian mothers were under mounting pressure to take personal responsibility for their sons' training in sexual morality. This demand certainly made a public impact, since it was supported by both the Social Purity Alliance and the White Cross Army. It is unfortunately impossible to tell how much practical change it brought about, since sex education is hardly ever mentioned in family memoirs, but as the latest stage in the shift of moral authority from father to mother it seems likely to have had some effect.[72]

In 1900 journalist Stephen Gwynn echoed a common sentiment when he remarked that fear was much less common among children than had been the case half a century before: 'the father is not that awe-inspiring person he once was'.[73] Yet this trend was not only a matter of parental attitude. It was also due to a greater assertiveness on the part of children. Perhaps the most revealing popular literary text of the period is F. Anstey's novel *Vice Versa*, which appeared in 1882. Subtitled 'A Lesson to Fathers', it recounts how a father's unbending and unsympathetic behaviour is humanized by the experience of being compelled by magic to change places with his son. The book has been justly called 'a landmark in the decline of Victorian patriarchy' because it gives vent to a schoolboy's ridicule of the pomposity and hypocrisy of old-style fathers.[74] There is plenty of evidence pointing to restiveness and disrespect in real life. Sometimes the filial challenge was a subtle, scarcely articulated one. Albert Spicer was a wealthy paper manufacturer and MP. Recalling family life at the turn of the century, his daughter wrote, 'Father ruled with benevolent autocracy. The benevolence was genuine but − truth compels me to state, though he himself might have objected − the autocracy was largely bluff'. When his children had good grounds for challenging Albert's decision, they usually got their way.[75] Sometimes the gestures against paternal authority were more provocative. Samuel Bligh was a doctor with a practice in Tooting, south London, in the 1890s. He was not a distant or harsh father − quite the reverse: his son Eric recalls 'the happy assurance of his giant comradeship' as he grew up. But Samuel never wavered from his strong Baptist faith, and he continued to try and impose a daily spiritual routine on his family. He moved prayers from the morning to the evening in order to make time for readings from both the Old and New Testaments. Eric experienced this as 'the real tyranny of his religious obsession', notwithstanding the warmth and love he had always received from his father. The children treated the ordeal with surreptitious mockery, as they continued to chatter in front of their father, made faces behind his back, flicked pellets at each other and caused as much disturbance as they could get away with. By the 1890s a culture of religious doubt and dilution made this kind of subversion much less shocking than it would have been half a century earlier. None of Bligh's children adopted his faith in later life.[76]

There was also more scope for children to prevail over their father in their choice of career. Daughters could still encounter severe obstacles, since they had to establish the principle of paid work as well as their particular preference. William Byles of Bradford was a professed supporter of John Stuart Mill's views on female education and helped to launch the Girls' Grammar School in 1875, but he believed that his daughters should grace the home rather than go to university or take employment. In 1877 Dr John Heaton reluctantly allowed his daughter Lucy to be assistant teacher at Leeds Girls' High School and then required her to resign after only two years in the post.[77] But sons were better placed. The growth of bureaucratization and professionalism meant that fathers were less likely to have attractive openings in their gift, and sons were better able to stick to their choice of career. Richard Meinertzhagen was just 16 when Cecil Rhodes offered him an opening in Africa in 1894. His father Daniel, so easygoing in other respects, held strong views about the proper destiny of his oldest surviving son. He refused to let him go and insisted that he start work at the family bank. Richard reluctantly submitted to the paternal will. But Daniel could not withstand his son's yearning for adventure indefinitely. After Richard had joined the part-time Hampshire Yeomanry, Daniel withdrew his objections, and in 1898 Richard received a commission in the regular Army.[78]

★

It is hardly surprising that late Victorian fatherhood was on the defensive, given that the traditional role of fathers had been steadily attenuated over quite a long period. Their position as moral authority in the home was more open to question than ever. There was little left of their role as educators. And they exercised less and less influence over their sons' choice of career. The decline of these more positive functions made the assertion of a father's authority, and the privileges of deference and service that went with it, appear all the more arbitrary. The uncertainty of paternal authority was compounded by comparable developments in relations between spouses. In both the legal sphere and everyday life the traditional hierarchy of family life was more openly questioned in the late Victorian period than at any time within living memory. A feminist movement securely rooted in the middle class had brought to the surface concerns about excessive patriarchal authority over both wives and children, and the public was periodically reminded of them by the grisly details of well-reported court cases. When a conservative writer like Eliza Lynn Linton could assert, as her guiding principles on the Woman Question, that women should have as good an education as men, that they should control their own property in marriage, and that their parental rights should be equal to those of their husbands, we can gauge how far the centre ground had moved.[79]

This open critique was not necessarily unwelcome to men. For many, the powers vested in the husband and father had long been an embarrassment, which they would not have dreamed of invoking. John Stuart Mill took these scruples to their logical extreme when he solemnly renounced his legal powers on his marriage to Harriet Taylor in 1851, but his egalitarianism was shared in progressive circles, as the case of Thomas Cobden-Sanderson illustrates. More typical was the middle-class man who, without subscribing to radical principles, regarded patriarchal rule as irrelevant to his own needs. Men like George Darling and Edward Hopkinson strove to be companionable husbands and responsive fathers because they valued intimacy and support above authority. For men of this stamp the liberalization of law and practice relating to the family was a breath of fresh air. But for those whose upbringing and experience had led them to think of relations between the sexes in more polarized terms, the changes caused considerable anxiety. The apprehension with which inexperienced bachelors so often anticipated marriage was intensified by the removal of powers on which they might have relied when relations soured. Men who instinctively thought of parent–child interaction in authoritarian terms found it hard to visualize themselves as fathers in a more liberal climate. For many the decline of deference represented net loss, and the advantages of domesticity were more open to question than ever. The legislation on wives' property and the rights of custody over children appeared to serve notice that power and privilege in the home, which had hitherto been largely beyond the reach of the law, were now subject to scrutiny and restraint. As the century drew to a close there was a sense that an era of stability in domestic life had drawn to an end. Additional instalments of reform seemed likely which could only curtail still further the historic power of men in the family.

CHAPTER EIGHT

The Flight from Domesticity

In 1890 Cornelius Stovin delivered a speech at the golden wedding celebrations of his parents-in-law, in which he struggled to find a metaphor which adequately expressed his faith in marriage. In a thinly veiled tribute to his own wife Elizabeth, he described woman as 'the finishing stroke of God's work in creation' and 'the summing up of all excellencies'. As for the married state, his first thought was to liken it to 'two or more railway carriages coupled together', but he settled on a more organic metaphor: man and wife were like 'the fingers of one hand'.[1] Cornelius would have found it difficult to use this kind of language of his own marriage, which was troubled by religious differences and financial anxieties.[2] But he never wavered in his reverence for the institution of marriage and the sanctity of its 'inward sentiments';[3] and since he was genuinely fond of his parents-in-law he easily cast them in the role of exemplars. As an elderly man's tribute to the previous generation in a remote corner of rural Lincolnshire, the language used by Cornelius was entirely appropriate. Outside that frame it was patently anachronistic. Railways had ceased to be the wonder of the age. Divine purpose was steadily surrendering its hold to evolutionary logic. And marriage itself no longer attracted the same veneration as it had done fifty years earlier.

Cornelius Stovin was not entirely out on a limb. His homespun encomiums on domesticity were still echoed in the more conservative advice books which continued to offer a blend of Evangelical and Ruskinian sentiment.[4] There were plenty of young men who strove to live by these values. The diary of the writer Maurice Hewlett, for example, repeatedly refers to his wife as 'noble' as well as 'dearest'; 'I can never say what I owe her from first to last', he wrote in his end-of-year review for 1894. 'I solemnly propose to work for her and our little son (and if God grant it, yet another child we have good hopes of) until the end'.[5] But Hewlett was the author of popular historical romances, for whom elevated sentiment was a stock-in-trade. In the more relaxed social atmosphere of the 1890s greater flexibility and realism were in evidence. As church attendance and firm belief declined, the social authority of the clergy was reduced – and with it the influence of their exacting vision of home life.

20. The Golden Wedding of Frank and Elizabeth Riggall, Dexthorpe, Lincolnshire, 1890.

Women themselves had undermined the 'pedestal' view of womanhood by voicing new rights and new freedoms based on an ideology of sexual equality. Once the demarcation between private and public had become blurred, woman's privileged status in the home became more difficult to sustain. The result was a new genre of didactic writing about marriage which had entirely lost the reverential tone of the early Victorians. The key concept was 'comradeship' – in Annie Swan's definition 'a standing shoulder to shoulder upholding each other through thick and thin'. The sensible husband would realize that 'he has married a very human woman, with a great many needs and wants'; far from being placed in a cage or on a pedestal, she needed to be well acquainted with her husband's financial situation.[6]

In fact this was the practical, no-nonsense form in which domesticity was eagerly adopted by the expanding ranks of the lower middle class at this time, both as a means of personal satisfaction and as a marker of social respectability. When the journalist Walter Besant characterized 'the average Englishman' as tame and tender-hearted – someone who 'sits at home with his wife and children and desires no other society' – he had in mind the clerk, the shopkeeper and the more 'respectable' of the working class.[7] The family memoirs of men of this background fully substantiate Besant's picture – notably Richard Church's recollection of his 'cosy, passionate, instinctive, and almost completely isolated' home.[8]

But alongside this modification in the mainstream ideology of marriage went a much more negative response. Among the professional and business classes who had lived by the code of domesticity for two generations or more, there was evidence of growing restlessness, amounting in some instances to outright rejection of marriage. 'Nowadays,' remarked Edward Hardy in 1896, 'it is often said that [young men] are giving up matrimony as if it were some silly old habit suited to their grandfathers and grandmothers.'[9] For them, domesticity no longer represented a fresh vision of comfort and reassurance, but a straitjacket. For some, like the men of the Bloomsbury Group, domesticity stultified proper relations between the sexes; for others like Edward Carpenter, its main drawback was the check it imposed on intimate relations between men. But though the avant-garde takes the limelight in the documentary record, the flight from domesticity was far from confined to them. Again and again one encounters young men who postponed marriage or refused it altogether: sometimes singly, as with John Heaton's eldest son, and sometimes almost an entire family, as with Edward Benson's three sons. Doubt about the future of the family name was a new experience in late Victorian England. It stemmed not primarily from birth control or loss of virility, but from a reluctance to marry.

★

In describing this reaction as 'the flight from domesticity' I do not mean to suggest that an entire generation renounced home life, nor even that there was a complete disenchantment with the comforts of the hearth. There is no symmetrical story of the 'rise' and 'fall' of domesticity. But in late Victorian England a much keener sense of the drawbacks of domestic life for men was articulated, and this coincided with a growing reluctance to marry, in circumstances where marriage would previously have been taken for granted as part of a natural progression from youth to manhood. Increasing numbers of middle-class men either chose not to marry, or delayed marriage until they were on the threshold of middle age. The declining incidence of marriage among middle-class men is, in theory at least, amenable to statistical treatment. But the marriage statistics which appeared every year in the *Reports of the Registrar-General* dealt with class and age independently. In order to put these two variables together, we have to be content with more fragmentary evidence. In 1874 Charles Ansell, an amateur statistician, concluded from a questionnaire of professional families that the mean age of first marriage for men currently stood at 30.51, and that it had gradually but steadily been rising since the early years of the century.[10] Sixteen years later W.J. Ogle constructed his own sample from the marriage registers in order to carry out statistical enquiries which were not attempted in the published *Reports*. He concluded that the mean age of first marriage among professional men was 31.2; he also observed that the proportion of men still unmarried at the age of 50 was much higher among professionals and men of independent income than in any other group.[11]

Further conclusions will have to await comprehensive demographic research on the marriage registers of late Victorian England. But the trend is clear – and it was clear to contemporaries too. English middle-class society had long been characterized by late marriage, on the assumption that it took time for a man to establish his 'independence' – that is a secure business or profession. Hence there was a well developed bachelor culture for young men in their twenties. But bachelorhood as a preferred rather than enforced status was frowned on, since it suggested an abdication from patriarchy and an indifference to lineage and posterity. From the 1860s onwards men's avoidance of marriage was blamed on two increasingly embarrassing social problems – the scourge of prostitution and the 'surplus woman'. Young men were not generally blamed for their immorality, except by purity campaigners, but it was obvious that if more of them married the clientele for vice would diminish. Spinsterhood lent itself to a similar logic. The numbers of New Women who rejected marriage were nothing compared with the many thousands who faced lifelong spinsterhood because too few eligible men were in the marriage market. Every man who opted for the single state was seen to condemn a woman to the denial of her 'natural' destiny as wife and mother.

The scale on which men avoided marriage in the late nineteenth century implies that there were strong considerations working to counterbalance the traditional association of bachelorhood with diminished manhood. Of course rejection of domesticity is by no means the whole story. Some commentators blamed men's preference for town pleasures, ranging from intellectual male company to the 'gay' life; the more moralistic railed against the selfishness of the confirmed bachelor.[12] Others blamed the devious scheming of mothers and daughters which brought marriage into disrepute and put off suitors.[13] Others again blamed both sexes for colluding in the view that marriage should be postponed until the newly married couple could enjoy the same level of luxury as their parents, and this interpretation has been amply borne out by modern research into the correlation between rising household budgets and the rising age of marriage.[14] But contemporaries were also aware that the taste for the single life must reflect on male attitudes towards domesticity itself. In one of the earliest treatments of this theme, W.R. Greg in 1869 itemized 'the fetters of a wife, the burden and responsibility of children, and the decent monotony of the domestic hearth' as deterrents to matrimony.[15] James Hussey presented the confirmed bachelor's case in a pastiche of 'To be or not to be':

> To marry – to live in peace –
> Perchance in war. Ay, there's the rub;
> For in the marriage state what ills may come,
> When we have shuffled off our liberty,
> Must give us pause. There's the respect
> That makes us dread the bonds of wedlock.
> For who could bear the noise of scolding wives,

The fits of spleen, the extravagance of dress,
The insolence of servants, and the spurns
That patient husbands from their consorts take,
When he himself might his quietus gain
By living single?[16]

Such objections were repeatedly aired during the last two decades of the century.[17] If these authors were right, middle-class society was witnessing a reappraisal of the claims of masculine domesticity.

That impression is confirmed by developments in the sphere of popular culture. Quite suddenly in the mid-1880s a new genre of bestselling adventure fiction was born. For a generation the most widely read novels had tended to deal with love and marriage, and thus to underwrite the claims of domesticity. A new group of writers headed by Robert Louis Stevenson and Henry Rider Haggard believed that the reading public had been starved of flesh-and-blood adventure. While earlier adventure writers like Marryat and Ballantyne had been read by juveniles, Stevenson and Rider Haggard aimed to provide adults with something heroic, exotic and bracingly masculine. Their heroes are fighters, hunters and frontiersmen distinguished by their daring and resourcefulness. Men set off into the unknown, to fulfil their destiny unencumbered by feminine constraint or by emotional ties with home; as the hunter Allan Quatermain reassures his readers in *King Solomon's Mines*, 'there is not a petticoat in the whole history'.[18] Support and companionship are provided by the silent bonds of male friendship – what Kipling in an early novel called 'the austere love that springs up between men who have tugged at the same oar together'.[19] Edmund Gosse believed that before Kipling 'the fiction of the Anglo-Saxon world ... had become curiously feminised'.[20] Arthur Conan Doyle later claimed that *Treasure Island* had marked the beginning of 'the modern masculine novel'. It is certainly true that from that point a sharp distinction grew up between men's and women's writing – sustained by Kipling, Conrad and Conan Doyle himself.[21]

A thin dividing line separated this fantasy world from Britain's actual empire. The process of exploration, expansion and 'pacification' during the era of the New Imperialism might be humdrum or squalid, but empire came to stand for the same attributes as the fictional characters of the novelist's imagination. Imperial reputation was grounded in a small repertoire of masculine qualities: stoicism as in the death of General Gordon, steely self-control exemplified by Kitchener, self-reliance in the case of Baden-Powell. All three of these men (and many other lesser exemplars) had one important thing in common: they travelled through life free of domestic ties (or in Baden-Powell's case until he married at the age of fifty-one, on his mother's urging). They gave credence to the belief that the empire, in which Britain's destiny seemed to lie at that time, was quintessentially a masculine arena, where men worked better without the company of women. Young men at this time could choose between a number of occupations which ruled out marriage, at least for the time being. There was a teaching career in the proliferating boarding schools; there were 'settlements' in the mould of Toynbee Hall (founded 1884) which reproduced the homo-social camaraderie of school and university. There was a growth of celibacy among Anglo-Catholic priests, and even a revival of celibate monastic orders within the Church of England (seventeen new foundations between 1865 and 1914).[22] But all of these paled into insignificance beside colonial careers, which included administration, the armed services, commerce and missionary work in most quarters of the globe. The empire was run by bachelors; in the public mind it represented devotion to duty or profit (and sometimes pleasure), undistracted by feminine ties.

This had not always been the meaning of empire. In the aftermath of the Indian Mutiny General Havelock had been admired as much for his family loyalties as his martial valour (see Chapter 6, p. 138). But when a fresh batch of Havelock biographies appeared in the 1880s and 1890s, the domestic side of his life was in nearly every case omitted.[23] Whether in the real-life exploits of empire-builders, or in the adventure yarns of Henty and Rider Haggard, the colonies now served to intensify the association between masculinity and empire, and correspondingly to weaken the imaginative power of the link between masculinity and domesticity. And for every young man who was prompted by the imperial fervour of the day to seek his fortune in the colonies, there were hundreds of others who were happy to escape for a while from the routines of domesticity into the make-believe of a frontier of the imagination. They experienced the thrill of the undomesticated life without incurring the resentment of the women in their lives; for, as readers of the *Girl's Own Paper* were informed, 'the reading young man makes a stay-at-home fireside-loving husband'.[24]

The relationship between imperialism and domesticity can be read in two ways. Renunciation of home comforts can be seen as a sacrifice which the young men of England were called upon to make in the cause of duty or in pursuit of fortune. The missionary societies were virtually alone in encouraging early marriage on the part of their male recruits in order to hold up a model of domesticity before their converts.[25] Every other overseas occupation was strongly associated with bachelorhood. The empire had long been a convenient means of disposing of the less conventional and less controllable elements of polite society. With the rapid expansion of the empire after 1880 – not to mention the growing fears for its security – this was no longer an adequate answer to imperial manpower requirements. If the colonial frontiers were to be populated and the new colonial subjects administered, the appeal of home comforts and feminine civilization must be actively countered among those who might otherwise be drawn to them. 'Strive to be ready when the call shall come . . .', intoned an imperial propagandist at Eton College in 1890, 'for you shall leave father and mother and wife and children for your Queen, your country or your faith'.[26] The novelist Grant Allen drew a direct link between the opportunities of empire and the incidence of spinsterhood in England. Whereas in America the young man had gone West, in England, Allen claimed,

> he is in the army, in the navy, in the Indian Civil Service, in the Cape Mounted Rifles. He is sheep-farming in New Zealand, ranching in Colorado, growing tea in Assam, planting coffee in Ceylon; he is a cowboy in Montana, or a wheat-farmer in Manitoba, or a diamond-digger at Kimberley, or a merchant at Melbourne: in short, he is anywhere, and everywhere, except where he ought to be, making love to the pretty girls of England.[27]

Allen was speaking of the middle and upper classes, which by the 1890s accounted for 26.5 per cent of all emigrants from Britain – a disproportionately high share in comparison with the lower classes.[28] As his list of colonial avocations suggests, many of those who left England were men who lacked the capital or connections to make good at home and were prepared to get their hands dirty overseas. But the appeal of imperial careers went right to the top of the educational ladder. Between 1875 and 1914, 27 per cent of men who entered Balliol College, Oxford, went on to work in the empire, half of them in India, and this does not include those who entered the Army.[29] Young men at this level were taught to regard themselves as members of an imperial service class, for whom marriage was a necessarily distant prospect. Those with less impressive educational credentials treated the colonies as a protected zone which owed them a living, and perhaps a fortune.

But celibacy and a preference for the homosocial life were more than the inevitable accompaniment to the young man's life overseas. They also provided motivation. In the late Victorian period disillusionment with domesticity and the hankering after a bracing men-only world were what attracted many to careers overseas. On the eve of his departure to join Milner's administration in the Transvaal in 1901, John Buchan described himself as 'thoroughly undomesticated'. While at home he had become alienated from the adhesive closeness of his family life, in South Africa he shared a bachelor house with other '*kindergarten*' members (Milner's young men) and was constantly on horseback.[30] The motives of emigrants and officials who spent a lifetime overseas are not easy to reconstruct, since their surviving private papers seldom predate the voyage out.[31] But that same sense of liberation is perfectly conveyed in the diary of a young mineral prospector who arrived in Bulawayo in 1888: an emigrant from Cumberland of one year's standing, Benjamin Wilson – known to Rhodesian posterity as 'Matabele' Wilson – happily took stock of his new circumstances:

> There is no old woman here to tell you 'You are looking pale' or 'Oh, I am sorry to see you looking so bad', or having people fooling around you with a cup of tea or soup or other things you do not want.[32]

Empire was actively embraced by young men as a *means* of evading or postponing the claims of domesticity. In England masculine identity was subject to constant negotiation with the opposite sex – and on domestic ground where they were often perceived to hold the advantage. By contrast the colonial world was thought of as a men-only sphere. Sexual relations with women of other races were of course comparatively commonplace, but this outlet could be kept in its rightful place – as a personal gratification and a means of acquiring masculine kudos, instead of a privilege to be paid for by conforming to domestic conventions.[33]

Domesticity was equally at odds with the values espoused by the public schools. As a result of the phenomenal expansion in the number and size of the public schools from the 1850s onwards, the proportion of middle-class boys who were exposed to these values was very much greater than in the early Victorian period. Public school had become the defining educational experience of boys in the upper middle class, and the public standing and self-confidence of the schools reached new heights.[34] The job of these schools was to instil manly self-reliance in boys who had been raised in comfortable conditions of domesticity (as discussed in Chapter 5). The level of anxiety felt by Victorian fathers and schoolmasters on this score meant that the balance was often tilted strongly in the direction of homosociality at the expense of domestic graces or home tastes. Dr Arnold had regretted how often boys at Rugby became distanced from their parents, but this was an integral part of the system.[35] The 1870s saw a significant modification to the traditional ethos of the public school, associated with a more explicitly imperial rationale. More emphasis was now placed on stoical endurance, group loyalty and team sports. By the 1890s some public schools (like Uppingham and Haileybury) were dispatching 30 per cent of their school-leavers overseas.[36] Young men emerged from these schools, it was said, with a veneer of good manners and social poise, but with scant respect for women of their own or any other class. As John Masefield put it, 'boys and young men are brought up as though they would always be boys, as though the world consisted of a playing-field and a tuck-shop, from which, when very weary or very bilious, they may go home to be contemptuous of their sisters'.[37] Habituated to an all-male society which thrived alternately on comradeship and competition, public school men gravitated towards a world of chambers and clubs. For many this was a sufficient emotional world. The late Victorian upper middle class was significantly over-populated with men who were permanently disqualified from family life. The characteristic stance of mid-Victorian fathers towards domesticity had been an appreciation of its material comforts and moral uplift, combined with the fear that it would emasculate their sons. Boarding education from the age of nine or thirteen – the preferred solution for those who had the means – resulted in a strong impulse on the part of the next generation to escape from the clutches of domesticity altogether. Marriage was still an essential stage in the attainment of full manhood, leading to household headship and offspring to continue the line.

But from the perspective of the products of the public schools, marriage both offered less and demanded less than in the heyday of domesticity. Often the intention was to continue after marriage with a bachelor style of living. Judged by the standards of the early Victorians, this was marriage without conviction.

The growing popularity of the public schools could certainly be blamed for a decline in commitment to family life among the upper middle class. But this was not the only cause, or even the most important one. The Victorian public schoolboy was scarcely a *tabula rasa* at 12 or 13. In most cases his early years had been passed in a home setting, and his attitude to domesticity formed there. Nor should it be forgotten that, even after the huge expansion in public school provision during the second half of Victoria's reign, boarding school was still the exception rather than the rule in middle-class boys' education. For those who attended day school the experience of a domestic upbringing was even more central in forming attitudes to family and marriage. The appeal of home itself must therefore be confronted directly in any account of the 'flight from domesticity' in these years.

★

That appeal had been grounded above all in a sense of alienation from the social and moral consequences of industrialism. Domesticity was the characteristic defence mechanism of a bourgeoisie whose own sense of personal security was felt to be at risk. It certainly cannot be assumed that this outlook persisted until the end of the century.[38] Nowadays the late Victorian period tends to be viewed as not truly Victorian at all, but as a watershed which clearly anticipated many developments of the new century. It is true that some of the more extreme symptoms of social dislocation in the 1840s had been modified. In particular the living conditions of the working class had been raised, public health had markedly improved, and a 'responsible' labour politics had developed. But the *fin de siècle* by no means represented all novelty. Early nineteenth-century domesticity had addressed a deep malaise in the middle class which was far from gone. Nothing had changed the conditions of bourgeois work in such a way as to undermine the countervailing charms of home. More men commuted to work than ever, and from the 1870s the economic climate in which they laboured was beset by recession, recalling the uncertainties of trade before the mid-Victorian boom. The great cities were still disfigured by the uncontrolled pollution of industrial production, confirming the appeal of suburban living. The centrality of childhood in the meaning of home was still strong – indeed by the end of the century the Romantic appreciation of the child (and the child within the adult) was making increasing inroads on the Evangelical view.[39] The doctrine of separate spheres was now made more absolute by the popular rendition of evolutionary biology.[40] Of the major props of domesticity, only religion had weakened. But so strong was the investment in the idea of home that it tended to persist as a quasi-religious belief in families which had long since abandoned 'serious Christianity'. In short, the conditions for social alienation which had led to the popularization of domesticity in the first place still obtained.

The really significant shift in the appeal of domesticity in the late Victorian period lay not in the sphere of education or in the broader social context, but in the atmosphere of the home itself. This was a recurrent theme among contemporary commentators from the late 1860s. The most insistent complaint was boredom. No doubt this is an occupational hazard for men at home, since the pleasures of evening society in the town will always seem sweeter to the man at the fireside. But very little public acknowledgement of this fact had been made in the mid-nineteenth century. W.R. Greg set something of a fashion going with his frank admission in 1869 of 'the decent monotony of the domestic hearth'.[41] The fastidious and sheltered wife – the Perfect Lady of the advice manuals – was not necessarily scintillating company. By the time Marianne Farningham declared twenty years later that 'home life is the only kind of life of which we do not tire',[42] she was contradicted by a mass of male opinion. A typical example was this outburst in the magazine *Temple Bar* in 1888:

> There is nothing more of the essence of home than dinner. I would sooner dine in public, with a play of life and character around me, exhibiting itself for my amusement, than *solus cum sola*, in the single society of one person, however charming. I consider the domestic dinner gruesome.[43]

Commentators were not short on explanations. Wives were blamed for keeping their husbands' bachelor friends out of the house in the interests of 'tone'. The cultural and intellectual gap between spouses was invoked – in spite of the steadily rising level of middle-class girls' education during this period. The man of intellect was represented as expending his energies on 'the acquisition of ugly millinery and uglier upholstery, and on spreading extravagant tables to feed uncultivated guests'. Robert Louis Stevenson counterposed the stifling conventions of home with heroism and adventure far away.[44] There was a surprising concurrence from advanced feminist opinion. Mona Caird, the most controversial critic of marriage at this time, conceded that the wife who played her domestic role strictly according to the rules was 'more exemplary than entertaining . . . The more admirable the wives the more profoundly bored the husbands!'[45]

Boredom was the acceptable face of men's discontent. Underneath lay a strong strain of sexual antagonism which arose from the perception that the home was a feminine – even a feminized – sphere. This was implicit in the removal of work from the domestic environment. If the husband was at home only in the evenings and on Sundays, the furnishing of the home was almost bound to become the exclusive responsibility of the wife; so too was the staging of domestic ceremonials from mealtimes through rituals of arrival and departure, to birthdays and Christmas. Two generations on from the 1820s and 1830s these aspects of middle-class living had become more elaborate and more

21. Family Tea in the 1860s.

formulaic, as a result of insecurities about social status which were ably exploited by the writers of household advice manuals.[46] Hence they appeared more stifling and more constraining to men. The drawing room was seen to enforce caution and dissembling on men's speech where there should have been manly directness; it led to misunderstandings where the stakes were highest – in courtship.[47] In 1879 the journalist T.H.S. Escott deplored 'the acceptance gained by the rite of five-o'clock tea'; it was, he declared, 'the symbol of the ascendancy of the softer over the sterner sex'.[48] Escott did not of course mean that women held the upper hand in society as a whole. Indeed, as Edward Carpenter pointed out, there was a certain mockery about men's drawing-room homage, since it hardly corresponded to the actual distribution of power between the sexes. But it did reflect women's control over the rituals and routines of the home which men had to respect as long as they lived by the code of domesticity.[49] Much the same could be said of the title 'queen', so freely lavished on the ideal wife and mother by writers like Patmore and Ruskin, doubtless taking their cue from Victoria's double identity as sovereign and wife.⁵⁰ If the lady's standing in the home was ultimately a fiction, it was one which demanded from men deference, self-control and a considerable expenditure of time.

This kind of homage was hard to square with any notion of manliness. Dancing to the tune of the wife or hostess reawakened the traditional fear that too much time spent in the company of women would encourage effeminacy. Kipling expressed precisely this anxiety in his early novel *The Light That Failed* (1890) where taking tea at five in the afternoon has become the tell-tale sign of the effeminate aesthete.⁵¹ Middle-class sensitivity on this issue was most clearly expressed in the condescending attitudes towards the suburban lifestyles of men of the lower middle class. Journalistic satire not only attacked the vulgarity and pretentiousness of the suburban clerk, but attributed these faults to his wife's control over the domestic sphere; in works like Thomas Crosland's *The Suburbans* (1905) the lower middle-class man had become a slave to his wife's vanity.⁵² The families of professional men and businessmen might agonize a little less over the finer points of social status, but in essentials their position was no different from that of the clerk or commercial traveller. Satirizing lower middle-class effeminacy was as much a means of displacing anxiety as of enforcing social distance on class inferiors. It acknowledged that a home controlled by women was not a fit abode for a manly breadwinner.

The homage which men were expected to pay in the home, like other expressions of chivalry, was premised on the fragility of the weaker sex. Yet these were the very years when, as we saw in the previous chapter, that premise was being undermined. The mere existence of an articulate feminism challenged the stereotype of female weakness, while its characteristic lines of argument placed male supremacists on the defensive. Feminist critics like Mona Caird were putting forward a new vision of marriage in which women would assert their equality instead of being forced to rely on the uncertain generosity of their spouses. The law was slowly but unmistakably catching up with the new thinking on inequality and exploitation within marriage, in the field of wives' rights to property and child custody. The Divorce Court, by accepting the principle of mental cruelty, served notice on husbands that wives were entitled to expect civilized standards of behaviour from their husbands, as of right. In 1891 a celebrated judgment by the Court of Appeal (in the Jackson case) laid down that husbands were not entitled to confine their wives in order to enforce their conjugal rights; this was widely glossed as placing liberty and power in the hands of the wife.⁵³ There was even talk of sexual autonomy and voluntary motherhood. The expansion of women's employment affected comparatively few middle-class wives, but by the end of the century a significant proportion had received a secondary education equal to that of their husbands, and they could not lightly be patronized as ignorant or empty-headed.

There can be little doubt that all these changes shifted the balance of advantage in men's attitude to marriage. It is easy to ridicule those opponents of the Married Women's Property Acts who believed that men would be put off matrimony altogether.[54] But the much-discussed changes in the law and the alarmist rhetoric which surrounded them certainly influenced the attitudes of young men. Misogyny and homosocial self-sufficiency are likely to have been intensified, while marriage was viewed as even more of a snare than before. The early Victorian model of domesticity had rested on an implied contract of master and protector in relation to dependent subordinate. Fifty years later that contract no longer seemed to hold. The husband still had the undivided duty of maintaining and protecting the home, but his domestic power and prestige were wilting; the 'weaker' sex, it seemed, was discovering its own strength.

These shifts in relations between the sexes were reflected in the changing spatial dynamics within the home. Faced with an uncompromisingly feminine ambience, middle-class men attached increasing importance to carving out their own exclusive space. They took their cue from the wealthy. Mark Girouard has described how from the 1850s onwards country houses were often equipped with a suite or wing of 'male' rooms – library, smoking room, billiard room, and sometimes bedrooms for bachelor friends – where men could relax away from the feminine constraint of the drawing room and the morning room.[55] In middle-class homes, it was already common for a room to be set aside for the husband's private use, but this was usually represented as a *professional* amenity, where a minister like William Gaskell or a lecturer like John Heaton performed an important part of his duties. By the 1880s, however, the role of the study or den as an escape from femininity was emphasized much more. Mary Haweis was abreast of the trend in 1889 when she recommended a 'smoking-den' for the husband even in the smaller house, where he could keep his 'books and ancient belongings, photographs of inscrutable people who were his early friends, gifts from unknown quarters which he still fancies he values', and to which his wife need only be admitted on sufferance. 'The tired master should have one place secure from the seamy side of domesticity.'[56] These sentiments were echoed by a correspondent who wrote to the *Daily Telegraph* in 1888 with an account of a bank manager oppressed by too many children and a live-in relative. 'His only happiness now is to shut himself up in his "growlery" away from the whole of his belongings to smoke the pipe of peace.'[57] The coach-house and stable yard were another masculine preserve. 'This region, far from women, and with that pleasant country smell of the home life of horses, was a favourite haunt of mine', recalled Eric Bligh of his Tooting childhood in the 1890s.[58]

★

It seems clear, then, from the periodicals and advice literature of the day that men's ambivalence towards domesticity represented a shift in sexual politics. Two or three generations on from the spread of the new moralized domesticity of the early nineteenth century, men were signalling a growing irritation with the rigid and exclusive association of domestic space with femininity. The gains in social and sexual equality which women were making as a result of statutory and judicial intervention not only placed sexual equality on the agenda as a general principle; they were also changing the balance of power quite specifically within the bourgeois home. Men's protest against domesticity therefore had something of the quality of a backlash. However, this theme of sexual antagonism must not be exaggerated. It is prominently on display in contemporary polemic, but much less obvious in the records of family life.[59] In fact the flight from domesticity was a turning away as much from patriarchy as from femininity. Many of the family narratives of the period record a rejection of the models of domestic manhood which late Victorian men had experienced during their upbringing. They were disenchanted both with the rewards of patriarchy, and with the character traits which had earned the patriarch his prestige within the home.

Samuel Butler was an early and well-known example. Both in his life and his novel *The Way of All Flesh* (completed in the 1880s) Butler is often cited as a classic instance of generational rebellion. But the character of Theodore Pontifex makes clear that Butler's anger against his father was about more than his own enforced subjection as a financial dependant; it extended to the whole practice of domestic patriarchy – its arbitrariness, meanness and deceit, its oppression of servants as well as junior family members. In both the novel and in Butler's own experience, the horrors of life in a parsonage were contrasted with the comforts of a bachelor existence in chambers – where there were no obligations to live-in dependants and no temptation to oppress them. Butler's own sexual needs as a middle-aged bachelor were met by a commercial arrangement with a mistress over many years. In Butler's eyes this renunciation of domestic patriarchy was the only 'independence' worth the name.[60] Edward Carpenter was someone else whose whole life was moulded by a reaction against the patriarchal household. His socialism was strongly influenced by the fact that his father had been, if not one of the idle rich, at any rate a comfortably positioned *rentier*. Carpenter's crusade for sexual openness – an end to 'the impure hush' – went back to the total censure of emotional and sexual disclosure in his childhood. And his lifelong commitment to women's emancipation was fired by the indignation he felt when he looked back at the futile idleness of his six sisters. All three of Edward's brothers also distanced themselves from domesticity, though in more conventional fashion by taking up careers which made marriage a distant contingency: one joined the Army, one the Navy, and one the Indian Civil Service.[61]

The negative appraisal of domestic patriarchy was also influenced by the polarization of sexual character which had disfigured so many mid-Victorian marriages. One of the deepest – though most intangible – influences on masculine domesticity in the late nineteenth century was the sharp divide experienced in childhood between the roles of mother and father. As was shown in Chapter 3, the theories of sexual difference which were popular in mid-Victorian England promised little in the way of convergence or companionship between husband and wife, and those differences were fully played out in the relations between parents and children. Maternal nurture implied softness, warmth, empathy and affection, and sons often experienced a real emotional openness from their mothers – all the greater if the mother herself felt put at a distance by her husband.[62] Fatherhood, on the other hand, suggested single-mindedness (particularly as regards breadwinning), discipline, rigidity and anxiety; many fathers subordinated their more human instincts to the overriding need to prepare their sons for a harsh and challenging market-place. Of course reality was more complex than this bleak picture would suggest: personal chemistry, not to mention the very considerable variation in education and taste between husbands and wives, saw to that. But the medical and psychological theories of the period undoubtedly influenced popular notions of what was appropriate in husband and wife – and what should be expected of mother and father. The masculinity of the paterfamilias was nicely caught by the French writer Edmond Demolins in 1898. Comparing English families with those at home, he wrote,

> A father's conversation with his children bears on serious, real, manly topics. Their talk does not run on the world of fashion (English fashion!), and Society tittle-tattle, nor on the good old time when life was so easy, so calm, so pleasant! No, they vaunt the Struggle for Existence, and Self-Help.[63]

Many of the late Victorian men who tried to break free of domesticity had been brought up in an environment of this kind. They were troubled not only by the distortion of their parents' natures, but by the threatened distortion of their own masculine sense of identity. For the message of polarized sexual character within the home for young men was severe: warmth and affection were feminine traits, to be exercised in the privacy of the home; masculinity was defined by its public destiny, in a way which excluded the so-called feminine qualities.

Two responses to this character formation can be clearly discerned in the lives of young men. The first was to assimilate the polarization of traits between father and mother as faithfully as possible, by suppressing the need to give or receive affection, and the impulse to express feelings. This was the posture of the 'stiff upper lip'. Silent, reserved and unshaken by waves of emotion, it represented the most extreme form of manliness as self-control. Sentiment and self-examination were dismissed as 'morbid'; to reveal inner pain, whether through tears or depression, was a sign of weakness. The stiff upper lip held out the hope of an unequivocal masculinity, while making intimate relations with the opposite sex almost impossible. The yearning for the feminine, instead of being pursued in courtship, was invested in the sentimentalized memory of the mother. This was what Edward Carpenter meant by 'man the ungrown'. To him it was a tragedy that the country was ruled by men of such diminished humanity.[64]

The other response entailed greater risks and often considerable frustration. Men who had been denied the warmth and affection which they craved from their fathers sometimes grew up determined to find these responses in other men, and only too ready to idealize those they thought might offer them. Bachelorhood and club or college life might be not merely a refuge from domesticity, but an alternative emotional resource. Among the more literary this aspiration was expressed in a self-conscious commitment to a 'Uranian' ideal – an attraction to younger men which was erotic in character though seldom given full sexual expression. Emotionally intense and physically demonstrative friendship between men was not new – in fact in most historical periods it has been taken for granted. What was new at the end of the nineteenth century was the numbers of men who tried to make this kind of friendship the focus of their lives, to the exclusion of marriage. Here in outline was a positive alternative to domesticity, but one which had its root in a disenchantment with the character of patriarch and the privileges which went with it.

Charles Ashbee exemplifies this second response. His parents certainly practised a fairly rigorous form of separate spheres. Elizabeth was never allowed to set foot in her husband's office in the City, while Henry's only contribution to the functioning of the household appears to have been to select the wines for their Tuesday dinner parties.[65] As described in the previous chapter, the Ashbees' separation in 1893 was the outcome of their growing divergence of interests. Charles had already become permanently estranged from his father over his own choice of career. He was therefore little inclined to sympathize with Henry's overbearing and rigid behaviour in the home, and he sided strongly with his mother; he was also influenced by her feminist friends like the educationalist Frances Mary Buss. These experiences affected not only Charles's attitude to his parents but his own approach to life. His early career as a designer was fired by an ideal of fraternity in work, played out in the Guild of Handicraft which he set up in London's East End, and he was strongly attracted to Edward Carpenter's ideal of homosexual comradeship. In 1897, at the age of 34, Charles proposed to the young Janet Forbes, but with intense misgivings and only after much internal debate. Janet greatly admired Charles's work and ideals. But during their marriage her desire for full intimacy often took second place to his immersion in the 'comrade friends', especially the boys of the Guild, and to his continuing devotion to his mother. For many years the marriage was almost certainly unconsummated.[66]

Charles Ashbee was sensitive to the inequalities and oppressions of domestic patriarchy, and at one level his life can be read as a principled stand against that inheritance. Such men were a small minority. The other response to the character gap between father and mother was less conscious and less principled. The many men who suppressed 'feminine' traits, maintained a stiff-upper-lip reserve, and shunned emotional intimacy with the opposite sex, were conforming to the gender prescriptions of middle-class society – even though the reproduction of that class was thereby called into doubt. They rejected the traditional patriarchal role for emotional rather than intellectual or moral reasons. This pattern is well represented among the empire-builders of the *fin de siècle*, and in no one more than Kitchener, imperial man *par excellence*. For the first fourteen years of his life, Herbert Kitchener was educated at home in Ireland, and thus experienced the full measure of the character gulf between his parents. His mother was warm and caring. When she died early from tuberculosis in 1864, Herbert accepted the blow stoically, but he was deeply affected. His father was a retired army officer with a short temper and an authoritarian disposition. He ruled over the household like a martinet, admired but feared by his son. Herbert's mother had worried that her son's sensitive nature would be crushed by his father, and so it proved: the son adapted all too well to the father's overbearing style, while repressing anything that smacked of the feminine. After Herbert entered the Royal Military Academy at the age of seventeen, he never again lived in conditions of domesticity. His reputation for steely reticence was well deserved. His emotional life was restricted to sentimental relationships with a few young officers, sometimes referred to as 'Kitchener's cubs'.[67]

Three years younger than Kitchener, Cecil Rhodes came from a different occupational niche and pursued a very different career path, but the masculine formation was similar. He was raised in an Essex vicarage, the sixth of nine children. Louise Rhodes was open-hearted and tender, and Cecil her favourite child. Francis Rhodes, already forty-six when Cecil was born, was detached from his family and preoccupied with the affairs of the parish; he was aloof, impatient and uncommunicative. Only one of their sons ever married; two entered the Army, and two sailed for South Africa. Cecil himself avoided female company and constructed his life as an exclusively man's world in which favoured subordinates were admitted to an inner circle. His most authoritative biographers have concluded that all his life Rhodes felt deprived of a close relationship with his father. Yet the model of masculine domesticity which Francis Rhodes presented was deeply unattractive.[68] Vicarage sons were particularly sensitive to the demerits of domestic patriarchy because their fathers were present in the home for so much of the time. It may be for this reason that they are disproportionately represented in the ranks of colonial officialdom. For example, of the two hundred or so who joined the administration of the British East African Protectorate (later Kenya) between 1895 and 1914, no fewer than forty-one were the sons of Anglican parsons.[69] Theodore Pontifex and his like cast a long shadow over late Victorian England.

★

An Ashbee, a Butler, a Kitchener or a Rhodes cannot stand for an entire generation. But the flight from domesticity which these lives exemplify is reflected in some highly distinctive features of late Victorian culture and society. One of these was the club. From the perspective of the habitué the late nineteenth and early twentieth centuries were the Golden Age of the club. This was true not only of the prestigious West End establishments, whose number grew by around 50 per cent in the second half of the century, but of the provinces also; the years 1870–1900 have been termed the heyday of the men's club in the northern cities.[70] Freemasonry became widespread over the country, with 2,329 new lodges founded between 1870 and 1912.[71] Every kind of taste and avocation was catered for, and almost every pocket. All the clubs excluded women, and nearly all of them were characterized by a bachelor ambience of smoking rooms, billiards, cards and manservants. The club was a refuge for the bachelor without a 'good' address of his own, the 'man's man' who kept female society at arm's length, and the administrator or soldier on leave from his posting overseas. Often the culture of misogyny was not far from the surface, especially in the more bohemian clubs which grew in number towards the end of the century.[72] In a burlesque of 1891 Israel Zangwill described the 'Bachelors' Club' in Leicester Square, whose members must never have been in love, must be bachelors from conviction, and must belong to the Anti-Anti-Tobacco League.[73] That so many club members were bachelors of long standing indicates that club culture had become a viable alternative to the married state. But (as stressed in Chapter 6) the clubs were also frequented by married men – those who, in Brian Harrison's words, 'spent a large part of their lives as though they were bachelors', dining, drinking, talking in an all-male setting, and depriving their wives of company and cash.[74] The prominence of this element is a good indication of widespread ambivalence towards the pleasures and duties of family life. One or two visits to the club each week might be consistent with domestic duties; as one advice book put it, the wife can then 'have a picnic dinner – always a joy to a woman – with a book propped up before her, can let herself go and let her cook go out'.[75] But the rebel against the feminized home contrived to spend as many of his leisure hours at the club as possible. This was a familiar grievance among wives, as shown by the lengthy correspondence on marriage which appeared in the *Daily Telegraph* in 1888.[76] The club had not become more attractive in itself; its intensified appeal was the consequence of external factors, among which the perceived deterioration in the conditions of domesticity was much the most significant.

One category of club grew with breathtaking speed during the late Victorian period – the sports club. Early and mid-Victorian men sought out an associational life for masculine conviviality, intellectual discussion, politics and culture. The addition of sport to this list represented a major increase in men's out-of-home activities. The range of amateur sports practised in England today still bears the strong imprint of the late nineteenth century. The origins of middle-class athleticism can be traced back to the promotion of team games by the public schools in the 1850s, as a means of providing an avenue of personal improvement for the academically less able boy – and later as a stratagem in the war on 'impurity'. 'Muscular Christianity' was a reflection of those concerns, but its impact on the Anglican clergy was not reflected in middle-class society at large. More important in disseminating sport were the periodic reminders – notably the invasion scare of 1859 – that the country needed men who were fit in body as well as in mind. In addition the competitive character of most sports

appealed to the bourgeois ethic of the market-place, while the growing influence of biological models of human development raised fears about physical
degeneration. By the 1870s an astonishing growth in athleticism was under way
in England. It included new sports like track athletics, Rugby Union, hockey,
tennis, badminton and cycling; the expansion of existing sports like cricket,
mountaineering and rowing; and one notable import, golf from Scotland.[77]

It has become customary to highlight the ideological and educational
rationale for this spectacular growth. But two very obvious gendered features of
the sporting craze need to be stressed: it was primarily a masculine affair, and it
took men out of the home.[78] Women were certainly not excluded in a
comprehensive way; their participation in tennis and cycling, for example, was
widely commented upon. But the organization and expression of late Victorian
sport were, to quote its most recent historian, 'aggressively masculine'.[79] For
many men sport held out the reassurance of an alternative way of life to the
feminized home. The sporting craze resulted in a massive encroachment on the
family weekend. Neither golf nor cricket could be played in less than half a day;
both of them were open to men who were past the vigour of early manhood
and had 'settled down' (golf was for some time strongly associated with the
over-35s). In *The Sorrows of a Golfer's Wife* (1896) the narrator recounted her
plight in being reduced 'to the humiliating position of a nonentity and a mere
golfer's wife', while her husband shied away from his domestic responsibilities
and discovered a new confidence to assert himself in the home.[80] Mountaineering and rock-climbing imposed a different rhythm, but with comparable
results; they involved a revival of the practice of men-only holidays, taken in
the Lake District or the Alps, but now justified by a rhetoric of almost spiritual
intensity. The out-of-season break in most sports was minimized by purely
social events in the clubhouse, where the camaraderie of team play and
competition could be kept in shape before play resumed. There is a rough
correlation between the growth of athleticism and the decline of religious
observance, summed up by the intrusion of weekend sport on the 'Victorian'
Sunday. But the religious analogy underestimates sport's impact on late
Victorian bourgeois society: it absorbed a great deal more time and money than
church activity had done, and it was overwhelmingly a masculine pursuit
(whereas church and chapel congregations attracted more women than
men).[81]

The high profile of organized sport was reflected in the heavily physical slant
now given to the concept of manliness. Indeed the statements of some
enthusiasts implied that athletic prowess was *all* that was required for full manly
credentials. The formative trials which tested manhood were increasingly seen
in sporting terms – the injury on the rugby field, the agonizing spurt to the
finishing line, the brush with death on a rock face. The headmaster of Loretto
declared, 'I have never yet known a genuine rugby forward who was not
distinctively a man'.[82] Such statements should not, however, be taken to
indicate a collapse of moral content. Sports were promoted not only for their

training in physical fitness, but for their character-building qualities of courage, self-control, stoical endurance, and the subordination of the ego to the team. The requirements of sport, taken in deadly earnest, were perfectly attuned to the 'stiff upper lip' character formation so common among men brought up in conventional middle-class families at this time. Pain and emotion were repressed, and individuality curtailed, in the cause of producing a type. The modified code of manliness at the end of the century was not, then, detached from morality. But it was uncoupled from domesticity. At the beginning of the century the Evangelical strategy to reform manliness had been to root it firmly in the home. Thomas Arnold and the first generation of reforming public school headmasters did not dissent from this, regarding family affections and respect for womanhood as essential to a manly character. Thomas Hughes was of this persuasion also, but by 1882 when he asserted that a man's relations within the home were those 'which most shrewdly test his manhood',[83] he was out of touch with mainstream opinion. Late Victorian manliness was a public, even military, code, to be exercised among men. Relations with the other sex were taken for granted, or else subsumed by a ritual call to chivalry. 'Purity' was promoted as a call to cleanness – a perfect manhood – rather than a moral obligation towards women.[84]

In retrospect the sexuality implied in late Victorian manliness seems decidedly ambivalent. Any code which is so resolutely homosocial and so indifferent towards women must, we suppose, be founded on a culture of same-sex desire. Certainly England at this time boasted a varied and extensive range of homosexual lifestyles.[85] As the trials of Oscar Wilde dramatically illustrated, there was by the 1890s a commercialized homosexual underworld in London and other cities which existed largely to service well-heeled men of the middle and upper classes. Most of the punters had acquired their forbidden tastes at public school, and the strongly homosocial slant of their code of manliness seems all of a piece with their sexual preferences. But that code gave no quarter to homosexuality; it was opposed to vice of every kind. Men's desires were supposed to be confined to proper relations with a member of the opposite sex. In that sense 'purity' was an even-handed principle. If manliness was taken seriously, it did not prompt men to prefer their own sex, but to submit to the frustration of curbing almost all their carnal impulses. Late Victorian men of the middle class included a disproportionate number who were in deep conflict with sexuality as well as domesticity.

But the code of manliness in its public renderings was no more a reliable guide to men's behaviour than it had been in the early Victorian period. Homosexual practice was almost certainly on the increase among middle-class men. The sexual radical Edward Carpenter thought so; so too did the homophobic standard-bearers of purity.[86] This view is not susceptible to demonstration; given the rigours of the law and the hounding of miscreants, homosexuality was seldom acknowledged. After the Criminal Law Amendment Act of 1885 against acts of gross indecency, homosexuality continued to find expression in two contrasted ways. On the one hand, it was serviced by a network of prostitution in the big cities which from time to time came to light in criminal proceedings. At the same time homosexuality flourished in a range of all-male institutions as a veiled identity and usually a sublimated practice. It sailed under the flag of celibacy, as for example among Anglo-Catholic clergy.[87] It appeared as concern for the welfare of boys, as in the case of youth-leaders and public school masters.[88] And it took refuge in a celebration of collegiate life, as among the resident members of the new 'settlements' in the slums.[89] All of these settings were a beacon for young middle-class men impatient of the bonds of domesticity.

In those pre-Freudian times homosexuality was not interpreted in terms of family dynamics. Proselytizing schoolmasters attributed it to moral weakness – by which they meant the habit of masturbation acquired in childhood, followed by collusion in 'corruption' by an older boy at school. Apologists for homosexuality, on the other hand, seized on scientific evidence of a 'third sex', formed before birth and beyond the scope of corrective treatment. They were also keen to rescue same-sex love from its popular association with vice. Homosexuals were as inhibited as anyone else by their exposure to the teachings of purity. Those who had attended public school would have learned of 'Greek love', but in a version which emphasized ideal beauty and cast a veil over genital contact.[90] The severity of the law – with the consequent licence for blackmail – reinforced the trend. These were the conditions for the emergence of a self-consciously 'higher' homosexual identity which stressed its emotional (even moral) features, rather than sexual pleasure. The more idealistic of the 'Uranians' followed Carpenter in advocating a 'homogenic love' across class barriers, as a means of social renewal.[91] In this somewhat rarefied form homosexuality represented a convincing and fulfilling emotional field in place of domesticity. This was probably the basis for much of its appeal for Charles Ashbee. He was strongly drawn to Carpenter, and much of his creative energy was taken up by his Guild of Handicraft, where East End boys were trained in craft work. However inhibited or sublimated the Uranian sensibility might be, it was strong enough to be the focus of Ashbee's emotional life for some years, and it came quite close to frustrating his plans for marriage.[92]

★

Several aspects of the flight from domesticity are well illustrated by the men of the Benson family. The contrast between generations is striking. Edward Benson had every reason to value domestic comfort and order because his hold on these things had been so precarious in early life. When he was 13 his father – an unbusinesslike chemical manufacturer – had died a bankrupt, leaving Edward responsible for his mother and her seven other children. Except for his four years as a student at Cambridge, he had exercised domestic responsibility all his life – first as a widow's eldest son, then as the senior male in another widow's family, and finally as paterfamilias in his own household. A secure and

22. Refuge from domesticity: Charles Ashbee and members of the Guild of Handicraft, Tintern Abbey, 1899.

appreciated place in the domestic sphere was integral to Edward's sense of himself and his place in the world. None of this was reproduced in the next generation. Edward and Mary Benson had six children, born between 1860 and 1871. As recounted in Chapter 5, Martin (the eldest) died young, as did his sister Nellie. One daughter and three sons remained. None of them married. The three sons gravitated towards homosocial settings. Arthur (A.C. Benson) became a public school teacher and Cambridge don; Fred (E.F. Benson) became a successful novelist, literary man about town and confirmed bachelor; and Hugh (R.H. Benson), after failing the Indian Civil Service exams, entered the priesthood, joined an Anglican celibate community and later went over to Rome. The Benson brothers were comparatively untouched by empire, although Arthur composed the words of 'Land of Hope and Glory' ('Wider still and wider shall thy bounds be set . . .'). But all three shared something of a 'Uranian' sensibility. This was most pronounced in the case of Arthur, whose

23. Refuge from domesticity: Arthur Benson and members of his house at Eton, 1893.

profession gave him ample opportunity to pursue romantic friendships with young men; his relations with them were chaste but all-engrossing, his ideal a 'concurrence of the soul'.[93] Fred subscribed to similar values. As a young man he mixed in the same circles as Oscar Wilde and Lord Alfred Douglas. In middle age he had a taste for the company of men half his age, and his most personal novel (*David Blaize*, 1916) was a record of a passionate schoolboy friendship.[94]

The strength of the Bensons' conviction against marriage varied. It was strongest in the case of Hugh who already regarded marriage as 'inconceivable' by the time he left Cambridge. It was least settled in the case of Arthur, but even he never came close to a proposal. Edward and Mary pressed him to marry, but in vain.[95] When Fred died in 1940, the family line died too. This outcome can be partly attributed to all-male education. The three brothers were deeply marked by their experience of public school and Cambridge. The mental instability which afflicted Edward, his son Arthur and (worst of all) his daughter Maggie also had an impact: in the late nineteenth century there was a strong presumption of heredity in such cases, and this weighed heavily with Arthur.[96] But the sons were reacting against more than the fear of insanity. Their parents were a pronounced case of the character gap found in so many Victorian marriages. After Mary Benson died in 1918, Arthur and Fred were able to read her diaries, in addition to Edward's papers which they had studied years before when he died in 1896. It was clearer to them than ever how ill-matched their parents had been. 'It seems to me now', Arthur wrote, 'that they were two very vivid and splendid people – but utterly antagonistic in temperament, and probably ought not to have married'; Edward had been intense, self-willed and dominating, while Mary had been loving and genuinely accepting of other people's faults.[97]

The contrast was a heavily gendered one. Edward never seemed to be truly off duty from his professional role as moral guide; his censorious and sometimes severe behaviour towards his sons stemmed from his conviction that they must be forearmed against an increasingly godless and amoral society – hence in Fred's words the 'watchfulness and responsibility' of his love.[98] Mary Benson was no less concerned with her sons' manliness, but she governed with a much lighter touch. Having delivered a dressing-down, she would quickly relax the tension with humour or an unexpected compliment. Her affection was never in doubt, and her sons could rely upon it in difficult times. As Fred put it, 'she loved with a swift eagerness'.[99] Mary Benson's sons remained under her spell all their lives. During her twenty-two years' widowhood, they were frequent visitors to her house in Sussex; Arthur, who went there three or four times a year, sometimes for weeks on end, called it 'the very sweetest home imaginable'; he treasured 'its perpetual feast of little simple, ancient, homely beauties'.[100] But for all three brothers, domesticity was something which belonged in the past; it was an extension of childhood, not a prescription for life. To assume the role of paterfamilias, as it had been discharged by their father, was inconceivable. This was not because they rejected their father and all his works. All of them retained a deep respect for him after he was dead; Arthur even wrote the official life – an act of duty which became an act of love.[101] The sons' reaction against their father was gradual and discriminating, and it focused most closely on his family life. Each in his own way sought a substitute for the warm relations denied to them by their father in romantic male friendship. But here too family upbringing took its toll. They might deplore the emotional restraint shown by their father, but they could not break away from it entirely. Arthur, who in his immense diary left much the fullest account of his feelings, could never approach the object of his affections too closely. Full emotional disclosure was impossible, and sexual expression was completely repressed. The best Arthur could achieve was to be 'on the edge of Paradise', as he described himself at the age of 48.[102]

★

Arthur Benson's bouts of tortured self-examination are proof enough that renunciation of domesticity was not always an easy option. But it was an increasingly common one. The accumulated and intensified tensions of bourgeois home life had reached the point where thousands of young men preferred to postpone marriage as long as possible, or to avoid it altogether. They were supported in their choice by a vigorous bachelor society in the major towns and cities, and by a new genre of adventure fiction which glamorized their condition. For those who had been to public school there was the sense of an almost seamless continuum of all-male institutions, where the emotional and material demands of women could be evaded indefinitely. The empire beckoned as the most unequivocal means of realizing the fantasy of a manly life free from feminine constraint. Of course the reproduction of patriarchy did not grind to a halt. Large numbers of men continued, as before, to contemplate matrimony happily, and many were deeply satisfied with the results. But even their conventional contentment was played out against a new backdrop. The merits of the married state were open to question, as never before. Marriage could not be taken for granted. The impact of the failure to marry on the national birth rate, and specifically on the survival of the 'superior' classes, was keenly debated. Domesticity, as men had experienced it during the mid-Victorian period, was no longer a destiny; it had become one option among several.

It is true that the declining incidence of marriage among middle-class men is open to other interpretations. Marriage has always been a highly sensitive indicator of wider economic and social trends, and this was no less true in the late nineteenth century. Since the middle class had made domestic show one of the main signs of social status, the tendency towards inflation in marital expectations was relentless; as the threshold of household outlay went up, more and more bachelors found that it was beyond their reach. Meanwhile other middle-class men of inferior education or uncertain capital found it difficult to secure rewarding employment in Britain; for them a career in the colonies, with its effective embargo on early marriage, was an obvious recourse. But there is surprisingly little evidence that delaying marriage for economic reasons was seen as a tragedy for those involved. What an earlier age had regarded as the regrettable postponement of full manhood now reflected a deeply felt suspicion of domesticity. The values of the public school, the armed services and the gentleman's club all testify to that suspicion, and popular fiction was remodelled during these years to take account of it. Both the public discourse about marriage, and the family histories of middle-class men themselves, show that the contradictions which had always been inherent in masculine domesticity had by the end of the century come into the open. Middle-class masculinity was more troubled and uncertain as a result, with social and cultural implications which extended far beyond the domestic sphere.

Conclusion

In contemporary British culture the label 'Victorian' continues to serve as a necessary shorthand to denote the past from which we are anxious to escape. Not even the vigorous defence of 'Victorian values' mounted by the Conservatives in the 1980s succeeded in dislodging the association of Victorianism with joyless and hypocritical repression. It seems we still cannot do without a negative and simplified image of Victorian sexuality.[1] The same applies to the Victorian family. We seize on stories of stifling ritual, Sunday boredom and rigid discipline to substantiate a picture of empty marriage, sexual hypocrisy and regimented childhood. Against this grim starting line we can plot the extent of our own emancipation, congratulating ourselves for our superiority, or reproaching ourselves for our backwardness.

As this book has shown, Victorian middle-class family life was far more varied than the popular stereotype allows. It was also more contradictory. It featured men who believed in an exalted ideal of domesticity and strove to live by it, and others who were defeated by its contradictions and registered their ambivalence in public. Intensely homosocial leisure pursuits flourished alongside a call to the hearth which was widely observed. The balance between patriarchal and companionate marriage was struck in countless different ways. Childhood occupied a larger place in the adult imagination than at any previous time, yet children themselves were often brought up in an inflexible domestic regime. Fatherhood encompassed every variant from the almost invisible breadwinner to the accessible and attentive playmate.

All this means that in the context of the family the label 'Victorian' is a very slippery one, and charting the gradual unpicking of 'Victorianism' over the last century is not likely to be a very enlightening enterprise. Indeed analogies between then and now are in some ways more instructive. For example, the recent attempt by Robert Bly[2] to recover a 'deep' masculinity on behalf of men who have grown up in feminized homes would have been instantly recognizable to all those Victorian fathers who patronized the new public schools in order to remove their sons to a more manly environment. But ultimately the nineteenth century matters, not because it furnishes an inspiring ideal or a cautionary tale, but because it witnessed both the climax of masculine domesticity and the first major reaction against it. In that sense the Victorians prefigured a dialectic which has continued from that day to this. The Edwardian period saw a continuation of the late Victorian pattern. Both the allure of empire as a men-only sphere and the male backlash against women's rights intensified, and they were reflected in the most successful reassertion of manly values at this time, the Boy Scouts. Baden-Powell believed his creation was a means of instilling the self-reliance of the frontiersman in boys attending day school who were too much under their mothers' influence.[3] After 1914 the confrontation between masculinity and domesticity would never be so starkly posed again. Two world wars profoundly conditioned men's attitudes to the home. The horror of the trenches undermined much of the appeal of the adventure fantasy which had animated the generation of Rider Haggard and Kipling. The male bonding of wartime failed to survive the armistice, and marriage was popular with men as never before.[4] In that context, the reaction against domesticity in modernist art and architecture between the wars seems little more than an aesthetic indulgence by the avant-garde.[5] The same pattern was repeated after the Second World War, the 1950s marking the beginning of modern DIY (as well as the growing vogue for open-plan interiors). In the meantime domestic service had largely disappeared from the middle-class household, except in the much attenuated form of the 'daily woman'. Domestic privacy became more absolute, and as labour-saving technology gradually took the place of the departed servants during the 1950s and 1960s there was the potential for more quality time between family members. In a more secular form the Victorian ethos of masculine domesticity was alive and well.

Yet if the overall tendency was for society to become more domestic, the gulf between the sexes became if anything more pronounced. Men spent longer hours at home, but they strictly observed the separation of marital roles, and – as a number of social enquiries in the 1950s confirmed – they tended to hold back from emotional intimacy.[6] There was little disposition to question this 'natural' masculinity until the revival of radical sexual politics in the 1970s. The interpretation then advanced by the anti-sexist men's movement was an interesting modification of the views current a hundred years before. Whereas the Victorians had placed their faith in domesticity as an antidote to the market-place, the men's movement of the early 1980s complained that they were disqualified from participating fully in domestic life by the wholesale distortion of their emotional selves by the capitalist system; at its most pessimistic, their assumption was that until men were emancipated from capitalist relations of production, no amount of individual breast-beating would change the face of masculinity. That view was an accurate reflection of how much more alienating the public world of work had become since the nineteenth century, in the wake of corporatism, bureaucratization and nationwide occupational mobility.

One difference between the Victorian age and our own is that 'the family' is no longer the undisputed article of faith which it once was. Its vociferous defence by the Right in Britain today is a good measure of how seriously the conventional family is under fire, not so much ideologically, as because of the life decisions of countless unmarried couples and single parents. Even among those who unequivocally support the family, there is a much more flexible attitude to sexual roles than existed in Victorian society. In a culture which acknowledges a relatively high degree of gender diversity, there is less need to put boys through the mill of a training in manliness. Domestic service is returning to the middle-class household, not to sustain the dignity of the lady of the house, but to service a two-income family. Fathers who wish to go beyond the stilted reserve of a generation ago and involve themselves in the routines of childcare may feel marginalized, but they receive more recognition than their grandfathers would have done.

However, this flexibility operates within a framework which would have been familiar to the Victorians. Their notions of domesticity were primarily a response to the fact that for the first time the paid employment of most bourgeois men took place away from the home. Today, despite the electronic revolution of the home computer and the Internet, the separation of work from home is still the condition of most people. Styles may have been transformed, but the home is still imagined and equipped as the antithesis of the workplace, and as a refuge from it. The Victorians established the 'common sense' of the proposition that, to be fully human and fully masculine, men must be active and sentient participants in domestic life. One hundred years on, we still contend with the practical and emotional implications of that belief.

A Note on Method

The principal source materials for the history of the family – the demographic, the didactic and the personal – reflect the somewhat fragmented character of this comparatively new field. Since my concern is with the family as experienced and represented at the time, I have made little use of demographic data, except to cite the findings of others in order to speak as precisely as possible about those aspects of family structure which can be quantified. Advice literature has been much drawn on by historians of all periods, and given the didactic bent of the Victorians there is no shortage of it for this study. Some of the advice-book writers of the period, like Sarah Ellis and John Angell James, achieved a very wide readership, and are among the most familiar names to the student of Victorian social history. Didactic writing of this kind is used here not as a short cut to discovering what domesticity meant in practice, but as an essential guide to the values which people regarded – with varying degrees of commitment – as the benchmark against which their home life should be judged.[1]

A fuller explanation is needed of the personal materials used for this study. They certainly exist in profusion, and they document the lives not only of the famous but of all classes where literacy was taken for granted. In many instances the scale of the record is prodigious.

> A hundred years hence, the laborious and comprehensive story told by Dr Heaton in the seven or eight closely written quarto volumes, each of many hundred pages, which formed the work of so many years, will be exceedingly valuable as a picture of domestic life in an English provincial town in the reign of Queen Victoria.[2]

This was the only reference made to John Heaton's massive journal in the Life written by Thomas Wemyss Reid in 1883. Like so many Victorian biographers, Wemyss Reid respected the privacy of his subject's family life; his interest was in Heaton's professional and public achievements. The journal belonged unequivocally to the private sphere. It was passed down through the family, and remains in private hands today. The journal was treated no differently from Heaton's letters to members of his family: they too were given the dignity of a leather binding and kept in the family circle.

As Wemyss Reid anticipated, the value of this kind of material is now fully recognized not only by the biographer but by the social historian. This is reflected in the very large number of family collections which are held in archives and libraries. They are, however, singularly unwieldy and uneven. Letters between separated spouses usually say much more about the travel itinerary and social introductions than they do about the couple's more intimate concerns. Diaries are not necessarily good sources for domestic life. At one extreme are devotional diaries intended to take the place of the confessional; Archibald Tait's, for example, was almost entirely restricted to spiritual matters. At the other extreme, many men treated the diary as a record of personal achievement; it was kept at home, but referred mostly to public life.[3] Diaries which shed light on men's domestic lives are harder to come by than might be imagined. Even John Heaton's journal is a good deal more informative on his varied public activities than his own domestic circle. All too often men's private papers are often not private at all, in the sense of being domestic or familial. A number of topics, like birth control or prostitution, are virtually never aired.

I have drawn on material relating to sixty families in all. Seven were explored in some depth through manuscript as well as published sources. These are the families of Joshua Pritchard, a Manchester exciseman; Edward Herford, a Manchester attorney; Cornelius Stovin, a Lincolnshire farmer; Isaac Holden, a Bradford mill-owner; John Heaton, a Leeds doctor; Daniel Meinertzhagen, a London banker; and Edward Benson, a priest and teacher. Although some effort was made to achieve a spread of region, occupation and religious denomination, this selection cannot be treated as a representative sample. Even when the remaining fifty-three families are included, there are gaps and imbalances. Nevertheless the case studies are more than merely illustrative. They offer a way into domesticity as it was experienced at the time. The analytical family historian deals in abstractions: developmental patterns, occupational routines, completed family size, ideologies of gender, and so on. Individual case-histories not only anchor these abstractions in lived experience; they also show us, as no other technique can do, how the compartmentalized categories of social analysis were articulated with each other on the ground. Social history is about the messiness of people's lives, as well as the structures which enable us to generalize about those lives. In this book I have tried to do justice to both.

Notes

Introduction: Masculinity and Domesticity

1. Betty Askwith, *Two Victorian Families*, London, 1971; David Williams, *Genesis and Exodus: a Portrait of the Benson Family*, London, 1979.
2. The most subtle exponent of these issues is R.W. Connell. See his *Gender and Power*, Cambridge, 1987, and his *Masculinities*, Cambridge, 1995.
3. Leonore Davidoff and Catherine Hall, *Family Fortunes: Men and Women of the English Middle Class, 1780–1850*, London, 1987.
4. Amy Louise Erickson, *Women and Property in Early Modern England*, London, 1993; F.K. Prochaska, *Women and Philanthropy in Nineteenth-Century England*, Oxford, 1980; Clare Midgley, *Women against Slavery: the British Campaigns, 1780–1870*, London, 1992.
5. John Tosh, 'What Should Historians Do With Masculinity? Reflections on Nineteenth-Century Britain', *History Workshop Journal* 38 (1994), pp. 179–202.
6. For England the most comprehensive guide is Anthony Fletcher, *Gender, Sex and Subordination in England, 1500–1800*, London, 1995.
7. On the question of patriarchy, see Judith Bennett, 'Feminism and History', *Gender & History* 1 (1989), pp. 251–72, and Michael Roper and John Tosh, 'Historians and the Politics of Masculinity', in Roper and Tosh (eds), *Manful Assertions: Masculinities in*

Britain since 1800, London, 1991, pp. 8–11.
8. The classic account is Keith Thomas, 'The Double Standard', *Journal of the History of Ideas* 20 (1959), pp. 195–216.
9. Laura Gowing, *Domestic Dangers: Women, Words and Sex in Early Modern London*, Oxford, 1996.
10. Carole Pateman, *The Sexual Contract*, Cambridge, 1988, pp. 77–92.
11. See Christopher Reed (ed.), *Not At Home: the Suppression of Domesticity in Modern Art and Architecture*, London, 1996, editor's Introduction, p. 7.
12. John Gillis, *A World of their Own Making: Myth, Ritual, and the Quest for Family Values*, Cambridge, MA, 1996, pp. xv, 61–2.
13. Gaston Bachelard, *The Poetics of Space*, trans. Maria Jolas, Boston, MA, 1964, pp. 5–7, 17.
14. E.J. Hobsbawm, *The Age of Capital, 1848–1875*, London, 1977, pp. 278–83.
15. Walter Benjamin, *Charles Baudelaire: a Lyric Poet in the Era of High Capitalism*, trans. Harry Zohn, London, 1973, p. 167.
16. There is a weaker case for claiming seventeenth-century Holland as the origin of modern domesticity. See Witold Rybczynski, *Home: a Short History of an Idea*, London, 1986.
17. G.M. Young, *Victorian England: Portrait of an Age*, Oxford, 1936, p. 150.

18. Jane Rendall, *The Origins of Modern Feminism*, Basingstoke, 1985, ch. 3; Davidoff and Hall, *Family Fortunes*, pp. 167–88; M. Jeanne Peterson, *Family, Love and Work in the Lives of Victorian Gentlewomen*, Bloomington, IN, 1989.

19. For an early recognition of this aspect of Victorian domesticity, see Walter E. Houghton, *The Victorian Frame of Mind, 1833–1870*, New Haven, CT, 1957, pp. 341–8.

20. Hobsbawm, *Age of Capital*, pp. 278–80.

21. David D. Gilmore, *Manhood in the Making: Cultural Concepts of Masculinity*, New Haven, CT, 1990.

Chapter 1: The Middle-Class Household

1. John Heaton, MS Diary, autobiographical introduction, and entry for 31 March 1851 (private collection, Leeds); Brian and Dorothy Payne, *Claremont*, Yorkshire Archaeological Society, Leeds, 1980.

2. Elizabeth Jennings, 'Sir Isaac Holden (1807–97)', Ph.D. thesis, Bradford University, 1982; John Tosh, 'From Keighley to St-Denis: Separation and Intimacy in Victorian Bourgeois Marriage', *History Workshop Journal* 40 (1995), pp. 193–206.

3. William Lucas, *A Quaker Journal*, 2 vols, London, 1934.

4. Margaret Hunt, *The Middling Sort: Commerce, Gender, and the Family in England, 1680–1780*, Berkeley, CA, 1996.

5. The calculations were made by Dudley Baxter. See John Seed, 'From "Middling Sort" to Middle Class in Late Eighteenth and Early Nineteenth Century England', in M.L. Bush (ed.), *Social Orders and Social Classes in Europe since 1500*, London, 1992, p. 121.

6. Tosh, 'From Keighley to St-Denis'.

7. Kathryn Hughes, *The Victorian Governess*, London, 1993, pp. 28–9, 48.

8. Daniel Cruikshank and Neil Burton, *Life in the Georgian City*, London, 1990; Shani d'Cruze, 'The Middling Sort in Eighteenth-Century Colchester: Independence, Social Relations and the Community Broker', in Jonathan Barry and Christopher Brooks (eds), *The Middling Sort of People*, Basingstoke, 1994, p. 181.

9. Peter Earle, *The Making of the English Middle Class: Business, Society and Family Life in London, 1660–1730*, London, 1989; Barry and Brooks, *Middling Sort*, passim; Lorna Weatherill, *Consumer Behaviour and Material Culture in Britain, 1660–1760*, London, 1988, p. 138. Joan Lane, *Apprenticeship in England, 1600–1914*, London, 1996, p. 196.

10. A.C. Benson, *The Life of Edward White Benson*, 2 vols, London, 1899, vol.1, p. 23.

11. Charlotte Sturge, *Family Records*, London, 1882, pp. 39–46.

12. Compare Leonore Davidoff and Catherine Hall, *Family Fortunes: Men and Women of the English Middle Class, 1780–1850*, London, 1987; Jane Rendall, *Women in an Industrialising Society, 1780–1880*, Oxford, 1990; Hunt, *Middling Sort*; Robert W. Shoemaker, *Gender in English Society, 1650–1850: The Emergence of Separate Spheres?* Harlow, 1998.

13. Shoemaker, *Gender in English Society*.

14. Isaac Holden to B. Holt, 9 June 1845, quoted in Jennings, 'Sir Isaac Holden', p. 32.

15. Theodore Koditschek, *Class Formation and Urban Industrial Society: Bradford, 1750–1850*, Cambridge, 1990, pp. 216–18.

16. Davidoff and Hall, *Family Fortunes*, pp. 57, 368–9; Maurice Spiers, *Victoria Park, Manchester*, Chetham Society Series, vol. 23, 1976; Donald Olsen, *The Growth of Victorian London*, Harmondsworth, 1979, ch. 5; Stefan

Muthesius, *The English Terraced House*, London, 1982, pp. 45–8.

17. Personal communication from Catherine Hall, with reference to her sample of the 1851 census. See also Davidoff and Hall, *Family Fortunes*, pp. 231–2.

18. A good example is William Gaskell, Unitarian minister in Manchester during the first half of Victoria's reign. Jenny Uglow, *Elizabeth Gaskell: a Habit of Stories*, London, 1993.

19. Davidoff and Hall, *Family Fortunes*; James Obelkevich, *Religion and Rural Society: South Lindsey, 1825–1875*, Oxford, 1976.

20. Sarah Ellis, *The Women of England*, London, 1839, p. 331.

21. Thomas Hughes, *Memoir of Daniel Macmillan*, London, 1882, pp. 44, 47.

22. Sarah Ellis, *The Wives of England*, London, 1843, pp. 316–22.

23. Clyde Binfield, *George Williams and the YMCA*, London, 1973.

24. Obelkevich, *Religion and Rural Society*, pp. 26, 56; Ann Kussmaul, *Servants in Husbandry in Early Modern England*, Cambridge, 1981, p. 130; Davidoff and Hall, *Family Fortunes*, pp. 256–60, 306–7.

25. Leonore Davidoff, *Worlds Between: Historical Perspectives on Gender and Class*, Cambridge, 1995, ch. 5.

26. Edward Higgs, 'Domestic Service and Household Production', in Angela John (ed.), *Unequal Opportunities: Women's Employment in England, 1800–1918*, Oxford, 1986, pp. 125–50; Koditschek, *Class Formation*, pp. 218–21.

27. John Burnett, *Useful Toil*, London, 1974, part 2; Davidoff, *Worlds Between*, ch. 5; Patty Seleski, 'Women, Work and Cultural Change in Eighteenth- and Early Nineteenth-Century London', in Tim Harris (ed.), *Popular Culture in England, c. 1500–1850*, Basingstoke, 1995; M.A. Simpson and T.H. Lloyd (eds), *Middle-Class Housing in Britain*, Newton Abbot, 1977.

28. Edward Higgs, 'The Tabulation of Occupations in the Nineteenth-Century Census with Special Reference to

Domestic Servants', *Local Population Studies* 28 (1982), pp. 58–66; Di Cooper and Moira Donald, 'Households and "Hidden" Kin in Early Nineteenth-Century England', *Continuity and Change* 10 (1995), pp. 257–78.

29. Robert Kerr, *The Gentleman's House: or How to Plan English Residences from the Parsonage to the Palace*, London, 1864, p. 76.

30. Davidoff, *Worlds Between*, ch. 5.

31. Hughes, *Victorian Governess*, pp. 85–116.

32. Raymond Williams, *Keywords*, 2nd edn, London, 1983, pp. 132–3; Naomi Tadmor, 'The Concept of the Household-Family in Eighteenth-Century England', *Past & Present* 151 (1996), pp. 111–40; Kussmaul, *Servants in Husbandry*, pp. 7, 129; Steven Ruggles, *Prolonged Connections: the Rise of the Extended Family in Nineteenth-Century England and America*, Madison, WI, 1987, pp. 37, 128, 131.

33. Simpson and Lloyd, *Middle-Class Housing*.

34. T. Wemyss Reid, *A Memoir of John Deakin Heaton, M.D.*, London, 1883, pp. 101–2; F.G. Byles, *William Byles*, Weymouth, 1932, p. 66.

35. T.H.S. Escott, *Club Makers and Club Members*, London, 1914, p. 200.

36. Arnold Palmer, *Movable Feasts*, London, 1952; John Burnett, *Plenty and Want: A Social History of Food in England from 1815 to the Present Day*, 3rd edn, London, 1989, pp. 67–8, 206.

37. Michael Curtin, *Propriety and Position: a Study of Victorian Manners*, New York, 1987.

38. Amanda Vickery, 'Sociability and Intimacy in Genteel Culture', paper presented at 62nd Anglo-American Conference of Historians, July 1993.

39. Robert Fishman, *Bourgeois Utopias: the Rise and Fall of Suburbia*, New York, 1987, pp. 51–62.

40. Leonore Davidoff, *The Best Circles*, London, 1973; Michael Brooks, 'Love and Possession in the Victorian House-

hold: the Example of the Ruskins', in Anthony S. Wohl (ed.), *The Victorian Family*, London, 1978, pp. 82–100.

41. Ellis, *Women of England* , p. 331.

42. E.J. Hobsbawm has said as much. See his *The Age of Capital, 1848–1875*, London, 1977, p. 279.

43. Neil McKendrick, John Brewer and J.H. Plumb, *The Birth of a Consumer Society*, London, 1982; John Brewer and Roy Porter (eds), *Consumption and the World of Goods*, London, 1993.

44. J.A. Banks, *Prosperity and Parenthood*, London, 1954, chs 4–6; Asa Briggs, *Victorian Things*, London, 1988, ch. 6.

45. Hester Chapone, *A Letter to a New-Married Lady*, 1777; repr. London, 1828, pp. 116, 122.

46. See, for example, Ellis, *Wives of England*.

Chapter 2: The Ideal of Domesticity

1. In the *OED* the first citations for 'homesickness' in this sense are 1798 and 1805.

2. John Heaton, autobiographical introduction, MS Diary (private collection, Leeds).

3. A. James Hammerton, *Cruelty and Companionship: Conflict in Nineteenth-Century Married Life*, London, 1992, pp. 74–9.

4. Hippolyte Taine, *Notes on England*, trans. E. Hyams, London, 1957, p. 78.

5. Henry Mayhew, 'Home Is Home, Be It Never So Homely', in Viscount Ingestre (ed.), *Meliora: Or Better Times to Come*, London, 1852, p. 261.

6. Catherine Tait to A.C. Tait, 29 April 1843, Tait MSS 102/173, Lambeth Palace Library.

7. W.L. Burn, *The Age of Equipoise*, London, 1964, p. 246.

8. Simon Schama, 'The Domestication of Majesty: Royal Family Portraiture, 1500–1850', *Journal of Interdisciplinary History* 17 (1986), pp. 155–83. He instances the paintings of Zoffany in particular.

9. Peter Earle, 'The Middling Sort in London', in J. Barry and C. Brooks (eds), *The Middling Sort of People*, London, 1994, p. 158; Margaret Hunt, *The Middling Sort: Commerce, Gender, and the Family in England, 1680–1780*, Berkeley, CA, 1996.

10. Randolph Trumbach, *The Rise of the Egalitarian Family*, New York, 1978; Lawrence Stone, *The Family, Sex and Marriage in England 1500–1800*, London, 1977; Anthony Fletcher, *Gender, Sex and Subordination in England, 1500–1800*, London 1995; Amanda Vickery, 'Women of the Local Elite in Lancashire, 1750–1825', Ph.D. thesis, University of London, 1991.

11. Hester Chapone, *Posthumous Works* (1808), vol. 2, p. 151, quoted in Stone, *Family, Sex and Marriage*, p. 327. See also Beth Kowaleski-Wallace, 'Home Economics: Domestic Ideology in Maria Edgeworth's *Belinda*', *The Eighteenth Century* 29 (1988), pp. 242–62.

12. William Cowper, *The Task* (1785), book 3. On Felicia Hemans, see Norma Clarke, *Ambitious Heights: Writing, Friendship, Love: the Jewsbury Sisters, Felicia Hemans and Jane Carlyle*, London, 1990, and Tricia Lootens, 'Hemans and Home', *PMLA* 109 (1994), pp. 238–53.

13. The aisles of Bath Abbey provide striking confirmation of this.

14. Compare Leonore Davidoff and Catherine Hall, *Family Fortunes: Men and Women of the English Middle Class, 1780–1850*, London, 1987 with Theodore Koditschek, *Class Formation and Urban Industrial Society: Bradford, 1750–1850*, Cambridge, 1990.

15. R.W. Emerson, *English Traits*, London, 1856; Taine, *Notes on England*.

16. Sarah Ellis, *The Mothers of England*, London, 1843, p. 308.
17. Sarah Ellis, *The Women of England*, London, 1839, p. 243.
18. W.R. Greg, review of W. Johnston, *England As It Is*, in *Edinburgh Review* 93 (1851), p. 326.
19. Mayhew, 'Home Is Home', p. 263.
20. Catherine Gallagher, *The Industrial Reformation of English Fiction*, Chicago, 1985, pp. 115–20.
21. Alexander Welsh, *Dickens and the City*, London, 1971; H.J. Dyos and M. Wolff (eds), *The Victorian City*, 2 vols, London, 1979.
22. Helene Roberts, 'Marriage, Redundancy or Sin: the Painter's View of Women in the First Twenty-Five Years of Victoria's Reign', in Martha Vicinus (ed.), *Suffer and Be Still*, London, 1972, p. 51; John R. Gillis, 'Ritualization of Middle-Class Family Life in Nineteenth-Century Britain', *International Journal of Politics, Culture and Society* 3 (1989), pp. 213–35.
23. T. Ragg, *Scenes and Sketches from Life and Nature* (1847), quoted in Davidoff and Hall, *Family Fortunes*, p. 369.
24. Welsh, *Dickens and the City*; Davidoff and Hall, *Family Fortunes*, pp. 188–90, 364–74; Leonore Davidoff, *Worlds Between: Historical Perspectives on Gender and Class*, Cambridge, 1995, pp. 46–50, 56–8; Stephen Constantine, 'Amateur Gardening and Popular Recreation in the 19th and 20th Centuries', *Journal of Social History* 14 (1981), p. 389.
25. Samuel Smiles, 'Music in the House', *Eliza Cook's Journal* 6 (1852), pp. 209–11.
26. Eliza Wilson to Walter Bagehot, 21 November 1857, in Mrs R. Barrington (ed.), *The Love-Letters of Walter Bagehot and Eliza Wilson*, London, 1933, p. 44.
27. J.A. Froude, *The Nemesis of Faith*, London, 1849, pp. 112–13.
28. Davidoff and Hall, *Family Fortunes*, ch. 3.
29. R.I. and S. Wilberforce, *The Life of William Wilberforce*, 5 vols, London,

1838, vol. 5, p. 77; Ford K. Brown, *Fathers of the Victorians*, Cambridge, 1961.
30. Christopher Hill, 'The Spiritualization of the Household', in *Society and Puritanism in Pre-Revolutionary England*, London, 1964, pp. 443–81; Lyndal Roper, *The Holy Household*, Oxford, 1989.
31. Alan Everitt, *The Pattern of Rural Dissent*, Leicester, 1972, p. 48; David Hempton, *Methodism and Politics in British Society, 1750–1850*, London, 1984, pp. 14–15.
32. Henry Abelove, *The Evangelist of Desire: John Wesley and the Methodists*, Stanford, CA, 1990, pp. 49–70.
33. Quoted in William W. Dean, 'The Methodist Class Meeting: its Significance and Decline', *Proceedings of the Wesley Historical Society* 43 (1981), p. 43.
34. Joseph Bush, *Elizabeth Riggall: a Memorial*, Derby, 1893, pp. 31–2.
35. See, for example, Jean Stovin (ed.), *Journals of a Methodist Farmer, 1871–75*, London, 1982, pp. 28, 119.
36. On the domestic roots of Methodism, see Leslie F. Church, *The Early Methodist People*, 2nd edn, London, 1949, pp. 153–81; A.D. Gilbert, *Religion and Society in Industrial England, 1740–1914*, London, 1976; Thomas Shaw, *A History of Cornish Methodism*, Truro, 1967, pp. 21–4; John Tosh, 'Methodist Domesticity and Middle-Class Masculinity in Nineteenth-Century England', in Robert N. Swanson (ed.), *Studies in Church History* 34 (1998); Deborah Valenze, *Prophetic Sons and Daughters: Female Preaching and Popular Religion in Industrial England*, Princeton, NJ, 1985.
37. Paul Sangster, *Pity My Simplicity: the Evangelical Revival and the Religious Education of Children, 1738–1800*, London, 1963; Doreen Rosman, *The Evangelicals and Culture*, London, 1984, ch. 4.
38. William Wilberforce to Zachary Macaulay, 1814, quoted in Christopher Tolly, *Domestic Biography: the Legacy of*

Evangelicalism in Four Nineteenth-Century Families, Oxford, 1997, p. 25.

39. See, for example, Edward Bickersteth, *A Treatise on Prayer*, 11th edn, London, 1828, p. 285.

40. Ibid., pp. 128–9; William Roberts, *The Portraiture of a Christian Gentleman*, London, 1829, pp. 95–6.

41. See, for example, Brewin Grant, *The Dissenting World: an Autobiography*, 2nd edn, London, 1869, p. 12.

42. John S. Reed, '"A Female Movement": the Feminization of 19th Century Anglo-Catholicism', *Anglican and Episcopal History* 57 (1988), pp. 216–24; Tolly, *Domestic Biography*, p. 45.

43. Rosman, *Evangelicals and Culture*, pp. 103–4; Pat Jalland, *Death in the Victorian Family*, Oxford, 1996, pp. 25–38, 271–6.

44. Gregory Schneider, *The Way of the Cross Leads Home: the Domestication of American Methodism*, Bloomington, IN, 1993, ch. 6.

45. Robert Fishman, *Bourgeois Utopias: the Rise and Fall of Suburbia*, New York, 1987, p. 53.

46. John R. Gillis, *A World of their Own Making: Myth, Ritual, and the Quest for Family Values*, Cambridge, MA, 1996, p. 103; J.A.R. Pimlott, *The Englishman's Christmas*, Hassocks, 1978.

47. Stone, *Family, Sex and Marriage*, pp. 435–9; Linda Pollock, *Forgotten Children: Parent–Child Relations from 1500 to 1900*, Cambridge, 1983, pp. 103–11, 116–24; Roy Porter, *English Society in the Eighteenth Century*, 2nd edn, London, 1990, pp. 266–8; Hugh Cunningham, *Children and Childhood in Western Society since 1500*, Harlow, 1995.

48. Anon., 'Childhood', *Blackwood's Edinburgh Magazine* 12 (1822), p. 143.

49. Peter Coveney, *The Image of Childhood*, Harmondsworth, 1967; David Grylls, *Guardians and Angels: Parents and Children in Nineteenth-Century Literature*, London, 1978; Hugh Cunningham, *The Children of the Poor: Representations of Childhood since the Seventeenth Century*, Oxford, 1991; Cunningham, *Children and Childhood*;

James Seward, *The New Child: British Art and the Origins of Modern Childhood, 1730–1830*, Berkeley, CA, 1995.

50. See, for example, G.E. Sargent, *Home Education*, London, 1854, p. 5.

51. This is caught by the contrasting attitudes of Augustus Hare's adopted mother and his grandmother in the 1830s. Augustus Hare, *The Years with Mother*, ed. Malcolm Barnes, London, 1984, pp. 18, 21, 27, 31.

52. Sangster, *Pity My Simplicity*; Philip Greven, *The Protestant Temperament*, New York, 1977; Tolly, *Domestic Biography*, ch. 1.

53. S. Tissot, *Onanism*, quoted in L.J. Jordanova, 'Naturalizing the Family: Literature and the Bio-Medical Sciences in the Late Eighteenth Century', in Jordanova (ed.), *Languages of Nature*, London, 1986, pp. 113–14; Abelove, *Evangelist of Desire*, pp. 53–4; Michael Mason, *The Making of Victorian Sexuality*, Oxford, 1994, pp. 205–15; Roy Porter and Lesley Hall, *The Facts of Life: the Creation of Sexual Knowledge in Britain, 1650–1950*, London, 1995, pp. 141–5; Janet Oppenheim, *Shattered Nerves: Doctors, Patients, and Depression in Victorian England*, New York, 1991, pp. 260–1.

54. David Newsome, *The Parting of Friends*, London, 1966, pp. 32–6; Standish Meacham, *Henry Thornton of Clapham*, Cambridge, MA, 1964, pp. 49–53; Rosman, *Evangelicals and Culture*, ch. 4; Tolly, *Domestic Biography*, pp. 7–14; Alan Richardson, *Literature, Education and Romanticism: Reading as Social Practice*, Cambridge, 1994, pp. 14–15.

55. John Angell James, *Female Piety*, 1856, quoted in Davidoff and Hall, *Family Fortunes*, p. 115.

56. Elizabeth Gaskell, *My Diary: the Early Years of My Daughter Marianne*, privately printed, 1923; Joshua Pritchard, MS Diary (1818–25), Manchester Central Reference Library, M375/1/3.

57. Mason, *Making of Victorian Sexuality*, pp. 195–205.

58. Mary Wollstonecraft, *A Vindication of the Rights of Woman* (1792), ed. C.H. Poston, New York, 1988, p. 63.

59. William Acton, *The Functions and Disorders of the Reproductive Organs in Youth, Adult Age and Advanced Life*, London, 1857, p. 27; for corroborating evidence in the USA, see G.J. Barker-Benfield, 'The Spermatic Economy: a Nineteenth-Century View of Sexuality', in Michael Gordon (ed.), *The American Family in Social-Historical Perspective*, 2nd edn, New York, 1978, p. 383.

60. On the development of thinking about sexual difference, see Fletcher, *Gender, Sex and Subordination*; Thomas Laqueur, *Making Sex: Body and Gender from the Greeks to Freud*, Cambridge, MA, 1990; Mary Poovey, *Uneven Developments: the Ideological Work of Gender in Mid-Victorian England*, London, 1988, pp. 7–10, 199–201; Michèle Cohen, *Fashioning Masculinity: National Identity and Language in the Eighteenth Century*, London, 1996, pp. 79–83; M. Jeanne Peterson, 'Dr Acton's Enemy: Medicine, Sex, and Society in Victorian England', *Victorian Studies* 29 (1986), pp. 569–90; Mason, *Making of Victorian Sexuality*, pp. 195–205.

61. Sarah Lewis, *Woman's Mission*, 7th edn, London, 1840, pp. 25, 95, 132.

62. Ruth Perry, 'Colonizing the Breast: Sexuality and Maternity in Eighteenth-Century England', *Journal of the History of Sexuality* 2 (1991), pp. 204–34. Amanda Vickery ('Women of the Local Elite', ch. 4) issues a timely caution against exaggerating the shift in attitudes towards motherhood between the early eighteenth and early nineteenth centuries, but the intensely moral view of motherhood was new.

63. Contemporary reticence about male sexuality is reflected in today's scholarly writing. Thus Peter Gay has much to say about men's view of women's sexuality and men's fear of women, but little about men's sexuality *per se*. (Peter Gay, *The Bourgeois Experience, Victoria to Freud*, vols 1 and 2, New York, 1984 and 1986).

64. John Tosh, 'What Should Historians Do With Masculinity? Reflections on Nineteenth-Century Britain', *History Workshop Journal* 38 (1994), pp. 179–202.

65. Carol Christ, 'Victorian Masculinity and the Angel in the House', in Martha Vicinus (eds), *A Widening Sphere*, London, 1977; Herbert Sussman, *Victorian Masculinities: Manhood and Manly Poetics in Early Victorian Literature and Art*, Cambridge, 1995, p. 13.

66. Barker-Benfield, 'Spermatic Economy'; Mason, *Making of Victorian Sexuality*, pp. 205–27; Oppenheim, *Shattered Nerves*, pp. 158–65; Lesley A. Hall, *Hidden Anxieties: Male Sexuality, 1900–1950*, Cambridge, 1991, pp. 17–18, 55–6.

67. John Ruskin, *Sesame and Lilies*, 1864, pocket edn, London, 1906, p. 107.

68. Lewis, *Woman's Mission*, p. 129.

69. The best treatment of polarity and gender in early Victorian culture is Poovey, *Uneven Developments*.

70. Quoted in Dorothy Thompson, *Queen Victoria: Gender and Power*, London, 1990, p. 46. See also Robert Rhodes James, *Albert, Prince Consort*, London, 1983, pp. 231, 244.

71. H.C. O'Donnoghue, *Marriage: the Source, Stability and Perfection of Social Happiness and Duty*, London, 1828, p. 98.

72. Jane Rendall, *The Origins of Modern Feminism*, Basingstoke, 1985.

Chapter 3: Husband and Wife

1. John Stuart Mill, speech in House of Commons, 20 May 1867, *Hansard*, vol. 187, cols 821–3.

2. Two years later, in *The Subjection of Women* (1869), Mill was more circumspect about the healthy state of mar-

riage; the more sanguine tone of his speech in the House of Commons was no doubt carefully adjusted to the occasion.

3. Eliza Wilson to Walter Bagehot, 10 January 1858, in Mrs R. Barrington (ed.), *The Love-Letters of Walter Bagehot and Eliza Wilson*, London, 1933, p. 93.

4. Hester Chapone, *A Letter to a New-Married Lady*, 1777, repr. London 1828, pp. 108–9; Sarah Ellis, *The Wives of England*, London, 1843, pp. 90–91; Dinah Mulock Craik, *A Woman's Thoughts about Women*, London, 1858, p. 154; William Landels, *The Marriage Ring*, London, 1883, pp. 174–85.

5. Benjamin Goodwin to John Goodwin, 20 November 1843, in Benjamin Goodwin,'Autobiography',1855,typescript copy in Bradford Public Library, p. 856.

6. A.C. Tait to Catherine Spooner, undated [June 1843], Tait Papers 192/300, Lambeth Palace Library; Catherine Spooner to A.C. Tait, 16 March 1843, Tait Papers 102/156; A.C. Tait, journals, Tait Papers 15, *passim*.

7. Daniel Macmillan to Frances Orridge, 7 June 1850, quoted in Thomas Hughes, *Memoir of Daniel Macmillan*, London, 1882, p. 179.

8. James Paget to Lydia North, 18 February 1837, quoted in M. Jeanne Peterson, *Family, Love, and Work in the Lives of Victorian Gentlewomen*, Bloomington, IN, 1989, p. 82.

9. John Heaton to Fanny Heaton, 24 September 1852, Heaton Papers (Leeds).

10. Frances Power Cobbe, *The Duties of Woman*, London, 1881, pp. 99–100.

11. John Heaton to Helen Heaton (daughter), 28 August 1870, Heaton Papers (Cornhill-on-Tweed).

12. Daniel Macmillan, journal, 19 May 1853, quoted in Hughes, *Memoir*, p. 193.

13. William Landels, *Woman: Her Position and Power*, London, 1870, p. 97. For the minority view, see John Angell

James, *The Family Monitor, or a Help to Domestic Happiness*, Birmingham, 1828, pp. 25–7, 36.

14. John Heaton to Helen Heaton, 5 August 1871, Heaton Papers (Cornhill-on-Tweed).

15. Cornelius Stovin to Elizabeth Stovin, 7 November and 9 November 1876, transcripts in Stovin Papers, in private hands.

16. Richard Meinertzhagen, *Diary of a Black Sheep*, Edinburgh, 1964, p. 99; Beatrice Webb, entry for 27 July 1910, MS diary, British Library of Political and Economic Science.

17. Peter Gay, *The Bourgeois Experience, Victoria to Freud,* vol. 1, *Education of the Senses*, New York, 1984; vol. 2, *The Tender Passion*, New York, 1986, esp. pp. 14–21, 30–34 (for Walter Bagehot), and 297–311 (for Charles Kingsley).

18. Michael Mason, *The Making of Victorian Sexuality*, Oxford, 1994, pp. 218–21.

19. Norman Vance, *The Sinews of the Spirit: the Ideal of Christian Manliness in Victorian Literature and Religious Thought*, Cambridge, 1985; Michael Mason, *The Making of Victorian Sexual Attitudes*, Oxford, 1994, pp. 17–19, 67, 134.

20. Charles Kingsley to Fanny Grenfell, 1843, quoted in Gay, *Tender Passion*, p. 309.

21. Quoted in Dorothy Thompson, *Queen Victoria; Gender and Power*, London, 1990, p. 59.

22. Joshua Pritchard to Mary Pritchard, 19 November 1836, 28 January 1837 and 15 August 1835, Pritchard Papers, M375/1/4, Manchester Central Reference Library.

23. Isaac Holden to Sarah Holden, 20 December 1850, Holden Papers/21, Bradford University Library; same to same, 13 June 1852, Holden Papers/23; Sarah Holden to Isaac Holden, undated [early November 1851], Holden Papers/44; John Tosh, 'From Keighley to St-Denis: Separation and Intimacy in Victorian Bourgeois

Marriage', *History Workshop Journal* 40 (1995), pp. 193–206.

24. Compare, for example, Peterson, *Family, Love, and Work* and Eric Trudgill, *Madonnas and Magdalens: the Origins and Development of Victorian Sexual Attitudes*, London, 1976.

25. Ian Bradley, *The Call to Seriousness*, London, 1974, p. 151.

26. 'Paterfamilas', letter to *Daily Telegraph*, 2 July 1868, quoted in John M. Robson, *Marriage or Celibacy? The Daily Telegraph on a Victorian Dilemma*, Toronto, 1995, p. 67.

27. See the case of Isaac Holden, discussed below (p. 73–6).

28. Elizabeth Gaskell to Charles Eliot Norton, 9 March 1859; same to Anne Robson, 10 May 1865, in J.A.V. Chapple and A. Pollard (eds), *The Letters of Mrs Gaskell*, Manchester, 1966, pp. 537, 758–61.

29. Craik, *Woman's Thoughts*, p. 153.

30. See, for example, Austin Harrison, *Frederic Harrison: Thoughts and Memoirs*, London, 1926, p. 197.

31. Anthony Fletcher, *Gender, Sex and Subordination in England, 1500–1800*, London, 1995; Susan Amussen, '"The Part of a Christian Man": the Cultural Politics of Manhood in Early Modern England', in S. Amussen and M. Kishlansky (eds), *Political Culture and Cultural Politics in Early Modern England*, Manchester, 1995, pp. 213–33.

32. *Tom* v. *Luckett* (1847), quoted in Megan Doolittle, 'Missing Fathers: Assembling a History of Fatherhood in Mid-Nineteenth Century England', Ph.D. thesis, University of Essex, 1996, p. 89.

33. A. James Hammerton, *Cruelty and Companionship: Conflict in Nineteenth-Century Married Life*, London, 1992, pp. 80, 149; Richard Kelly, 'Mrs Caudle, a Victorian Curtain Lecturer', *University of Toronto Quarterly* 38 (1969), pp. 295–309.

34. Barbara Taylor, *Eve and the New Jerusalem*, London, 1983; Elizabeth Gaskell to Eliza Fox, April 1850, in Chapple and Pollard, *Letters of Mrs Gaskell*,

p. 109; Jenny Uglow, *Elizabeth Gaskell: a Habit of Stories*, London, 1993, pp. 77–8.

35. Hammerton, *Cruelty and Companionship*.

36. For the first, see Sarah Sugden to Isaac Holden, 6 October 1849, Holden Papers/52; for the second, see Catherine Spooner to A.C. Tait, 11 February 1843, Tait Papers 102/143.

37. Wally Seccombe, 'Patriarchy Stabilized: the Construction of the Male Bread-winner Wage Norm in Nineteenth-Century Britain', *Social History* 11 (1986), pp. 53–76. The first citation for 'breadwinner' in this sense in the *OED* is dated 1821.

38. The last two paragraphs distil many of the findings of Hammerton, *Cruelty and Companionship*.

39. See, for example, Henry Venn, *The Complete Duty of Man*, London, 1836 (first published 1763), pp. 246–7; James, *Family Monitor*, p. 48.

40. Peterson, *Family, Love, and Work*, pp. 183–4; John Tosh, 'Domesticity and Manliness in the Victorian Middle Class: the Family of Edward White Benson', in M. Roper and J. Tosh (eds), *Manful Assertions: Masculinities in Britain since 1800*, London, 1991, pp. 50–51; Betty Askwith, *Two Victorian Families*, London, 1971, pp. 130–31; Virginia Woolf, *Moments of Being*, London, 1976, pp. 124–6.

41. See especially the case of John Curtis, tried in 1858: Hammerton, *Cruelty and Companionship*, pp. 89–94.

42. Richard G. White, *England Without and Within*, Boston, MA, 1881, p. 208. See also Harriet Beecher Stowe, *Little Foxes: or the Insignificant Little Habits Which Mar Domestic Happiness*, London, 1866, pp. 106–13.

43. Hammerton, *Cruelty and Companionship*, pp. 89–94, 98, 114–15, 129–33.

44. Ibid., pp. 79, 131–3, 151–3.

45. Cornelius Stovin to Elizabeth Stovin, 14 November 1874, in Jean Stovin (ed.), *Journals of a Methodist Farmer, 1871–75*, London, 1982, p. 153.

46. Margaret Forster, *Elizabeth Barrett*

Browning, London, 1988, pp. 14, 65; C.R. Ashbee, *'Grannie'*, privately printed, 1939, p. 34.

47. Hippolyte Taine, *Notes on England*, trans. E. Hyams, London, 1957, p. 79.

48. Mandell Creighton to Louise von Glehn, 12 December 1871, quoted in Louise Creighton, *Life and Letters of Mandell Creighton*, 2 vols, London, 1904, vol. 1, p. 122.

49. Ibid.

50. Anthony Howe, *The Cotton Masters, 1830–1860*, Oxford, 1984, pp. 76–8.

51. Cornelius Stovin to Elizabeth Stovin, 17 October 1876, transcribed into Diary, Stovin Papers.

52. Mary Benson, Diary, 8 March 1898, Benson Papers 1/77, Bodleian Library, Oxford.

53. Peterson, *Family, Love, and Marriage*, ch. 2.

54. Sarah Ellis, *The Women of England*, London, 1839, p. 338.

55. J.A. and Olive Banks, *Feminism and Family Planning in Victorian England*, London, 1964, pp. 66–70; Eliza Lynn Linton, quoted in Trudgill, *Madonnas and Magdalens*, p. 268; T.H.S. Escott, *England: its People, Polity, and Pursuits*, 2 vols, London, 1879, vol. 2, pp. 13–15.

56. Barbara Caine, *Destined to be Wives: the Sisters of Beatrice Webb*, Oxford, 1986, pp. 94–6; Meinertzhagen Papers, *passim*, in private hands.

57. Quoted in Trudgill, *Madonnas and Magdalens*, p. 80.

58. E.g. Edward Benson to Mary Sidgwick, 7 June 1859, Benson Papers 3/15.

59. Ellis, *Wives of England*, pp. 90–91; K.C. Phillipps, *Language and Class in Victorian England*, Oxford, 1984, p. 161.

60. Beatrice Webb, entry for 26 November 1889, MS Diary, BLPES.

61. Edward Benson to Mary Sidgwick, 2 May 1859 and 7 June 1859, Benson Papers 3/15; Mary Benson, Diary, 8 March 1898, Benson Papers 1/77.

62. Mary Benson, retrospective Diary, 1875, Benson Papers 1/79; Tosh, 'Domesticity and Manliness', pp. 51–9.

63. Mary Benson's Diary, undated entry reproduced in E.F. Benson, *Mother*, London, 1925, p. 14; E.F. Benson, *Our Family Affairs, 1867–1896*, London, 1920; A.C. Benson, *The Trefoil: Wellington College, Lincoln, and Truro*, London, 1923; David Newsome, *Godliness and Good Learning*, London, 1961, pp. 184–92.

64. Edward Benson to Mary Sidgwick, 7 June 1859, Benson Papers 3/15; Mary Benson, retrospective Diary, 1875, Benson Papers 1/79; Tosh, 'Manliness and Domesticity', pp. 51–9; Askwith, *Two Victorian Families*, pp. 120–45.

65. David G. Pugh, *Sons of Liberty: the Masculine Mind in Nineteenth-Century America*, Westport, CT, 1983, p. 83.

66. A.C. Benson, *Trefoil*, p. 253; E.F. Benson, *Mother*, pp. 22–3.

67. Joshua Pritchard, MS Diaries, Pritchard Papers, M375/1/3; letters from Joshua to Mary Pritchard, 1835–7, Pritchard Papers, M375/1/4. See also John Tosh, 'Methodist Domesticity and Middle-Class Masculinity in Nineteenth-Century England', in Robert N. Swanson (ed.), *Studies in Church History* 34 (1998).

68. A.C. Tait, journals, Tait Papers; W. Benham (ed.), *Catharine and Craufurd Tait*, London, 1879.

69. William Austin, unpublished Diary (1851–2), quoted in Leonore Davidoff and Catherine Hall, *Family Fortunes: Men and Women of the English Middle Class, 1780–1850*, London, 1987, p. 270.

70. John Wesley, quoted in Philip Greven, *The Protestant Temperament*, New York, 1977, p. 127.

71. Colleen McDannell, *The Christian Home in Victorian America, 1840–1900*, Bloomington, IN, 1986, pp. 109, 127, 130–35; Pat Jalland, *Death in the Victorian Family*, Oxford, 1996, pp. 98–104.

72. Hammerton, *Cruelty and Companionship*, pp. 93, 100.

73. Tosh, 'From Keighley to St-Denis'; Elizabeth Jennings, 'Sir Isaac Holden (1807–97)', Ph.D. thesis, Bradford University, 1982.

74. Sarah Holden to Isaac Holden, 11 December 1850, Holden Papers/44.

75. *A Class-Book Containing Directions for Class-Leaders*, n.d.; Sarah Holden to Isaac Holden, 4 December 1850, Holden Papers/21; Sarah Sugden to Isaac Holden, 6 October 1849, Holden Papers/52.

76. Isaac Holden to Sarah Holden, 23 April 1861, Holden Papers/32; John Hodgson, *Textile Manufacture and Other Industries in Keighley*, Keighley, 1879, p. 116; Isaac Holden to Sarah Holden, 20 December 1850, Holden Papers/21.

77. Isaac Holden to Sarah Holden, 10 January 1851, Holden Papers/22. See also Tosh, 'Keighley to St-Denis'.

78. For the wider religious context of the Holdens' marriage, see Tosh, 'Methodist Domesticity'.

79. Theodore Koditschek, 'The Triumph of Domesticity and the Making of Middle-Class Culture', *Contemporary Sociology* 18 (1989), p. 180.

80. See the useful critique by Amanda Vickery, 'Golden Age to Separate Spheres? A Review of the Categories and Chronologies of English Women's History', *Historical Journal* 36 (1993), pp. 383–414.

81. Peterson, *Family, Love, and Work*, esp. ch. 6.

82. Representative examples are: Taine, *Notes on England*, and R.W. Emerson, *English Traits*, London, 1856.

Chapter 4: Father and Child

1. Catharine Beecher, quoted in Kathryn Kish Sklar, *Catharine Beecher: a Study in American Domesticity*, New York, 1976, p. 265.

2. Charles Kingsley to Fanny Kingsley, 7 November 1844, quoted in Susan Chitty, *The Beast and the Monk: a Life of Charles Kingsley*, London, 1974, p. 98.

3. Walter Houghton, *The Victorian Frame of Mind, 1833–1870*, New Haven, CT, 1957, pp. 201–2; Michael St. J. Packe, *The Life of John Stuart Mill*, London, 1954, pp. 317–20; Phyllis Rose, *Parallel Lives: Five Victorian Marriages*, Harmondsworth, 1985, pp. 92, 95, 127.

4. H.L. Malchow, *Gentlemen Capitalists: the Social and Political World of the Victorian Businessman*, Basingstoke, 1991, pp. 33, 70, 344.

5. Diary of John Heaton, 27 January 1851 and 22 June 1855, Heaton Papers (Leeds).

6. The same was true of Cornelius Stovin's firstborn, named Cornelius Denison Stovin in 1864.

7. Roy Porter and Lesley Hall, *The Facts of Life: the Creation of Sexual Knowledge in Britain, 1650–1950*, London, 1995,

pp. 39–53, 69–81; Thomas Laqueur, *Making Sex: Body and Gender from the Greeks to Freud*, Cambridge, MA, 1990; John R. Gillis, *A World of Their Own Making: Myth, Ritual, and the Quest for Family Values*, Cambridge, MA, 1996, pp. 183–93.

8. J. Jill Suitor, 'Husbands' Participation in Childbirth: a Nineteenth-Century Phenomenon', *Journal of Family History* 6 (1981), pp. 278–93; Judith S. Lewis, *In the Family Way: Childbearing in the British Aristocracy, 1760–1860*, New Brunswick, NJ, 1986, pp. 171–3, 188; Pat Jalland, *Women, Marriage and Politics, 1860–1914*, Oxford, 1986, pp. 144–5; Gillis, *World of Their Own Making*, pp. 168–9, 191.

9. John Angell James, *The Young Man's Friend*, London, 1851, p. 298.

10. Marianne Farningham, *Boyhood*, London, 1870, p. 102; idem, *Home Life*, London, 1889, p. 11.

11. David Roberts, 'The Paterfamilias of the Victorian Governing Classes', in A.S. Wohl (ed.), *The Victorian Family*, London, 1978, pp. 59–81.

12. Joshua Pritchard to Mary Pritchard, 31 August 1835, Pritchard Papers, Man-

chester Central Reference Library M375/1/4.

13. Mary Holden to Isaac Holden, 28 November 1856, in Eustace Illingworth (ed.), *The Holden–Illingworth Letters*, Bradford, 1927, pp. 206–7.

14. Quoted in Derek Hudson, *Man of Two Worlds: the Life and Diaries of Arthur J. Munby, 1828–1910*, London, 1972, pp. 203–4.

15. Richard Church, *Over the Bridge*, London, 1955, p. 43.

16. Gillis, *World of Their Own Making*, pp. 87–108.

17. Sarah Ellis, *The Mothers of England*, London, 1843, p. 108; Barbara Fass Leavy, 'Fathering and *The British Mother's Magazine*, 1845–1864', *Victorian Periodicals Review* 13 (1980), pp. 10–16.

18. J.R. Seeley, *Lectures and Essays*, London, 1870, p. 271. Other examples of this opinion are referred to in Claudia Nelson, *Invisible Men: Fatherhood in Victorian Periodicals, 1850–1910*, Athens, GA, 1995, pp. 45–6.

19. Ellis, *Mothers of England*, p. 136.

20. Margaret Forster, *Elizabeth Barrett Browning*, London, 1988.

21. Sarah Ellis, *The Daughters of England*, London, 1842, p. 301.

22. See, for example, Austin Harrison, *Frederic Harrison: Thoughts and Memoirs*, London, 1926 (recalling his early childhood in the 1870s).

23. Dinah Mulock Craik, quoted in Nelson, *Invisible Men*, p. 60.

24. David Newsome, *The Parting of Friends*, London, 1966, p. 2; Leonore Davidoff and Catherine Hall, *Family Fortunes: Men and Women of the English Middle Class, 1780–1850*, London, 1987, pp. 225–7.

25. William Denny to Lelia Denny, 1 July 1884, in Alexander Bruce, *The Life of William Denny*, London, 1889, p. 288.

26. Alexander Macmillan, 'The Child in the Midst: a Fragment', in George Macmillan (ed.), *Letters of Alexander Macmillan*, privately printed, 1908, p. 338.

27. William Buchan, *Domestic Medicine*, 1772, quoted in Lewis, *In the Family Way*, p. 67.

28. Randolph Trumbach, *The Rise of the Egalitarian Family: Aristocratic Kinship and Domestic Relations in Eighteenth-Century England*, New York, 1978, p. 248.

29. Quoted in Davidoff and Hall, *Family Fortunes*, p. 330.

30. William Cobbett, *Advice to Young Men*, 1830, repr. London, 1926, p. 176.

31. James Stephen, *Essays in Ecclesiastical Biography*, London, 1849, p. 273.

32. E.g. in Dinah Mulock Craik, *John Halifax, Gentleman*, London, 1856.

33. Quoted in Norma Clarke, 'Strenuous Idleness: Thomas Carlyle and the Man of Letters as Hero', in Michael Roper and John Tosh (eds), *Manful Assertions: Masculinities in Britain since 1800*, London, 1991, pp. 31–3.

34. Trumbach, *Rise of the Egalitarian Family*, p. 248.

35. Harrison, *Frederic Harrison*, pp. 48–9.

36. John R. Gillis, 'Ritualization of Middle-Class Family Life in Nineteenth-Century Britain', *International Journal of Politics, Culture and Society* 3 (1989), p. 230.

37. Doreen Rosman, *The Evangelicals and Culture*, London, 1984, p. 107. See also G.E. Sargent, *Home Education*, London, 1854, pp. 16, 26.

38. Joshua Pritchard to Mary Pritchard, 16 August 1836, Pritchard Papers, M375/1/4.

39. Jenny Uglow, *Elizabeth Gaskell: a Habit of Stories*, London, 1993, pp. 136–7, 159, 301, 497.

40. Harrison, *Frederic Harrison*, pp. 61–3.

41. John Heaton to Helen Heaton, 29 October 1876, Heaton Papers (Cornhill-on-Tweed); John Heaton to Fanny Heaton, 11 September 1875, Heaton Papers (Leeds); T. Wemyss Reid, *A Memoir of John Deakin Heaton, M.D.*, London, 1883, p. 299.

42. William Lucas, *A Quaker Journal*, 2 vols, London, 1934, vol. 2, pp. 395, 474.

43. For other examples of playful fathering, see Edna Lyall, *The Burges Letters: a Record of Child Life in the Sixties*,

London, 1902, and James Sully, *My Life and Friends: a Psychologist's Memoirs*, London, 1918, pp. 15–18.

44. Christopher Anderson, *The Genius and Design of the Domestic Constitution*, 2nd edn, Edinburgh, 1847, p. 319.

45. Harrison, *Frederic Harrison*, p. 58; John Stuart Mill, *On Liberty* (1859), repr. Harmondsworth, 1974, p. 175.

46. Froude, *Shadows of the Clouds*, London, 1847, p. 25.

47. John Angell James, *The Family Monitor, or a Help to Domestic Happiness*, Birmingham, 1828, p. 129; Theodore Dwight, *The Father's Book*, London, 1834, *passim*. (Dwight was an American, but his didactic writings circulated in England.)

48. Davidoff and Hall, *Family Fortunes*, pp. 89, 108–10.

49. J.M. Kemble to W.B. Donne, 24 September 1838, quoted in John Killham, *Tennyson and 'The Princess'*, London, 1958, pp. 163–4.

50. Joshua Pritchard to Mary Pritchard, 15 August 1835 and 18 September 1836, Pritchard Papers M375/1/4.

51. Isaac Holden to Margaret Holden, 26 November 1856, 10 June 1858 and 14 April 1859, in *Holden–Illingworth Letters*; Joshua Murgatroyd to Thomas Murgatroyd, 2 August 1870, Murgatroyd Papers, Manchester Central Reference Library, M478/15/1.

52. Craik, *John Halifax, Gentleman*, vol. 3, p. 180.

53. See above, Chapter 2, p. 45.

54. For example, Jacob Abbott, *Parental Duties in the Promotion of Early Piety*, London, 1834.

55. Quoted in Hugh Cunningham, *Children and Childhood in Western Society since 1500*, Harlow, 1995, p. 66.

56. Mrs John Sandford, *Woman in Her Social and Domestic Character*, 6th edn, London, 1839, p. 219.

57. Ellis, *Mothers of England*, pp. 27, 160, 366. See also Nelson, *Invisible Men*, pp. 14–16.

58. Sarah A. Sewell, *Woman and the Times We Live In*, 2nd edn, Manchester, 1869, p. 52.

59. Steven Mintz, *A Prison of Expectations: The Family in Victorian Culture*, New York, 1983, pp. 27–39; Nelson, *Invisible Men*, p. 15.

60. This transition has not been studied for England, but see Colleen McDannell, *The Christian Home in Victorian America, 1840–1900*, Bloomington, IN, 1986.

61. William Roberts, *The Portraiture of a Christian Gentleman*, London, 1829, pp. 95–6.

62. M. Jeanne Peterson, *Family, Love, and Work in the Lives of Victorian Gentlewomen*, Bloomington, IN, 1989, pp. 37–9; Deborah Gorham, 'Victorian Reform as a Family Business: the Hill Family', in A.S. Wohl (ed.), *The Victorian Family*, London, 1978, pp. 119–47.

63. Seeley, *Lectures and Essays*, pp. 269–71.

64. For a discussion of this issue in relation to the working class, see Megan Doolittle, '"Missing Fathers": Assembling a History of Fatherhood in Mid-Nineteenth Century England', University of Essex, Ph.D. thesis, 1996, pp. 217–21.

65. James Payn in *Chambers' Journal* 1868, quoted in David Grylls, *Guardians and Angels: Parents and Children in Nineteenth-Century Literature*, London, 1978, p. 55. Dinah Mulock Craik concurred: see Nelson, *Invisible Men*, pp. 62–3. See also Hugh Cunningham, *The Children of the Poor: Representations of Childhood since the Seventeenth Century*, Oxford, 1991.

66. John Tosh, 'Authority and Nurture in Middle-Class Fatherhood: the Case of Early and Mid-Victorian England', *Gender & History* 8 (1996), p. 53.

67. Priscilla Robertson, 'Home as a Nest: Middle-Class Childhood in Nineteenth-Century Europe', in Lloyd De Mause (ed.), *The History of Childhood*, London, 1976, p. 422.

68. Horace Bushnell, *Christian Nurture*, London, 1861, p. 206.

69. Linda Pollock, *Forgotten Children: Parent–Child Relations from 1500 to 1900*,

Cambridge, 1983, pp. 173–87. See also Mintz, *Prison of Expectations*, pp. 30–39.

70. Andrew Halliday, quoted in Nelson, *Invisible Men*, p. 63.

71. Other texts in this vein are Lant Carpenter, *Principles of Education, Intellectual, Moral and Physical*, London, 1820, and Theodore Dwight, *The Father's Book*, London, 1834.

72. See Doolittle, '"Missing Fathers"'.

73. Mark C. Carnes, *Secret Ritual and Manhood in Victorian America*, New Haven, CT, 1989, esp. pp. 107–27.

74. Daniel to Georgina Meinertzhagen, 22 August 1876 and 21 September 1878, Meinertzhagen Papers, privately held.

75. Richard Meinertzhagen, *Diary of a Black Sheep*, Edinburgh, 1964, p. 106. Beatrice Mayor, 'One Family of Ten', MS in private hands, p. 15.

76. Roberts, 'Paterfamilias of the Victorian Governing Classes'; Gillis, *World of Their Own Making*, pp. 179, 190.

77. Froude's autobiographical fragment is reproduced in W.H. Dunn, *James Anthony Froude: a Biography, 1818–56*, Oxford, 1961, pp. 17, 39–44. Butler's appeared in thinly veiled form in his novel, *The Way of All Flesh* (1903).

78. The relevance of these records to the history of the family is now well established for this period. See A. James Hammerton, *Cruelty and Companionship: Conflict in Nineteenth-Century Married Life*, London, 1992, and Doolittle, '"Missing Fathers"'.

79. Hammerton, *Cruelty and Companionship*, pp. 89–94, 127–8. I am indebted to Megan Doolittle for showing me her copies of the court proceedings relating to the Curtis case.

80. Frances Curtis to Mrs Flood, March 1852, quoted in Hammerton, *Cruelty and Companionship*, p. 90.

81. See, for example, Lucas, *Quaker Journal*, vol. 2, p. 395; Davidoff and Hall, *Family Fortunes*, pp. 332–3.

82. E.F. Benson, *Our Family Affairs, 1867–1896*, London, 1920, pp. 39, 104; A.C. Benson, quoted in David Newsome, *On the Edge of Paradise: A.C. Benson the Diarist*, London, 1980, p. 16; A.C. Benson, *The Trefoil: Wellington College, Lincoln and Truro*, London, 1923, p. 42; John Tosh, 'Domesticity and Manliness in the Victorian Middle Class: the Family of Edward White Benson', in Roper and Tosh, *Manful Assertions*, pp. 61–5.

83. E.F. Benson, *Our Family Affairs*, p. 103. See also Lee Krenis, 'Authority and Rebellion in Victorian Autobiography', *Journal of British Studies* 18 (1978), p. 117, and Mintz, *Prison of Expectations*, pp. 28–35.

84. J.R. Seeley to Edith Seeley, undated, and J.R. Seeley to Bessie Seeley, 9 April 1881, Seeley Papers, London University Library.

85. E.g. Lyall, *Burges Letters*. See also Harrison, *Frederic Harrison*, pp. 52–5.

86. Barbara Caine, *Destined to be Wives: the Sisters of Beatrice Webb*, Oxford, 1986, pp. 15–21.

87. Cornelius Stovin, diary entries for 12 January and 22 January 1875, 1 October 1872, 11 February 1875, 12 January 1875, in Jean Stovin (ed.), *Journals of a Methodist Farmer 1871–75*, London, 1982, pp. 178, 181, 104, 190, 177.

88. Cornelius Stovin to Elizabeth Stovin, 14 November 1874, in Stovin, *Journals*, p. 152.

89. E.W. Benson to Mary Benson, undated, in A.C. Benson, *The Life of Edward White Benson*, 2 vols, London, 1899, vol. 1, p. 644.

90. Henry Ashworth to Richard Cobden, 8 September 1861 and 27 January 1862, Cobden Papers, BM Add. MSS 43654/101 and 43654/147.

91. Lawrence Stone has been particularly influential here. See his *The Family, Sex and Marriage in England 1500–1800*, London, 1977, pp. 112–14, 206–14, 247–9.

92. Benjamin Goodwin to John Goodwin, 25 June 1849, quoted in Theodore Koditschek, 'Class Formation and the Bradford Bourgeoisie', Ph.D. thesis, Princeton University, 1981, p. 576.

93. Cornelius Stovin, Diary, 19 November 1874, in Stovin, *Journals*, p. 155.

94. David Newsome, *Godliness and Good Learning*, London, 1961, ch. 3.
95. John Heaton, entry for 12 August 1878, MS Diary; John Heaton to Helen Heaton, 24 August 1878,

Heaton Papers (Cornhill-on-Tweed). Other examples are given in Pat Jalland, *Death in the Victorian Family*, Oxford, 1996, esp. ch. 6.

Chapter 5: Boys into Men

1. Edward Herford, Diary, 5 February 1835, 2 April 1832, 23 April 1832, 30 June 1834, Manchester Central Reference Library, MS 923.4/H32. I have also drawn on an unpublished paper on Edward Herford by John Seed.
2. Edward Herford, Diary, 30 June 1834, 7 April 1832 and 28 January 1839; Sarah Ellis, *The Mothers of England*, London, 1843, pp. 305–6.
3. Robert Holt to Richard Holt, 31 May 1882, Holt Papers, Liverpool Record Office DUR 14/1.
4. Anthony Fletcher, *Gender, Sex and Subordination in England, 1500–1800*, London, 1995, p. 297.
5. William Cobbett, *Advice to Young Men*, 1830, repr. London, 1926, p. 292; J.R. Seeley, *Lectures and Essays*, London, 1870, pp. 269–70; J.R. Seeley to Edith Seeley (sister), 2 April 1872, Seeley Papers, London University Library.
6. E.g. Sarah Lewis, *Woman's Mission*, 7th edn, London, 1840, p. 32.
7. Thomas T. Spicer, *Masculine Education*, London, 1855, p. 14; Joshua Murgatroyd to Thomas Murgatroyd, 12 August 1868, Murgatroyd Papers, Manchester Central Reference Library M478/15/1.
8. Amongst a large and uneven literature, see especially David Newsome, *Godliness and Good Learning*, London, 1961, and J.R. de S. Honey, *Tom Brown's Universe: the Development of the Victorian Public School*, London, 1977.
9. Ludwig Wiese, *German Letters on English Education*, trans. W.D. Arnold, London, 1854, pp. 46–52; Hippolyte Taine, *Notes on England*, trans. E. Hyams, London, 1957, p. 206.
10. Leonore Davidoff and Catherine Hall, *Family Fortunes: Men and Women of the English Middle Class, 1780–1850*, London, 1987, p. 344.
11. F.G. Byles, *William Byles*, Weymouth, 1932, pp. 95, 103; Rhodes Boyson, *The Ashworth Cotton Enterprise*, Oxford, 1970, pp. 40–44, 252.
12. G.E. Milburn (ed.), *The Diary of John Young, Sunderland Chemist and Methodist Lay Preacher, 1841–1843*, Surtees Society Publications, vol. 195 (1983), pp. 92–3.
13. Byles, *William Byles*, p. 61.
14. James Watts to mother, and James Watts to Harriet Rigby, both undated, Watts Papers, Manchester Central Reference Library C/1/1.
15. Mary Thale (ed.), *The Autobiography of Francis Place*, Cambridge, 1972; Clyde Binfield, *George Williams and the YMCA*, London, 1973.
16. Bruce Haley, *The Healthy Body and Victorian Culture*, Cambridge, MA, 1978, pp. 167–8; George R. Parkin, *Edward Thring, Headmaster of Uppingham School*, 2 vols, London, 1898, vol. 2, pp. 156, 159.
17. John R. Gillis, 'Servants, Sexual Relations and the Risks of Illegitimacy in London, 1801–1900', in Judith L. Newton *et al.* (eds), *Sex and Class in Women's History*, London, 1983, pp. 114–45; Françoise Barret-Ducrocq, *Love in the Time of Victoria*, trans. John Howe, London, 1991.
18. Joan Lane, *Apprenticeship in England, 1600–1914*, London, 1996, pp. 194–5.
19. Anthony Trollope, *An Autobiography*, 1883, repr. Oxford, 1980, pp. 51–2.
20. The evidence for these statements is

21. Edward Herford, Diary, 3 November 1839, 12 November 1844.

22. Herbert Sussman, *Victorian Masculinities: Manhood and Manly Poetics in Early Victorian Literature and Art*, Cambridge, 1995; John S. Reed, '"A Female Movement": the Feminization of 19th Century Anglo-Catholicism', *Anglican and Episcopal History* 57 (1988), pp. 199–238.

23. J.A. Banks, *Prosperity and Parenthood*, London, 1954; John M. Robson, *Marriage or Celibacy? The Daily Telegraph on a Victorian Dilemma*, Toronto, 1995; Simon Gunn, 'The Manchester Middle Class, 1850–1880', Ph.D. thesis, University of Manchester, 1992.

24. Angus Holden to Isaac Holden, 1 March 1854 and 4 October 1860, in Eustace H. Illingworth (ed.), *Holden–Illingworth Letters*, Bradford, 1927, pp. 183, 321; Angus Holden to Sarah Holden, 13 April 1858, ibid., p. 245.

25. Cf. E. Anthony Rotundo, *American Manhood: Transformations in Masculinity from the Revolution to the Modern Era*, New York, 1993, pp. 101–5.

26. The point is further discussed in John Tosh, 'Domesticity and Manliness in the Victorian Middle Class: the Family of Edward White Benson', in M. Roper and J. Tosh (eds), *Manful Assertions: Masculinities in Britain since 1800*, London, 1991, p. 57.

27. John Clive, *Thomas Babington Macaulay: the Shaping of the Historian*, London, 1976, pp. 258–9, 267, 499; T.B. Macaulay to John Moultrie, 11 February 1835, quoted in Christopher Tolly, *Domestic Biography: the Legacy of Evangelicalism in Four Nineteenth-Century Families*, Oxford, 1997, pp. 206–9.

28. Mandell Creighton to Robert Raikes, 8 August 1866, in Louise Creighton (ed.), *Life and Letters of Mandell Creighton*, 2 vols, London, 1904, vol. 1, p. 33.

29. The issues are reviewed in Alan Sin-field, *Alfred Tennyson*, Oxford, 1986, pp. 127–53.

30. On male friendship, see Jeffrey Richards, '"Passing the Love of Women": Manly Love and Victorian Society', in J.A. Mangan and James Walvin (eds), *Manliness and Morality: Middle-Class Masculinity in Britain and America, 1800–1940*, Manchester, 1987, pp. 92–122.

31. William Landels, *How Men Are Made*, London, 1859, pp. 8–9, and *True Manhood: Its Nature, Foundation and Development*, London, 1861, p. 43.

32. Edward Herford, Diary, 9 July 1832.

33. Robert Holt to Richard Holt, 1 November 1883, Holt Papers, 920 DUR/14/1.

34. V.G. Kiernan, *The Duel in European History*, Oxford, 1988, ch. 12; Anna Clark, *The Struggle for the Breeches*, London, 1995; Fletcher, *Gender, Sex and Subordination*, pp. 342–6; Linda Colley, *Britons: Forging the Nation, 1707–1837*, London, 1992, pp. 164–93.

35. Isaac Taylor, *Advice to the Teens: or Practical Helps towards the Formation of One's Own Character*, 3rd edn, London, 1820, p. 93.

36. See generally Davidoff and Hall, *Family Fortunes*; Marjorie Morgan, *Manners, Morals and Class in England, 1774–1858*, London, 1994, esp. p. 64.

37. Margaret Hunt, 'English Urban Families in Trade, 1660–1800: the Culture of Early Modern Capitalism', Ph.D. thesis, New York University, 1986, pp. 246–76; Fletcher, *Gender, Sex and Subordination*; Anon., *Female Government*, 1779, quoted in Paul Langford, *A Polite and Commercial People: England, 1727–1783*, Oxford, 1989, p. 606. Michèle Cohen, 'The Grand Tour: Constructing the English Gentleman in Eighteenth-Century France', *History of Education* 21 (1992), pp. 241–57.

38. Mary Sewell, quoted in Mary Bayly, *The Life and Letters of Mrs Sewell*, London, 1889, p. 117.

39. T.B. Macaulay to John Moultrie, 11

February 1835, quoted in Tolly, *Domestic Biography*, p. 207; Deborah Gorham, *The Victorian Girl and the Feminine Ideal*, London, 1982.

40. John Angell James, 'The Young Man from Home' (1839), repr. in *Works*, London, 1860, vol. 5, p. 423; Ellis, *Mothers of England*, pp. 37, 305–6.

41. John Taylor, *The Autobiography of a Lancashire Lawyer*, Bolton, 1883, pp. 129–30.

42. Thomas Binney, *Address on the Subject of Middle Class Female Education* (1873), quoted in Davidoff and Hall, *Family Fortunes*, p. 116.

43. For some stimulating reflections on this theme, see Bruce Mazlish, *James and John Stuart Mill: Father and Son in the Nineteenth Century*, London, 1975, esp. p. 33.

44. Isaac Holden to Angus Holden, 12 March 1859, and Angus Holden to Isaac Holden, 17 March 1859, *Holden–Illingworth Letters*, pp. 258, 262.

45. Lant Carpenter, *Principles of Education, Intellectual, Moral and Physical*, London, 1820, pp. 183–4.

46. Letters from Isaac Holden to Margaret Holden, *Holden–Illingworth Letters*, passim. Beatrice Potter, entry for 26 November 1889, MS Diary, British Library of Political and Economic Science. See also Gorham, *Victorian Girl*, ch. 3.

47. 'An Old Boy' [Thomas Hughes], *Notes for Boys (and their Fathers) on Morals, Mind and Manners*, London, 1885, p. 91.

48. Benjamin Goodwin to John Goodwin, 16 March 1840, in Benjamin Goodwin, 'Reminiscences of Three Score Years and Ten', MS (1855), typescript copy in Bradford Public Library, p. 823; William Lucas, *A Quaker Journal*, 2 vols, London, 1934, vol. 2, p. 395.

49. Revd John Breay, quoted in Davidoff and Hall, *Family Fortunes*, pp. 332–3.

50. The literature on the other kinds of school patronized by middle-class families is frustratingly inadequate. School histories tend to be less fully

documented, and there are fewer surviving collections of letters home (partly because of the large number of day schools).

51. Banks, *Prosperity and Parenthood*, pp. 228–9. The best studies of the public school during the period of transition are Newsome, *Godliness and Good Learning* and Honey, *Tom Brown's Universe*.

52. Thomas Hughes, *Tom Brown's Schooldays*, 1857, repr. Oxford, 1989, p. 237; Leslie Stephen, 'Thoughts of an Outsider: Public Schools', *Cornhill Magazine* 27 (1873), p. 286; Peter Cominos, 'Late Victorian Sexual Respectability and the Social System', *International Review of Social History* 8 (1963), p. 26.

53. On this transition, see Newsome, *Godliness and Good Learning*, pp. 43–9, and Honey, *Tom Brown's Universe*, pp. 191–3.

54. John Oxley Parker to Christopher Oxley Parker, 2 February 1863, in J. Oxley Parker, *The Oxley Parker Papers*, Colchester, 1964, pp. 241–2.

55. Quoted in John Chandos, *Boys Together: English Public Schools, 1800–1864*, London, 1984, p. 329.

56. Parkin, *Edward Thring*, vol. 2, pp. 195–6.

57. E.W. Benson, speech at inaugural meeting, 25 May 1883, *Report of the Church of England Purity Society*, London, 1883, pp. 29–30; extract from Martin's copybook, reproduced in Newsome, *Godliness and Good Learning*, p. 155.

58. Letters from E.W. Benson to Martin Benson, no dates given (1870), quoted in Newsome, *Godliness and Good Learning*, pp. 166–7; same to same, 20 February 1874, Benson Papers 3/43, Bodleian Library, Oxford.

59. The life and death of Martin Benson are movingly recounted in Newsome, *Godliness and Good Learning*, ch. 3. On oppressive parental expectations, see Lee Krenis, 'Authority and Rebellion in Victorian Autobiography', *Journal of British Studies* 18 (1978), pp. 110–11.

60. John Heaton, entry for 5 August 1864,

MS Diary, Heaton Papers, Leeds; John Heaton to Helen Heaton, 10 May 1866, Heaton Papers, Cornhill-on-Tweed.

61. John Heaton to Fanny Heaton, 17 September 1873, Heaton Papers, Leeds; John Heaton to Helen Heaton, 14 August 1873, Heaton Papers,

Cornhill-on-Tweed; John Heaton, Diary, 25 January 1878, Heaton Papers, Leeds.

62. John Heaton, Diary, 31 December 1875; John Heaton's will of 1 April 1879; John Heaton to Fanny Heaton, 15 January 1877, all in Heaton Papers, Leeds.

Chapter 6: Convivial Pleasures and Public Duties

1. Hippolyte Taine, *Notes on England*, trans. E. Hyams, London, 1957, pp. 254–5.

2. Leonore Davidoff and Catherine Hall, *Family Fortunes: Men and Women of the English Middle Class, 1780–1850*, London, 1987, pp. 436–45. F.M.L. Thompson, *The Rise of Respectable Society*, London, 1988, pp. 255, 304.

3. John Burnett, *Plenty and Want: a Social History of Food in England from 1815 to the Present Day*, 3rd edn, London, 1989.

4. E.g. Austin Harrison, *Frederic Harrison: Thoughts and Memoirs*, London, 1926, p. 24. See also Leonore Davidoff, *The Best Circles*, London, 1973, pp. 42–6; Michael Curtin, *Propriety and Position: a Study of Victorian Manners*, New York, 1987.

5. Samuel Smiles, 'Music in the House', *Eliza Cook's Journal* 6 (1852), pp. 209–11; Nicholas Temperley, *The Romantic Age*, London, 1981, p. 120.

6. Peter Clark, *The English Alehouse*, London, 1983, pp. 306–7.

7. T.B. Dudley (ed.), *Memoir of James Bisset* (1904), quoted in Davidoff and Hall, *Family Fortunes*, p. 418. For another example, see ibid., p. 427.

8. John Angell James, *The Family Monitor, or a Help to Domestic Happiness*, Birmingham, 1828, pp. 19–20.

9. William Cobbett, *Advice to Young Men*, 1830, repr. London, 1926, p. 166.

10. William Thompson, *Appeal of One Half of the Human Race, Women, against

the Pretensions of the Other Half, Men*, 1825, repr. London, 1983, p. 77.

11. E.g. James M. Hussey, *Home*, London, 1878, pp. 30–32.

12. Personal communication from Simon Gunn.

13. Brian Harrison, *Drink and the Victorians*, London, 1971, pp. 46–7; idem, 'Pubs', in H.J. Dyos and M. Wolff (eds), *The Victorian City*, London, 1979, pp. 166–7; Dagmar Hoher, 'The Composition of Music Hall Audiences', in Peter Bailey (ed.), *Music Hall: the Business of Pleasure*, Milton Keynes, 1986, pp. 73–92.

14. 'Unit', letter to *Daily Telegraph*, 15 July 1868, quoted in John M. Robson, *Marriage or Celibacy? The Daily Telegraph on a Victorian Dilemma*, Toronto, 1995, p. 75.

15. W.M. Thackeray, 'Mr Brown's Letters to his Nephew' (1849), in *Works*, vol. 8, Oxford, 1908, pp. 334–5.

16. John Stuart Mill, speech in House of Commons, 20 May 1867, *Hansard*, vol. 187, cols 821–3.

17. John Clubbe (ed.), *Froude's Life of Carlyle*, London, 1979, p. 112; Norma Clarke, 'Strenuous Idleness: Thomas Carlyle and the Man of Letters as Hero', in Michael Roper and John Tosh (eds), *Manful Assertions: Masculinities in Britain since 1800*, London, 1991, pp. 30–33.

18. Nathaniel Hawthorne, *The Marble Faun* (1860), quoted in Samuel Smiles, *Character*, London, 1871, p. 307.

19. Thomas Hughes to Lord Ripon, 13

November 1881, quoted in E.C. Mack and W.H.G. Armytage, *Thomas Hughes*, London, 1952, p. 252.

20. John Walton, *The English Seaside Resort: a Social History, 1750–1914*, Leicester, 1983, pp. 23–4.

21. Margaret Watts to James Watts, no date [*c.* 1836], Watts Papers, Manchester Central Reference Library C/1/1.

22. Elizabeth Gaskell to John Forster, May 1854, in J.A.V. Chapple and A. Pollard (eds), *The Letters of Mrs Gaskell*, Manchester, 1966, p. 282. See also Jenny Uglow, *Elizabeth Gaskell: a Habit of Stories*, London, 1993.

23. Alan Crawford, *C.R. Ashbee*, London, 1985, p. 6.

24. Peter Clark, *Sociability and Urbanity: Clubs and Societies in the Eighteenth-Century City*, Leicester, 1986; Paul Langford, *A Polite and Commercial People: England, 1727–1783*, Oxford, 1989, p. 100; John Brewer, Neil McKendrick and J.H. Plumb, *The Birth of a Consumer Society: the Commercialization of Eighteenth-Century England*, London, 1983, pp. 217–44; John Brewer, *The Pleasures of the Imagination*, London, 1997, pp. 39–50, 507–12.

25. For the development of clubs in this period, see Ralph Nevill, *London Clubs: Their History and Treasures*, London, 1911; F.R. Cowell, *The Athenaeum: Club and Social Life in London, 1824–1974*, London, 1975, pp. 2–5; Davidoff, *The Best Circles*, p. 24; Stefan Collini, *Public Moralists: Political Thought and Intellectual Life in Britain, 1850–1930*, Oxford, 1991, p. 17.

26. Alan P. White, 'Formation and Development of Middle-Class Urban Culture and Politics', Ph.D. thesis, University of Leeds, 1990, p. 31.

27. Ibid., p. 31.

28. Walter Besant, *London in the Nineteenth Century*, London, 1909, p. 262 (written in 1900); Nevill, *London Clubs*, p. 153.

29. *Leeds Mercury*, 29 December 1849, quoted in White, 'Middle-Class Urban Culture and Politics', p. 31.

30. From verses by Theodore Hook (1788–1841), quoted in Nevill, *London Clubs,* p. 143.

31. Leonore Davidoff, *Worlds Between: Historical Perspectives on Gender and Class*, Cambridge, 1995, p. 259.

32. Richard Kelly, 'Mrs Caudle, a Victorian Curtain Lecturer', *University of Toronto Quarterly* 38 (1969), pp. 295–309; see also A. James Hammerton, *Cruelty and Companionship: Conflict in Nineteenth-Century Married Life*, London, 1992, p. 80.

33. Henry N. Dixon, unpublished Diary, 13 January 1842, quoted in Davidoff and Hall, *Family Fortunes*, p. 333. I am also grateful to Simon Gunn for allowing me to consult Chapter 6 of his forthcoming book, *The Rites of Power: Bourgeois Culture and the Industrial City, 1840–1900*, Manchester, forthcoming.

34. The flood began with Steven Marcus, *The Other Victorians*, London, 1966. It continued with Ronald Pearsall, *The Worm in the Bud: the World of Victorian Sexuality*, London, 1969; Eric Trudgill, *Madonnas and Magdalens: the Origins and Development of Victorian Sexual Attitudes*, London, 1976; Fraser Harrison, *The Dark Angel: Aspects of Victorian Sexuality*, London, 1977; Frances Finnegan, *Poverty and Prostitution*, Cambridge, 1979; Judith R. Walkowitz, *Prostitution and Victorian Society*, Cambridge, 1980; Peter Gay, *The Bourgeois Experience: Victoria to Freud*, vols 1 and 2, New York, 1984, 1986; Judith R. Walkowitz, *City of Dreadful Delight: Narratives of Sexual Danger in Late-Victorian London*, London, 1992; Michael Mason, *The Making of Victorian Sexuality*, Oxford, 1994; idem, *The Making of Victorian Sexual Attitudes*, Oxford, 1994.

35. See, for example, William Tait, *Magdalenism*, Edinburgh, 1840, and William Logan, *The Great Social Evil*, London, 1871.

36. Peter Cominos, 'Late Victorian Sexual Respectability and the Social System', *International Review of Social History* 8 (1963), pp. 18–48, 216–50; Sheila

Rowbotham, *Hidden from History*, London, 1973, pp. 51–3.

37. Walkowitz, *Prostitution*, pp. 13–31, 71–7, 153–7.

38. Ibid., p. 23; Finnegan, *Poverty*, pp. 114–16; Mason, *Making of Victorian Sexuality*, pp. 101–3.

39. Arthur Engel, '"Immoral Intentions": the University of Oxford and the Problem of Prostitution, 1827–1914', *Victorian Studies* 23 (1979), pp. 79–107.

40. *Journals and Miscellaneous Notebooks of Ralph Waldo Emerson*, vol. 10, Cambridge, MA, 1973, pp. 50–51.

41. Caroline Peters, *The King of Inventors: a Life of Wilkie Collins*, London, 1991, ch. 3.

42. Gail Savage, '"The Wilful Communication of a Loathsome Disease": Marital Conflict and Venereal Disease in Victorian England', *Victorian Studies* 34 (1990), pp. 35–54; Lucy Bland, *Banishing the Beast: English Feminism and Sexual Morality, 1885–1914*, London, 1995.

43. Georgina to Daniel Meinertzhagen, 22 October 1878 and 1 May 1878, Meinertzhagen Papers, in private hands.

44. Georgina to Daniel Meinertzhagen, 25 July 1876, and Daniel to Georgina Meinertzhagen, 20 July 1877, ibid.

45. Daniel to Georgina Meinerstzhagen, 4 April 1881, ibid.

46. Barbara Caine, *Destined to be Wives: the Sisters of Beatrice Webb*, Oxford, 1986, pp. 95–6, 118; Beatrice Mayor, 'One Family of Ten', MS in private hands, p. 30.

47. Theodore Koditschek, *Class Formation and Urban Industrial Society: Bradford, 1750–1850*, Cambridge, 1990, pp. 148–9, 296–7.

48. *Bradford Observer*, 5 October 1868, quoted in Koditschek, *Class Formation*, p. 249.

49. Notably in R.J. Morris, *Class, Sect and Party: the Making of the British Middle Class, 1820–1850*, Manchester, 1990.

50. Cornelius Stovin, Diary, 5 September 1872, in Jean Stovin (ed.), *Journals of a Methodist Farmer, 1871–75*, London, 1982, p. 96.

51. Davidoff and Hall, *Family Fortunes*, pp. 99–106, 130–48; F.K. Prochaska, *Women and Philanthropy in Nineteenth-Century England*, Oxford, 1980.

52. Davidoff and Hall, *Family Fortunes*, pp. 426–7; Mary Ann Clawson, *Constructing Brotherhood: Class, Gender, and Fraternalism*, Princeton, NJ, 1989.

53. Arnold Thackray, 'Natural Knowledge in Cultural Context: the Manchester Model', *American Historical Review* 79 (1974), pp. 672–709; R.J. Morris, 'Middle-class Culture, 1700–1914', in Derek Fraser (ed.), *A History of Modern Leeds*, Manchester, 1980, pp. 200–22; idem, *Class, Sect and Party*.

54. When John Heaton Sr retired from business in 1827, he was worth between £30,000 and £40,000. He had only one other child apart from Dr Heaton. John Heaton, MS Diary, undated entry, Heaton Papers (Leeds).

55. E.g. Diary, 23 November 1867, and review of the year 1870, ibid.

56. Asa Briggs, *Victorian Cities*, Harmondsworth, 1968, pp. 159–65.

57. The sources for the preceding two paragraphs are: John Heaton, MS Diary, *passim*, Heaton Papers (Leeds); T. Wemyss Reid, *A Memoir of John Deakin Heaton, M.D.*, London, 1883, pp. 105, 167–70; Brian and Dorothy Payne, 'An Eye-Witness Account of the Meeting of the Royal Archaeological Institute at Ripon, July 1874', *The Archaeological Journal* 128 (1972), pp. 186–90; B.P.S. Scattergood, *A Short History of the Leeds Musical Soirées, 1848–1931*, Leeds, 1932, pp. 28–9, 106–7.

58. Reid, *Memoir*.

59. John Heaton, MS Diary, entry for 27 January 1851.

60. Ibid., entry for 23 November 1877.

61. John Heaton to Helen Heaton, 14 August 1873, Heaton Papers (Cornhill-on-Tweed).

62. John Heaton, MS Diary, entries for 23 November 1871, December 1875 and 23 November 1877; John Heaton to Fanny Heaton, 17 October 1870 Heaton Papers (Leeds).

63. J.J. Ruskin to Margaret Ruskin, 13 February 1840, in V.A. Burd (ed.), *The Ruskin Family Letters*, vol. 2, Ithaca, NY, 1973, p. 640.

64. James, *The Family Monitor*, p. 22.

65. Isaac Holden to Sarah Holden, 15 December 1850, Holden Papers/21, Bradford University Library.

66. Austin Harrison, *Frederic Harrison: Thoughts and Memoirs*, London, 1926, p. 61.

67. John Tosh, 'Domesticity and Manliness in the Victorian Middle Class: the Family of Edward White Benson', in M. Roper and J. Tosh (eds), *Manful Assertions: Masculinities in Britain since 1800*, London, 1991, pp. 61–2.

68. John Heaton to Fanny Heaton, 28 July 1849, Heaton Papers (Leeds).

69. Edward Herford, entry for 28 January 1839, MS Diary, Manchester Central Reference Library, MS 923. 4 H32.

70. Patrick Joyce, *Democratic Subjects: the Self and the Social in Nineteenth-Century England*, Cambridge, 1994, pp. 116–24.

71. Graham Dawson, *Soldier Heroes: British Adventure, Empire and the Imagining of Masculinities*, London, 1994, pp. 134–44.

72. Thomas Hughes, *Memoir of Daniel Macmillan*, London, 1882, p. 178. See also Smiles, *Character*, pp. 308–9.

73. Walter Bagehot to Richard Hutton, 20 September 1847, in Mrs R. Barrington, *Life of Walter Bagehot*, London, 1914, p. 168.

74. S.S. Pugh, *Christian Manliness*, London, 1880, p. 4.

75. Dror Wahrman, '"Middle-Class" Domesticity Goes Public: Gender, Class and Politics from Queen Caroline to Queen Victoria', *Journal of British Studies* 32 (1993), pp. 396–432; idem, *Imagining the Middle Class: the Political Representation of Class in Britain, c.* 1780–1840, Cambridge, 1995, pp. 377–408; Anna Clark, *The Struggle for the Breeches*, London, 1995, pp. 264, 268; Richard Cobden, speech in House of Commons, 6 July 1848, quoted in Patricia Hollis, *Class and Conflict in Nineteenth-Century England, 1815–1850* London 1973, p. 354. See also Keith McClelland, 'Rational and Respectable Men: Gender, the Working Class and Citizenship in Britain, 1850–1867', in Laura Frader and Sonya Rose (eds), *Gender and Working-Class Formation in Modern Europe*, Ithaca, NY, 1995.

76. John Vincent, *The Formation of the British Liberal Party, 1857–68*, Harmondsworth, 1972, p. 242. See also Joyce, *Democratic Subjects*, pp. 122–3.

77. William Hale White, *The Deliverance of Mark Rutherford*, 1885, repr. London, 1923, p. 106. See also Catherine M. Maclean, *Mark Rutherford: a Biography of William Hale White*, London, 1955, pp. 150–51.

78. Sarah Ellis, *The Mothers of England*, London, 1843, p. 308.

79. H.L. Malchow, *Gentlemen Capitalists: the Social and Political World of the Victorian Businessman*, Basingstoke, 1991, p. 8.

80. Edward Baines, *The Life of Edward Baines* (1851), quoted in Clyde Binfield, *So Down to Prayers*, London, 1977, p. 65.

81. Edwin Hodder, *The Life of Samuel Morley*, London, 1887, pp. 179–80, 164–5, 185.

82. F.G. Byles, *William Byles*, Weymouth, 1932, *passim*.

83. Elizabeth Gaskell to Charles Eliot Norton, 9 March 1859, and Elizabeth Gaskell to Anne Robson, 10 May 1865, in Chapple and Pollard, *Letters of Mrs Gaskell*, pp. 537, 758.

Chapter 7: The Decline of Deference

1. David Rubinstein, *Before the Suffragettes: Women's Emancipation in the 1890s*, Brighton, 1986.

2. R.J. Helmstadter, 'The Nonconformist Conscience', in Gerald Parsons (ed.), *Religion in Victorian Britain*, vol. 4, Manchester, 1988.

3. Ibid.; Frank Turner, 'The Victorian

Crisis of Faith and the Faith that was Lost', in R.J. Helmstadter and B. Lightman (eds), *Victorian Faith in Crisis*, Basingstoke, 1990; Hugh McLeod, *Religion and Society in England, 1850–1914*, Basingstoke, 1996, ch. 4.

4. See, for example, William Dawson, *The Threshold of Manhood*, London, 1889, pp. 242–8.

5. Richard G. White, *England Without and Within*, Boston, MA, 1881, pp. 260–61; Pat Thane, 'Late Victorian Women', in T.R. Gourvish and A. O'Day (eds), *Late Victorian Britain, 1867–1900*, Basingstoke, 1988, p. 191. Cf. Colleen McDannell, *The Christian Home in Victorian America, 1840–1900*, Bloomington, IN, 1986.

6. Edwin Lees writing in *Notes and Queries*, 1879, quoted in J.A.R. Pimlott, *The Englishman's Christmas*, Hassocks, 1978, p. 114.

7. Pimlott, *Englishman's Christmas*, pp. 111–19; Penne Restad, *Christmas in America*, New York, 1995; John Lionel Tayler, *The Story of a Life*, London, 1931, p. 112.

8. Claudia Nelson, *Invisible Men: Fatherhood in Victorian Periodicals, 1850–1910*, Athens, GA, 1995, ch. 3.

9. See for example Katharine Chorley, *Manchester Made Them*, London, 1950, pp. 178–9.

10. Leslie Stephen to Julia Duckworth, 7 August 1877, quoted in Noel Annan, *Leslie Stephen: the Godless Victorian*, London, 1984, p. 83.

11. Ernest Newton, quoted in Donald J. Olsen, *The Growth of Victorian London*, Harmondsworth, 1979, p. 209.

12. This point is well substantiated by studies of Victorian children's literature. See Peter Coveney, *The Image of Childhood*, Harmondsworth, 1967, and David Grylls, *Guardians and Angels: Parents and Children in Nineteenth-Century Literature*, London, 1978.

13. Carolyn Steedman, *Strange Dislocations: Childhood and the Idea of Human Interiority, 1780–1930*, London, 1995. See also Hugh Cunningham, *Children*

and Childhood in Western Society since 1500*, Harlow, 1995, p. 74.

14. Anna Davin, *Growing Up Poor: Home, School and Street in London, 1870–1914*, London, 1996; George Behlmer, *Child Abuse and Moral Reform in England, 1870–1908*, Stanford, CA, 1982.

15. Kelly Boyd, ' "Wait Till I'm a Man": Ideals of Manliness in British Boys' Story Papers, 1855–1940', Ph.D. thesis, Rutgers University, 1991.

16. Cunningham, *Children and Childhood*, p. 76.

17. Linda Pollock, *Forgotten Children: Parent–Child Relations from 1500 to 1900*, Cambridge, 1983, pp. 173–87; Nelson, *Invisible Men*, pp. 63–7.

18. Rubinstein, *Before the Suffragettes*; Elaine Showalter, *Sexual Anarchy: Gender and Culture at the Fin de Siècle*, London, 1991; Lucy Bland, *Banishing the Beast: English Feminism and Sexual Morality, 1885–1914*, London, 1995.

19. Walter Besant, *The Revolt of Man*, London 1882. This text is briefly discussed in Peter Gay, *The Bourgeois Experience, Victoria to Freud*, vol. 1, *Education of the Senses*, New York, 1984, pp. 194–5, and Showalter, *Sexual Anarchy*, pp. 41–3.

20. Official labour statistics, cited in Rubinstein, *Before the Suffragettes*, p. 70.

21. Emma C. Hewitt, 'The "New Woman" in Relation to the "New Man" ', *Westminster Review* 147 (1897), pp. 335–7.

22. Rubinstein, *Before the Suffragettes*.

23. Susan Pedersen, 'Rathbone and Daughter: Feminism and the Father at the Fin de Siècle', *Journal of Victorian Culture* 1 (1996), pp. 98–117; Olive Banks, *Becoming a Feminist: the Social Origins of 'First Wave' Feminism*, Brighton, 1976, pp. 25–31.

24. Rubinstein, *Before the Suffragettes*, chs 2–3; Bland, *Banishing the Beast*, pp. 143–9; Sally Ledger, *The New Woman: Fiction and Feminism at the Fin de Siècle*, Manchester, 1997.

25. 'Mrs Caird's First Reply', in Harry

Quilter (ed.), *Is Marriage a Failure?*, London, 1888, p. 41.

26. Bland, *Banishing the Beast*, ch. 4; Elaine Showalter, *A Literature of Their Own: British Women Novelists from Brontë to Lessing*, London, 1978; Sally Mitchell, *The New Girl: Girls' Culture in England, 1880–1915*, New York, 1995.

27. Bram Djikstra, *Idols of Perversity*, Oxford, 1986; Judith R. Walkowitz, *City of Dreadful Delight: Narratives of Sexual Danger in Late-Victorian London*, London, 1992.

28. Josephine Butler, *Social Purity*, London, 1879, pp. 10–11.

29. Edward Bristow, *Vice and Vigilance: Purity Movements in Britain since 1700*, Dublin, 1977, pp. 94–104; F.K. Prochaska, *Women and Philanthropy in Nineteenth-Century England*, Oxford, 1980, p. 217; *DNB Supplement 1901–11*, article on Jane Ellice Hopkins.

30. Butler, *Social Purity*, pp. 10–11; *The Shield*, 21 January 1873, quoted in Myna Trustram, *Women of the Regiment: Marriage and the Victorian Army*, Cambridge, 1984, p. 132.

31. Austin Harrison, *Frederic Harrison: Thoughts and Memoirs*, London, 1926, pp. 59–60.

32. Ellice Hopkins, *The Power of Womanhood*, London, 1899.

33. Olive Schreiner to Karl Pearson, 19 July 1885, in Ruth First and Anne Scott, *Olive Schreiner: a Biography*, London, 1980, p. 157.

34. Bland, *Banishing the Beast*, pp. 146–9; Norma Clarke, 'Feminism and the Popular Novel of the 1890s', *Feminist Review* 20 (1985), pp. 91–104.

35. Bland, *Banishing the Beast*, pp. 135, 138; Sandra Stanley Holton, 'Free Love and Victorian Feminism: the Divers Matrimonials of Elizabeth Wolstenholme and Ben Elmy', *Victorian Studies* 37 (1994), pp. 199–222; Mary Lyndon Shanley, *Feminism, Marriage and the Law in Victorian England, 1850–1895*, London, 1989, pp. 177–88; William Acton, *The Functions and Disorders of the Reproductive Organs in Youth, Adult Age and Ad-* vanced *Life*, 6th edn, London, 1875, p. 142.

36. These figures are adapted from those of the Registrar-General in 1911 by J.A. Banks, *Victorian Values: Secularism and the Size of Families*, London, 1981, pp. 40, 98. See also Michael Anderson, 'The Social Implications of Demographic Change', in F.M.L. Thompson (ed.), *Cambridge Social History of Modern Britain*, vol. 2, Cambridge, 1990, p. 44.

37. J.A. Banks, *Prosperity and Parenthood*, London, 1954, chs 3–6.

38. Simon Szreter, *Fertility, Class and Gender in Britain, 1860–1940*, Cambridge, 1996. See also Angus McLaren, *Birth Control in Nineteenth-Century England*, London, 1978; Roy Porter and Lesley Hall, *The Facts of Life: the Creation of Sexual Knowledge in Britain, 1650–1950*, London, 1995; Michael Mason, *The Making of Victorian Sexuality*, Oxford, 1994.

39. Szreter, *Fertility, Class and Gender*, p. 420.

40. Shanley, *Feminism, Marriage and the Law*.

41. Extracts from *Hansard* in Shanley, *Feminism, Marriage and the Law*, pp. 69, 73–4.

42. Ibid., p. 124.

43. Married Women's Property Committee, *Final Report*, London, 1882, p. 34, quoted in Shanley, *Feminism, Marriage and the Law*, p. 103.

44. Montague Lush, 'Changes in the Law Affecting the Rights, Status and Liabilities of Married Women', in *A Century of Law Reform: Twelve Lectures*, London, 1901, p. 342.

45. E.E. Kellett, *As I Remember*, London, 1936, p. 236.

46. A. James Hammerton, *Cruelty and Companionship: Conflict in Nineteenth-Century Married Life*, London, 1992, ch. 4.

47. Thomas de Witte Talmage, *The Marriage Tie*, London, 1890, p. 56.

48. Geoffrey Mortimer, *Chapters on Human Love*, London, 1898, p. 237.

49. Hammerton, *Cruelty and Companion-*

ship, pp. 80–81, 153; Jose Harris, *Private Lives, Public Spirit: Britain, 1870–1914*, London, 1994, pp. 89–91.

50. William Fowler, MP, quoted in Shanley, *Feminism, Marriage and the Law*, p. 147.

51. Ibid., ch. 5; Megan Doolittle, 'Missing Fathers: Assembling a History of Fatherhood in Mid-Nineteenth Century England', Ph.D. thesis, University of Essex, 1996, pp. 128–37.

52. Quoted in Grylls, *Guardians and Angels*, p. 101.

53. Quoted in Nelson, *Invisible Men*, p. 53.

54. Mona Caird, *The Morality of Marriage*, London, 1897, p. 126.

55. Nelson, *Invisible Men*, ch. 2; Doolittle, 'Missing Fathers', p. 25.

56. Henry Ashbee, Diary for 27 June 1875, quoted in Hammerton, *Cruelty and Companionship*, p. 145.

57. Ibid., pp. 143–9; C.R. Ashbee, '*Grannie*', privately printed, 1939, p. 62.

58. Elizabeth Wolstenholme Elmy, writing in the *Journal of the Vigilance Association*, 1881, quoted in Holton, 'Free Love and Victorian Feminism', p. 216.

59. A.B. Hopkins, *Elizabeth Gaskell: Her Life and Work*, London, 1952, p. 303.

60. Tayler, *Story of a Life*, pp. 252–5.

61. T.J. Cobden-Sanderson, *Journals, 1879–1922*, 2 vols, privately printed, London, 1926, vol. 1, esp. pp. 41–2, 62, 121, 245–50; Marianne Tidcombe, *The Bookbindings of T.J. Cobden-Sanderson*, London, 1984, pp. 1–30.

62. Annan, *Leslie Stephen*.

63. Leonore Davidoff and Catherine Hall, *Family Fortunes: Men and Women of the English Middle Class, 1780–1850*, London, 1987, p. 229. See also Bland, *Banishing the Beast*, p. 182.

64. Annie S. Swan, *Courtship and Marriage and the Gentle Art of Home-Making*, London, 1893, pp. 103–5. See also Stephen Gwynn, 'The Modern Parent', *Cornhill Magazine*, 3rd series, 8 (1900), p. 667.

65. Beatrice Webb, entry for 15 June 1906, MS Diary, British Library of Political and Economic Science.

66. Chorley, *Manchester Made Them*, pp. 171–2.

67. T.J. Cobden-Sanderson, entry for 17 June 1885, Cobden-Sanderson, *Journals*, p. 217.

68. Ibid., pp. 222, 226–7, 284–5, 294, 300–1, 356.

69. L.P. Jacks, *Life and Letters of Stopford Brooke*, 2 vols, London, 1917, vol. 2, pp. 421–5.

70. Thomas Darling to Kenneth and Malcolm Darling, 25 January 1890, and Thomas Darling to Malcolm Darling, 16 September 1892, Darling Papers, Cambridge Centre of South Asian Studies, 15/3; Clive Dewey, *Anglo-Indian Attitudes: the Mind of the Indian Civil Service*, London, 1993, pp. 105–14

71. Mary Mildred Darling to Malcolm Darling, 22 February 1895, Darling Papers 16/2; see also same to same, 5 January 1895, Darling Papers 16/3.

72. Elizabeth Blackwell, *Counsel to Parents on the Moral Education of Their Children in Relation to Sex*, London, 1878, pp. 61–2; Hopkins, *Power of Womanhood*; Nelson, *Invisible Men*, pp. 78–9.

73. Gwynn, 'The Modern Parent', p. 677.

74. Grylls, *Guardians and Angels*, p. 103.

75. Anon., *Albert Spicer, 1847–1934: a Man of His Time*, London, 1938, pp. 64–5.

76. Eric Bligh, *Tooting Corner*, London, 1946, pp. 160–63; Hammerton, *Cruelty and Companionship*, pp. 142–3.

77. F.G. Byles, *William Byles*, Weymouth, 1932, pp. 97, 120–21; John Heaton, entries for January 1877 and December 1878, MS Diary, Heaton Papers (Leeds).

78. Richard Meinertzhagen, *Diary of a Black Sheep*, Edinburgh, 1964, pp. 211–13. My grandfather, Arnold Sillem, had a closely comparable experience in the 1880s. His stockbroker father was at first unwilling to let him enter the Army and insisted that he join the firm. But after four years he relented, and Arnold was commissioned into the Queen's Royal West Surrey Regiment in 1887. Rosamond

Estcourt Tosh, 'Arnold Frederick Sillem, 1865–1949', unpublished typescript (1976) in the author's possession.

79. Eliza Lynn Linton, *The Autobiography of Christopher Kirkland*, 3 vols, London, 1885, vol. 3, p. 2.

Chapter 8: The Flight from Domesticity

1. Cornelius Stovin, entry for 18 March 1890, MS Diary, Stovin Papers, in private hands; Joseph Bush, *Elizabeth Riggall: a Memorial*, Derby, 1893, p. 56.
2. See above, pp. 57, 66.
3. Cornelius Stovin, entry for 31 August 1870, MS Diary, Stovin Papers.
4. E.g. J.R. Miller, *Secrets of Happy Home Life*, London, 1894; George Bainton, *The Wife as Lover and Friend*, London, 1896; J.G. Greenhough, *Our Dear Home Life*, London, 1896.
5. Maurice Hewlett, entry for 31 December 1894, MS Diary, BL Add. MSS 41075.
6. Annie Swan, *Courtship and Marriage and the Gentle Art of Home-Making*, London, 1893, pp. 32–4, 40–41. See also E.J. Hardy, *How To Be Happy Though Married*, 2nd edn, London, 1896.
7. Walter Besant, *The Rise of the Empire*, London, 1897, pp. 14–15.
8. Richard Church, *Over the Bridge*, London, 1955, p. 119. For the context, see A. James Hammerton, *Cruelty and Companionship: Conflict in Nineteenth-Century Married Life*, London, 1992, pp. 139–42.
9. Hardy, *How To Be Happy*, p. 12.
10. Charles Ansell, *On the Rate of Mortality at Early Periods of Life, the Age of Marriage, the Number of Children to a Marriage, the Length of a Generation, and Other Statistics of Families in the Upper and Professional Classes*, London, 1874.
11. William Ogle, 'On Marriage-Rates and Marriage-Ages, with Special Reference to the Growth of Population', *Journal of the Royal Statistical Society* 53 (1890), pp. 253–89. The figure of 31.2 is actually Michael Anderson's extrapolation from the figures produced by Ogle. Michael Anderson, 'The Social Implications of Demographic Change', in F.M.L. Thompson (ed.), *Cambridge Social History of Modern Britain*, vol. 2, Cambridge, 1990, pp. 32–4.
12. Sarah Sewell, *Women and the Times We Live In*, 2nd edn, Manchester, 1869, pp. 120–21; W.R. Greg, *Why Are Women Redundant?*, London, 1869, p. 21.
13. Harry Quilter (ed.), *Is Marriage a Failure?*, London, 1888, p. 146.
14. Swan, *Courtship and Marriage*, pp. 81–2; J.A. Banks, *Prosperity and Parenthood*, London, 1954.
15. Greg, *Why Are Women Redundant?* p. 21.
16. James Hussey, *Home*, London, 1878, p. 26.
17. For references, see below, notes 41–5, 47–9.
18. H. Rider Haggard, *King Solomon's Mines*, London, 1885, p. 9.
19. Rudyard Kipling, *The Light That Failed* (1891), repr. London, 1988, p. 58.
20. Edmund Gosse in *Century* magazine (1891), quoted in Martin Seymour-Smith, *Rudyard Kipling*, London, 1989, p. 123.
21. Arthur Conan Doyle, quoted in J.A. Hammerton (ed.), *Stevensoniana*, London, 1903, p. 243. For the literary history of the period, see Elaine Showalter, *Sexual Anarchy: Gender*

and Culture at the Fin de Siècle, London, 1991, ch. 5.

22. Seth Koven, 'From Rough Lads to Hooligans: Boy Life, National Culture and Social Reform', in Andrew Parker *et al.* (eds), *Nationalisms and Sexualities*, New York, 1992, pp. 365–91; Peter F. Anson, *The Call of the Cloister*, London, 1955, pp. 78, 133, 590–91.

23. Graham Dawson, *Soldier Heroes: British Adventure, Empire and the Imagining of Masculinities*, London, 1994, pp. 144–54.

24. *Girl's Own Paper* 2 (1881), p. 7, quoted in Kate Flint, *The Woman Reader, 1837–1914*, Oxford, 1993, p. 82.

25. Catherine Hall, *White, Male and Middle Class: Explorations in Feminism and History*, Cambridge, 1992, pp. 222–31.

26. Geoffrey Drage, *Eton and the Empire*, Eton, 1890, pp. 39–40.

27. Grant Allen, 'Plain Words on the Woman Question', *Fortnightly Review* 46 (1889), pp. 454–5

28. F. Musgrove, *The Migratory Elite*, London, 1963, pp. 19–21.

29. Richard Symonds, *Oxford and Empire: the Last Lost Cause?*, London, 1986, pp. 306–7. On the less educated 'gentleman emigrant', see Thomas Hughes, *Rugby, Tennessee*, London, 1881, and A.G. Bradley, 'Gentlemen Emigrants', *Macmillan's Magazine* 58 (1888), pp. 30–40.

30. Janet Adam Smith, *John Buchan*, London, 1965, pp. 43–5, 165.

31. This is my conclusion after trawling the archives of the Royal Commonwealth Society, Rhodes House Library, the India Office Library and the Imperial War Museum.

32. Benjamin Wilson, quoted in Ronald Hyam, *Britain's Imperial Century, 1815–1914*, London, 1974, p. 138.

33. Ronald Hyam, *Empire and Sexuality: the British Experience*, Manchester, 1990.

34. E.C. Mack, *Public Schools and British Opinion since 1860*, New York, 1941; J.R. de S. Honey, *Tom Brown's Universe: the Development of the Victorian Public School*, London, 1977.

35. Peter Cominos, 'Late Victorian Sexual Respectability and the Social System', *International Review of Social History* 8 (1963), p. 26.

36. Patrick Dunae, *Gentlemen Emigrants: from the British Public Schools to the Canadian Frontier*, Vancouver, 1981, p. 60. On the cult of physical endurance, see J.A. Mangan, *Athleticism in the Victorian and Edwardian Public School*, Cambridge, 1981.

37. John Masefield, *My Faith in Women's Suffrage*, London, 1910, p. 7.

38. See, for example, Jose Harris, *Private Lives, Public Spirit: Britain, 1870–1914*, Oxford, 1993; J.F.C. Harrison, *Late Victorian Britain, 1875–1901*, London, 1990.

39. David Grylls, *Guardians and Angels: Parents and Children in Nineteenth-Century Literature*, London, 1978; Hugh Cunningham, *Children and Childhood in Western Society since 1500*, Harlow, 1995, pp. 74–8.

40. Cynthia Russett, *Sexual Science: the Victorian Construction of Womanhood*, Cambridge, MA, 1989.

41. Greg, *Why Are Women Redundant?* p. 21.

42. Mary Farningham, *Home Life*, London, 1889, p. 2.

43. 'One of Us', 'Why We Men Do Not Marry', *Temple Bar* 84 (1888), p. 219.

44. See Eliza Lynn Linton, *The Girl of the Period and Other Social Essays*, London, 1883, pp. 335–43; 'Eugenius', 'The Decline of Marriage', *Westminster Review* 135 (1891), pp. 11–27; Philip Hamerton, *The Intellectual Life*, London, 1873, pp. 249, 251; Robert Louis Stevenson, *Virginibus Puerisque*, 1881, repr. London, 1918, p. 5.

45. Mona Caird, 'Marriage', *Westminster Review* 130 (1888), p. 197.

46. Banks, *Prosperity and Parenthood*, pp. 86–102. On the 'feminization' of the home, see also John Burnett, *A Social History of Housing, 1815–1970*, London, 1978, p. 110.

47. Geoffrey Mortimer, *Chapters on Human Love*, London, 1898, pp. 230–5.

48. T.H.S. Escott, *England: its People, Polity and Pursuits*, 2 vols, London, 1879, vol. 2, p. 17.

49. Edward Carpenter, *Love's Coming of Age* (1896), repr. London, 1914, pp. 44–5. See also his 'The Drawing-Room Table in Literature', *The New Age*, 17 March 1910, p. 464.

50. Elizabeth Langland, *Nobody's Angels: Middle-Class Women and Domestic Ideology in Victorian Culture*, Ithaca, NY, 1995, pp. 66–71.

51. Kipling, *The Light That Failed*, p. 40.

52. Crosland's writing is analysed in A. James Hammerton, 'Masculinity and Marriage in the Lower Middle Class: the Making of "Moral Manliness", England, 1870–1920', paper presented to conference on the English Middle Class, Manchester Metropolitan University, September 1996.

53. Edward Manson, 'Marital Authority', *Law Quarterly Review* 7 (1891), p. 255; Eliza Lynn Linton, 'The Judicial Shock to Marriage', *Nineteenth Century* 29 (1891), pp. 691–700.

54. See above, p. 157.

55. Mark Girouard, *Life in the Victorian Country House*, Harmondsworth, 1980, pp. 292–8.

56. Mary Haweis, *The Art of Housekeeping: a Bridal Garland*, London, 1889, pp. 33–4.

57. Quilter, *Is Marriage a Failure?* p. 133.

58. Eric Bligh, *Tooting Corner*, London, 1946, p. 234.

59. In earlier writings I did not sufficiently take account of this point. John Tosh, 'Imperial Masculinity and the Flight From Domesticity in Britain, 1880–1914', in T.P. Foley et al. (eds), *Gender and Colonialism*, Galway, 1995, pp. 72–85, and 'The Making of Masculinities: the Middle Class in Late Nineteenth-Century Britain', in Angela V. John and Claire Eustance (eds), *The Men's Share? Masculinities, Male Support and Women's Suffrage in Britain,*

1890–1920, London, 1997, pp. 38–61.

60. Generational rebellion is stressed in Lee Krenis, 'Authority and Rebellion in Victorian Autobiography', *Journal of British Studies* 18 (1878), pp. 107–30, and in Steven Mintz, *A Prison of Expectations: the Family in Victorian Culture*, New York, 1983, ch. 5. For the biographical context, see Peter Raby, *Samuel Butler: a Biography*, London, 1991.

61. Edward Carpenter, *My Dreams and Days*, London, 1916. See also C. Tsuzuki, *Edward Carpenter, 1844–1929: Prophet of Human Fellowship*, Cambridge, 1980.

62. The Oedipal implications of this pattern are addressed in Peter Gay, *The Bourgeois Experience, Victoria to Freud*: vol. 2, *The Tender Passion*, New York, 1986, p. 98.

63. Edmond Demolins, *Anglo-Saxon Superiority: To What It Is Due*, London, 1898, p. 100.

64. Drage, *Eton and the Empire*, p. 39; John E. Adamson, *The Theory of Education in Plato's Republic*, London, 1903, p. 51; Carpenter, *Love's Coming of Age*, pp. 25–33.

65. Charles Ashbee, 'Grannie', privately printed, 1939, pp. 34, 36.

66. Hammerton, *Cruelty and Companionship*, pp. 144–8; A. James Hammerton, 'From Patriarchy to Comradeship: Problems in the Reconstruction of Middle-Class Marriage and Masculinity in Late Victorian and Edwardian England', paper presented to Canadian Historical Association, Charlottetown, Prince Edward Island, May 1992.

67. Philip Magnus, *Kitchener: Portrait of an Imperialist*, London, 1958, ch. 1; Trevor Royle, *The Kitchener Enigma*, London, 1985, pp. 13, 17–18.

68. Robert I. Rotberg and M.F. Shore, *The Founder: Cecil Rhodes and the Pursuit of Power*, New York, 1988, pp. 14–28.

69. T.H.R. Cashmore, 'Studies in District Administration in the East Africa

70. Walter Besant, *London in the Nineteenth Century*, London, 1909 (written in 1900), pp. 260–61, 264; Simon Gunn, *The Rites of Power: Bourgeois Culture and the Industrial City, 1840–1900*, Manchester, forthcoming, ch. 6.

71. John Lowerson, *Sport and the English Middle Classes, 1870–1914*, Manchester, 1993, p. 22.

72. Gunn, *Rites of Power*.

73. Israel Zangwill, *The Bachelors' Club*, London, 1891.

74. Brian Harrison, *Separate Spheres: the Opposition to Women's Suffrage in Britain*, London, 1978, p. 97.

75. Maud Churton Braby, *Modern Marriage and How to Bear It* (1909), quoted in Flint, *Woman Reader*, p. 100.

76. Quilter, *Is Marriage a Failure?*.

77. Bruce Haley, *The Healthy Body and Victorian Culture*, Cambridge, MA, 1978; Lowerson, *Sport and the English Middle Classes;* David Rubinstein, 'Cycling in the 1890s', *Victorian Studies* 21 (1977), pp. 47–71.

78. This aspect is briefly acknowledged in Lowerson, *Sport and the English Middle Classes*, p. 18.

79. Ibid., p. 191.

80. Mary E. Kennard, *The Sorrows of a Golfer's Wife*, London, 1896, p. 9.

81. Peter H. Hansen, 'Albert Smith, the Alpine Club and the Invention of Mountaineering in Britain', *Journal of British Studies* 34 (1995), pp. 300–24; Lowerson, *Sport and the English Middle Classes*.

82. H.H. Almond, 'Football as a Moral Agent' (1893), quoted in Mangan, *Athleticism*, p. 302.

83. Thomas Hughes, *Memoir of Daniel Macmillan*, London, 1882, p. 178. For similar views, see Thomas de Witt Talmage, *The Marriage Tie*, London, 1890, pp. 55–6.

84. See, for example, John Brookes, *Manliness and Culture*, London,1877, and William Dawson, *The Making of Manhood*, London,1894. More generally, see David Newsome, *Godliness and Good Learning*, London, 1961, and Mangan, *Athleticism*.

85. Jeffrey Weeks, *Coming Out: Homosexual Politics in Britain, from the Nineteenth Century to the Present*, London, 1977.

86. For Social Purity, see Judith R. Walkowitz, *Prostitution and Victorian Society*, Cambridge, 1980, pp. 90–113, 233–45, and Lucy Bland, *Banishing the Beast: English Feminism and Sexual Morality, 1885–1914*, London, 1995, pp. 95–123. For Carpenter, see his *Dreams and Days*.

87. David Hilliard, 'UnEnglish and Unmanly: Anglo-Catholicism and Homosexuality', *Victorian Studies* 25 (1982), pp. 181–210.

88. Honey, *Tom Brown's Universe*, pp. 189–94; Jeffrey Richards, '"Passing the Love of Women": Manly Love and Victorian Society', in J.A. Mangan and J. Walvin (eds), *Manliness and Morality: Middle-Class Masculinity in Britain and America, 1800–1940*, Manchester 1987, pp. 92–122.

89. Koven, 'From Rough Lads to Hooligans', pp. 365–91.

90. Richard Jenkyns, *The Victorians and Ancient Greece*, Oxford, 1980.

91. Timothy D'Arch Smith, *Love in Earnest*, London, 1970.

92. Alan Crawford, *C.R. Ashbee*, London, 1985, pp. 29–31; Hammerton, 'From Patriarchy to Comradeship'.

93. Arthur Benson, Diary, 1924, quoted in David Newsome, *On the Edge of Paradise: A.C. Benson the Diarist*, London, 1980, p. 195.

94. Brian Masters, *The Life of E.F. Benson*, London, 1991, esp. pp. 175–80.

95. R.H. Benson, *Confessions of a Convert*, London, 1913, p. 29; Newsome, *On the Edge of Paradise*, pp. 42, 144.

96. Ibid., p. 61.

97. Arthur Benson, Diary, August 1923, quoted in Newsome, *On the Edge of Paradise*, p. 15; Geoffrey Palmer and Noel Lloyd, *E.F. Benson As He Was*, Luton, 1988, pp. 56–7.

Protectorate, 1895–1918', Ph.D. thesis, London University, 1965, pp. 15–23, 28–9.

98. E.F. Benson, *Our Family Affairs: 1867–1896*, London, 1920, p. 103. See also A.C. Benson, *The Trefoil: Wellington College, Lincoln and Truro*, London, 1923, pp. 273–5.

99. E.F. Benson, *Our Family Affairs*, p. 105.

100. Arthur Benson, Diary, quoted in Newsome, *On the Edge of Paradise*, p. 131.

101. A.C. Benson, *The Life of Edward White Benson*, 2 vols, London, 1899. See also Newsome, *On the Edge of Paradise*, p. 164.

102. Newsome, *On the Edge of Paradise*, p. 243. See also John Tosh, 'Domesticity and Manliness in the Victorian Middle Class: the Family of Edward White Benson', in M. Roper and J. Tosh (eds), *Manful Assertions: Masculinities in Britain since 1800*, London, 1991, pp. 61–7.

Conclusion

1. Michael Mason, *The Making of Victorian Sexuality*, Oxford, 1994, pp. 1–8.

2. Robert Bly, *Iron John: a Book about Men*, Shaftesbury, 1990.

3. Tim Jeal, *Baden-Powell*, London, 1989.

4. Joanna Bourke, *Dismembering the Male: Men's Bodies, Britain, and the Great War*, London, 1996, pp. 155–74. See also Alison Light, *Forever England: Femininity, Literature and Conservatism between the Wars*, London, 1991, pp. 8–14.

5. Christopher Reed (ed.), *Not At Home: the Suppression of Domesticity in Modern Art and Architecture*, London, 1996.

6. Lynne Segal, *Slow Motion: Changing Masculinities, Changing Men*, London, 1990, pp. 1–13.

A Note on Method

1. On the perils of reading social practice from didactic texts, see Jay Mechling, 'Advice to Historians on Advice to Mothers', *Journal of Social History* 9 (1975–76), pp. 44–63.

2. Thomas Wemyss Reid, *A Memoir of John Deakin Heaton*, London, 1883, p. 286.

3. For example, the MS Diary of Robert Holt, Liverpool Record Office 920/DUR/1.

Sources

1. Manuscript Collections

Bodleian Library, Oxford
Papers of Edward White Benson and his family

Bradford University Library
Papers of Sir Isaac Holden

The British Library
Papers of Richard Cobden
Diary of Maurice Hewlett

The British Library of Political and Economic Science
The Diaries of Beatrice Webb

Brotherton Library, University of Leeds
Papers of Sir Isaac Holden

The Cambridge Centre of South Asian Studies
Papers of Sir Malcolm Darling

Lambeth Palace
Papers of A.C. Tait

Liverpool Record Office
Papers of Robert Holt and his family

London University Library
Papers of Sir John Seeley

Manchester Central Reference Library
Diary of Edward Herford
Papers of Joshua Murgatroyd
Papers of Joshua Pritchard
Papers of James Watts

Trinity College, Cambridge
Diary of Edward White Benson

In private hands
Papers of John Deakin Heaton
Papers of Daniel Meinertzhagen
Papers of Cornelius Stovin

Unpublished family memoirs
Goodwin, Benjamin 'Reminiscences of Three Score Years and Ten', MS (1855), typescript copy in Bradford Public Library.
Mayor, Beatrice, 'One Family of Ten', typescript in private hands.
Tosh, Rosamond Estcourt 'Arnold Frederick Sillem, 1865–1949', typescript (1976) in the author's possession.

2. Published Family Records (including Diaries and Letters, Autobiographies, and Biographies Written with First-hand Knowledge)

Anon., *Albert Spicer, 1847–1934: a Man of His Time*, London, 1938.
Ashbee, C.R. *'Grannie'*, privately printed, 1939.
Barrington, Mrs R. *Life of Walter Bagehot*, London, 1914.
Barrington, Mrs R. (ed.) *The Love-Letters of Walter Bagehot and Eliza Wilson*, London, 1933.
Bayly, Mary *The Life and Letters of Mrs Sewell*, London, 1889.
Benham, W. (ed.) *Catharine and Craufurd Tait*, London, 1879.
Benson, A.C. *The Life of Edward White Benson*, 2 vols, London, 1899.
Benson, A.C. *The Trefoil: Wellington College, Lincoln and Truro*, London, 1923.
Benson, E.F. *Our Family Affairs, 1867–1896*, London, 1920.
Benson, E.F. *Mother*, London, 1925.
Benson, R.H. *Confessions of a Convert*, London, 1913.
Bligh, Eric *Tooting Corner*, London, 1946.
Bruce, Alexander *The Life of William Denny*, London, 1889.
Burd, V.A. (ed.) *The Ruskin Family Letters*, vol. 2, Ithaca, NY, 1973.
Bush, Joseph *Elizabeth Riggall: a Memorial*, Derby, 1893.
Bush, Joseph *Francis Riggall: a Memorial*, Derby, 1893.
Byles, F.G. *William Byles*, Weymouth, 1932.
Carpenter, Edward *My Dreams and Days*, London, 1916.
Chapple, J.A.V. and A. Pollard (eds) *The Letters of Mrs Gaskell*, Manchester, 1966.
Chorley, Katharine *Manchester Made Them*, London, 1950.
Church, Richard *Over the Bridge*, London, 1955.
Clarke, J.B.B. (ed.) *An Account of the Infancy, Religious and Literary Life of Adam Clarke*, 3 vols, London, 1833.
Clubbe, John (ed.) *Froude's Life of Carlyle*, London, 1979.
Cobden-Sanderson, T.J. *Cosmic Vision*, London, 1922.
Cobden-Sanderson, T.J. *Journals, 1879–1922*, 2 vols, privately printed, London, 1926.
Creighton, Louise (ed.) *Life and Letters of Mandell Creighton*, 2 vols, London, 1904.
Dent, H.R. (ed.) *The Memoirs of J.M. Dent*, London, 1928.
Gaskell, Elizabeth *My Diary: the Early Years of My Daughter Marianne*, privately printed, 1923.

Gisborne, John *A Brief Memoir of the Life of John Gisborne Esq.*, London, 1852.

Grant, Brewin *The Dissenting World: an Autobiography*, 2nd edn, London, 1869.

Hardy, R.S. *Commerce and Christianity: Memorial of Jonas Sugden of Oakworth House*, London, 1857.

Hare, Augustus *The Years with Mother*, ed. Malcolm Barnes, London, 1984.

Harrison, Austin *Frederic Harrison: Thoughts and Memoirs*, London, 1926.

Harvey, W.F. *We Were Seven*, London, 1936.

Hodder, Edwin *The Life of Samuel Morley*, London, 1887.

Hughes, Thomas *Memoir of a Brother*, London, 1873.

Hughes, Thomas *Memoir of Daniel Macmillan*, London, 1882.

Illingworth, Eustace H. (ed.) *The Holden–Illingworth Letters*, Bradford, 1927.

Jacks, L.P. *Life and Letters of Stopford Brooke*, 2 vols, London, 1917.

Kellett, E.E. *As I Remember*, London, 1936.

Linton, Eliza Lynn *The Autobiography of Christopher Kirkland*, 3 vols, London, 1885.

Lucas, William *A Quaker Journal*, 2 vols, London, 1934.

Lyall, Edna *The Burges Letters: a Record of Child Life in the Sixties*, London, 1902.

Macmillan, George (ed.) *Letters of Alexander Macmillan*, privately printed, 1908.

Meinertzhagen, Richard *Diary of a Black Sheep*, Edinburgh, 1964.

Milburn, G.E. (ed.) *The Diary of John Young, Sunderland Chemist and Methodist Lay Preacher, 1841–1843*, Surtees Society Publications, vol. 195, 1983.

Parker, J. Oxley *The Oxley Parker Papers*, Colchester, 1964.

Parkin, George R. *Edward Thring, Headmaster of Uppingham School*, 2 vols, London, 1898.

Reid, T. Wemyss *A Memoir of John Deakin Heaton, M.D.*, London, 1883.

Ryland, J.E. *Memoirs of John Kitto*, Edinburgh, 1856.

Stanley, A.P. *The Life and Correspondence of Thomas Arnold*, 2 vols, London, 1844.

Stovin, Jean (ed.) *Journals of a Methodist Farmer, 1871–75*, London, 1982.

Sturge, Charlotte *Family Records*, London, 1882.

Sully, James *My Life and Friends: a Psychologist's Memoirs*, London, 1918.

Tayler, John Lionel *The Story of a Life*, London, 1931.

Taylor, John *The Autobiography of a Lancashire Lawyer*, Bolton, 1883.

Thale, Mary (ed.) *The Autobiography of Francis Place*, Cambridge, 1972.

Trollope, Anthony *An Autobiography*, 1883, repr. Oxford, 1980.

Wilberforce, R.I. and S. *The Life of William Wilberforce*, 5 vols, London, 1838.

Woolf, Virginia *Moments of Being*, London, 1976.

3. Advice Literature

Abbott, Jacob *Parental Duties in the Promotion of Early Piety*, London, 1834.

Anderson, Christopher *The Genius and Design of the Domestic Constitution*, 2nd edn, Edinburgh, 1847.

Arthur, Timothy Shay *Advice to Young Men on Their Duties and Conduct in Life*, London, 1854.

Bainton, George *The Wife as Lover and Friend*, London, 1896.

Bickersteth, Edward *A Treatise on Prayer*, 11th edn, London, 1828.

Blackwell, Elizabeth *Counsel to Parents on the Moral Education of Their Children in Relation to Sex*, London, 1878.

Brookes, John *Manliness and Culture*, London, 1877.

Brown, James Baldwin *The Home in its Relation to Man and Society*, London, 1883.

Bushnell, Horace *Christian Nurture*, London, 1861.

Butler, Josephine *Social Purity*, London, 1879.

Caird, John *Christian Manliness*, Glasgow, 1871.
Caird, Mona *The Morality of Marriage*, London, 1897.
Carpenter, Edward *Love's Coming of Age*, 1896, repr. London, 1914.
Carpenter, Lant *Principles of Education, Intellectual, Moral and Physical*, London, 1820.
Chapone, Hester *A Letter to a New-Married Lady*, 1777; repr. London, 1828.
Cobbe, Frances Power *The Duties of Woman*, London, 1881.
Cobbett, William *Advice to Young Men*, 1830, repr. London, 1926.
Craik, Dinah Mulock *A Woman's Thoughts about Women*, London, 1858.
Dawson, William *The Threshold of Manhood*, London, 1889.
Dawson, William *The Making of Manhood*, London, 1894.
Dwight, Theodore *The Father's Book*, London, 1834.
Ellis, Sarah *The Women of England*, London, 1839.
Ellis, Sarah *The Daughters of England*, London, 1842.
Ellis, Sarah *The Mothers of England*, London, 1843.
Ellis, Sarah *The Wives of England*, London, 1843.
Farningham, Marianne *Boyhood*, London, 1870.
Farningham, Marianne *Home Life*, London, 1889.
Greenhough, J.G. *Our Dear Home Life*, London, 1896.
Gwynn, Stephen 'The Modern Parent', *Cornhill Magazine* 3rd series, 8 (1900), pp. 662–78.
Hardy, E.J. *How To Be Happy Though Married*, 2nd edn, London, 1896.
Haweis, Mary *The Art of Housekeeping: a Bridal Garland*, London, 1889.
Hopkins, Ellice *The Power of Womanhood*, London, 1899.
Hussey, James M. *Home*, London, 1878.
James, John Angell *The Family Monitor, or a Help to Domestic Happiness*, Birmingham, 1828.
James, John Angell 'The Young Man from Home', 1839, repr. in *Works*, London, 1860, vol. 5.
James, John Angell *The Young Man's Friend*, London, 1851.
Landels, William *How Men Are Made*, London, 1859.
Landels, William *True Manhood: Its Nature, Foundation and Development*, London, 1861.
Landels, William *Woman: Her Position and Power*, London, 1870.
Landels, William *The Marriage Ring*, London, 1883.
Lewis, Sarah *Woman's Mission*, 7th edn, London, 1840.
Mayhew, Henry 'Home Is Home, Be It Never So Homely', in Viscount Ingestre (ed.) *Meliora: Or Better Times to Come*, London, 1852.
Miller, J.R. *Secrets of Happy Home Life*, London, 1894.
Mortimer, Geoffrey *Chapters on Human Love*, London, 1898.
O'Donnoghue, H.C. *Marriage: the Source, Stability and Perfection of Social Happiness and Duty*, London, 1828.
'An Old Boy' [Thomas Hughes] *Notes for Boys (and their Fathers) on Morals, Mind and Manners*, London, 1885.
Pugh, S.S. *Christian Manliness*, London, 1880.
Roberts, William *The Portraiture of a Christian Gentleman*, London, 1829.
Ruskin, John *Sesame and Lilies*, 1864 pocket edn, London, 1906.
Sandford, Mrs John *Woman in Her Social and Domestic Character*, 6th edn, London, 1839.
Sargent, G.E. *Home Education*, London, 1854.
Sewell, Sarah *Woman and the Times We Live In*, 2nd edn, Manchester, 1869.
Smiles, Samuel 'Music in the House', *Eliza Cook's Journal* 6 (1852), pp. 209–11.
Smiles, Samuel *Character*, London, 1871.
Spicer, Thomas T. *Masculine Education*, London, 1855.
Stowe, Harriet Beecher *Little Foxes: or the Insignificant Little Habits Which Mar Domestic Happiness*, London, 1866.
Swan, Annie S. *Courtship and Marriage and the Gentle Art of Home-Making*, London, 1893.
Talmage, Thomas de Witte *The Marriage Tie*, London, 1890.

Taylor, Isaac *Advice to the Teens: or Practical Helps towards the Formation of One's Own Character*, 3rd edn, London, 1820.

Venn, Henry *The Complete Duty of Man*, 1763, repr. London, 1836.

4. Other Primary Works

Acton, William *The Functions and Disorders of the Reproductive Organs in Youth, Adult Age and Advanced Life*, London, 1857; 6th edn, 1875.

Adamson, John E. *The Theory of Education in Plato's Republic*, London, 1903.

Allen, Grant 'Plain Words on the Woman Question', *Fortnightly Review* 46 (1889), pp. 448–58.

Anon. 'Childhood', *Blackwood's Edinburgh Magazine* 12 (1822), pp. 139–45.

Ansell, Charles *On the Rate of Mortality at Early Periods of Life, the Age of Marriage, the Number of Children to a Marriage, the Length of a Generation, and Other Statistics of Families in the Upper and Professional Classes*, London, 1874.

Besant, Walter *The Revolt of Man*, London, 1882.

Besant, Walter *The Rise of the Empire*, London, 1897.

Besant, Walter *London in the Nineteenth Century*, London, 1909.

Bradley, A.G. 'Gentlemen Emigrants', *Macmillan's Magazine* 58 (1888), pp. 30–40.

Caird, Mona 'Marriage', *Westminster Review* 130 (1888), pp. 186–201.

Carpenter, Edward 'The Drawing-Room Table in Literature', *The New Age*, 17 March 1910, pp. 464–5.

Craik, Dinah Mulock *John Halifax, Gentleman*, London, 1856.

Demolins, Edmond *Anglo-Saxon Superiority: To What It Is Due*, London, 1898.

Drage, Geoffrey *Eton and the Empire*, Eton, 1890.

Emerson, Ralph Waldo *English Traits*, London, 1856.

Emerson, Ralph Waldo *Journals and Miscellaneous Notebooks*, vol. 10, Cambridge, MA, 1973.

Escott, T.H.S. *England: its People, Polity and Pursuits*, 2 vols, London, 1879.

Escott, T.H.S. *Club Makers and Club Members*, London, 1914.

'Eugenius', 'The Decline of Marriage', *Westminster Review* 135 (1891), pp. 11–27.

Froude, J.A. *Shadows of the Clouds*, London, 1847.

Froude, J.A. *The Nemesis of Faith*, London, 1849.

Greg, W.R. *Why Are Women Redundant?* London, 1869.

Greg, Mrs Samuel *A Layman's Legacy in Prose and Verse*, London, 1877.

Haggard, H. Rider *King Solomon's Mines*, London, 1885.

Hamerton, Philip *The Intellectual Life*, London, 1873.

Hammerton, J.A. (ed.) *Stevensoniana*, London, 1903.

Hewitt, Emma C. 'The "New Woman" in Relation to the "New Man"', *Westminster Review* 147 (1897), pp. 335–7.

Hodgson, John *Textile Manufacture and Other Industries in Keighley*, Keighley, 1879.

Hughes, Thomas *Tom Brown's Schooldays*, 1857, repr. Oxford, 1989.

Hughes, Thomas *Rugby, Tennessee*, London, 1881.

Kennard, Mary E. *The Sorrows of a Golfer's Wife*, London, 1896.

Kerr, Robert *The Gentleman's House: or How to Plan English Residences from the Parsonage to the Palace*, London, 1864.

Kipling, Rudyard *The Light That Failed*, 1891, repr. London, 1988.

Linton, Eliza Lynn *The Girl of the Period and Other Social Essays*, London, 1883.

Linton, Eliza Lynn 'The Judicial Shock to Marriage', *Nineteenth Century* 29 (1891), pp. 691–700.

Logan, William *The Great Social Evil*, London, 1871.

Lush, Montague 'Changes in the Law Affecting the Rights, Status and Liabilities of Married Women', in *A Century of Law Reform: Twelve Lectures*, London, 1901.

Manson, Edward 'Marital Authority', *Law Quarterly Review* 7 (1891), pp. 244–55.

Masefield, John *My Faith in Women's Suffrage*, London, 1910.

Mill, John Stuart *On Liberty*, 1859, repr. Harmondsworth, 1974.

Mill, John Stuart *The Subjection of Women*, London, 1869.

Ogle, William 'On Marriage-Rates and Marriage-Ages, with Special Reference to the Growth of Population', *Journal of the Royal Statistical Society* 53 (1890), pp. 253–89.

'One of Us', 'Why We Men Do Not Marry', *Temple Bar* 84 (1888), pp. 218–23.

Quilter, Harry (ed.) *Is Marriage a Failure?* London, 1888.

Report of the Church of England Purity Society, London, 1883.

Seeley, J.R. *Lectures and Essays*, London, 1870.

Stephen, James *Essays in Ecclesiastical Biography*, London, 1849.

Stephen, Leslie 'Thoughts of an Outsider: Public Schools', *Cornhill Magazine* 27 (1873), pp. 281–92, 605–15.

Stevenson, Robert Louis *Virginibus Puerisque*, 1881, repr. London, 1918.

Taine, Hippolyte *Notes on England*, trans. E. Hyams, London, 1957.

Tait, William *Magdalenism*, Edinburgh, 1840.

Thackeray, W.M. 'Mr Brown's Letters to His Nephew' (1849), in *Works*, vol. 8, Oxford, 1908.

Thompson, William *Appeal of One Half of the Human Race, Women, against the Pretensions of the Other Half, Men*, 1825, repr. London, 1983.

White, Richard G. *England Without and Within*, Boston, MA, 1881.

White, William Hale *Mark Rutherford's Deliverance*, 1885, repr. London, 1923.

Wiese, Ludwig *German Letters on English Education*, trans. W.D. Arnold, London, 1854.

Wollstonecraft, Mary *A Vindication of the Rights of Woman*, 1792, repr. ed. C.H. Poston, New York, 1988.

Zangwill, Israel *The Bachelors' Club*, London, 1891.

5. Published Secondary Works

Abelove, Henry *The Evangelist of Desire: John Wesley and the Methodists*, Stanford, CA, 1990.

Amussen, Susan '"The Part of a Christian Man": the Cultural Politics of Manhood in Early Modern England', in S. Amussen and M. Kishlansky (eds) *Political Culture and Cultural Politics in Early Modern England*, Manchester, 1995.

Amussen, Susan and Mark Kishlansky (eds) *Political Culture and Cultural Politics in Early Modern England*, Manchester, 1995.

Anderson, Michael 'The Social Implications of Demographic Change', in F.M.L. Thompson (ed.) *Cambridge Social History of Modern Britain*, vol. 2, Cambridge, 1990.

Annan, Noel *Leslie Stephen: the Godless Victorian*, London, 1984.

Anson, Peter F. *The Call of the Cloister*, London, 1955.

Askwith, Betty *Two Victorian Families*, London, 1971.

Bachelard, Gaston *The Poetics of Space*, trans. Maria Jolas, Boston, MA, 1964.

Banks, J.A. *Prosperity and Parenthood*, London, 1954.

Banks, J.A. *Victorian Values: Secularism and the Size of Families*, London, 1981.

Banks, J.A. and Banks, Olive *Feminism and Family Planning in Victorian England*, London, 1964.

Banks, Olive *Becoming a Feminist: the Social Origins of 'First-Wave' Feminism*, Brighton, 1976.

Barker-Benfield, G.J. 'The Spermatic Economy: a Nineteenth-Century View of Sexuality', in Michael Gordon (ed.) *The American Family in Social-Historical Perspective*, 2nd edn, New York, 1978.

Barret-Ducrocq, Françoise *Love in the Time of Victoria*, trans. John Howe, London, 1991.

Barry, Jonathan and Christopher Brooks (eds) *The Middling Sort of People*, Basingstoke, 1994.

Behlmer, George *Child Abuse and Moral Reform in England, 1870–1908*, Stanford, CA, 1982.

Benjamin, Walter *Charles Baudelaire: a Lyric Poet in the Era of High Capitalism*, trans. Harry Zohn, London, 1973.

Bennett, Judith 'Feminism and History', *Gender & History* 1 (1989), pp. 251–72.

Binfield, Clyde *George Williams and the YMCA*, London, 1973.

Binfield, Clyde *So Down to Prayers*, London, 1977.

Bland, Lucy *Banishing the Beast: English Feminism and Sexual Morality, 1885–1914*, London, 1995.

Bly, Robert *Iron John: a Book about Men*, Shaftesbury, 1990.

Bourke, Joanna *Dismembering the Male: Men's Bodies, Britain, and the Great War*, London, 1996.

Boyson, Rhodes *The Ashworth Cotton Enterprise*, Oxford, 1970.

Bradley, Ian *The Call to Seriousness*, London, 1974.

Brewer, John *The Pleasures of the Imagination*, London, 1997.

Brewer, John and Roy Porter (eds) *Consumption and the World of Goods*, London, 1993.

Briggs, Asa *Victorian Cities*, Harmondsworth, 1968.

Briggs, Asa *Victorian Things*, London, 1988.

Bristow, Edward *Vice and Vigilance: Purity Movements in Britain since 1700*, Dublin, 1977.

Brooks, Michael 'Love and Possession in the Victorian Household: the Example of the Ruskins', in Anthony S. Wohl (ed.) *The Victorian Family*, London, 1978.

Brown, Ford K. *Fathers of the Victorians*, Cambridge, 1961.

Burn, W.L. *The Age of Equipoise*, London, 1964.

Burnett, John *Useful Toil*, London, 1974.

Burnett, John *A Social History of Housing, 1815–1970*, London, 1978.

Burnett, John *Plenty and Want: a Social History of Food in England from 1815 to the Present Day*, 3rd edn, London, 1989.

Caine, Barbara *Destined to be Wives: the Sisters of Beatrice Webb*, Oxford, 1986.

Carnes, Mark C. *Secret Ritual and Manhood in Victorian America*, New Haven, CT, 1989.

Chandos, John *Boys Together: English Public Schools, 1800–1864*, London, 1984.

Chitty, Susan *The Beast and the Monk: a Life of Charles Kingsley*, London, 1974.

Christ, Carol 'Victorian Masculinity and the Angel in the House', in Martha Vicinus (ed.) *A Widening Sphere*, London, 1977.

Church, Leslie F. *The Early Methodist People*, 2nd edn, London, 1949.

Clark, Anna *The Struggle for the Breeches*, London, 1995.

Clark, Peter *The English Alehouse*, London, 1983.

Clark, Peter *Sociability and Urbanity: Clubs and Societies in the Eighteenth-Century City*, Leicester, 1986.

Clarke, Norma 'Feminism and the Popular Novel of the 1890s', *Feminist Review* 20 (1985), pp. 91–104.

Clarke, Norma *Ambitious Heights: Writing, Friendship, Love: the Jewsbury Sisters, Felicia Hemans and Jane Carlyle*, London, 1990.

Clarke, Norma 'Strenuous Idleness: Thomas Carlyle and the Man of Letters as Hero', in Michael Roper and John Tosh (eds) *Manful Assertions: Masculinities in Britain since 1800*, London, 1991.

Clawson, Mary Ann *Constructing Brotherhood: Class, Gender, and Fraternalism*, Princeton, NJ, 1989.

Clive, John *Thomas Babington Macaulay: the Shaping of the Historian*, London, 1976.

Cohen, Michèle 'The Grand Tour: Constructing the English Gentleman in Eighteenth-Century France', *History of Education* 21 (1992), pp. 241–57.

Cohen, Michèle *Fashioning Masculinity: National Identity and Language in the Eighteenth Century*, London, 1996.

Colley, Linda *Britons: Forging the Nation, 1707–1837*, London, 1992.

Collini, Stefan *Public Moralists: Political Thought and Intellectual Life in Britain, 1850–1930*, Oxford, 1991.

Cominos, Peter 'Late Victorian Sexual Respectability and the Social System', *International Review of Social History* 8 (1963), pp. 18–48, 216–50.

Connell, R.W. *Gender and Power*, Cambridge, 1987.

Connell, R.W. *Masculinities*, Cambridge, 1995.

Constantine, Stephen 'Amateur Gardening and Popular Recreation in the 19th and 20th Centuries', *Journal of Social History* 14 (1981), pp. 387–406.

Cooper, Di and Moira Donald, 'Households and "Hidden" Kin in Early Nineteenth-Century England', *Continuity and Change* 10 (1995), pp. 257–78.

Coveney, Peter *The Image of Childhood*, Harmondsworth, 1967.

Cowell, F.R. *The Athenaeum: Club and Social Life in London, 1824–1974*, London, 1975.

Crawford, Alan *C.R. Ashbee*, London, 1985.

Cruikshank, Daniel, and Neil Burton *Life in the Georgian City*, London, 1990.

Cruze, Shani de 'The Middling Sort in Eighteenth-Century Colchester: Independence, Social Relations and the Community Broker', in Jonathan Barry and Christopher Brooks (eds) *The Middling Sort of People*, Basingstoke, 1994.

Cunningham, Hugh *The Children of the Poor: Representations of Childhood since the Seventeenth Century*, Oxford, 1991.

Cunningham, Hugh *Children and Childhood in Western Society since 1500*, Harlow, 1995.

Curtin, Michael *Propriety and Position: a Study of Victorian Manners*, New York, 1987.

Davidoff, Leonore *The Best Circles*, London, 1973.

Davidoff, Leonore *Worlds Between: Historical Perspectives on Gender and Class*, Cambridge, 1995.

Davidoff, Leonore and Catherine Hall, *Family Fortunes: Men and Women of the English Middle Class, 1780–1850*, London, 1987.

Davin, Anna *Growing Up Poor: Home, School and Street in London, 1870–1914*, London, 1996.

Dawson, Graham *Soldier Heroes: British Adventure, Empire and the Imagining of Masculinities*, London, 1994.

De Mause, Lloyd (ed.) *The History of Childhood*, London, 1976.

Dean, William W. 'The Methodist Class Meeting: its Significance and Decline', *Proceedings of the Wesley Historical Society* 43 (1981), pp. 41–8.

Dewey, Clive *Anglo-Indian Attitudes: the Mind of the Indian Civil Service*, London, 1993.

Djikstra, Bram *Idols of Perversity*, Oxford, 1986.

Dunae, Patrick *Gentlemen Emigrants: from the British Public Schools to the Canadian Frontier*, Vancouver, 1981.

Dunn, W.H. *James Anthony Froude: a Biography, 1818–56*, Oxford, 1961.

Dyos, H.J. and M. Wolff (eds) *The Victorian City*, 2 vols, London, 1979.

Earle, Peter *The Making of the English Middle Class: Business, Society and Family Life in London, 1660–1730*, London, 1989.

Earle, Peter 'The Middling Sort in London', in J. Barry and C. Brooks (eds) *The Middling Sort of People*, Basingstoke, 1994.

Engel, Arthur '"Immoral Intentions": the University of Oxford and the Problem of Prostitution, 1827–1914', *Victorian Studies* 23 (1979), pp. 79–107.

Erickson, Amy Louise *Women and Property in Early Modern England*, London, 1993.

Everitt, Alan *The Pattern of Rural Dissent*, Leicester, 1972.

Finnegan, Frances *Poverty and Prostitution*, Cambridge, 1979.

First, Ruth and Anne Scott *Olive Schreiner: a Biography*, London, 1980.

Fishman, Robert *Bourgeois Utopias: the Rise and Fall of Suburbia*, New York, 1987.

Fletcher, Anthony *Gender, Sex and Subordination in England, 1500–1800*, London, 1995.

Flint, Kate *The Woman Reader, 1837–1914*, Oxford, 1993.

Forster, Margaret *Elizabeth Barrett Browning*, London, 1988.

Gallagher, Catherine *The Industrial Reformation of English Fiction*, Chicago, 1985.

Gay, Peter *The Bourgeois Experience, Victoria to Freud*, vols 1 and 2, New York, 1984 and 1986.

Gilbert, A.D. *Religion and Society in Industrial England, 1740–1914*, London, 1976.

Gillis, John R. 'Servants, Sexual Relations and the Risks of Illegitimacy in London, 1801–1900', in Judith L. Newton *et al.* (eds) *Sex and Class in Women's History*, London, 1983.

Gillis, John R. 'Ritualization of Middle-Class Family Life in Nineteenth-Century Britain', *International Journal of Politics, Culture and Society* 3 (1989), pp. 213–35.

Gillis, John R. *A World of Their Own Making: Myth, Ritual, and the Quest for Family Values*, Cambridge, MA, 1996.

Gilmore, David D. *Manhood in the Making: Cultural Concepts of Masculinity*, New Haven, CT, 1990.

Girouard, Mark *Life in the Victorian Country House*, Harmondsworth, 1980.

Gorham, Deborah 'Victorian Reform as a Family Business: the Hill Family', in A.S. Wohl (ed.) *The Victorian Family*, London, 1978.

Gorham, Deborah *The Victorian Girl and the Feminine Ideal*, London, 1982.

Gowing, Laura *Domestic Dangers: Women, Words and Sex in Early Modern London*, Oxford, 1996.

Greven, Philip J. *The Protestant Temperament*, New York, 1977.

Grylls, David *Guardians and Angels: Parents and Children in Nineteenth-Century Literature*, London, 1978.

Gunn, Simon *The Rites of Power: Bourgeois Culture and the Industrial City, 1840–1900*, Manchester, forthcoming.

Haley, Bruce *The Healthy Body and Victorian Culture*, Cambridge, MA, 1978.

Hall, Catherine *White, Male and Middle Class: Explorations in Feminism and History*, Cambridge, 1992.

Hall, Lesley A. *Hidden Anxieties: Male Sexuality, 1900–1950*, Cambridge, 1991.

Hammerton, A. James *Cruelty and Companionship: Conflict in Nineteenth-Century Married Life*, London, 1992.

Hansen, Peter H. 'Albert Smith, the Alpine Club and the Invention of Mountaineering in Britain', *Journal of British Studies* 34 (1995), pp. 300–24.

Harris, Jose *Private Lives, Public Spirit: Britain, 1870–1914*, Oxford, 1993.

Harrison, Brian *Drink and the Victorians*, London, 1971.

Harrison, Brian *Separate Spheres: the Opposition to Women's Suffrage in Britain*, London, 1978.

Harrison, Brian 'Pubs', in H.J. Dyos amd M. Wolff (eds) *The Victorian City*, London, 1979.

Harrison, Fraser *The Dark Angel: Aspects of Victorian Sexuality*, London, 1977.

Harrison, J.F.C. *Late Victorian Britain, 1875–1901*, London, 1990.

Helmstadter, R.J. 'The Nonconformist Conscience', in Gerald Parsons (ed.) *Religion in Victorian Britain*, vol. 4, Manchester, 1988.

Hempton, David *Methodism and Politics in British Society, 1750–1850*, London, 1984.

Higgs, Edward 'The Tabulation of Occupations in the Nineteenth-Century Census with Special Reference to Domestic Servants', *Local Population Studies* 28 (1982), pp. 58–66.

Higgs, Edward 'Domestic Service and Household Production', in Angela John (ed.) *Unequal Opportunities: Women's Employment in England, 1800–1918*, Oxford, 1986.

Hill, Christopher *Society and Puritanism in Pre-Revolutionary England*, London, 1964.

Hilliard, David 'UnEnglish and Unmanly: Anglo-Catholicism and Homosexuality', *Victorian Studies* 25 (1982), pp. 181–210.

Hobsbawm, E.J. *The Age of Capital, 1848–1875*, London, 1977.

Hoher, Dagmar 'The Composition of Music Hall Audiences', in Peter Bailey (ed.) *Music Hall: the Business of Pleasure*, Milton Keynes, 1986.

Hollis, Patricia *Class and Conflict in Nineteenth-Century England, 1815–1850*, London, 1973.

Holton, Sandra Stanley 'Free Love and Victorian Feminism: the Divers Matrimonials of Elizabeth Wolstenholme and Ben Elmy', *Victorian Studies* 37 (1994), pp. 199–222.

Honey, J.R. de S. *Tom Brown's Universe: the Development of the Victorian Public School*, London, 1977.

Hopkins, A.B. *Elizabeth Gaskell: Her Life and Work*, London, 1952.

Houghton, Walter *The Victorian Frame of Mind, 1833–1870*, New Haven, CT, 1957.

Howe, Anthony *The Cotton Masters, 1830–1860*, Oxford, 1984.

Hudson, Derek *Man of Two Worlds: the Life and Diaries of Arthur J. Munby, 1828–1910*, London, 1972.

Hughes, Kathryn *The Victorian Governess*, London, 1993.

Hunt, Margaret *The Middling Sort: Commerce, Gender, and the Family in England, 1680–1780*, Berkeley, CA, 1996.

Hyam, Ronald *Britain's Imperial Century, 1815–1914*, London, 1974.

Hyam, Ronald *Empire and Sexuality: the British Experience*, Manchester, 1990.

Jalland, Pat *Women, Marriage and Politics, 1860–1914*, Oxford, 1986.

Jalland, Pat *Death in the Victorian Family*, Oxford, 1996.

James, Robert Rhodes *Albert, Prince Consort*, London, 1983.

Jeal, Tim *Baden-Powell*, London, 1989.

Jenkyns, Richard *The Victorians and Ancient Greece*, Oxford, 1980.

Jordanova, L.J. 'Naturalizing the Family: Literature and the Bio-Medical Sciences in the Late Eighteenth Century', in Jordanova (ed.) *Languages of Nature*, London, 1986.

Joyce, Patrick *Democratic Subjects: the Self and the Social in Nineteenth-Century England*, Cambridge, 1994.

Kelly, Richard 'Mrs Caudle, a Victorian Curtain Lecturer', *University of Toronto Quarterly* 38 (1969), pp. 295–309.

Kiernan, V.G. *The Duel in European History*, Oxford, 1988.

Killham, John *Tennyson and 'The Princess'*, London, 1958.

Koditschek, Theodore 'The Triumph of Domesticity and the Making of Middle-Class Culture', *Contemporary Sociology* 18 (1989), pp. 178–81.

Koditschek, Theodore *Class Formation and Urban Industrial Society: Bradford, 1750–1850*, Cambridge, 1990.

Koven, Seth 'From Rough Lads to Hooligans: Boy Life, National Culture and Social Reform', in Andrew Parker *et al.* (eds) *Nationalisms and Sexualities*, New York, 1992.

Kowaleski-Wallace, Beth 'Home Economics: Domestic Ideology in Maria Edgeworth's *Belinda*', *The Eighteenth Century* 29 (1988), pp. 242–62.

Krenis, Lee 'Authority and Rebellion in Victorian Autobiography', *Journal of British Studies* 18 (1978), pp. 107–30.

Kussmaul, Ann *Servants in Husbandry in Early Modern England*, Cambridge, 1981.

Lane, Joan *Apprenticeship in England, 1600–1914*, London, 1996.

Langford, Paul *A Polite and Commercial People: England, 1727–1783*, Oxford, 1989.

Langland, Elizabeth *Nobody's Angels: Middle-Class Women and Domestic Ideology in Victorian Culture*, Ithaca, NY, 1995.

Laqueur, Thomas *Making Sex: Body and Gender from the Greeks to Freud*, Cambridge, MA, 1990.

Leavy, Barbara Fass 'Fathering and *The British Mother's Magazine*, 1845–1864', *Victorian Periodicals Review* 13 (1980), pp. 10–16.

Ledger, Sally *The New Woman: Fiction and Feminism at the Fin de Siècle*, Manchester, 1997.

Lewis, Judith S. *In the Family Way: Childbearing in the British Aristocracy, 1760–1860*, New Brunswick, NJ, 1986.

Light, Alison *Forever England: Femininity, Literature and Conservatism between the Wars*, London, 1991.

Lootens, Tricia 'Hemans and Home', *PMLA* 109 (1994), pp. 238–53

Lowerson, John *Sport and the English Middle Classes, 1870–1914*, Manchester, 1993.

McClelland, Keith 'Rational and Respectable Men: Gender, the Working Class and Citizenship in Britain, 1850–1867', in Laura Frader and Sonya Rose (eds) *Gender and Working-Class Formation in Modern Europe*, Ithaca, NY, 1995.

McDannell, Colleen *The Christian Home in Victorian America, 1840–1900*, Bloomington, IN, 1986.

Mack, E.C. *Public Schools and British Opinion since 1860*, New York, 1941.

Mack, E.C. and W.H.G. Armytage, *Thomas Hughes*, London, 1952.

McKendrick, Neil, John Brewer and J.H. Plumb *The Birth of a Consumer Society*, London, 1982.

McLaren, Angus *Birth Control in Nineteenth-Century England*, London, 1978.

Maclean, Catherine M. *Mark Rutherford: a Biography of William Hale White*, London, 1955.

McLeod, Hugh *Religion and Society in England, 1850–1914*, Basingstoke, 1996.

Magnus, Philip *Kitchener: Portrait of an Imperialist*, London, 1958.

Malchow, H.L. *Gentlemen Capitalists: the Social and Political World of the Victorian Businessman*, Basingstoke, 1991.

Mangan, J.A. *Athleticism in the Victorian and Edwardian Public School*, Cambridge, 1981.

Mangan, J.A. and James Walvin (eds) *Manliness and Morality: Middle-Class Masculinity in Britain and America, 1800–1940*, Manchester, 1987.

Marcus, Steven *The Other Victorians*, London, 1966.

Mason, Michael *The Making of Victorian Sexual Attitudes*, Oxford, 1994.

Mason, Michael *The Making of Victorian Sexuality*, Oxford, 1994.

Masters, Brian *The Life of E.F. Benson*, London, 1991.

Mazlish, Bruce *James and John Stuart Mill: Father and Son in the Nineteenth Century*, London, 1975.

Meacham, Standish *Henry Thornton of Clapham*, Cambridge, MA, 1964.

Midgley, Clare *Women against Slavery: the British Campaigns, 1780–1870*, London, 1992.

Mintz, Steven *A Prison of Expectations: The Family in Victorian Culture*, New York, 1983.

Mitchell, Sally *The New Girl: Girls' Culture in England, 1880–1915*, New York, 1995.

Morgan, Marjorie *Manners, Morals and Class in England, 1774–1858*, London, 1994.

Morris, R.J. 'Middle-class Culture, 1700–1914', in Derek Fraser (ed.) *A History of Modern Leeds*, Manchester, 1980.

Morris, R.J. *Class, Sect and Party: the Making of the British Middle Class, 1820–1850*, Manchester, 1990.

Musgrove, F. *The Migratory Elite*, London, 1963.

Muthesius, Stefan *The English Terraced House*, London, 1982.

Nelson, Claudia *Invisible Men: Fatherhood in Victorian Periodicals, 1850–1910*, Athens, GA, 1995.

Nevill, Ralph *London Clubs: Their History and Treasures*, London, 1911.

Newsome, David *Godliness and Good Learning*, London, 1961.

Newsome, David *The Parting of Friends*, London, 1966.

Newsome, David *On the Edge of Paradise: A.C. Benson the Diarist*, London, 1980.

Newton, Judith *et al.* (eds) *Sex and Class in Women's History*, London, 1983.

Obelkevich, James *Religion and Rural Society: South Lindsey, 1825–1875*, Oxford, 1976.

Olsen, Donald *The Growth of Victorian London*, Harmondsworth, 1979.

Oppenheim, Janet *Shattered Nerves: Doctors, Patients, and Depression in Victorian England*, New York, 1991.

Packe, Michael St J. *The Life of John Stuart Mill*, London, 1954.

Palmer, Arnold *Movable Feasts*, London, 1952.

Palmer, Geoffrey and Noel Lloyd *E.F. Benson As He Was*, Luton, 1988.

Pateman, Carole *The Sexual Contract*, Cambridge, 1988.

Payne, Brian and Payne, Dorothy 'An Eye-Witness Account of the Meeting of the Royal Archaeological Institute at Ripon, July 1874', *The Archaeological Journal* 128 (1972), pp. 186–90.

Payne, Brian and Payne, Dorothy *Claremont*, Yorkshire Archaeological Society, Leeds, 1980.

Pearsall, Ronald *The Worm in the Bud: the World of Victorian Sexuality*, London, 1969.

Pedersen, Susan 'Rathbone and Daughter: Feminism and the Father at the Fin de Siècle', *Journal of Victorian Culture* 1 (1996), pp. 98–117.

Perry, Ruth 'Colonizing the Breast: Sexuality and Maternity in Eighteenth-Century England', *Journal of the History of Sexuality* 2 (1991), pp. 204–34.

Peters, Caroline *The King of Inventors: a Life of Wilkie Collins*, London, 1991.

Peterson, M. Jeanne 'Dr Acton's Enemy: Medicine, Sex, and Society in Victorian England', *Victorian Studies* 29 (1986), pp. 569–90.

Peterson, M. Jeanne *Family, Love and Work in the Lives of Victorian Gentlewomen*, Bloomington, IN, 1989.

Phillipps, K.C. *Language and Class in Victorian England*, Oxford, 1984.

Pimlott, J.A.R. *The Englishman's Christmas*, Hassocks, 1978.

Pollock, Linda *Forgotten Children: Parent–Child Relations from 1500 to 1900*, Cambridge, 1983.

Poovey, Mary *Uneven Developments: the Ideological Work of Gender in Mid-Victorian England*, London, 1988.

Porter, Roy *English Society in the Eighteenth Century*, 2nd edn, London, 1990.

Porter, Roy and Lesley Hall *The Facts of Life: the Creation of Sexual Knowledge in Britain, 1650–1950*, London, 1995.

Prochaska, F.K. *Women and Philanthropy in Nineteenth-Century England*, Oxford, 1980.

Pugh, David G. *Sons of Liberty: the Masculine Mind in Nineteenth-Century America*, Westport, CT, 1983.

Raby, Peter *Samuel Butler: a Biography*, London, 1991.

Reed, Christopher (ed.) *Not At Home: the Suppression of Domesticity in Modern Art and Architecture*, London, 1996.

Reed, John S. '"A Female Movement": the Feminization of 19th Century Anglo-Catholicism', *Anglican and Episcopal History* 57 (1988), pp. 199–238.

Rendall, Jane *The Origins of Modern Feminism*, Basingstoke, 1985.

Rendall, Jane *Women in an Industrialising Society, 1780–1880*, Oxford, 1990.

Restad, Penne *Christmas in America*, New York, 1995.

Richards, Jeffrey '"Passing the Love of Women": Manly Love and Victorian Society', in J.A. Mangan and James Walvin (eds) *Manliness and Morality: Middle-Class Masculinity in Britain and America, 1800–1940*, Manchester, 1987.

Richardson, Alan *Literature, Education and Romanticism: Reading as Social Practice*, Cambridge, 1994.

Roberts, David 'The Paterfamilias of the Victorian Governing Classes', in A.S. Wohl (ed.) *The Victorian Family*, London, 1978.

Roberts, Helene 'Marriage, Redundancy or Sin: the Painter's View of Women in the First Twenty-Five Years of Victoria's Reign', in Martha Vicinus (ed.) *Suffer and Be Still*, London, 1972.

Robertson, Priscilla 'Home as a Nest: Middle-Class Childhood in Nineteenth-Century Europe', in Lloyd De Mause (ed.) *The History of Childhood*, London, 1976.

Robson, John M. *Marriage or Celibacy? The Daily Telegraph on a Victorian Dilemma*, Toronto, 1995.

Roper, Lyndal *The Holy Household*, Oxford, 1989.

Roper, Michael and John Tosh (eds) *Manful Assertions: Masculinities in Britain since 1800*, London, 1991.

Rose, Phyllis *Parallel Lives: Five Victorian Marriages*, Harmondsworth, 1985.

Rosman, Doreen *The Evangelicals and Culture*, London, 1984.

Rotberg, Robert I. and M.F. Shore *The Founder: Cecil Rhodes and the Pursuit of Power*, New York, 1988.

Rotundo, E. Anthony *American Manhood: Transformations in Masculinity from the Revolution to the Modern Era*, New York, 1993.

Rowbotham, Sheila *Hidden from History*, London, 1973.

Royle, Trevor *The Kitchener Enigma*, London, 1985.

Rubinstein, David 'Cycling in the 1890s', *Victorian Studies* 21 (1977), pp. 47–71.

Rubinstein, David *Before the Suffragettes: Women's Emancipation in the 1890s*, Brighton, 1986.

Ruggles, Steven *Prolonged Connections: the Rise of the Extended Family in Nineteenth-Century England and America*, Madison, WI, 1987.

Russett, Cynthia *Sexual Science: the Victorian Construction of Womanhood*, Cambridge, MA, 1989.

Rybczynski, Witold *Home: a Short History of an Idea*, London, 1986.

Sangster, Paul *Pity My Simplicity: the Evangelical Revival and the Religious Education of Children, 1738–1800*, London, 1963.

Savage, Gail '"The Wilful Communication of a Loathsome Disease": Marital Conflict and Venereal Disease in Victorian England', *Victorian Studies* 34 (1990), pp. 35–54.

Scattergood, B.P.S. *A Short History of the Leeds Musical Soirées, 1848–1931*, Leeds, 1932.

Schama, Simon 'The Domestication of Majesty: Royal Family Portraiture, 1500–1850', *Journal of Interdisciplinary History* 17 (1986), pp. 155–83.

Schneider, Gregory *The Way of the Cross Leads Home: the Domestication of American Methodism*, Bloomington, IN, 1993.

Seccombe, Wally 'Patriarchy Stabilized: the Construction of the Male Bread-winner Wage Norm in Nineteenth-Century Britain', *Social History* 11 (1986), pp. 53–76.

Seed, John 'From "Middling Sort" to Middle Class in Late Eighteenth and Early Nineteenth Century England', in M.L. Bush (ed.) *Social Orders and Social Classes in Europe since 1500*, London, 1992.

Segal, Lynne *Slow Motion: Changing Masculinities, Changing Men*, London, 1990.

Seleski, Patty 'Women, Work and Cultural Change in Eighteenth- and Early Nineteenth-Century London', in Tim Harris (ed.) *Popular Culture in England, c. 1500–1850*, Basingstoke, 1995.

Seward, James *The New Child: British Art and the Origins of Modern Childhood, 1730–1830*, Berkeley, CA, 1995.

Seymour-Smith, Martin *Rudyard Kipling*, London, 1989.

Shanley, Mary Lyndon *Feminism, Marriage and the Law in Victorian England, 1850–1895*, London, 1989.

Shaw, Thomas *A History of Cornish Methodism*, Truro, 1967.

Shoemaker, Robert W. *Gender in English Society, 1650–1850: The Emergence of Separate Spheres?* Harlow, 1998.

Showalter, Elaine *A Literature of Their Own: British Women Novelists from Brontë to Lessing*, London, 1978.

Showalter, Elaine *Sexual Anarchy: Gender and Culture at the Fin de Siècle*, London, 1991.

Simpson, M.A. and T.H. Lloyd (eds) *Middle-Class Housing in Britain*, Newton Abbot, 1977.

Sinfield, Alan *Alfred Tennyson*, Oxford, 1986.

Sklar, Kathryn Kish *Catharine Beecher: a Study in American Domesticity*, New York, 1976.

Smith, Janet Adam *John Buchan*, London, 1965.

Smith, Timothy D'Arch *Love in Earnest*, London, 1970.

Spiers, Maurice *Victoria Park, Manchester*, Chetham Society Series, vol. 23, 1976.

Steedman, Carolyn *Strange Dislocations: Childhood and the Idea of Human Interiority, 1780–1930*, London, 1995.

Stone, Lawrence *The Family, Sex and Marriage in England 1500–1800*, London, 1977.

Suitor, J. Jill 'Husbands' Participation in Childbirth: a Nineteenth-Century Phenomenon', *Journal of Family History* 6 (1981), pp. 278–93.

Sussman, Herbert *Victorian Masculinities: Manhood and Manly Poetics in Early Victorian Literature and Art*, Cambridge, 1995.

Symonds, Richard *Oxford and Empire: the Last Lost Cause?* London, 1986.

Szreter, Simon *Fertility, Class and Gender in Britain, 1860–1940*, Cambridge, 1996.

Tadmor, Naomi 'The Concept of the Household-Family in Eighteenth-Century England', *Past and Present* 151 (1996), pp. 111–40.

Taylor, Barbara *Eve and the New Jerusalem*, London, 1983.

Temperley, Nicholas *The Romantic Age*, London, 1981.

Thackray, Arnold 'Natural Knowledge in Cultural Context: the Manchester Model', *American Historical Review* 79 (1974), pp. 672–709.

Thane, Pat 'Late Victorian Women', in T.R. Gourvish and A. O'Day (eds) *Late Victorian Britain, 1867–1900*, Basingstoke, 1988.

Thomas, Keith 'The Double Standard', *Journal of the History of Ideas* 20 (1959), pp. 195–216.

Thompson, Dorothy *Queen Victoria: Gender and Power*, London, 1990.

Thompson, F.M.L. *The Rise of Respectable Society*, London, 1988.

Thompson, F.M.L. (ed.) *Cambridge Social History of Modern Britain*, vol. 2, Cambridge, 1990.

Tidcombe, Marianne *The Bookbindings of T.J. Cobden-Sanderson*, London, 1984.

Tolly, Christopher *Domestic Biography: the Legacy of Evangelicalism in Four Nineteenth-Century Families*, Oxford, 1997.

Tosh, John 'Domesticity and Manliness in the Victorian Middle Class: the Family of Edward White Benson', in M. Roper and J. Tosh (eds) *Manful Assertions: Masculinities in Britain since 1800*, London, 1991.

Tosh, John 'What Should Historians Do With Masculinity? Reflections on Nineteenth-Century Britain', *History Workshop Journal* 38 (1994), pp. 179–202.

Tosh, John 'From Keighley to St-Denis: Separation and Intimacy in Victorian Bourgeois Marriage', *History Workshop Journal* 40 (1995), pp. 193–206.

Tosh, John 'Imperial Masculinity and the Flight from Domesticity in Britain, 1880–1914', in T.P. Foley *et al.* (eds) *Gender and Colonialism*, Galway, 1995.

Tosh, John 'Authority and Nurture in Middle-Class Fatherhood: the Case of Early and Mid-Victorian England', *Gender & History* 8 (1996), pp. 48–64.

Tosh, John 'The Making of Masculinities: the Middle Class in Late Nineteenth-Century Britain', in Angela V. John and Claire Eustance (eds) *The Men's Share? Masculinities, Male Support and Women's Suffrage in Britain, 1890–1920*, London, 1997.

Tosh, John 'Methodist Domesticity and Middle-Class Masculinity in Nineteenth-Century England', in Robert N. Swanson (ed.) *Studies in Church History* 34 (1998), pp. 323–45.

Trudgill, Eric *Madonnas and Magdalens: the Origins and Development of Victorian Sexual Attitudes*, London, 1976.

Trumbach, Randolph *The Rise of the Egalitarian Family: Aristocratic Kinship and Domestic Relations in Eighteenth-Century England*, New York, 1978.

Trustram, Myna *Women of the Regiment: Marriage and the Victorian Army*, Cambridge, 1984.

Tsuzuki, C. *Edward Carpenter, 1844–1929: Prophet of Human Fellowship*, Cambridge, 1980.

Turner, Frank 'The Victorian Crisis of Faith and the Faith that was Lost', in R.J. Helmstadter and B. Lightman (eds) *Victorian Faith in Crisis*, Basingstoke, 1990.

Uglow, Jenny *Elizabeth Gaskell: a Habit of Stories*, London, 1993.

Valenze, Deborah *Prophetic Sons and Daughters: Female Preaching and Popular Religion in Industrial England*, Princeton, NJ, 1985.

Vance, Norman *The Sinews of the Spirit: the Ideal of Christian Manliness in Victorian Literature and Religious Thought*, Cambridge, 1985.

Vickery, Amanda 'Golden Age to Separate Spheres? A Review of the Categories and Chronologies of English Women's History', *Historical Journal* 36 (1993), pp. 383–414.

Vincent, John *The Formation of the British Liberal Party, 1857–68*, Harmondsworth, 1972.

Wahrman, Dror '"Middle-Class" Domesticity Goes Public: Gender, Class and Politics from Queen Caroline to Queen Victoria', *Journal of British Studies* 32 (1993), pp. 396–432.

Wahrman, Dror *Imagining the Middle Class: the Political Representation of Class in Britain, c. 1780–1840*, Cambridge, 1995.

Walkowitz, Judith R. *Prostitution and Victorian Society*, Cambridge, 1980.

Walkowitz, Judith R. *City of Dreadful Delight: Narratives of Sexual Danger in Late-Victorian London*, London, 1992.

Walton, John *The English Seaside Resort: a Social History, 1750–1914*, Leicester, 1983.

Weatherill, Lorna *Consumer Behaviour and Material Culture in Britain, 1660–1760*, London, 1988.

Weeks, Jeffrey *Coming Out: Homosexual Politics in Britain, from the Nineteenth Century to the Present*, London, 1977.

Welsh, Alexander *Dickens and the City*, London, 1971.

Williams, David *Genesis and Exodus: a Portrait of the Benson Family*, London, 1979.

Williams, Raymond *Keywords*, 2nd edn, London, 1983.

Wohl, A.S. (ed.) *The Victorian Family*, London, 1978.

Young, G.M. *Victorian England: Portrait of an Age*, Oxford, 1936.

6. Unpublished Theses and Papers

Boyd, Kelly '"Wait Till I'm a Man": Ideals of Manliness in British Boys' Story Papers, 1855–1940', Ph.D. thesis, Rutgers University, 1991.

Cashmore, T.H.R. 'Studies in District Administration in the East Africa Protectorate, 1895–1918', Ph.D. thesis, London University, 1965.

Doolittle, Megan 'Missing Fathers: Assembling a History of Fatherhood in Mid-Nineteenth Century England', Ph.D. thesis, University of Essex, 1996.

Gunn, Simon 'The Manchester Middle Class, 1850–1880', Ph.D. thesis, University of Manchester, 1992.

Hammerton, A. James 'From Patriarchy to Comradeship: Problems in the Reconstruction of Middle-Class Marriage and Masculinity in Late Victorian and Edwardian England', paper presented to Canadian Historical Association, Charlottetown, Prince Edward Island, May 1992.

Hammerton, A. James 'Masculinity and Marriage in the Lower Middle Class: the Making of "Moral Manliness", England, 1870–1920', paper presented to conference on the English Middle Class, Manchester Metropolitan University, September 1996.

Hunt, Margaret 'English Urban Families in Trade, 1660–1800: the Culture of Early Modern Capitalism', Ph.D. thesis, New York University, 1986.

Jennings, Elizabeth 'Sir Isaac Holden (1807–97)', Ph.D. thesis, Bradford University, 1982.

Koditschek, Theodore 'Class Formation and the Bradford Bourgeoisie', Ph.D. thesis, Princeton University, 1981.

Vickery, Amanda 'Women of the Local Elite in Lancashire, 1750–1825', Ph.D. thesis, University of London, 1991.

Vickery, Amanda 'Sociability and Intimacy in Genteel Culture', paper presented to 62nd Anglo-American Conference of Historians, July 1993.

White, Alan P. 'Formation and Development of Middle-Class Urban Culture and Politics', Ph.D. thesis, University of Leeds, 1990.

Index

Acton, Dr William
on marital sex, 155–6; on masturbation, 42; on sexuality, 44
adolescence, 105, 107
adultery, 3, 131, 155
affection, 115, 118–19, 166 *and see* emotion; love
age of consent, 154 *and see* sexual activity
agnosticism, 146
Albert, Prince of Wales, *48*
and childbirth, 82; and domesticity, 49
alcohol, 125
alienation
and cities, 50; and industrialism, 178–9; and redeeming power of children, 86; and work, 6, 31, 178–9, 196
Allen, Grant, on empire and spinsterhood, 175–6
Anderson, Christopher, on patriarchal authority, 89
angel
definitions of, 55; angel in the house, 55; Angel Mother, 45, 47, 68, 71
Ansell, Charles, on marriage, 172
Anstey, F.W., on fathers, 166–7
apprenticeships, 15, 18, 105, 107
Arnold, Thomas
and manliness, 189; and public schools, 117, 177
Ashbee, Charles, *191*
career, 185; and father, 161, 185; marriage, 185; sexuality, 190
Ashbee, Elisabeth, marriage, 160–61, 185
Ashbee, Henry
and children, 161; and home/work divide, 64; marriage, 160–61, 185; separate apartment, 127
Ashworth, George, marriage, 106
Ashworth, Henry
family life, 100, and sons' occupations, 115
Ashworth, John, marriage, 106
associations and committees, 6, 132–6 *and see* homosociality; public service
Austin, William, marriage, 72

authority
and apprenticeships, 18; and fatherhood, 89–92; within marriage, 29, 54, 62; and religion, 29, 34–5, 37, 73, 83–4, 146, 170; *and see* domestic authority; patriarchal authority

Bachelard, Gaston, 4–5
bachelors, 55, 173–7, 185
apartments, 57, 127; and clubs, 128, 185, 187; and sexual activity, 108, 171, 183, 185; status of, 108
Baden-Powell, Robert, 103, *104*, 174, 196
Bagehot, Walter
letter from fiancée, 33; marriage, 54; on marriage, 139
Baines, Edward, 140
Barrett, Edward, 64, 85
Beecher, Catharine, on paternity, 79–80
Benjamin, Walter, 5
Benson, Arthur (A.C.), *192*
emotional life, 120, 191, 192; and father, 98, 193
Benson, Edward, *22*, *69*
career of, 71, 72; childhood, 15; and domestic management, 63; and domesticity, 190–91; family life, 98, 100, children, 119–20, 141, on death of son, 100; marriage, 68–71, 109, 192–3; reputation, 137
Benson, Fred (E.F.)
emotional life, 191, 192; on parents, 98, 193
Benson, Hugh (R.H.), 191, 192
Benson, Margaret, 120
Benson, Martin, 100
education, 119–20
Benson, Mary, *70*
children, 119–20, 191; lack of education, 66; marriage, 68–71, 192–3; and religion, 70–71, 72
Benson, Nellie, 191
Besant, Walter, on English men, 171
Binney, Thomas, on mothers, 114